Overview

This book offers a six-step system for designing social science research. You start by developing a good research question on the topic that you wish to investigate. You then choose a logical structure that will lead you to an answer. Together, the question and the logical structure identify the type of data you need to produce that answer. Once you know what type of data you need, you can pick the best data collection method for gathering it, the data collection site where you are apt to find it, and the best data analysis method to use. Do the six steps, and you've designed your research. Then all you have to do is carry it out.

The cover picture shows this relationship graphically. The book describes each step in detail, with examples.

SAGE was founded in 1965 by Sara Miller McCune to support the dissemination of usable knowledge by publishing innovative and high-quality research and teaching content. Today, we publish over 900 journals, including those of more than 400 learned societies, more than 800 new books per year, and a growing range of library products including archives, data, case studies, reports, and video. SAGE remains majority-owned by our founder, and after Sara's lifetime will become owned by a charitable trust that secures our continued independence.

Los Angeles | London | New Delhi | Singapore | Washington DC | Melbourne

Research Basics

Design to Data Analysis
in Six Steps

James V. Spickard

University of Redlands

Los Angeles | London | New Delhi
Singapore | Washington DC | Melbourne

FOR INFORMATION:

SAGE Publications, Inc.
2455 Teller Road
Thousand Oaks, California 91320
E-mail: order@sagepub.com

SAGE Publications Ltd.
1 Oliver's Yard
55 City Road
London EC1Y 1SP
United Kingdom

SAGE Publications India Pvt. Ltd.
B 1/I 1 Mohan Cooperative Industrial Area
Mathura Road, New Delhi 110 044
India

SAGE Publications Asia-Pacific Pte. Ltd.
3 Church Street
#10-04 Samsung Hub
Singapore 049483

Acquisitions Editor: Leah Fargotstein
Development Editor: Eve Oettinger
Editorial Assistant: Yvonne McDuffee
eLearning Editor: Laura Kirkhuff
Production Editor: Kelly DeRosa
Copy Editor: Amy Marks
Typesetter: C&M Digitals (P) Ltd.
Proofreader: Scott Oney
Indexer: Sheila Bodell
Cover Designer: Rose Storey
Marketing Manager: Susannah Goldes

Printed in the United States of America

Library of Congress Cataloging-in-Publication Data

Names: Spickard, James V., author.

Title: Research basics : design to data analysis in six steps / James V. Spickard, University of Redlands.

Description: Los Angeles : SAGE, [2017] | Includes bibliographical references and index.

Identifiers: LCCN 2016026731 | ISBN 9781483387215 (pbk. : alk. paper)

Subjects: LCSH: Social sciences—Research—Methodology. | Research—Methodology.

Classification: LCC H62 .S72984 2017 | DDC 001.4/2—dc23
LC record available at https://lccn.loc.gov/2016026731

This book is printed on acid-free paper.

SUSTAINABLE FORESTRY INITIATIVE

Certified Chain of Custody
Promoting Sustainable Forestry
www.sfiprogram.org
SFI-01268

SFI label applies to text stock

16 17 18 19 20 10 9 8 7 6 5 4 3 2 1

Brief Contents

Detailed Contents

---

[1]Unlike the rest of this book, these guides and handouts may be photocopied and distributed under the Creative Commons Attribution-Noncommercial-ShareAlike 4.0 United States License. To view a copy of this license, visit http://creativecommons.org/licenses/by-nc-sa/4.0/ or send a letter to Creative Commons, PO Box 1866, Mountain View, CA 94042.

List of Figures and Tables

Figures

Tables

For Instructors: Why This Book?

There are lots of books about research, but none quite like this one. Thirty years of teaching social science research has convinced me that the standard approaches need revision. They're not wrong, if you already know what you're doing. Yet most students don't. Even graduate students make simple errors, because their textbooks don't show them how to think through the research process clearly.

Three problems with most research textbooks get in the way of student learning.

First, most texts are titled something like *Research Methods*. They focus on various data gathering techniques: from survey research to questionnaire construction to detached and participant observation to content analysis, and so on. Such data gathering methods are important, but that isn't where research must start.

Instead, research starts with developing a good research question and a logical structure for what it takes to produce an answer. The question identifies exactly what you are looking for. The logical structure describes exactly what you have to do to find it. Students often don't know how to create clear research questions and they frequently neglect to think through their research logic. They need to be taught how to do both. *Research Basics* starts with these two steps. It teaches readers how to craft a research question and how to identify a logical process for answering it. That's where research begins, so it is the first focus of this book.

Second, even those texts that provide a *pro forma* chapter on the research question typically jump directly from that chapter to a series of chapters on various data gathering techniques. This leaves out a crucial intermediate step. Before you can choose a research method, you have to identify the type of data that you need to answer the question you have posed. In my experience, most students don't know how to do this, and most textbooks don't cover it very clearly.

For example, I've seen even top-notch graduate students think that they can get a deep understanding of people's worldviews with a mailed questionnaire. This is not an appropriate data collection method for getting at deep understandings. Surveys are fine for eliciting shallow opinions, but they are inadequate for tapping deep, nuanced ways of thinking. Standard textbooks have chapters on how to gather both types of data, but they usually don't teach students how to identify the type of data their particular research question needs. *Research Basics* does. It draws a clear connection between the type of data one needs and the best ways to gather it. This helps research succeed.

Research Basics also highlights how to choose a data collection site—where you think you'll be able to find the data you need.

This brings us to the third problem with standard textbooks: They typically divide data collection methods into two categories: quantitative and qualitative. This approach reflects a misunderstanding of what methods do. Whether a study is quantitative or qualitative depends on how one analyzes the data, not on the method one uses to collect it. If you intend to count your data, the study is quantitative. If you don't, your study is qualitative. Most data collection methods can be used with either quantitative or qualitative research.

For example, content analysis can generate either quantitative or qualitative studies. A researcher may find that television program X has, on average, twice as many scenes of violence as does television program Y. That's a quantitative matter. A different researcher may be interested in how television program Z portrays marriages, as opposed to how it portrays unmarried relationships. That's a qualitative project. Both projects examine the content of television programs, and both do so in similar ways. However, they respond to very different research questions.

Here's another example, from a study based on structured interviews. A quantitative approach may find that 30% of people agreed with statement A while only 20 percent of people agreed with statement B. That's useful for answering certain research questions. A qualitative approach, by contrast, may look in detail at what people think about statements A and B, regardless of whether they agree with these statements or not. In either case, the choice of a research question pushes the study in one direction or another.

In short, choosing whether you are going to analyze your data quantitatively or qualitatively is the last step in research design, not the first. *Research Basics* puts things in their proper order.

Of course, I don't discard the standard elements found in many research textbooks. I just reorganize them so that they make sense. For example, most texts do talk about the importance of the research question; I just give it more priority than usual. I also cover the standard types of research design—descriptive, experimental, quasi-experimental, and so on. The difference is that I treat these as examples of different ways of making a logical argument, rather than as simply a list from which students can choose. I want students to think about why one logical structure is better than another for answering their research question. Moreover, outlining the logic of your argument is just one step in designing research; it's not the whole thing. The *Research Basics* six-step process makes this abundantly clear.

Finally, I do distinguish between quantitative and qualitative research, as data analysis methods. I simply put them at the end of the design process rather than at the beginning. This doesn't mean that you start collecting data before you've decided how to analyze it. That would be shoddy work. Good designers think through all six steps before they begin their research.

Identifying the type of data (Step 3) is absolutely central. The research question and the logical structure tell you what type of data you need, and that type of data in turn steers you to an appropriate data collection method, a data collection site, and a data analysis method. *Research Basics* shows this through many examples. Students will make far fewer research mistakes once they learn the pattern.

Research Basics shows how these six steps flow, one from another. Here is a graphic representation of the process:

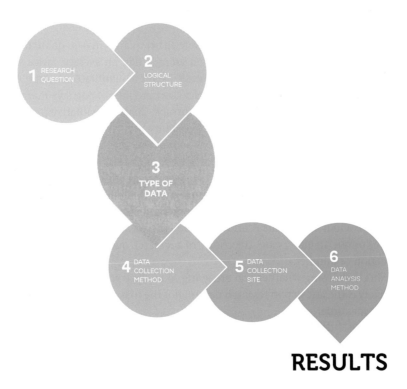

Research Basics walks students through this process step by step, laying out the choices they have to make. I have written the book so that students can simultaneously grasp the whole process and get a reasonable sense of the details. Once they have their overall research design worked out, they can consult other, more specialized resources for fine details.

What Lies Ahead

I have organized this book into two parts:

- Part I outlines the basic model by presenting the six steps and showing how they flow together to make a coherent whole. This is the heart of my approach, so I'll take a good deal of time showing your students how it works.
- Part II is organized around different types of data, along with the different data collection and data analysis methods that are appropriate for each.

Part I shows the design process as a whole; Part II focuses on the connection between the types of data and the methods of gathering it. This is the key concept that sets this book apart from others.

I use lots of examples throughout the book. In my experience, students learn best when they can work through good solid examples. Part II, particularly, uses examples to teach how to compare areas and organizations, how to conduct surveys, how to construct interviews, and so on. It does this, however, without ever losing sight of why you might choose a given data collection method.

Chapter 14, the final one, is also an example—this time an extended one. It explores various attempts to count America's homeless population. It identifies the issues that this research topic raises and examines various efforts to come up with an accurate figure. Chapter 14 gives students a chance to see how research works, from start to finish. They get to see the six-step model in action.

The central point of this book is that these six steps go together. Once you've developed a good research question and chosen a logical structure for your research, everything flows directly: Your question determines your type of data, which determines the data collection method you use to gather it. The type of data also leads you to the data collection site where you can find that kind of data, and it determines the data analysis method you need to draw conclusions from what you've found. Each step connects to the others; that's why keeping them aligned matters.

You will notice that I do not treat research ethics as a separate step in the design process. That's because it is integral to the choice of data collection method. I provide an overview of ethics in Chapter 4, which is about choosing the best way to gather the type of data you need. That's where your students will learn about the Belmont Report, about institutional review boards, and about the things they need to know as they design ethical research. I then integrate ethics into each chapter in Part II. There, I show the specific issues that are raised by that chapter's data collection methods, and how each of that chapter's research examples dealt with those issues.

1. Research Question
2. Logical Structure
3. Type of Data
4. Data Collection Method
5. Data Collection Site
6. Data Analysis Method

Your students will thus get both the theory and the practice of research ethics, integrated into their other learning. I have identified those sections with headings, in case you wish to have students reflect on them all together.

Teaching your students the *six key steps* will help them learn how to design good social science research. Teaching them how to put those steps in the right logical order will help even more.

The text includes some other tools to help your students learn:

- A set of Research Handouts for you to use in teaching.
- Review questions at the end of each chapter that cover the main points.
- "Think About It" questions alongside the text to stimulate reflection.
- A glossary of key terms; those terms are bold-faced in the text.
- An open-access Student Study Site at *study.sagepub.com/spickard* with a variety of useful study tools, including SAGE journal articles, video & web resources, eFlashcards, and quizzes.

Each of these resources should help your students learn more effectively.

Acknowledgments

I thank Adrienne Redd for extensive brainstorming and Janaki Spickard-Keeler for invaluable editorial assistance. Thanks to my colleagues at the Fielding Graduate University, where I taught research design for many years, especially Miguel Guilarte, Gary Schulman, Lita Furby, David Rehorick, and Matt Hamabata. Thanks to my many students at Fielding and at the University of Redlands who have used parts of this book as I have been developing it. Special thanks to Vicki Knight, Eve Oettinger, Leah Fargotstein, and Amy Marks of Sage Publishing for advice about how best to structure the book and for their fine suggestions about how to revise it. Thanks also to several reviewers who provided helpful comments:

Edward E. Ackerley, Northern Arizona University

Eric R. Bressler, Westfield State University

Rebekah Cole, Old Dominion University

Tam Q. Dinh, Saint Martin's University

Keith F. Donohue, North Dakota State University

Laci A. Fiala, Walsh University

Donna Goyer, California State University San Marcos

Stephanie J. Jones, Texas Tech University

Sue Kavli, Dallas Baptist University

Roger Klomegah, Fayetteville State University

Jason LaTouche, Tarleton State University

Jann W. MacInnes, University of Florida

Anna Ya Ni, California State University San Bernardino

Beverly J. Ross, California University of Pennsylvania

Angela L. Snyder, Notre Dame of Maryland University

Bhoomi K. Thakore, Elmhurst College

Victor Thompson, Rider University

Robert G. Wonser, College of the Canyons

Ryan Yeung, The College at Brockport, State University of New York

Tina M. Zappile, Stockton University

About the Author

James V. Spickard is Professor of Sociology & Anthropology at the University of Redlands, in California, where he teaches courses on research design and methods, social theory, the sociology of religion, homelessness, and world hunger. Most of his research focuses on the role that religion plays in contemporary society. He also investigates movements for social change. He has written or edited several books, most recently on non-Western sociological theory, on the transnational dynamics of African Pentecostalism, on social statistics, and on reflexive ethnography.

Introduction

This book shows you how to design empirical research. Simply. Coherently. It gives you a clear model that you can apply to any research project. You may be interested in the natural world. You may be interested in people's individual behavior. Or you may want to know more about the forces that structure our society. No matter what your topic, the research process is the same. For any project, you have to complete six basic steps:

1. Develop a good **research question**. This is different from a *research topic*. A topic is broad, but a question is narrow. A question identifies the exact part of the topic that you want to explore.
2. Choose a **logical structure** for your research. This tells you how to organize your research project so that it can answer the question you have posed.
3. This logical structure plus a properly formed question help you to identify the **type of data** you need. This is the central step of the design process. Doing this well makes everything flow easily.
4. Once you know what type of data you need, pick a **data collection method** to find it.
5. Choose your **data collection site**, where you expect to find your data.
6. The research question, the type of data, and the data collection method together tell you how to pick a **data analysis method**.

Once you've done your analysis, you can answer the research question that you've posed. Expressed graphically,

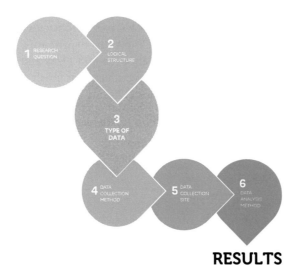

RESULTS

This book tells you how to design research so that these six elements all work together.

Why a Six-Step Formula?

Why, you might ask, should you follow a formula? Isn't doing research just a matter of going out and looking for things, and then writing up what you find? Not really. True, if you are interested in people's opinions, for example, you can locate some people and ask them a bunch of questions. But unless you have chosen the right people to ask, have thought through your questions beforehand, and have figured out how you are going to draw conclusions from what people tell you, you probably won't come up with anything useful.

I once met a graduate student who wanted to learn about executive coaching. An executive coach is someone who advises an inexperienced business leader, to help him or her learn how to lead more effectively. The student put an ad in a local newspaper asking for volunteers to talk with him about how coaching works. Ten people responded, whom he met for conversations over coffee. He recorded the interviews. Later, though, he found that his recordings were useless. He couldn't draw any valid conclusions from them. The problem? He had forgotten to construct a clear research question. He hadn't thought through what he needed to ask, so his interviews wandered all over the place. As a result, he couldn't find any patterns in his interviewees' answers. His data were worthless.

This is an example of bad research design. This student skipped an important step in his reasoning (Step 1 in our six-step system): He forgot to develop a good research question. Had he identified clearly what he wanted to know, he would have designed a better set of questions to ask his interviewees, and he would have been able to draw better conclusions from what they told him. He would have received his degree much more quickly than he actually did.

Students aren't the only ones to make such errors, but they usually have less experience than seasoned professionals. We all know that experience is a good teacher. I have been carrying out research projects since the mid-1970s and have been teaching research methods to graduates and undergraduates for nearly that long. Over the years, I have learned that every research project has six basic steps. I have written this book to describe each of these steps and to show you how they make your research more productive. My design formula shows you how to avoid the pitfalls that can leave you with a lot of data but no real answers.

Looking Ahead

This book is organized into two parts.

Part I

In Part I, I describe the six steps in detail and show the relationship between them. I give examples, to make everything clear. Here are some of the things you'll learn:

1. How to develop a good, solid *research question*.

    a. How to tell a *research topic* from a *research question* and why that difference matters.
    b. How to review the scholarly literature on a topic. This tells you what's already known about it. It also tells you what *isn't* known. Your research question should lead you to something that no one has discovered before.

2. How to choose a *logical structure* for your research, so that your research project actually answers the question you have posed.

    You'll learn, for example, about the difference between a *descriptive* study and a study that tries to identify *causal relationships*. (These are just two of many logical structures.)

3. How to identify the *type of data* you need to answer that question.

    Some questions ask you to describe people's behavior. Others ask you to collect people's *reports* about their behavior. Still others ask for people's opinions—perhaps about some behavior they've observed. These different types of data call for different research designs.

4. How to pick a *data collection method* so that you can collect the type of data you need.

5. How to choose an appropriate *data collection site* where your data can be found.

6. How to pick a *data analysis method* to turn your data into a clear answer.

    a. Different types of data call for different methods of analysis.
    b. Choosing your data analysis method is the *last* step in the design process.

Each of the six steps leads to the next. Developing a good research question (1) helps you to choose a logical structure (2) for your research. The question and this logic let you identify the type of data (3) you need. Identifying the data you need tells you what data collection methods (4) are possible, the data collection site (5) where you can collect the data, and how to choose a data analysis method (6).

Everything flows smoothly. That's the point of this book: to make designing research easy and clear.

Each of the chapters in Part I covers a single step.

There are lots of ways to collect data.

Part II

Part II shows you how to use this six-step design method, with examples. It is organized around Step 3 (identifying the type of data your project needs to gather). Each chapter focuses on a particular type of data—or in some cases several related types of data. It shows what makes that data type unique, what data collection methods you can use, and what data analysis methods you can use to interpret what you've found. These relationships among *types of data, data collection methods*, and *data analysis methods* are central to the research process.

Chapter 11, for example, focuses on various ways of recording people's behavior. It shows how to observe and record that behavior directly, but it also discusses ways of collecting people's *reports* about their own behavior. As noted earlier, these are two different types of data. Watching what people do and asking them what they have done are two different things. They both, however, concern what people *do* rather than what they *think*. They are thus related data types, but they are not the same.

Similarly, Chapter 9 focuses on the various things we can interview people about: such things as root attitudes toward life, actual experiences, the things that "everyone" knows, and the things that only experts know. These are all related, but they are still somewhat different. For example, if you want to know how to fly an airplane, you are apt to ask experts rather than people you meet in the grocery store or at a party. By contrast, pretty much everyone knows the norms of politeness: how you are supposed to act around your grandparents, your boss, and your coworkers. Expert opinion and what everyone knows are two different kinds of information, and they call for different data collection methods. You need to use a method that produces the kind of data that your research question requires.

Part II goes into plenty of detail, with lots of examples. These examples will help you learn how to identify the type of data you need to answer your research question. They will also help you choose the data collection and data analysis methods you need. And they will identify the ethical issues that each method raises.

An Extended Example: Counting Homeless People

The final chapter deserves special mention. Chapter 14 contains an extended example of efforts to count the number of homeless people in the United States. It points out the importance to researchers of having good definitions: How many homeless people you find depends in part on how you define the term *homelessness*. The chapter describes the history of homeless counts and provides a detailed analysis of several recent efforts. It gives you an example of how a single research project can combine surveys, censuses, and observations to produce a reasoned estimate of the extent of a social problem. It also shows the strengths and weaknesses of several research techniques.

Chapter 14 also shows you how a single topic can be broad enough to generate a large number of research questions. Those questions ask for different types of data, and these various types of data call for different forms of data collection and data analysis. You will see our six-step formula in action.

Research Guides and Handouts

Finally, the book ends with a series of handouts and study guides that I have developed for my teaching. Most of these guides appear in the text as well, but I have collected them here to make them easier for you to locate and use. Unlike the rest of this book, these guides and handouts may be photocopied and distributed under the Creative Commons Attribution-Noncommercial-ShareAlike 4.0 United States License.[1] You can use them in your own research, if you wish—or give them to others who may need them.

The text contains several other useful tools. These include a glossary, which defines the terms that you'll find boldfaced in the text; review questions at the end of each chapter; and "Think About It" questions that encourage you to reflect on key ideas. You'll find more tools online at *study.sagepub.com/spickard*, including SAGE journal articles, video & web resources, eFlashcards, and quizzes. Each of these resources should help you learn.

Let's begin.

Note

1. To view a copy of this license, visit http://creativecommons.org/licenses/by-nc-sa/4.0/ or send a letter to Creative Commons, PO Box 1866, Mountain View, CA 94042.

1 RESEARCH QUESTION

2 LOGICAL STRUCTURE

3 TYPE OF DATA

4 DATA COLLECTION METHOD

5 DATA COLLECTION SITE

6 DATA ANALYSIS METHOD

RESULTS

THE SIX STEPS

PART I

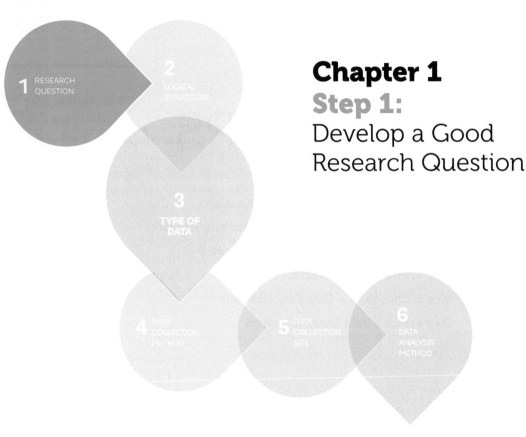

Chapter 1
Step 1:
Develop a Good Research Question

Research is designed to answer questions. We investigate things because we want to find out something about them.

We may, for example, want to know how something works. Biologists wonder how cells metabolize energy. Weather watchers want to know how storm clouds form. Environmental scientists want to understand people's interactions with their environment. Educators want to know how teachers learn to teach well. Urban planners want to know how people can improve their neighborhoods. Both traffic planners and environmentalists want to know how we can get people to drive less. These "how" questions focus on processes. They tell us the steps involved in getting something done.

Alternatively, we may want to know about people's opinions and attitudes. What do people really think of their political leaders? What do they like about their jobs? What do they think would make their cities more livable? These "what" questions ask us to describe people's thoughts. This is not a matter of accomplishing something, but of understanding people. We want to know how they see the world.

Or we may want to know what people actually do. Do men and women use language differently? How much good food do people throw away? Do people lie about how much they recycle? "Do" questions ask about people's behavior. This is different from their opinions and attitudes, because thoughts are not deeds. Both are interesting, however, and are worth investigation.

Research Question

There's a problem, however. These questions are all pretty general. They cover a lot of territory and aren't specific enough for in-depth research projects. Take the question of what people like about their jobs. What kind of jobs are we talking about? There are several thousand different kinds of occupations, and people can do similar things for wildly different organizations. An elementary school teacher, for example, has a much different set of responsibilities than someone who teaches adults in a corporate setting—even though they share the same profession. Broad questions typically produce shallow research, because they aren't focused enough to be useful. Good research questions are much more specific and take a lot more effort to craft.

That's the topic of this chapter: *how to develop a good research question*. This may be the most important step in the research process. It is certainly the first one. Taking time with your research question will save you lots of time later. It will also make it much more likely that your project succeeds. In this chapter you'll learn

- How to identify a good research topic.
- How to narrow this topic, so that it can become a research question.
- How to search the literature to learn what others have written on your topic.
- How to recraft your research question so that it can guide you through the next steps in the research process.
- How to start writing your research proposal.

Let's go!

Start With a Research Topic

Research begins with a **research topic**. This is just a fancy word for what you want to study. There are lots of choices. For example, you might want to know how to improve people's lives. You might want to figure out how economies create jobs, or what makes nonprofit organizations succeed, or how people can build better neighborhoods. Alternatively, you might be interested in individuals: what makes people happy, why some relationships thrive, or why others go nowhere. Or you might care about people's differences: the ideas, views, and experiences that distinguish one individual from another. There are many such topics, maybe an infinite number of them. Each of them is worth investigating.

Choosing the right research topic *for you*, however, is a very personal matter. What fascinates one researcher can easily bore another. We've all met people who wax poetic about tree snails, or Star Trek fan groups, or what happened in Wales in the 1840s. Sometimes we understand their enthusiasm, but other times not so much. They, in turn, might not be much interested in the topics that appeal to you. The point is, you need to pick a topic you find exciting—or, to put it more colloquially, for which you have some passion. You want to pick a topic that you find interesting enough to get you through the inevitable dull moments. That's what will keep you going. No passion means no finished project. Nobody can tell you what general topic will work. That's something you have to find on your own.

I, for example, am fascinated by human behavior. I like to understand people, and I want to know what makes them tick. I want to know what they're thinking about, how they think about it, and the ways that they view the world. And I love to encounter differences—the stranger, the better.

My first serious research was an ethnographic study of American converts to one of the new Japanese religions. Did you know there are new religions? There are, and lots of them, particularly in times of major social changes. Mid-20th-century Japan saw more than its share of social change and gave birth to more than 700 new religions between 1920 and 1980.[1] I spent almost two years hanging out with the members of one of these groups in and around San Francisco, California. They told me their beliefs, I observed their healing practices, I saw their method of nature farming, and I listened to their ideas about the coming New Age. I also learned how difficult it was for them to create clear lines of communication between the Japanese "Mother Church" and a congregation made up mainly of American converts.[2] It was a fun project for someone with my interests. I'll tell you about it in Chapter 13, when I show you how do design an **ethnography**.

Not everyone likes such things, however. Some people would rather explore the natural environment. They'd like to know what happens when you dam a river, when chemicals are spilled during transport, or when genetically modified seeds are introduced into particular farming communities. Maybe you want to learn how to develop better water treatment systems. Or maybe you want to figure out how to improve poor people's diets while still protecting wild animals and farmland.

The point is, any topic will do. You just need to choose one that you feel strongly enough about to see through to the finish.

From Topic to Question

An exciting topic, though, isn't enough. Research topics are broad and are typically complex. They can take a lifetime to investigate. You've got only one life, so you need to focus your research on something you can investigate in a reasonable amount of time. Your first step as a researcher, after specifying a general topic, is to whittle that topic down to a manageable size.

You might think this would be easy to do, but it's not. Even the most seasoned researchers have to spend a lot of time on this step.

An Example: Mass Transit

Let's take an example. Maybe you're interested in mass transit. You know: the buses, streetcars, light rail systems, and commuter trains that move people around cities. Some cities have well-developed transit systems—New York, Boston, and Philadelphia, among others. Other cities don't and are clogged with cars as a result. As I write this passage, officials in San Antonio, Texas, and Tucson, Arizona, among other places, are considering how to move people more efficiently. You can imagine how many issues are involved! Here are just a few of them:

- Where should the most efficient transit system go?
- What kind of transit system reduces traffic congestion and pollution the most?
- What changes does mass transit make in the neighborhoods through which it passes?
- How does mass transit affect people's everyday lives?

Each of these questions is important. Each of them is part of the overall mass transit picture. Each is, however, still too broad to be a good a research question.

Why? None of these questions would take a lifetime to answer—the concern that made us narrow the topic in the first place—but each of them is still too unfocused.

Take that first question: "Where should the most efficient transit system go?" This sounds straightforward, until we ask ourselves what we mean by *efficient*. Do we mean moving people the farthest? If so, we'll spotlight commuter rail projects instead of inner-city buses. Do we mean moving the most people at once? If that's efficiency, then we'll want to improve transit downtown, leaving suburban commuters to their own devices. Do we mean the cheapest? That puts cost-per-person or cost-per-mile front and center. The point is, even the topic of efficient transportation covers a lot of possible research projects. We need to be much more specific before we're ready to investigate.

Okay, so let's narrow this down. For the sake of argument, we'll define *efficient* as the ability to minimize the total time a city's residents spend commuting to work. We'll say that a transit system is efficient if it gets the most people to work in the shortest amount of time. My own commute might be longer, but the sum total of everyone's commute time, added together, will be as small as we can make it.

We could, of course, focus on getting shoppers to market; partiers to a city's nightclubs, theaters, and bars; and so on. That's okay. Focusing our research on how to shorten commute time doesn't mean that the other ideas are unimportant. It just means that they are different research projects. We need to concentrate on one project at a time.

> **The Rule: A good research question tells you immediately what type of data you need to produce an answer.**

So our question becomes: "How should we route a transit system that minimizes the total time that commuters spend getting to work?" Clearly, we've narrowed our topic. But is this good enough? How do we know that we are no longer dealing with a research topic but with a **research question**?

Here's the rule: *A good research question tells you immediately what type of data you need to produce an answer.* It tells you exactly what to look for. It may ask you to observe people's behavior. It may ask you to collect their attitudes and opinions. It may ask you to weigh air molecules. You'll know what data to gather because the research question will tell you. If it doesn't, then it's still a topic and you have to narrow it further.

For our mass transit question, once we define *efficiency* as a matter of minimizing the total amount of time that a city's residents spend commuting to work, we know exactly what data to collect. We need to collect commute times. How much time does it take people to get to work, using various means of transportation? How long does it take them on city buses? How long do they have to drive? Can people walk? Ultimately, we'll be seeking the ideal transit mix that will lower the aggregate time that people spend getting to work. Some people's times might increase, but others' commute times should decrease by more than enough to make the system as a whole more efficient.

Again, we could have defined *efficiency* in a different way. That would produce a different research question. The point is to find a question that tells you exactly what data you need.

Once you know what you need to look for, research design is actually quite simple. Identifying the **type of data** lets you choose a **data collection method** to use for collecting it. It lets you choose a **data collection site** from which to gather that data. It also helps you choose how to analyze that data, because different types of data call for different **data analysis methods**. These are Steps 3, 4, 5, and 6 in our six-step design process. They flow directly from a properly designed research question. (So does Step 2, **logical structure**, which we'll meet in the next chapter.)

In short, framing your research question properly sets you on the road to drawing good conclusions. It makes successful research possible.

THINK ABOUT IT
Why is the data type your key to good research design?

Making Decisions

Here's another example, taken from one of the other questions related to mass transit: "What changes does mass transit make in the neighborhoods through which it passes?" This question is still too general and is therefore best thought of as a research topic. Are we talking about physical changes? Changes to the length of people's commutes? Changes in pollution levels? Changes to people's perceived quality of life? Or something else? A research topic includes many such questions, each of which collects a different type of data; a research question includes just one. By identifying a single data type, a research question makes it easy to see exactly how the research is to proceed.

Of course, we can undertake a **research project** to investigate several related research questions, especially if we have a team among whom to divide the labor. Susan can investigate pollution levels, Ralph can gather people's ideas about quality of life, and Ginny can measure people's commutes. Each will have her or his own research question, even while sharing ideas, resources, and so on. The key is that each question tells us exactly what we want to find.

Let's pursue for a moment the fourth question related to mass transit: "How does mass transit affect people's everyday lives?" What do we have to do to move this from being a research topic to being a research question?

The short answer is that we have to narrow it further, until we reach a question that makes clear the kind of data we need. In this case, first, we have to decide what kind of mass transit we're talking about. For example, bus lines affect nonriders differently than do light rail and commuter trains. Buses use regular roadways, stop frequently, and can cause as much local congestion as they cure. But people can board them in more places, and they can easily shift their routes to cope with snow or street repairs. A city might even use them to evacuate people in case of a major emergency. So we can't just talk about "mass transit" in the abstract; we have to specify which kind.

Second, we have to decide which people we are going to consider. Some people use mass transit, but others do not; we should probably include both, but we may wish to focus on just one group, not forgetting the other's existence. Do we want to poll residents or tourists? Mass transit affects both of them, but differently. Home owners or renters? They often have different stakes in their communities, so mass transit may affect them differently as well.

Here are a few other decisions to make: Do we want to study people from all over the city or just those who live near the transit lines? Young people? People who work? People who don't work? The elderly? Mass transit likely affects them all.

Third, we have to decide what kind of effects to look for. Are we interested in economic effects (e.g., cost of living, property values, savings in commute times and costs)? Are we interested in quality-of-life issues (e.g., how pleasant or unpleasant it is to be in the neighborhoods that mass transit serves, changes in the availability of grocery stores and restaurants, the growth or absence of street crime)? Are we interested in social effects (e.g., changes in how people spend their time, an increase or a decrease in their sense of community)? These are just a few of the possible effects that mass transit might bring. We have to decide which of them is worth reviewing.

You get the point. Designing good research is a matter of winnowing down our interests until we can produce a research question that is specific enough to accomplish two things. First, we need it to be focused enough for us to finish given our available time and resources. Second, that question needs to tell us exactly what we should be looking for. Otherwise, it's still too general.

To summarize the ground we've just covered: A *research topic* describes an area you want to investigate; a *research question* identifies exactly what you want to find out about a small piece of that topic. It's something you can answer given the time and resources you have available. It also identifies the type of data you need to find. What's next?

Search the Literature

Before you can proceed, you need to take two additional steps. First you have to find out what other people have discovered about your topic. Then you have to fine-tune your research question. Using mass transit as an example, I'll demonstrate the first step in this section and the second in the section that follows.

You have to learn what other people have already found out about your topic, so that you can build on their work. No one likes to duplicate effort, and in the research business, you don't get paid unless you do something new. Doctoral and master's-level students clearly have to do original work, so they'd better know what others have done before them. Contract researchers also get paid more for new work, though they can sometimes make money by summarizing what others have already found. In neither case do you want to start a project and invest lots of time and effort in it, only to discover that you could have easily found the answers in a library or online. So search the literature! It will make your life much easier.

Let's see how this works concretely. Let's imagine we've chosen to explore a narrow subtopic of our transit study: "What effects does mass transit have on the lives of people who *don't* use it?" What might existing research tell us about this issue? Speaking broadly, existing studies demonstrate four areas of benefit, which vary according to the kind of transit and the geography of the transit system:

- Mass transit systems either lower traffic congestion, compared with highway construction, or they lower the rate at which that congestion increases, compared with highway construction.
- They decrease pollution and save fuel; this improves air quality and lowers the price of gasoline for everyone.
- They reduce car expenses, especially for families with school-age children and those who need cars only occasionally.
- They raise residential property values in areas they serve.

Let's start with traffic congestion. Here's the problem: The number of registered vehicles in the United States more than quadrupled in the 50 years between 1960 and 2010, while the number of available miles of highway increased by only 14%. That's more cars per square foot of roadway than we had before.[3] Taking only urban and suburban areas (there's not much traffic in the countryside), we find that total lane-miles (the number of miles multiplied by the number of available lanes) increased by 77%. That's still a lot less than the growing number of vehicles. Roads are definitely getting more crowded.

Does building more highways help? Quite the opposite. Reviewing the situation in California, Mark Hansen reported that "adding lane-miles does induce substantial new traffic."[4] Norman Marshall found a similar pattern in Texas.[5] As far as roads are concerned, it seems that if you build it, they will come. Mass transit, by contrast, seems either to reduce vehicle traffic or at least to reduce its increase. Mobility Planning Associates, for example, reported that traffic congestion in large and very large urban areas without rail systems increased nearly twice as much (59%) as in similar areas with such systems (32%).[6] Lyndon Henry reported that Denver rail ridership during peak commute hours on a major corridor was just under a third of the total load.[7] These and other studies show that light rail systems, at least, benefit nonriders by lowering traffic congestion—if not absolutely, then at least below what it would have been otherwise. That makes it easier for nonriders to drive.

THINK ABOUT IT
How can searching the literature improve your research project?

We do not, however, know exactly how this works in particular cities, and we cannot yet predict what specific mass transit mix works best in which kinds of settings. These topics are open for further investigation.

We do know, however, that all forms of mass transit use less energy and pollute less than cars. Electric railways, for example—both light rail and commuter rail—use about one sixth of the energy as cars per passenger-mile.[8] A 2005 flyer put out by Portland, Oregon's TriMet transportation agency claimed that the city's transit system saves 65 million car trips a year for a net reduction of 4.2 tons of air pollution per day.[9] This improves everyone's air quality, including nonriders'. It would be worthwhile investigating other cities' savings, especially in regions that receive less hydropower than northwestern Oregon. Mass transit increases electricity use while lowering gasoline consumption. Especially when it comes to coal-powered electricity, a researcher would need to take into account the pollution produced by electrical generators before he or she could gauge just how much a particular mass transit system would clean up the air.

Calculating costs also requires balancing both sides of the equation. Mass transit provides both costs and savings, even for nonusers. Unfortunately, most of the efforts to measure such things for nonriders rely on anecdotes, not evidence. We know, for example, that nonriders have to pay the increased sales (and other) taxes used to fund transit systems, but we also know that those same nonriders use mass transit while their cars are being fixed or when they want to attend special events and leave their cars at home. We just don't know how much, except in special cases. San Diego's light rail system, for instance, carries 9% to 10% of the fans to Padres (baseball) games, saving a measureable number of car trips.[10]

Here's another anecdotal situation: Mom and dad may need cars for work, but the $30 they spend each month on the kids' transit passes saves the $250 it costs to maintain a third car for Tommy or Terri Teen. How many families actually do this? We have anecdotes because we don't (yet) have clear studies. This, too, is fertile ground for empirical research.

Finally, there's the matter of property values. Several studies point to increased property values around mass transit stations—in part because easy access to transportation makes homes and businesses more attractive. A study of "gentrification" in Chicago found that "properties closest to transit stations increased in value much more than those farther away."[11] A study of the San Francisco area's Bay Area Rapid Transit (BART) system reported that the average home in two East Bay counties was worth $3,200 to $3,700 more for each additional mile it was closer to a BART station.[12] Robert Cervero found increased single- and multiple-family housing values near commuter and light rail stations in San Diego County, California, accompanied by slight drops in the value of commercial property along the tracks between stations.[13] Again, the effect of increased property values on nonriders will vary depending on the kind of transit system in question, where nonriders live, and whether they are selling or buying property. Research can usefully uncover the patterns that affect different areas.

So much for the positive effects; what about negative ones? There's not as much empirical research on this question as one might think, in part because the opposition to mass transit is often ideological. Some people think driving cars is a human right or a central part of the American way. Others, as a matter of principle, don't want the government to organize mass transit systems. Still others don't want to be taxed to pay for transit, even if it ends up benefiting everyone, including themselves.

This isn't to say that all (or just) those on the center-right of the political spectrum oppose mass transit. Paul Weyrich and William Lind, both prominent political activists, have written several policy papers favoring mass transit on conservative political grounds.[14] These papers make good reading, in part because they cite empirical data and in part because they take conservative arguments seriously.

Transit critic Wendell Cox did produce some empirical research on this topic, however. He used commute-to-work data from the 2000 U.S. Census to question official mass transit ridership figures.[15] It turns out that fewer people reported on the census that they used mass transit than transit authorities had claimed. Cox thus concluded that official figures were wrong.

In a study I cited earlier, Lyndon Henry took issue with Cox's method. He pointed out some major flaws in the way that opinions were surveyed on the census and argued that one cannot deduce people's actual behavior from what they report they do. Weighing the evidence, he concluded that one can't rely on people's reports of their own behavior. Memories fail, people want to appear more virtuous than they are, and so on. Henry argued that actual passenger counts are the only way to go.[16]

Literature searches often produce such conflicts. One of your jobs, as a researcher, is to examine the evidence each side brings to the table and to draw conclusions about what is and is not correct. That's the only way you can learn what's known and unknown about your topic. You are particularly interested in the latter—what is *not* known—because it opens the door to your own work.

I'll say a bit more about literature searches in a moment, but I have another point to make first. I've heard too many beginning scholars try to justify their research by saying, "Nothing's been written about my topic." That's hogwash. There's *always* something that's been written about your topic. If you haven't found anything, then

THINK ABOUT IT

When do *you* use public transportation? What might encourage you to use it more?

you aren't looking hard enough. The real question is whether so much has been written about it that there's no point in investigating the topic any more. That's for you to decide. But don't cop out by claiming that your ideas are so unique that nothing relevant has been written about them before.

The fact is, a good literature search always turns up something useful. You may end up taking ideas from several previous studies, combining them in new ways. You may be able to replicate an old study with a new, more suitable population. You may even fix a badly designed study, making sense out of nonsense. The point is this: What you find in the literature tells you what is and isn't known about your topic. Once you know that, you're ready to move forward.

Recraft Your Research Question

I've spent a lot of time on literature searches because it's such an important part of the research process. Now let's move on. Consider our first research subtopic: "What effects does mass transit have on the lives of people who *don't* use it?" How do we turn this subtopic into a good research question?

First, remember what typifies a research question: *A good research question tells you immediately what type of data you need.* We need a question that specifies the type of data we'll need to collect, which sets us on the road to collecting it.

Questions Based on the Literature

Remember what we found in the literature. We know that mass transit reduces congestion, but we also know that the reduction varies from place to place. It also depends on the kind of mass transit involved. That suggests several research options, including these two:

1. We could compare traffic before and after a particular transit system is built, asking, "How much did this transit project reduce congestion on nearby highways?" We would measure the amount of congestion after the project and compare it with previous records, adjusting our results to allow for the growth or decline in regional traffic overall.
2. If we couldn't get before-and-after figures, we could compare congestion along transit and nontransit corridors, asking, "How much lower (or higher) is congestion in one corridor than in another?" We would have to pick corridors that are similar, to be sure that transit made the difference.

Both of these questions tell us what we're looking for: traffic congestion, which we would probably define as traffic above a certain number of vehicles per hour. Most states keep traffic logs for their most congested roads, so we could use this already-collected data for our study. If our area of interest doesn't keep such data, we would have to use automated traffic monitors or count the cars ourselves. Both techniques work, which is one reason these two research questions are relatively straightforward.

THINK ABOUT IT
Do these questions tell you what kind of data you need to gather? Why does that make things easier for you?

What if we can't or don't want to count cars? Are there other ways to manage things? Here's a third question that involves asking commuters to count for us.

3.   We could give commuters logbooks and ask them to record their commute times. Pairing transit with nontransit neighborhoods, we would compare their figures. We would have to make sure to match our neighborhoods on commute distances, times of day, and so on, because these differences could really mess up the results. Our research question then is, "How many hours do people report commuting in paired mass transit and non–mass transit neighborhoods?"

Note that this question asks people to report their behaviors. That's a bit different from observing those people's behaviors directly. Both are legitimate and possible, but behaviors and reports of behaviors are different types of data and thus call for different research methods. We'll see in Step 3 how important this is.

Enough on congestion; how about pollution? We could easily turn questions 1 and 2, above, into questions about pollution:

4.   "How much less (or more) pollution do we find after the construction of mass transit systems, compared with before?" (We would also have to factor in changes to overall pollution levels from other sources.)
5.   "How much lower (or higher) is air pollution in a transit area than in a nontransit area?"

Again, both of these questions tell us exactly what we're looking for: levels of air pollution, most likely measured with standard instruments. The questions themselves make the data type clear.

Note, however, that we can't create an exact parallel to our third question about traffic congestion—the one about reported commuting hours and mass transit. The problem is, people don't typically know how much pollution they encounter each day. You can't, for example, see ozone. Yes, we could collect people's impressions, but impressions about pollution and actual pollution levels are two different things. Measuring pollution calls for special equipment; measuring mileage, by contrast, needs only a working odometer in the commuter's car. There's little point in asking people to share knowledge that they aren't likely to have.

Moving on to some other possibilities, we could ask nonriders in transit and nontransit neighborhoods to record their transportation costs:

6.   "How much do people in each of these neighborhoods spend on transportation in a typical month?" We would have to make sure to include all

costs, because insurance payments, car repairs, and registration fees often come up just once or twice a year.

To get a real comparison, though, we need to modify this question a bit: "How much do *families* in each of these neighborhoods spend on transportation in a typical month?" This will catch the amounts that teenagers spend on bus passes, for example—something the previous question might miss. These are transportation costs, after all, so we need to count them.

7. Alternatively, we could ask non-transit-riding car owners in both neighborhoods, "How much do you use your car during a typical month?" and "For what kinds of events?" We should specifically ask what they do for transportation when their car(s) are being repaired. This wouldn't capture all of their transport costs, but it would let us see whether people who *could* ride transit do so when they have no other way to get around. They benefit from its availability, even if they don't use it much. That was our starting subtopic, after all: "What effects does mass transit have on the lives of people who *don't* use it?" Being able to get around without a car is one of those benefits, so we need to see how much they actually do so.

Again, both of these questions ask people to report their behavior—something different from actually measuring congestion and pollution. A good research question is clear about this: It lets us know exactly what kind of data we need. A research topic doesn't. That's one of the differences between the two.

Finally, we could track property values:

8. "How do property values change after the construction of mass transit?" This research would compare real estate prices before and after, to show which areas and types of buildings increased in value and which decreased. We would have to allow for the overall trend of prices during the period, weighing whether the prices in transit areas increased (or decreased) faster or slower than in the overall region. (This replicates the research mentioned earlier, but in different cities; each city is likely to be unique, despite overall similarities.)

9. "Are there systematic differences in property values between similar neighborhoods with and without access to mass transit?" This research question parallels the other neighborhood comparisons that cover congestion, pollution, and transportation costs. Like the congestion and pollution questions, it calls for externally measured data. We would search public records to compare sales prices, property assessments, and so on.[17] This approach can be both time-consuming and complex, but it gives a relatively firm sense of the effects that mass transit can bring.

THINK ABOUT IT

What kinds of things can we learn from observing street life?

Either of these questions would produce interesting research. Depending on the answers, communities might decide to invest in mass transit projects, in the hope that they would improve local wealth.

Three More Possibilities

So far, we've stayed pretty close to the research we found in the literature. Now let's look at a few alternatives. The following projects highlight additional effects that mass transit may or may not have on neighborhoods. They also highlight different research techniques than the ones we've used so far.

10. Existing research (not cited above) demonstrates that some mass transit stations—especially well-maintained light rail lines, subways, and so on—often attract restaurants, bookstores, movie houses, and similar businesses. Increased foot traffic brings them customers. They, in turn, become destinations in themselves, as nonriders seek out the entertainment they provide. Other stations, however, are not well maintained and can attract crime and vagrants, driving away customers and businesses. A research project could pose this question: "What is the observable character of street life in places with and without mass transit hubs?" It could look for patterns that differentiate these two kinds of stations, and also find patterns that differentiate transit-served areas from those without transit at all. Unlike the congestion and pollution projects, this would not involve mere counting. It would involve a more holistic system of observation that captures qualitative differences as well.

11. The previous projects have looked at things that are relatively easy to measure: congestion, pollution, travel time, and so on. What about people's subjective sense of things? Do people have a different sense of neighborliness in areas served by mass transit? Or do they feel estranged from their neighbors, perhaps because it's so easy to get away from them? We could interview people living in neighborhoods with and without mass transit, asking them to describe what it's like to live there. The research question would be, "Are there any systematic differences in the ways that residents of transit-served and transit-less neighborhoods describe the quality of life in their area?" This question requires a different kind of data than we have seen before: people's reflections on their lives.

12. Finally, we could interview long-term residents of neighborhoods recently served by mass transit, asking them to reflect on the changes they have experienced. Our research question would be, "What changes do people report that mass transit has brought to their lives?" We would have to be careful to get a range of views, as different people will have different experiences. We would also have to be careful to interview

people long enough after a transit system was put in place, so that our responses would not be colored by the inevitable construction problems. In essence, we want people to compare the "new normal" with the "old normal." We should not expect shallow answers. If we do our interviews right, though, we should expect rich ones.

These last three projects call for a different kind of data than do most of our previous ones: They ask us to collect people's deeply held opinions and attitudes. I explore this type of data in Step 3 and then again in Chapter 9. First, though, I need to address one last step on the path to a good research question: writing a research proposal.

Start Your Research Proposal

You've chosen a research topic. You've read the existing literature on that topic. You've created a good, solid research question. Now you have to make the case that this research is worth doing. There are three main reasons for doing so:

- You need research funding.
- You need to convince people to participate in your study.
- You need to demonstrate that the research is ethical.

The first of these reasons ought to be obvious. Research costs money, and most researchers (especially students) don't have any! You need to find someone to pay for your research, and then you need to convince them that your project is worth doing. The second reason also should be obvious. You can't carry out a survey, an interview study, or any other project involving people unless you can convince those people to cooperate.

The third reason may be less obvious, unless you remember some history. A lot of unethical research has been carried out over the years. Nazi pain experiments, the Tuskegee syphilis study, the Milgram obedience studies, and the like have made people very concerned about harming research participants—physically, psychologically, or socially, or by involving them in research against their will. The United States now prohibits unethical research, as do most other countries. Research proposals must now be approved by **Institutional Review Boards (IRBs)**, which examine them to make sure that researchers treat participants properly. (We'll learn more about this in Step 4.)

A good research proposal accomplishes all of these tasks. It helps you get money, by showing funders what you are planning to do. It helps you get participants, by showing them what you are asking of them. And it helps you convince an IRB that you will protect your participants. It shows all of them why your research is important.

Learning how to craft a research proposal is an important skill.

The Parts of a Proposal

What goes into a proposal? Different schools and funding agencies require different degrees of detail, but they all follow the same logic. Six points are central—three of which you are ready to finish as soon as you have your research question in hand. They are as follows:

1. A clear description of the research topic, including a summary of what is already known about that topic.
2. A one-sentence statement of the research question that the project will seek to answer. (This is almost always something that is not known.) The proposal should connect this question to the existing literature, something that almost always takes more than one sentence to accomplish.
3. A demonstration of why it is important to answer this research question: What good comes of this answer? Why is this project worth anybody's time?

These three parts focus on the research question—the topic of the present chapter. The rest of this book will help you to write the rest of your proposal, which covers the remaining three parts:

4. A description of how the researcher plans to answer the research question. This includes

   a. An outline of how the proposed project will be logically structured to answer the research question. (*This is Step 2 in our six-step method.*)
   b. A description of the type of data that the researcher plans to collect or use (*Step 3*)
   c. A description of how the researcher will collect these data (*Step 4*)
   d. A description of where the researcher will collect these data (*Step 5*)
   e. A description of how the researcher will analyze these data (*Step 6*)

Chapters 2 through 6 will show you how to complete these steps, in great detail. A typical research proposal also addresses two other matters:

5. A statement of the **limitations** of this research, specifically the things that it cannot discover (and why).
6. A summary of any ethical issues that may arise in the research process.

Your choice of logical structure (Step 2) will identify your study's limitations. Your reflections on your data collection technique (Step 4) will help you to identify ethical issues. We'll visit these topics in their appropriate chapters in Part I of this book. Each chapter in Part II also has a section on research ethics, geared specifically to the kind of methods the chapter addresses.

A Proposal in Brief: The Concept Paper

An abbreviated version of a research proposal is known as a concept paper. A concept paper is a short, easily readable proposal, used for settings in which a full proposal is too long. You'll want to write both. The longer version is useful when you need the details, and the shorter version is valuable when you need to leave them out. Once you have mastered the six-step method to design your research, you will find both versions easy to write. You can find a one-page handout summarizing this material in the "Research Guides and Handouts" section at the back of the book.

That's it for this chapter. Congratulations! You now know much more about how to craft a good research question than you did when you began.

Review Questions

1. What are the differences between a research topic and a research question?

2. Why do you need to search the existing literature on a topic before choosing your research question?

3. How do you know when you've narrowed your topic enough?

4. What should your research question tell you about the kind of data that you need to answer it?

5. Why is choosing a research question the first step in designing research?

The open-access Student Study Site at study.sagepub.com/spickard has a variety of useful study tools, including SAGE journal articles, video & web resources, eFlashcards, and quizzes.

Notes

1. For details, see Horace Neill McFarland, *Rush Hour of the Gods: A Study of the New Religious Movements in Japan.* Harper & Row, 1970.

2. See James Spickard, "Globalization and Religious Organizations: Rethinking the Relationship Between Church, Culture, and Market," *International Journal of*

(Continued)

(Continued)

Politics, Culture, and Society 18 (2004): 47–63.

3. Bureau of Transportation Statistics, *National Transportation Statistics*. Retrieved from http://www.bts.gov/publications/national_transportation_statistics/

4. Mark Hansen, "Do New Highways Generate Traffic?" *Access* 7 (Fall 1995). See M. Hansen and Y. Huang, "Road Supply and Traffic in California Urban Areas," *Transportation Research Part A: Policy and Practice* 31 (1997): 205–218.

5. Norman L. Marshall, "Evidence of Induced Demand in the Texas Transportation Institute's Urban Roadway Congestion Study Data Set." Paper presented at the Transportation Research Board 79th annual meeting, January 9–13, 2000.

6. Mobility Planning Associates (using data compiled from the Texas Transportation Institute), "Study: Rail Transit May Slow Growth in Traffic Congestion," October 2000. Retrieved from http://www.lightrailnow.org/facts/fa_00017.htm

7. Lyndon Henry, "Light Rail and Urban Mobility," Transportation Research Circular E-C058: 9th National Light Rail Transit Conference, 2003, p. 383.

8. Robert J. Shapiro et al., *Conserving Energy and Preserving the Environment: The Role of Public Transportation*. American Public Transportation Association, 2002. Based on actual ridership, not capacity.

9. "Facts About TriMet," October 2005. Retrieved from http://www.cts.pdx.edu/prof_courses/LRT_Policy/trimetfactsheet.pdf

10. Judith Leitner, "Event Ridership Helps Trolly Grow," *San Diego Sun/Sentinel*, June 6, 2002.

11. Jeffrey Lin, "Gentrification and Transit in Northwest Chicago," *Transportation Quarterly* 56 (2002): 175.

12. The Sedway Group, "BART's Contributions to the Bay Area." Report prepared for the Bay Area Rapid Transit District, July 1999, p. iv.

13. Robert Cervero, "Effects of Light and Commuter Rail Transit on Land Prices: Experiences in San Diego County," 2003. Retrieved from http://www.uctc.net/research/papers/769.pdf

14. See, for example, Paul M. Weyrich and William S. Lind, *How Transit Benefits People Who Do Not Ride It: A Conservative Inquiry*. Free Congress Foundation, 2003; and *Twelve Anti-Transit Myths*. Free Congress Foundation, 2001.

15. Wendell Cox, "Mass Transit Rider Increase Largely an Illusion," *Cincinnati Business Courier*, August 16, 2002. For a more ideological view, see Cox, *Why Light Rail Doesn't Work*. Texas Policy Foundation, 2000.

16. Henry, "Light Rail and Urban Mobility," 371. See p. 45ff for a different example of this phenomenon.

17. We have to be careful about property assessments, because different states have different laws about how assessments are carried out. In some states, for example, assessments for tax purposes bear little relationship to actual property values. Public records research is seldom as straightforward as it seems.

1 RESEARCH QUESTION

2 LOGICAL STRUCTURE

3 TYPE OF DATA

4 DATA COLLECTION METHOD

5 DATA COLLECTION SITE

6 DATA ANALYSIS METHOD

RESULTS

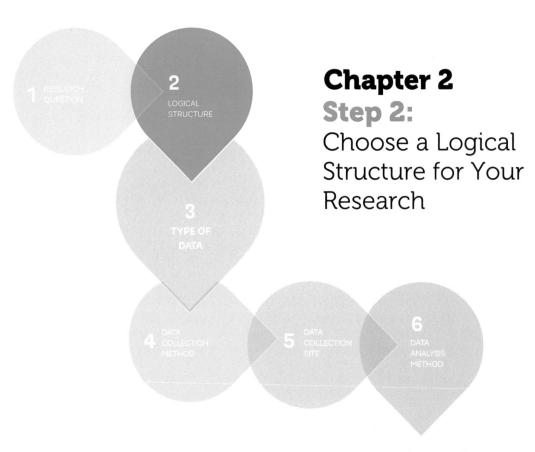

Chapter 2
Step 2:
Choose a Logical Structure for Your Research

RESULTS

Once you've developed your research question, you have to figure out how to answer it. This starts with logic. You need to look at your question and recognize what it is asking you to do. Is it asking you to compare things? To describe something in detail? To show how something happens? To develop new skills for solving practical problems? These are a few of the many possibilities we will encounter in this chapter. You first identify which of these possibilities applies to your project. Then you outline the **logical structure** you need to follow as you carry out your research.

Let's start with some examples, to make things concrete. Then we'll take a look at a variety of possible logical structures. By the end of this chapter, you should be familiar with a range of possibilities.

Three Examples

For Step 1, we took our examples from research on mass transit. For Step 2, we'll focus on a different research topic: education and schooling. Some of our examples are general, looking at various aspects of school life. Some, however, focus on a more specific subtopic: "What educational practices are most effective in helping students learn?" This is a hugely important issue, one that has generated lots

Logical Structure

of research and also lots of controversy. We won't get bogged down in any ideological battles, though. Instead, we'll see how different research questions produce research with different logical structures. No one structure is better than another, in the abstract. Each is designed to answer different kinds of research questions. Your job is to find the logical structure that your research question needs.

1. Comparing Outcomes

Let's imagine you are a third-grade teacher working in an urban elementary school. You are trying to teach your students basic geometry, but you're not having much luck at it. Some of your students succeed right away, but others flounder. You want to reach everybody, and you're willing to experiment with different teaching techniques. You've read about several promising methods but are unclear about which will work best with the kinds of students in your school. You want to design a research project that will let you know.

First, you identify three techniques that you could try. Your old standard involves the chalkboard, colored paper, scissors, and pencils. You begin the lesson from the front of the class, describing the day's concepts; then you have the students work alone at their desks, cutting out geometrical shapes and filling out worksheets. You circulate to help those who are having trouble. Each student takes a short quiz when the lesson is done.

A second technique is similar, but instead of working alone, students work in groups around big tables. They cooperate with cutting out shapes and then put those shapes together to answer a set of questions. Individual students then fill out worksheets, but they bring these back to the group, so that they can share (and correct) their answers. Each student takes the same short quiz when the lesson is done.

The third technique is a bit more active. Rather than talking from the front of the room while students listen from their seats, everyone gets up for a session of "geometry yoga." At your direction, students make shapes with their bodies, both individually and together. Some form circles, tangents, arcs, and so on. Others measure these elements, charting how they change when students change position. After doing this as a whole class, the students break up into groups to complete collective worksheets based on physical movements. Again, each student takes a short quiz when the lesson is done.

Your research question is, "Which teaching technique produces the best overall quiz scores for my students?" You need to compare the three techniques, to see which gives you the best results.

This kind of research calls for an **experiment**. You might try each of your three techniques with a different group of students, seeing which scores are best. Each group gets a different lesson, and you see which one creates the most learning. For this to work, you have to make sure that your three groups are pretty much alike. If one of them had all the "smart" kids, for example, then you wouldn't know whether your results came from the children's native ability or from the style of teaching. Experimenters have to minimize the differences between **experimental groups** and **control groups**, or the research doesn't work. In this case, you don't really have a control group, because you have to teach every child something. However, you can treat your standard teaching technique as the control and the other two techniques as the experimental treatments. It doesn't matter what you call them; you are still comparing all three techniques.

The question is, how are you going to get three groups that you can compare? Ideally, you would assign students to each group randomly. Each student would have an equal chance of being part of any one of the groups. If you do this well, the odds are that the groups will be a mix of bright kids, slow kids, verbal kids, quiet kids, and so on. If the groups are pretty much alike, then any difference in their quiz scores will result from the effectiveness of the lesson they get. That's what you want to test.

In real life, you might have trouble doing this in a school setting. Principals usually don't let teachers mix their kids randomly, and kids can get uncomfortable when they get pulled out of their ordinary routine. This means you'll probably have to use existing groups, because that's what the kids are used to. You just have to make them as equal as possible.

Perhaps you teach in a team setting in which several third-grade classes have the same teacher for math. That makes things easy: First period gets the standard treatment, second period gets group work, third period gets geometry yoga, and so on. If you're not in a team setting, however, you have other options. You can recruit two other teachers for your project, with each teacher using a different technique. Or you can try the three techniques yourself with the same group of students, but on different topics. You teach shapes in the standard way, areas with groups, and angles with geometry yoga. You quiz the students before and after to see how much they've learned.

In each case, you try to structure things so that the main difference between the three groups is the teaching technique you use. That's where you want to focus. That's what your experiment is designed to examine.

I think you get the idea. In this case, the logic comes right out of your research question: "Which teaching technique produces the best overall quiz scores for my students?" You are comparing groups while controlling the extraneous differences among them. Different quiz scores tell you which technique works best.

Note that there are some clear limitations to this study. For one thing, it's aimed at *your* students, not at students in general. Schools can be small or large, the students' families can be wealthy or poor, and school populations can be ethnically diverse or monocultural. You can't claim that what works for your students will work for students everywhere. This is a **limitation** of your research design, but it does not negate what you learn. It just means that you can't generalize to other groups.

Second, your study is small, and it depends on your own teaching abilities. Maybe you're really enthusiastic about geometry yoga but not so good at traditional chalk-talk. Perhaps a different teacher would get different results. Ideally, you'd follow up your small study with a larger one that eliminates such personal influences. Small size and dependence on individual skills are further design limitations. You try to work around these limitations the best you can.

The logic of experimental studies remains the same, though. Find two or more closely matched groups, give one lesson to one and another lesson (or nothing) to another, and then measure the differences. If you've matched the groups well, then you can attribute the differences to the different lessons the groups have received.

Here's an actual case. In 2015, a group of educational researchers led by Maria Blanton examined the effectiveness of an early algebra program for third graders.[1] They were trying to find a new way to introduce algebraic reasoning, so that students would have something to build on once they enrolled in middle-school algebra classes. Scores of studies have documented the difficulties that early adolescents have with learning algebra. Would a well-designed third-grade program help younger students learn the subject?

Blanton and her colleagues compared 39 students who received an early algebra program with 67 students who received their school district's standard mathematics instruction. Each group was tested before and after, to see how well they understood key algebraic concepts and how often they used key elements of algebraic thinking. The researchers found that the students who had received the early intervention did much better than the control group. They concluded that "provided the appropriate instruction, children are capable of engaging successfully with a broad and diverse set of big algebraic ideas."

Experiments like this are a good way to compare outcomes for two or more groups.

2. Systematic Description

Not all research questions ask you to compare groups in this way. Sometimes, you just want to find out what is happening in a particular place and time. What do kids do in a particular classroom? How do they sit? Are they engaged or bored? Do they fidget, flirt, and zone out, or do they concentrate on their lessons? How are those lessons structured? Such questions call for systematic description. They ask the researcher to *describe* what is going on and to do so in a clear, detailed way.

Here's a good example. In 1969, a team of educational anthropologists examined how Eskimo children were being educated in several locations in Alaska.[2] They visited schools run by the state of Alaska, by the Bureau of Indian Affairs (BIA), and by missionary groups. They wanted to see what kind of education was taking place and how that education either meshed or did not mesh with what Eskimo children were learning in their out-of-school hours. The researchers were not looking for measureable outcomes:

test scores, graduation rates, and so on. Instead, they were trying to identify school practices that helped Eskimo children stay engaged. They were also trying to learn how both Eskimo and White cultural patterns encouraged or discouraged the connection between classroom education and the education that inevitably occurs in everyday life.

For his part of the study, visual anthropologist John Collier wanted to see how Eskimo children behaved in the classroom.[3] He wanted to track their engagement and disengagement, particularly the effect (if any) of teachers' attempts to integrate their lessons with the children's out-of-school world. Like many anthropologists, he had noticed that White teachers in Eskimo communities tended to live apart from their students, interacting little outside the formal school setting. They weren't bad people; they just came from elsewhere and didn't know much about local life. They saw themselves as service workers, "bringing education" to people who had little of it. Collier suspected that this made school a harder place for children to thrive, but he wanted to find out. Specifically, he wanted to see if he could find visual evidence in the children's behavior of whether they were connecting school-time learning to the rest of their lives.

His research questions were, "What patterns of engagement and non-engagement do we see among Eskimo children in various kinds of schools?" and "Do these patterns vary, depending on the degree that the teachers and/or the curriculum connect school-based learning with the education children receive in the rest of their daily lives?"

Clearly, this research does not lend itself to the kind of experiments described earlier. Experiments compare two situations, to see what factors cause different outcomes. The anthropologists wanted to describe what they saw going on. Their study is a **descriptive study**. Such studies describe an event, a site, a situation, or an area of interest factually and accurately. They then draw conclusions from what they see.

Collier's piece of the project was particularly interesting. He filmed classrooms, and then he trained graduate students to note the students' behavior. With the sound turned off, they looked at such things as gestures, body postures, eye and hand movements, the amount of space between people, the degree to which the children faced or didn't face the teacher and each other, and so on. Collier developed a coding system that took into account both White and Eskimo patterns of interaction. Perhaps unsurprisingly, he found much greater engagement among the younger students when teachers used Eskimo cultural patterns and when they connected classroom learning with what students experienced at home. Lessons that didn't fit the Alaskan landscape produced much less engagement. For example, the rhyme "April showers bring May flowers" appeared in all the Eskimo textbooks even though that's not true of April and May in the far north. Younger students couldn't relate to this rhyme. Older students were better able to handle White cultural references. Collier found the same patterns, whether the schools were under BIA, missionary, or state control.

THINK ABOUT IT
What can film tell you that simple note taking can't?

I won't go into details, but Collier's book is well worth reading. The point is, he used film to help him describe what went on in Eskimo classrooms. Description was key. A descriptive study observes what is going on as clearly and objectively as possible.

Here's a second example of a descriptive study. In the early 1980s, a team led by Joseph Tobin spent time in three classrooms for 4-year-olds in three countries: Japan, China, and the United States.[4] They observed these schools' classrooms, getting to know the teachers, the students, the parents, and the school leaders. They, too, took video footage to illustrate the patterns they saw. Unlike Collier, they showed that footage to the parents and to school personnel to get their reactions. This let the researchers describe what went on in those classrooms, but it also let them describe the attitudes of the adults toward what they saw happening.

For example, Japanese viewers were generally supportive of the hands-off approach that a Japanese teacher took toward a student's unruly behavior. Japanese customs favor letting peer groups control their members, so teaching preschoolers to do this was culturally appropriate. Americans, however, favored the ways their teachers intervened to insist that their students "use words" to express themselves. Japanese were politely critical, finding the American approach "a lot like marriage counseling."

Tobin's point was not to say that one approach is right and another is wrong. He merely described the differences between the three cultures' ways of shaping behavior in 4-year-olds. Even though the study compared three preschools, it was also a descriptive study, not an experiment. It made no attempt to measure results; it sought only to describe what happened and how the people involved explained things.

3. Seeking Correlations

Sometimes you are interested in outcomes, but you can't experiment. Maybe you can't find two matched groups to compare. Maybe you don't have enough authority over those groups to experiment on one while leaving the other as a control. Yet you still want to know whether Factor A and Outcome B have anything to do with one another. You want to see if there's a pattern, even if you can't prove causation.

Or maybe you don't care about outcomes at all. Maybe you just want to see if there is a relationship between two or more different things that seem to be happening in the same places or to the same people. Do weaker high school students tend to smoke more? Are students who are taught by inexperienced teachers more troubled? Or are they more creative? Without an experiment, you can't draw a direct line between such things, but you can tell if they happen together. **Correlational research** is a good choice for questions like these.

What is a **correlation**? The term gets thrown around a lot, but it has a precise meaning in social research. *Saying that two things are correlated means that there is a measurable patterned relationship between them.* Both parts are important. There has to be a relationship, and it has to be measureable. Correlational studies look for such patterns, and they measure them to find out if they are important.

Let's take a simple example. Let's say we've heard that school districts with high numbers of impoverished children typically have lower reading scores than do school districts with lower percentages of poor students. We've also heard that they have larger class sizes, spend less on educating each student, and so on. We can think of examples that fit, but we can think of some others that don't. How do we tell if these factors go together, generally? We look for correlations.

First, we start with some figures. The U.S. Department of Education collects data from all the school districts in the country. We know where classes are large and small, where per-pupil spending is high and low, where test scores are above or below average, where more families are rich or poor, and so on. Which of these things happen in the same places? Which show no relationships? That's what a correlational study seeks to find out.

To make this simple, I'm going to use data from the 50 U.S. states rather than data from the school districts. That lets me show you a simple map of these data. Figure 2.1 shows the percentage of fourth graders who are reading below grade level. States with higher numbers of poor readers are more darkly shaded; lighter shades mean that more kids read at or above the norm. New Mexico, Mississippi, and Louisiana have it the worst; more than 75% of their fourth graders read less well than they should. Massachusetts is the only state with less than 50% reading below grade level (49.6% in 2012).

FIGURE 2.1   Percentage of Fourth Graders Reading Below Grade Level

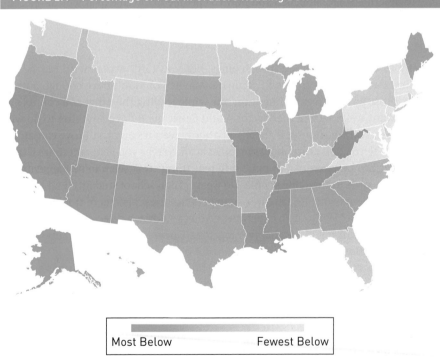

Most Below   Fewest Below

Source: Data from U.S. Department of Education.

Figure 2.2 is another map, showing the percentage of public school students defined as "economically disadvantaged." Once again, dark colors indicate higher rates of disadvantage, whereas light colors indicate less poverty. Mississippi is high, at 71%; New Hampshire is low, at 25%. That's nearly a three-to-one spread. Mississippi is the top state on other poverty measures, by the way, whereas New Hampshire is at the bottom.[5] Other states shift around, though, which is why we don't try to correlate just two data points. Correlational studies work with large numbers of cases—the more, the better. A pattern that covers just two states is much less interesting than a pattern that covers them all.

Are these maps similar? More or less. Southern states are shaded more darkly on both, which means that more of their children can't read well and more live in poverty. The states in the northern tier are lighter, which means that a higher percentage of their children read well and a smaller percentage are economically disadvantaged. Yes, reading scores are lower in the Southwest and poverty is higher in the Southeast, relatively speaking, but the maps are more alike than they are different.

Just looking at maps isn't good enough, however. Correlational studies need clear measurements, and there are several ways to measure exactly how similar these

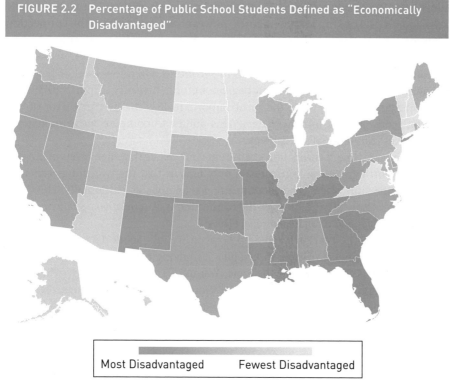

FIGURE 2.2   Percentage of Public School Students Defined as "Economically Disadvantaged"

Most Disadvantaged   Fewest Disadvantaged

Source: Data from U.S. Department of Education.

patterns are. The most common is the Pearson product-moment coefficient—commonly called the **correlation coefficient** or **Pearson's r**. The Pearson's *r* for these two maps is 0.72. That's very high. Such a high *r* value tells us that low fourth-grade reading scores and high levels of poverty happen in the same places. We'll learn the details in Step 6, but the highest possible Pearson's *r* is 1.0, which means the maps are exactly alike; the lowest possible value is 0.0, which means they are not alike at all.[6]

I could make similar maps for other things, because it turns out that several factors correlate with the percentage of a state's fourth graders who are reading below grade level. Here are a few of them:

- Low levels of per-pupil spending in schools (*r* = 0.49: Utah spends the least, at $7,149; New York spends the most, at $19,569)
- Low levels of adult participation in the workforce (*r* = 0.53: West Virginia is lowest, at 67.3%; Nebraska is highest, at 83%)
- High levels of ethnic minorities in a state's population (*r* = 0.39: Hawaii is highest, at 77.3%; Maine is lowest, at 5.6%)

These numbers don't mean that Hawaii, Utah, and West Virginia have the most low-level readers. Correlations describe overall patterns, not one-to-one rank-orderings. Looking at these figures, however, we can say that the connection between low reading scores and high levels of child poverty is stronger (0.72) than the connection between low reading scores and the other variables. A low level of adult workforce participation comes in second (0.53), a low level of per-pupil spending is third (0.49), and a high degree of ethnic diversity is fourth (0.39). All are important, but poverty is the most important. It is the best predictor of low reading scores among fourth graders. This ability to compare measurements is what makes correlational studies tick.

At the same time, a correlation coefficient can't tell us that high levels of poverty *cause* low fourth-grade reading scores; it only tells us that the two things generally happen in the same places. They accompany one another, at least usually. The closer the Pearson's *r* is to 1.0, the stronger the connection is. *A correlational study can tell us about relationships, but it can't tell us about cause.*

We'll revisit the Pearson's *r* in Step 6, when we talk about data analysis. We'll then spend a good deal of time in Chapter 7 studying correlational research itself. The point here is to understand the logic. You use a correlational study when your research question asks whether there is a relationship between two things, regardless of whether one causes another. Sometimes that relationship turns out to be causal; sometimes it does not. There is still a relationship. Correlational research is a powerful tool for investigators to use.

Not all correlational studies deal with things happening in particular places. Some deal with things happening in different organizations. Others deal with things happening to individuals. The latter are important, because they let us see whether two different aspects of individual behavior typically go together. Here are a few examples, taken from studies of schools:

- Murat Bursal and Lynda Paznokas studied 65 beginning teachers and found a correlation between a measure of those teachers' math anxiety and another measure of their self-confidence at teaching math and science. Those teachers with higher scores on a non-math-related self-efficacy test were also more likely to report being confident about their teaching ability than were those whose scores were low.[7]
- George Domino and Amanda Morales found strong correlations between a nonverbal test of intelligence and both grade point averages and ability-test scores among both Mexican American and Anglo college students. Neither ethnicity nor gender made any difference to these correlations. Verbally based intelligence tests seem not to work well with Mexican American students, so the correlations on this nonverbal test indicate its potential usefulness.[8]
- Philip DeCicca and Justin Smith examined the relationship between the length of time that students spend in kindergarten and later academic performance. They found a correlation between longer kindergarten attendance, increased grade repetition, and lower 10th-grade test scores.[9]

Each of these studies used a correlational structure to answer a research question about the relationship between two or more aspects of individuals' lives. None of them proved causality. All of them found relationships that warrant further exploration.

Ten Logical Structures for Research

There are a lot of different ways to structure social research. Ten common ones cover most of the bases:

1. True experiments
2. Quasi-experiments
3. Ex post facto research
4. Correlational research
5. Descriptive research
6. Case studies
7. Historical research
8. Longitudinal research
9. Meta-analysis
10. Action research

In the sections that follow, I'll describe each of these methods briefly and give you a few guidelines for their use. I'll also provide some brief examples. Part II of this book has extended examples of each.

> The ten research logics are the key to good social science research.

1. True Experiments

I described experiments earlier, in the "Comparing Outcomes" example. You use experiments when you want to understand cause-and-effect relationships. You compare two groups: an **experimental group** that receives the treatment you wish to test and a **control group** that does not. You need to make sure that your groups are as close to equivalent as you can make them before you begin. Then you start the treatment with one group and leave the other alone. Any difference between the groups at the end is likely to be a result of whatever it was you did to the treatment group.

The teaching experiment described earlier, involving three methods for teaching geometry, is a good example of this logical structure.

2. Quasi-Experiments

As the name indicates, **quasi-experiments** approximate the conditions of a true experiment, but they don't quite control all the factors involved. This is usually a matter of circumstance. Not every situation lends itself to experiments, particularly when you are investigating things that happen in ordinary life. Maybe you can't assign participants randomly to treatment and control groups. Maybe bringing people into the laboratory will distort their behavior so much that you can't explore a particular research question there. Like experiments, quasi-experiments look for cause-and-effect relationships and try to figure out why groups have different outcomes. The inability to control all the factors that might affect those outcomes, however, means that researchers must think through the implications of whatever compromises they have to make.

Sometimes you get lucky. Life occasionally sets up quasi-experiments for you. By chance, different things may happen to two similar groups. We can look at the outcomes and trace at least some of the different results to those groups' different experiences. We typically call these **natural experiments**, because they occur without our overt intervention. They fall into the quasi-experimental category.

Here's a recent example. A team led by Shin-Yi Chou took advantage of one such natural experiment, to gauge the effect of mothers' education on child health in Taiwan.[10] In 1968, the Taiwanese government expanded compulsory education from six years to nine years. To do so, the government opened 254 new junior high schools—an 80% increase over the number that had existed previously. They didn't, however, open all of them at the same time across the country. Chou and her colleagues took advantage of this fact to identify treatment and control groups, made up of men and women who either did or didn't get access to this new schooling right away. They then looked at the birth records of children who were born to these men and women 10 to 20 years later. They wanted to see whether there were any systematic differences in infant health.

They found that there were. Parents who had more schooling had fewer low-weight births and fewer child deaths than parents who had not had access to the new school system. This was particularly true for women who received the new junior high education. Chou and her associates estimated that this factor alone accounted for a decline in infant mortality of about 11%.

This is a typical quasi-experiment. Obviously, you can't divide a country's boys and girls randomly into two groups, sending one group to junior high and the other group out into the workforce. Your Institutional Review Board would be all over you for that ethical lapse. But the inability of the Taiwanese government to open new schools simultaneously in all parts of the country produced a natural—and random—division. Chou and her colleagues looked for resulting differences, and they found them.

3. Ex Post Facto Research

The third logical structure is similar to quasi-experiments, but it gives you even less control over the factors that you think might be causing a particular outcome. *Ex post facto* is Latin for "after the fact." **Ex post facto research** begins with an outcome and seeks that outcome's causes, retrospectively. It uses existing data to answer the research question.

Let's say that you are interested in why students drop out of high school. There are lots of ways to investigate this, but one good way is to identify people who have already dropped out and then examine their school records for any patterns. That's what John Alspaugh, from the University of Missouri, did in 1999.[11] He collected data from 45 high schools to see if the dropout rate varied according to the grade level at which individual students entered. He found that students who entered high school later had higher dropout rates. Longevity in a particular school seemed to reduce the likelihood of a student dropping out. In parallel, high schools with just three grades (10–12) had higher dropout rates than did schools with four grades (9–12) and six grades (7–12). In short, the earlier their transition to high school, the more apt students were to stay enrolled. This worked for both boys and girls, though boys' dropout rates were higher at all levels and the effect of later high school entry was stronger for them.

This ex post facto study began with students' dropout status and then looked backward to find possible causes. Though Alspaugh found a relatively strong trend, he was not able to control all of the possible variables. It is hard to do so in retrospective studies.

Elaine Humphrey conducted a similar ex post facto study to examine the differences between first-generation college students and students whose parents had had a college education.[12] She assembled data on 3,966 students who completed a survey toward the end of their first year of college, and then she compared survey answers across the two types of students. She found significant differences

THINK ABOUT IT
What's the difference between true experiments, quasi-experiments, and ex post facto research? Why and when would you choose one over the others?

between first-generation and non-first-generation students, particularly around issues of jobs and money. She argued that a family's familiarity with college education makes a great deal of difference to students' early college experience.

True experiments, quasi-experiments, and ex post facto studies lie on a continuum. All look for differences between groups, and all try to locate the source of those differences. Experiments give investigators the most control, whereas ex post facto studies give them the least. These logical structures are appropriate for research questions that try to find out why groups differ from one another.

4. Correlational Research

Correlational research is one step further along this continuum. I described this logical structure earlier, in the "Seeking Correlations" example. It is, however, worth emphasizing the key points.

First, **correlational research** checks to see if two (or more) things are associated with one another, or if they are independent. There are many kinds of association. Things can happen in the same places, they can happen at the same times, they can happen in the same organizations, or they can happen to the same people. Correlational logic is good for answering research questions about what kinds of things go together. In general, do students who were born right after the grade cutoff—and are thus older—do better socially than students who were born just before the cutoff? Or do they, in general, get bored more easily and thus get into more trouble? The phrase "in general" is a good clue that you are looking for a relationship without trying to claim that age necessarily produces good or bad behavior.

A correlation between A and B could result from several different causal relationships (Figure 2.3). This leads to our second point: *Correlation is not cause.* Just because two or more things are associated with one another does not mean that one of them causes the other. There are lots of possibilities. Factor A could cause Factor B, but conversely Factor B could cause Factor A. Or Factor C could cause both Factors A and B. In that case, A and B would be correlated only because they both result from the same thing. There are other possibilities, but the point is that just showing that two things are associated doesn't tell us there is a **causal relationship** between them. Correlational logic is good for finding associations, but not for discovering which way causality runs.

Third, *correlational research requires measurement.* We have to have some way of measuring how closely two or more things are related; otherwise, it's not an actual correlation. (This is one of those times when you have to be very careful with language, so that you don't make claims you can't support.)

As noted earlier, we return to correlational logic in Step 6 and Chapter 7. Step 6 takes a closer look at data analysis, and Chapter 7 looks at research that compares areas,

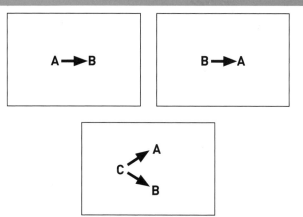

FIGURE 2.3   Three Possible Causal Relationships

organizations, and other aggregate groups. Correlational studies are particularly pow-erful ways to make such comparisons. They are not the only ways to do so, however.

Let's pause here to notice something about the four logical structures described so far. Experiments, quasi-experiments, ex post facto research, and correlational research all share something in common. They all try to discover the relationships between two or more things. Experimental projects try to trace causal relationships between Factor A and Factor B. Correlational projects try to see whether there is any patterned relationship between those same factors, without regard to cause. Quasi-experimental and ex post facto research fall somewhere in between.

These four ways of structuring research are thus all suitable for certain kinds of research questions. Sticking with our focus on schools, these include such questions as "Does increasing per-pupil spending improve student test scores?" "Do students who attend smaller schools get better grades?" and "Does giving schools more autonomy from their districts improve the quality of their students' education?" Each of these "do" questions identifies two or more factors and asks if there is a relationship between them.

These logical structures are particularly appropriate for research questions that seek to identify relationships between different variables. They also frequently lend themselves to **quantitative data analysis**. Other kinds of analysis can be used, so don't get in the habit of thinking that some logical structures are naturally quantita-tive and others are naturally qualitative. It's not that simple. (We'll explore this idea when we reach Step 6.)

The next several logical structures also have something in common. They answer research questions that ask what is going on in a particular situation. Descriptive stud-ies answer "what" questions, but so do case studies and historical research. They all describe things, but in different ways.

5. Descriptive Research

I presented two descriptive projects earlier, in the "Systematic Description" example. Both projects used film to study various social scenes. Most descriptive projects don't use film. They all, however, seek to understand the details of whatever it is they are studying. They want to know *what* is happening, *how* it happens, and *what* the people involved in those happenings think about it. Some projects compare two or more research sites, to highlight differences between them. They seldom, however, focus on causes and outcomes. Instead, descriptive researchers try to paint as clear a picture as possible of what is happening in the setting they have chosen to investigate.

The results can be very rich. For example, sociologist Barrie Thorne spent a year observing students in each of two elementary schools, one in California and the other in Michigan. She looked for the ways that children learn, create, and enforce gender norms.[13] She tracked children in the classroom, on the playground, at lunch, and in their neighborhoods. She wanted to see *how* they learn what it is to be boys and girls, *what* those identities mean to them and to the adults nearby, *when* those identities are enforced and when they are not, and *how* this whole process happens. Among other things, she observed that gender division does not rule all parts of children's lives. Neighborhood play, for example, is often gender mixed, but recess play is usually not. Teachers and other adults often highlight boy-versus-girl divisions by such things as dividing the class into gender-based teams. Children replicate this in their free play, but also by passing on child folklore about things such as "cooties," "chase-and-kiss," and "goin' with." Children don't begin school using gender as an organizing principle, and most teachers don't consciously force it on them. Yet by the end of grade school, the division is clear-cut. Thorne described how this happens, in very complex detail.

There were good reasons for her to do so. Sociologists at the time argued that sex roles are inevitable, though clearly they vary from society to society. They saw sex roles as a matter of *socialization,* the process by which adults train children to act according to social norms. In this vision, adults were active and children were passive. Thorne suspected that the real picture was much more complicated.

Her research showed that it was. Yes, adults do influence children. However, children also train themselves to take gender roles. They engage in what Thorne called "borderwork": dividing boys from girls and enforcing the division. This is a social process, not an individual one. Thorne's descriptions of children at play showed that gender boundaries can take center stage, can be sidelined, or can even be challenged. The process, however, always happens collectively. In her words,

> When gender boundaries are activated, the loose aggregation "boys and girls" consolidates into "the boys" and "the girls" as separate and reified groups. In the process, categories of identity that on other occasions have minimal relevance for interaction become the basis of separate collectivities. . . . These stylized moments evoke recurring themes that are deeply rooted in our cultural conceptions of gender, and they suppress awareness of patterns that contradict and qualify them.[14]

Thorne described in great detail how this was done.

Thorne's study was an **ethnography**—a data gathering method that we will meet again in Step 4 and in Chapter 13. Ethnographies require long-term immersion in a specific social scene. This gives one time to notice the scene's social patterns, including those of which the participants are not fully aware. Ethnographers are trained to identify these patterns. They are also trained to listen to the ways that people explain their own behavior. Ethnographic writing describes what the scene's participants understand about what is happening, but it also describes those participants' unconscious patterns of behavior. This makes it a particularly powerful technique for understanding social life.

Not all descriptive studies are ethnographic, however. Much **survey research** is also descriptive. Investigators use **social surveys** to collect and then describe what a particular set of people reports about their own beliefs, experiences, and behavior. They do not typically attempt to assess causation.

Elias Avramidis and his colleagues, for example, surveyed 81 primary and secondary school teachers in a school district in the southwest of England.[15] They were interested in these teachers' attitudes toward what school authorities call "mainstreaming": enrolling students with various kinds of disabilities in regular classrooms, usually (though not always) with special assistance to help them keep up with their class. Their study described the range of attitudes found among the teachers. They were also able to show that teachers who were already including "special needs" children in their classes were more positive about the program, as were teachers with more university education. Their study did not argue that either experience or education *caused* the positive attitudes; it merely *described* the attitudes the investigators found among the sets of teachers.

Descriptive studies do not answer research questions about cause and effect. Though they can shed light on factors that might well be influential, they do not directly test them. Instead, they focus on painting as thorough a picture as possible of whatever area of interest an investigator has chosen.

6. Case Studies

Case studies are another kind of descriptive research. They are, however, even more focused on details than are studies that cover a wider range of cases. They typically examine a single example, to shed light on a wider social trend. They are quite common in anthropology, education, and certain subfields of psychology. Ludwig Binswanger's famous "Case of Ellen West," for example, launched the subfield of existential psychology. He portrayed in great detail the psycho-emotional life of one of his patients, whose own internal despair led her to commit suicide.[16] Case studies need not be so grim, but they do need to be detailed. Readers come away from them with a clear sense of how wider social, psychological, biological, environmental, or other processes operate in a particular setting.

THINK ABOUT IT
When do you choose descriptive research?

Jay MacLeod wrote a famous case study about the educational aspirations of two youth gangs in a Boston housing project.[17] One gang, whose members were mostly African American teenagers, believed their teachers when they said that education was a route to success. They worked hard at school, though not terribly successfully, so they blamed themselves for their failures. The members of the other gang, mostly White, thought this was stupid. They saw no meaningful jobs, didn't think schools helped anyone get ahead, and told MacLeod that in 10 years they "would be dead or in jail." MacLeod showed how both gangs' attitudes reinforce the American class system. The Black gang members blamed themselves for their failures, while the White gang members quit trying. When MacLeod interviewed them again some years later, neither group's members had found much success.

MacLeod's interview data were rich, and he gave the reader a quite detailed sense of these boys' lives. What made the book a good case study, though, was the way that he used his interviews to shed light on wider theories of educational and social class stratification. He evaluated six different approaches that ranged from an emphasis on the power of social structures in keeping the poorer classes down to those that stress the role of class culture in preventing advancement. His teens illustrated elements of each, but he ultimately found the cultural theories more plausible.

Case studies can also be smaller affairs. For example, Reba Page wrote a useful case study of lower-track classes at a college preparatory high school, showing how students and staff handled the cognitive dissonance of preparing weaker students for a university education they may never attain. In the same volume, Kathryn Anderson-Levitt wrote a case study of how teachers in France use general cultural knowledge to teach first grade. Norman Chance wrote a case study of village-level education in China. Margaret Gibson wrote a case study of Punjabi immigrant children in an American high school. Each of these case studies showed how general social processes work in a particular setting.[18] Details matter for case study research.

7. Historical Research

Historical research is similarly descriptive, but in this case the descriptions are about the past, not the present. The logic of this approach is like that of case studies. Historical research follows a particular topic through time, showing in detail how it either changed or stayed the same across a historical period.

Bob Schlagal, for example, outlined a history of teaching spelling in American schools, as part of his effort to understand the variety of ways in which empirical research does and does not influence classroom practices.[19] He identified the periods during which scientific approaches dominated educational systems and those periods (sometimes more recent) in which science took a backseat to pedagogical prejudice.

In a different historical vein, Jacquelyn Dowd Hall described the ways that the American civil rights movement has been presented, both in classrooms and for the public at large.[20] She noted that the dominant narrative presents the civil rights movement as relatively short (1954–1965), as located mainly in the South, and as focused on combating formal legal barriers to full citizenship rather than on socioeconomic discrimination. "The master narrative," she wrote,

> simultaneously elevates and diminishes the movement. It ensures the status of the classical phase as a triumphal moment in a larger American progress narrative, yet it undermines its *gravitas*. It prevents one of the most remarkable mass movements in American history from speaking effectively to the challenges of our time.[21]

To the extent that American school textbooks have embraced this version of a short Civil Rights Movement—and many have[22]—they present a distorted picture of American life and of African Americans' efforts to change the society in which they live. Historical descriptive research examines such things in great detail.

As noted, descriptive research, case study research, and historical research all describe things in as much detail as possible. They answer research questions that focus on such details: *What* is happening? *How* does it unfold? *What* do the participants think about? and so on. If your research question asks you to describe things in detail, then one of these three logical structures may be the way to go.

THINK ABOUT IT
What are the main differences between "Do?" questions and "What?" questions? Why do they call for different logical structures?

The remaining three kinds of research are different. They, too, can be either qualitative or quantitative—though I hope that by now you recognize that this distinction belongs to Step 6 in our design process, not to this one. Longitudinal research and meta-analysis are fine research strategies. They are both reasonably clear, so I can keep my introductions short. Action research, by contrast, is more complex. I'll say quite a bit about it here and give some examples of it in later chapters.

8. Longitudinal Research

If historical research looks to the past for answers, **longitudinal research** looks to the future, tracing change over a long period. Longitudinal research on people typically follows a set of people to see what happens to them. Longitudinal research on an ecosystem measures changes in that system, looking for long-term trends. Both call for an initial assessment to establish a baseline for future comparison. Then you revisit the people, the place, or whatever it is you are studying, tracking the changes that you find. Sometimes you do this every year, sometimes every 5 or 10 years, though occasionally less often. (That's where the "long" in longitudinal research comes in: This logical structure takes time.)

Educational researchers have frequently carried out longitudinal studies. The National Center for Educational Statistics (NCES) has sponsored at least five such studies, each of which has traced students from high school through their young adult years.[23]

The first—the National Longitudinal Study of the High School Class of 1972 (NLS-72)—surveyed a representative sample of 19,000 American high school seniors in 1972 and then resurveyed the same individuals five times between 1973 and 1986. The most recent study—the High School Longitudinal Study of 2009 (HSLS:09)—surveyed more than 23,000 ninth-graders from 944 schools, plus a selection of parents, teachers, school counselors, and school administrators. The study team resurveyed the students in 2012, when they were high school seniors. The next follow-up will be in 2016, after these young people have spent time in college, the military, or the workforce.

Each of these studies had a different focus. The NLS-72 asked general questions about students' expectations and life experiences, seeking to find out how young people of this generation reported their transition from school to adulthood. This was a descriptive project. It captured the early experience of a generation that hit the job market during a decade-long economic downturn. The changing U.S. economy undercut the stable jobs and marriages that these students' parents had experienced in the 1950s, and that the students were raised to expect. Instead, many of these young people found transient employment, serial careers, and (sometimes) serial relationships.[24] The NLS-72 longitudinal follow-ups give us a glimpse of how these young people coped with this situation, over time.

The HSLS:09 study was more specific. It asked three research questions. Quoting from the NECS website:

- "What are students' trajectories from the beginning of high school into postsecondary education, the workforce, and beyond?"
- "What majors and careers do students decide to pursue when, why, and how?"
- "How do students choose science, technology, engineering, and math (STEM) courses, majors, and careers?"

This ongoing study is also collecting more general information. Like the NLS-72, this information will help researchers find out how today's student generation copes with whatever social changes occur while they make their own transition from school to adulthood. Given the major shifts in the U.S. economy over the past 50 years, we can expect their experiences to be different. Just how, though, we don't yet know.

The NCES studies are quantitative research—something that is almost inevitable when one wants to collect results from so many people over such a long period of time. As we will see in Step 6, one of the strengths of quantitative studies is their ability to draw conclusions for an entire population based simply on a sample. The 19,000 and 23,000 students in the two studies I've mentioned were carefully chosen to represent the full student cohorts of which they are a part. Investigators can thus reliably generalize their answers to their student generations as a whole.

Not all longitudinal studies are quantitative, however. Anthropologists are well known for designing qualitative research to study communities over time. George and Louise Spindler, for example, studied the south German village of Beutelsbach over a 10-year period starting in the early 1960s.[25] They traced changes in demographics, social attitudes, land use, and the local economy. They focused particularly on the village schools, where they examined the ways that different approaches to education mirrored social divisions within the village. The fact that the Spindlers could spread their study over several years let them see things about village life that would have remained hidden to anyone attempting a short-term investigation. That is the strength of longitudinal research. It can trace developments over time that are invisible to other ways of structuring research.

This tells us the kinds of research questions that lend themselves to a longitudinal logical research structure: questions that ask about *development over time*. Here are a few examples:

- "How did/do young people of Generation ____ adjust to adulthood, as they move from high school through college and into the adult world?"
- "What are the long-term effects, if any, of the Head Start program on participants' learning, as they proceed through their later schooling?"
- "What are the long-term effects of different systems for teaching beginning readers (such as whole language learning and Hooked on Phonics) on children's reading ability and school scores 5, 10, 15, and 20 years afterward?"

Such research questions are not limited to education. Medical research has produced several important longitudinal studies, including the Australian Longitudinal Study on Women's Health, the Canadian Longitudinal Study on Aging, the Framingham Heart Study, and the Nurses' Health Study. Longitudinal research in environmental studies tracks ecosystems over time, asking such questions as "How does the level of atmospheric carbon dioxide change over time in various parts of the world?" "How does increased carbon dioxide affect tree growth rates in tropical and boreal forests?" and "What are the effects of climate change on [a particular location or ecosystem]?" From the study of organizational development, we find questions such as "What key crises do nonprofit organizations typically encounter, as they move from startup to success (or failure)?" Other fields have their own examples.

All such studies require sufficient funding and interest to sustain a long-term research commitment. That is both their chief weakness and their chief value. Longitudinal research produces insights into long-term processes that short-term research projects cannot provide.

9. Meta-Analysis

Meta-analysis is a hybrid research structure. It combines several previous studies into one and then reanalyzes their data so as to draw more general conclusions than any of the individual studies could do alone. This research strategy is often quantitative: As we'll see in Step 6, small studies often do not contain enough data to reveal clear patterns. Combining several such studies together lets the patterns show through.

Here are two examples, both of them evaluating the practice of putting students of similar abilities and characteristics in the same classroom. An early meta-analysis by Chen-Lin and James Kulik combined 52 studies that measured the effects of ability grouping on high school students.[26] Whereas the individual studies showed only small increases in average test scores, the combined dataset showed that ability grouping aided high-achieving students considerably, while aiding lower achieving students hardly at all. Conrad Carlberg and Kenneth Kavale looked at 50 studies of the effects of tracking low-IQ and special needs children into their own classes.[27] They found that special classes were significantly inferior to regular class placement for low-IQ students but were significantly better for students with emotional problems, learning disabilities, and behavioral disorders.

Both of these studies were interesting, because they were able to identify influential factors that the smaller individual studies had missed. Those small studies didn't have enough students in them to locate all of the patterns. Both studies, however, had some problems. As Robert Slavin pointed out in a subsequent reevaluation,[28] systemic **biases** in the meta-analysis process may have produced results that simply were not there.

Slavin argued that the studies that formed the basis of the Kuliks' work typically matched students in ability-grouped classes with other students of equal IQ who were not. The former students did better, but the studies failed to say why the latter students were not in the advanced classes. Was their lower achievement the result of the different classes? Or did it stem from whatever unknown factors had led school administrators to leave those students on the regular track? IQ is not the only factor in such assignments. Maturity, ability to focus, emotional development, and so on also make a difference to school success. The Kuliks' studies did not provide this information. Slavin made similar complaints about the studies on which Carlberg and Kavale relied. His point was that grouping a series of flawed studies together does not overcome their flaws. It compounds them. Meta-analysis does not have to fail, but it does have to take such factors into account.

An additional problem stems from publication bias. This is the tendency of academic journals to publish research that shows positive results and not to publish research that shows no difference between treatment groups. If there is even a moderately lower publication rate for projects that find no difference between students on various ability tracks, then a meta-analysis of published studies will overemphasize whatever difference exists. This is a serious problem with medical research, where drug companies frequently do not report negative results.[29]

These limitations do not mean that you should not chose meta-analysis as a research strategy. It just means you have to be careful that your conclusions from combining various studies are based on firm ground.

10. Action Research

The final logical structure is a bit different from the rest. The first four structures compared things. Experiments, quasi-experiments, ex post facto research, and correlational research work best for research questions that ask whether there are patterns or connections between two or more variables. The next three structures described things. Descriptive research, case studies, and historical research work best for research questions that ask for close observations. Longitudinal research and meta-analysis can either compare or describe, depending on the research question they are attempting to answer.

Action research also answers research questions, but these are questions of a different kind. Rather than "do" or "what" questions, action research best answers "how" questions.

- "How do we teach students to take responsibility for their own learning?"
- "How do we engage low-income parents as equal partners in their children's schools?"
- "How do we shift the balance between homework and in-class work, to maximize student learning?"

These are questions about processes. They are questions about skills. They are also questions that call for considerable study. They are perfect questions for research projects that involve learning how to get something done.

Let's look at an example. Starting in the late 1990s, Crichton Casbon and Lucy Walters, of England's Qualifications and Curriculum Authority (QCA), worked with local schools to find ways to use physical education and school support to improve school performance.[30] They began with eight schools, later adding 120 more. They worked with staff from each school to identify one or more areas that needed improvement—from improved attendance and behavior to improved academic work to increased involvement in healthy, active lifestyles. Each school chose its own goal, and the QCA staff worked with the schools to develop programs through which better physical education could improve these other aspects of school life. Two things were key. First, each school identified its own goals for improvement. Second, each school chose a program that it could apply and then test for effectiveness. That is what typifies action research: the process of developing and implementing a program and then testing that program to see whether it works.

In Casbon and Walters's case, this involved working with each school to identify a specific, measurable goal. "For example, a school that identified a need to improve behaviour might have the following specific objective: *We want to increase the amount of positive play happening at lunchtimes amongst our year 6 pupils.*"[31] The school team identified a program to encourage such behavior, applied it, tested it, and then changed it as needed so that it would work. The teams kept good records throughout, so that they could track their successes and failures. They specifically kept good records of their decision making and of their own learning. Action research is a process of learning *how* to do things, so the teams' observations of their own work processes are a central part of the project results. So are records of any midcourse modifications that a team finds necessary.

This characteristic distinguishes action research from other logical research structures. Whereas experimental research does not alter its procedures midcourse, action research does. Action research wants to find out what works, and if something isn't working, then it's fine to change it. You can't, however, just change things willy-nilly. Instead, you document your failures and the reasons for any midcourse changes. Then you document the outcomes. In Casbon and Walters's case, other teams that want to use physical education and sports to improve school life will be able to read this documentation and learn a lot from what worked and what didn't at the various

- Plan
- Act
- Observe
- Reflect

schools. Action research is thus practical. It collects data as rigorously as do other types of research, but it uses them in a different way.

Usually, action research projects in education are much smaller in scale. Rebecca Wisniewski described a small project at her inner-city elementary school in Lowell, Massachusetts.[32] Her school had a group of semibilingual Cambodian students who could not read. She and several other teachers decided to try a number of strategies to increase their reading ability. Each teacher chose a different method, all documented their work and their results, and they shared their successes and failures. For her part, she worked with two fourth-grade students to write a few sentences about what they were doing in school. The students turned this into a short "newspaper" that went home to their parents.

The students had to read the newspapers to their parents, as the parents could not read English. Gradually, the "newspapers" became longer and editions soon began to include parents' comments on the school, their children, and the project.

At the end, Wisniewski and her colleagues interviewed the students to find out which of the techniques worked best, from the students' point of view. They also had test scores and other objective measures, but the team found that the student feedback was crucial to improving instruction. This piece of action research, like many, used a "plan-act-observe-reflect" model.[33] Planning is followed by action; that action is observed; you reflect on the results; and then you plan new actions for further improvement. Each step is important.

Action research comes in several flavors. Each involves a plan-act-observe-reflect process. They differ in who designs the research and who makes up the research team.

Regular action research is much like the other logical structures reviewed in this chapter. The investigator chooses the project, decides how it will be carried out, runs the investigation, and organizes the reflection. When a team of investigators is involved, that team makes these decisions. In both cases, research is run from the top.

Participatory action research—sometimes called PAR—is different. PAR is run from the bottom. A community decides that it wants to learn how to do something. Perhaps it has a problem that needs solving, or maybe it needs to learn a new skill. The community decides what the problem is and then (often) hires an outside consultant to help it organize the effort. The consultant's role is typically not to make research decisions. Instead, she or he advises the community about its options and then teaches the community members whatever skills they need to carry out the research process. The "participatory" part of this research comes from the fact that the community itself makes all the decisions—including whether to do the research at all. If it decides to abandon the project halfway through, so be it. That's not the consultant's worry.

There is no clear line between action research and participatory action research; they are on a continuum. The difference is a matter of who makes decisions, and to what degree. Both are appropriate for "how" research questions. Both use a plan-act-observe-reflect model. Both are logical ways in which to structure research.

Matching Logical Structure to the Research Question

We've looked at 10 logical structures, which are summarized in Table 2.1. All of these structures are good, but they produce very different kinds of research. Your choice depends on your research question. To summarize:

- Experiments, quasi-experiments, ex post facto research, and correlational research work well for questions that ask about relationships between two or more things. Does A affect B? Do C and D typically happen together? If you have a "do" question, start looking here.
- Descriptive research, case studies, and historical research all answer "what" questions. What does E look like in the real world? What happened in the case of F? These logical structures describe things in depth. Choose one of them if your research question calls for such description.
- Longitudinal research, meta-analysis, and action research are all a bit special. The first asks what happens over time; the second draws conclusions by combining previous studies; the third answers "how" questions. Each is an appropriate structure for certain research inquiries.

The point is, you need to choose a logical structure that matches your research question. Figure 2.4 (on the next page) captures the ideal relationship. First, you develop your question. Then you choose a logical structure for your research that will let you answer it.

Now, I'll let you in on a secret: *Real research isn't that simple.* Sometimes, you start the way things are supposed to be, but then you run into trouble.

Sometimes the issue is power. Maybe your research question calls for description, but your funding agency insists that you do an experiment. They're paying the bills, so you have to conform. Or maybe you're in a discipline that doesn't like working with numbers. Certain subfields of anthropology, for example, insist that all research should be descriptive. Certain subfields of psychology, by contrast, insist that numerical comparisons are the only way to go. Such situations are unfortunate, but they're not unusual.

TABLE 2.1   Ten Logical Structures for Research
1. True experiments
2. Quasi-experiments
3. Ex post facto research
4. Correlational research
5. Descriptive research
6. Case studies
7. Historical research
8. Longitudinal research
9. Meta-analysis
10. Action research

FIGURE 2.4   Letting Your Research Question Determine Your Logical Structure

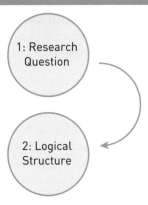

More benignly—though with the same result—you may find that your research question suggests a logical structure that you can't, in fact, carry out. This may be a matter of data: Suppose that you want to measure the effectiveness of a particular kind of charter school on improving elementary students' enjoyment of their education. This calls for a comparative study. The data for doing such a study, though, currently don't exist. Unless you can generate those data yourself—not likely, unless you have a very large research budget—you can't do your comparison.

In such cases, you need a Plan B. If you can't do a large charter school study, maybe you can do a small one. If you can't make the comparisons you want, maybe you can do some very good descriptions. In short, when the perfect logical research structure isn't possible, you can go back and revise your research question. Choose a question close to your first one, making sure that it calls for a logical research structure that you have the resources to accomplish.

Figure 2.5 illustrates this situation. The right-hand arrow indicates that the logical structure still has to match the research question. That hasn't changed. The left-hand

FIGURE 2.5   Matching Your Logical Structure to Your Research Question

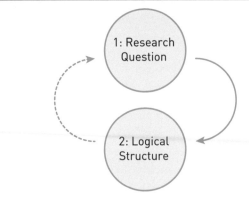

arrow (with the dashed line) indicates that you're allowed to work backward if you have to. The point is to get the two things to match. Usually, the question determines the structure, but sometimes the influence has to run the other way.

Review Questions

1. Why do you identify your research question before choosing a logical structure for your research?

2. Why is choosing a logical structure important?

3. What are the main differences between comparative research and descriptive research?

4. What are some of the strengths and drawbacks of each of the ten logical research structures presented in this chapter?

5. Why might you want to alter your research question after examining the possible logical structures for your project?

The open-access Student Study Site at **study.sagepub.com/spickard** has a variety of useful study tools, including SAGE journal articles, video & web resources, eFlashcards, and quizzes.

Notes

1. Maria Blanton et al., "The Development of Children's Algebraic Thinking: The Impact of a Comprehensive Early Algebra Intervention in Third Grade," *Journal for Research in Mathematics Education* 46 (2015): 39–87.

2. John Connelly led this project. It was part of a larger study described by Estelle Fuchs and Robert Havighurst in *To Live on This Earth: American Indian Education*. Albuquerque: University of New Mexico Press, 1972.

3. John Collier, Jr., *Alaskan Eskimo Education: A Film Analysis of Cultural Confrontation in the Schools*. New York: Holt, Rinehart, and Winston, 1973.

4. Joseph Tobin et al., *Preschool in Three Cultures: Japan, China, and the United States*. New Haven, CT: Yale University Press, 1989. A follow-up study and two videos are available at www.joetobin.net.

5. Here are two of the other measures: the overall poverty rate (Mississippi, 22.4%; New Hampshire, 8.3%), and the percentage of kids under age 6 living in poverty (Mississippi, 37.8%; New Hampshire, 13.8%).

6. I'll discuss negative correlations in Step 6. Briefly, positive correlations mean that two things happen in the same places or to the same people, whereas negative correlations mean that where

(Continued)

(Continued)

one happens, the other doesn't. In either case, the two variables are related. A zero-correlation means there is no relationship between them.

7. Murat Bursal and Lynda Paznokas, "Mathematics Anxiety and Pre-service Teachers' Confidence to Teach Mathematics and Science," *School Science & Mathematics*, 106 (2006): 173–180.

8. George Domino and Amanda Morales, "Reliability and Validity of the D-48 with Mexican American College Students," *Hispanic Journal of Behavioral Sciences*, 22 (2000): 382–389.

9. Philip DeCicca and Justin Smith, "The Long-Run Impacts of Early Childhood Education: Evidence From a Failed Policy Experiment," *Economics of Education Review* 36 (2013): 41–59.

10. Shin-Yi Chou et al., "Parental Education and Child Health: Evidence From a Natural Experiment in Taiwan," *National Bureau of Economic Research, Working Paper 13466*. Retrieved from http://www.nber.org/papers/w13466.pdf

11. John W. Alspaugh, "The Effect of Transition Grade to High School, Gender, and Grade Level Upon Dropout Rates," *American Secondary Education* 29 (2000): 2–9.

12. Elaine Humphrey, "An Ex-Post Facto Study of First Generation Students," master's thesis, Department of Education, Virginia Polytechnic Institute and State University, Blacksburg, Virginia, 2000.

13. Barrie Thorne, *Gender Play: Girls and Boys in School*. New Brunswick, NJ: Rutgers University Press, 1993.

14. Thorne, *Gender Play*, 65–66.

15. Elias Avramidis et al., "A Survey Into Mainstream Teachers' Attitudes Towards the Inclusion of Children With Special Educational Needs in the Ordinary School in One Local Education Authority," *Educational Psychology* 20 (2000): 191–211.

16. Ludwig Binswanger, "The Case of Ellen West," pp. 237–364 in Rollo May et al. (eds.), *Existence: A New Dimension in Psychiatry and Psychology*. New York: Basic Books, 1958 (original in German, 1944). See also Walter Vandereycken, "New Documentation on the Famous Case of 'Ellen West,'" *History of Psychiatry* 14 (2003): 133–134; and Naamah Akavia, "Writing the Case of Ellen West: Clinical Knowledge and Historical Representation," *Science in Context* 21 (2008): 119–144.

17. Jay MacLeod, *Ain't No Makin' It: Leveled Aspirations in a Low-Income Community*. Boulder, CO: Westview Press, 1987.

18. All four articles are from George and Louise Spindler, eds. *Interpretive Ethnography of Education at Home and Abroad*, Mahwah, NJ: Lawrence Erlbaum, 1987.

19. Bob Schlagal, "Classroom Spelling Instruction: History, Research, and Practice," *Reading Research and Instruction* 42 (2002): 44–57.

20. Jacquelyn Dowd Hall, "The Long Civil Rights Movement and the Political Uses of the Past," *Journal of American History* 91 (2005): 1233–1263.

21. The quote is from p. 1234.

22. See Terrie L. Epstein, "Tales From Two Textbooks: A Comparison of the Civil Rights Movement in Two Secondary History Textbooks," *Social Studies* 85 (1994): 121–126.

23. Details of these studies can be found at the National Center for Educational Statistics website, https://nces.ed.gov/surveys/hsb/. Data for some of these studies are readily available.

24. Beth Rubin, *Shifts in the Social Contract: Understanding Change in American Society.* Thousand Oaks, CA: Pine Forge Press, 1996.

25. George Spindler, *Burgbach: Urbanization and Identity in a German Village.* New York: Holt, Rinehart, & Winston, 1973. I contributed in a small way to this study when I was an undergraduate taking the Spindlers' courses.

26. Chen-Lin Kulik and James Kulik, "Effects of Ability Grouping on Secondary School Students: A Meta-Analysis of Evaluation Findings," *American Educational Research Journal* 19 (1982): 415–428.

27. Conrad Carlberg and Kenneth Kavale, "The Efficacy of Special Versus Regular Class Placement for Exceptional Children: A Meta-Analysis," *Journal of Special Education* 14 (1980): 295–309.

28. Robert E. Slavin, "Meta-Analysis in Education: How Has It Been Used?" *Educational Researcher* 13 (1984): 6–15.

29. P. Easterbrook et al., "Publication Bias in Clinical Research," *Lancet* 337 (8746): 867–872, 1991; K. Dwan et al., "Systematic Review of the Empirical Evidence of Study Publication Bias and Outcome Reporting Bias," *PLOS One* 3(2008).

30. Crichton Casbon and Lucy Walters, "Using an Action Research Model to Bring About School Improvement Through PE and School Sport." Paper presented at the Australian Association for Research in Education annual conference, Melbourne, Australia, November 28–December 2, 2004. Retrieved from http://education.qld .gov.au/staff/development/performance/ resources/readings/example-school-action-research-project.pdf

31. Casbon and Walters, 6.

32. Rebecca Wisniewski, "Stories From the Field," pp. 16–21 in *Action Research* by Eileen Ferrance, Northeast and Islands Regional Educational Laboratory at Brown University, 2000. Retrieved from http:// www.brown.edu/academics/education-alliance/sites/brown.edu.academics .education-alliance/files/publications/ act_research.pdf

33. Stephen Kemmis and Robin McTaggart, *The Action Research Planner.* Victoria, Australia: Deakin University Press, 1982.

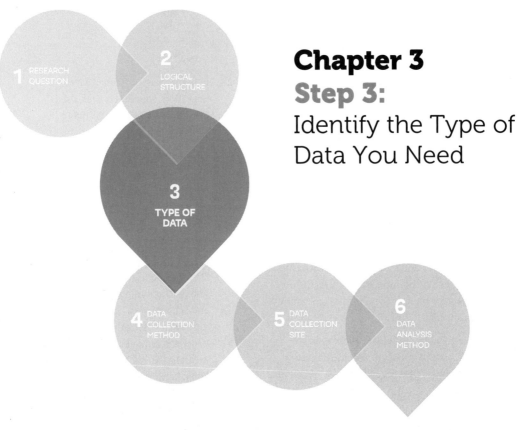

Chapter 3
Step 3:
Identify the Type of Data You Need

RESULTS

Y ou've developed a good research question and have chosen a logical structure for your project. Now you have to figure out what **type of data** you need to find. Each research question asks for a different type of data. Some questions ask you to focus on acts and behavior: what people, animals, and other things *do*. Others ask you to focus on beliefs and attitudes: what people (though probably not animals and plants) *think*. Still others—and here I'll focus on the social sciences—look for such things as personal feelings, psychological traits, or hidden social patterns. Each of these is a different type of data. You need to figure out what type of data your research question is asking you to find. Only then can you pick a method for collecting the data (Step 4), a site in which to find it (Step 5), and a method for analyzing the data you have discovered (Step 6).

You probably noticed that each of the research questions I outlined in Chapter 1 calls for a specific kind of information. For example, the question "How much did this transit project reduce congestion on nearby highways?" asks us to measure "congestion." How should we define this concept, to make our research project most useful? We've got some choices. We can think of congestion as the amount of traffic on the road at any given time (number of cars per lane-mile), or we can think of it as the amount of time each driver loses from not being able to drive the speed limit. In either case, we are measuring behavior. We are looking for things that people *do*. True, they

Type of Data

don't choose to get stuck in traffic: Crowded highways force people to drive slowly. It's still behavior, though. It's an action that we can observe.

Other questions ask for different kinds of information. The survey question "How much do you use your car during a typical month?" asks people to report on their behavior. Here we don't observe people. We ask them to tell us what they do. *Behavior* and *reports of behavior* are two different types of data. The first are acts: things that actually happen in the real world. These are things that we can (potentially) observe. The second are *reports* of those acts, either by the parties involved or by knowledgeable observers. People tell us what happens—which is not the same thing as our observing them directly. We have to be clear about the type of data we are getting.

An example will make the difference clear. Americans have a far higher rate of church participation than do people in other highly developed countries. This is not in doubt. Yet, how many people actually attend church, synagogue, mosque, or other religious services in any given week?

The Gallup Organization has polled Americans about their religious participation for decades. The General Social Survey interviews a representative sample of Americans on this topic every 2 years. The Princeton Religious Research Center and the Pew Research Center have carried out numerous surveys since the 1990s. Though numbers vary a bit, about 40% of the poll respondents report attending a religious service within the past 7 days. The General Social Survey percentages have dropped since about 2000, to the low 30s, but that's still much higher than religious participation is in Canada, Europe, Japan, and other industrialized countries.

These are self-reports, however. What happens if you try to measure attendance directly? Kirk Hadaway, Penny Marler, and Mark Chaves did that in the early 1990s. They counted attendance at all Protestant churches in a county in northwestern Ohio and compared the results with reported attendance from a contemporaneous poll. They also obtained attendance figures from 18 Catholic dioceses, which they compared with poll results in those areas. In each case, they found the actual attendance level to be about half of the amount obtained from the poll results. Americans reported high church attendance, but their behavior was significantly different.[1]

THINK ABOUT IT
What are the differences between "behavior" and "reports of behavior"?

As Chaves later pointed out,[2] poll respondents probably aren't lying, nor are they likely to have forgotten. Many Americans consider themselves to be religious, and one of the signs of "being religious" is attendance at church services. Telling a pollster that you attended last week, when you did not, may be a way of affirming your identity as a religious person. Or it may be a way of saying, "Well, I usually attend, and if you'd asked me any time in the past several weeks, I could have said 'yes' legitimately. So saying 'yes' now is truer than saying 'no,' at least in the overall scheme of things." People think like that, by the way, and they don't consider it untruthful. Still, it makes self-reported data less reliable. It makes survey research more difficult to conduct than it would otherwise be.

Does this mean that we can't trust people to report their own behavior? Not necessarily. In the mid-1990s, Stanley Presser and Linda Stinson had people fill out time diaries, listing their activities and the time they spent on them.[3] Looking at Christians' Monday entries, which reported the previous day's behavior, they found that about 29% attended some sort of religious service. That's about a third lower than the Gallup and GSS polls at that time and just a bit higher than the actual counts. It seems that you can get people to report accurately about church attendance, if you don't ask them directly.

The take-away for us, however, is simpler. *Behavior* and *reports of behavior* are different types of data. They can answer different research questions. Our question should always specify exactly which type of data we need.

Fourteen Types of Data

What types of data are there? Here are 14 of the most important types of data that researchers seek. I've already described the first two, behaviors and reports of behaviors, though I expand on them here to include **events** and **reports of events**—similar phenomena that have a similar distinction between them.

1. Acts, Behavior, or Events

Acts, behavior, or events are either the things that people, animals, and the like *do* or the things that happen. Going to church is an act; the church service itself is an event. They both happen in real time, right in front of us. To capture them, we have to observe them directly. The same is true when environmental researchers observe animal behavior, or when they track what goes on in a particular ecosystem. Both things involve the direct observation of acts, behavior, or events.

Scientists call these **first-order phenomena**, which means that we can experience them directly, if we are present. If we are *not* present, then we have a choice. If we are investigating people, we can get second-order reports about them from others, or we can ask them directly. (See the next item.) If we are investigating animals or ecosystems, we can set up video cameras or make audio recordings. These are not quite first-order phenomena, because what is captured is only what the camera or microphone picks up. These data are closer than reports, but they're not as good as being there. Still, cameras and recorders are useful—particularly for recording behavior that is difficult to observe. Environmental researchers often use cameras to capture the movements of rare nocturnal animals. Social researchers occasionally review security camera footage to obtain records of illicit human behavior. (Be sure to check with your Institutional Review Board [IRB] before planning research using this technique; see Step 4.)

2. Reports of Acts, Behavior, or Events

Reports of acts, behavior, or events are the accounts that people provide about acts, behavior, or events. They are **second-order phenomena**, such as people telling us they went to church last week or what they heard at a concert last night. Sometimes you want to observe things directly; other times you want to learn what people have to say about them. Your research question needs to be very specific about which type of data you are after.

Clearly, if you can't observe acts, behavior, or events, either directly or by remote means, you'll have to settle for reports. In some situations, however, you'll want the reports rather than direct observations. Going back to our church example, the fact that more people report attending religious services than actually attend them tells us something about the high status of religion in U.S. society. The decline in reported attendance over time, however, tells us that religion is not as important a part of American life as it once was. Direct observation would not give us this information. Only people's reports of their behavior (and the fact that we can check those reports for accuracy) give us the data we need. This is a case in which reports are *better* than observations.

The point, though, is that observations of behavior (or acts or events) and reports of behavior (or acts or events) are different types of data. You need to make sure that your research question asks about the type of data that you really need.

3. Economic Data

Economic data are related to the economy: what's been bought, sold, and traded; how much money people make at various occupations; what kinds of goods get produced; and so on. These are almost always reports of acts or events, systematically collected by government agencies, banks, and businesses. For example, gross domestic product (GDP) is the total value of all goods and services produced in a given country. Companies report the value of the things they make each month, writers report how much they earned on their books and articles, hospitals report the costs of treating patients, newspapers report their circulation and their ad sales, and so on. Each of these pieces of data reports an action: products made, articles sold, patients treated, and so forth. Though we could conceivably count this stuff, no one typically does so. Instead, we rely on people to report what they do. Add up the reports, and you've got economic data.

Some figures are more reliable than others. For example, you can hook up a meter to the local power plant to see how much electricity it has produced. The meter will capture this information directly. Someone, however, has to read the meter and report the results, so you're still dealing with a report, though it's probably a good one.

By contrast, I'd bet that few gamblers report their winnings accurately, either to their spouses or to the government at tax time. Casinos may do a better job (they're easier to audit), but they probably don't keep track of how much small bettors win or lose.

Some research questions ask us to examine economic data. We need to be wise about how these data are produced. Sometimes they are very reliable, but other times they are not. If the data we want are apt to be inaccurate, we should design our research to use something better.

4. Organizational Data

Economic data describe an economy, either a large one, like the economy of the United States, or a smaller one, like the economy of San Antonio, Texas, where I live. **Organizational data** describe organizations: schools, businesses, governments, and similar entities. Like economic data, they mainly describe behavior and characteristics: How many employees does an organization have? How is the organization structured? How many customers does it have? What are the objective results of its operation? Such questions ask you to describe the behavior of the organization as a whole or—sometimes—the behavior of people in it. You can also compare organizations, just as you can compare economies. Organizational data are open to both comparative and descriptive research projects.

A word of caution here: Some organizational data are not behavioral. You may, for example, want to ask what an organization sees as its mission—a matter of ideas, not behavior. Similarly, the question of how the organization's leaders see it working is a matter of collecting their informed opinions. Such questions really belong to one of the nonbehavioral data types, not to this one. *Mission* is a matter of organizational identity (self-identity), and *informed opinions* are a matter of expert knowledge. These are different from the kind of organizational data I include here and are described later in this chapter.

5. Demographic Data

THINK ABOUT IT
What do economic, organizational, and demographic data have in common?

The term *demographic* comes from two Greek terms, *demos* and *graphie*. Roughly translated, it means "descriptions of a people." **Demographic data** describe the collective characteristics of a population. Like economic data, these data are usually collected by government agencies, businesses, and other organizations, often through required reports. Universities, for example, have to report the percentage of students who identify as White, Black, Asian, Native American, and so on. They also have to report the number who identify themselves as Hispanic, Spanish-surnamed, Latino/a,

Chicano/a, and the like—all identities that point to one of the fastest-growing American ethnic groups, people of Latin American descent.[4] According to the U.S. Census Bureau, "Hispanics can be of any race." This is a rather clumsy way to acknowledge that many Latin American countries don't use the North American racial model to categorize their populations.[5]

Besides race, demographic data include gender, age, generation, social class, level of education, and sometimes wealth or poverty. They can include such things as the ability to speak and read other languages, whether or not one owns a home, and the extent to which people have had various life experiences, such as illness and travel. Some of these are social identities, while others are reports of acts, behavior, or events. Research questions that call for demographic data need to be thought through carefully, keeping the differences between social identities and reports of acts in mind.

6. Self-Identity

Self-identity consists of the labels we use to describe ourselves. I, for example, am an American of mixed Norwegian, German, English, Irish, French, and Dutch ancestry. I am male, a father, a teacher, politically progressive, West Coast raised, and a Quaker. (I'm also technically a senior citizen, but I don't like to think about that.) One of my former students, by contrast, is female, pagan/agnostic, middle-aged, a mother, also an American, an East Coaster, left-liberal, a teacher, and a community builder.

As you can see, self-identities are complex. Each one of us affirms certain things about ourselves, ignoring others. Understood deeply, self-identities are hard to compare. They are, however, rich sources of information about people. Ask someone, "Who are you?" when you have time to listen, and the response is likely to teach you a lot.

We can also collect shallower identities. Nearly every American can answer the question "Are you a Republican, a Democrat, or an Independent?" The same is true for the question "What race are you: White or Caucasian, Black or African American, Asian or Asian American, Native American, mixed-race, or other?" Culturally, Americans believe they can change the former but not the latter. We can switch political parties but can't change our race—at least so we think.[6]

I have a colleague, however, who says (correctly), "I grew up White, was Black in my early adulthood, and have spent the last few decades struggling to be Asian." This makes sense when you know his story. His parents were from Pakistan and he grew up in the United States, where Pakistanis are considered White. He moved to England, where Pakistanis are considered Black—as are many other people from Britain's former colonies in South Asia, Africa, and the Caribbean. As a politically engaged scholar, he has been at the forefront of the movement to have the British government recognize "Asian" as a separate racial category.[7]

Self-identities can be powerful things. You'll need to keep in mind that each person constructs her or his identity differently, so the words that you use to describe people may not match what they use to describe themselves. Be careful here: You don't want to alienate your research subjects from the start.

7. Shallow Opinions and Attitudes

We all have opinions. Until we think about it, however, we seldom realize that personal opinions are of two types. Some are relatively shallow. If someone asks us, for example, whether we like a particular movie, we can easily toss off an answer. The same is true if we're asked if we approve of a politician's stand on the economy, war, or abortion. These **shallow opinions and attitudes** sit relatively close to the surface of people's lives and cover a variety of topics.

For example, I believe that eggplants are probably good for you, and I've learned several ways to cook them. I still don't much like them, though. Moreover, I don't think my opinion about them is very important. This is how shallow personal opinions work. As we'll see in Chapter 4, questionnaires capture such opinions easily, though you should never overinterpret the results; these opinions might not be very important, even to the people who hold them.

The Argentinian author Jorge Luis Borges wrote, "When you come right down to it, opinions are the most superficial things about anyone." You don't have to agree with him to recognize that some opinions are, indeed, shallow.

> **THINK ABOUT IT**
>
> Can you name some of your own shallow opinions? Some of your deep opinions? How are these different?

8. Deeply Held Opinions and Attitudes

Other opinions are more deeply held. For instance, it is very hard to answer a question like "Do you have a sense of purpose in life?" Almost everyone has an opinion on the matter, but those opinions are complex and nuanced. The same is true of the question "Do you believe in God?" Taken seriously, this is a matter for deep reflection. Surprisingly, many religious people find this question hard to answer, because it depends on what one means by the terms *God* and *believe.* I've interviewed religious people who certainly don't think that the world is run by an old guy with a long white beard who sits on clouds throwing thunderbolts. These same people, however, find their lives to be led by a power higher than they can comprehend. Some call this "believing in God"; others don't, and yet others are not sure. This is typical of **deeply held personal opinions and attitudes.** They are subtle and multifaceted. Questionnaires don't capture them well at all. Interviews do. We'll see how interviews do this when we cover data collection methods in Step 4 and in Chapter 11, when we cover various kinds of interviewing. We'll also see lots of examples in Part II of this book.

The point here is that shallow and deep opinions are different types of data.

9. Personal Feelings

I'll be brief with this data type. If personal opinions are the things that individuals think and believe (either shallowly or deeply), then **personal feelings** are the emotions individuals have in certain situations. These are not usually shallow. Yes, people can have shallow feelings, but few scholars are interested in them. Sociologists and psychologists who study emotions typically find deeper feelings more interesting and also more significant. They also find them to be more complex—a clear parallel with the deep personal opinions that I mentioned earlier.

Emotions can be studied socially. Arlie Hochschild demonstrated this in *The Managed Heart*: a study of how work and gender roles call for people to have certain emotions and suppress others.[8] The point here is to know when your research question asks you to locate opinions and when it asks you to locate feelings. Ideas and emotions, though related, are different things. Thus they are different types of data.

10. Cultural Knowledge

Personal opinions are things that individuals know or think they know. **Cultural knowledge**, in contrast, consists of things that *everyone* knows—at least everyone in a particular society, subculture, or social scene. For example, almost every suburban American teenager over the age of 16 knows how to drive a car. Getting a driver's license is a coming-of-age ritual in this subculture, one that both signifies and produces greater independence. One is no longer a child, dependent on others for transportation. Knowing how to drive—and being certified as a good driver—is a core cultural competence. Were you to investigate teen driving, then, you could interview almost anyone in the suburbs about it. This knowledge is shared, not simply personal.

Similarly, most long-term homeless people know how to make their own alcohol. As James Spradley learned from studying Seattle "tramp culture" in the late 1960s,[9] one needs just raisins, sugar, bread yeast, water, and a bucket to mix them in. Fermentation starts quickly in warm weather, and one can produce drinkable hooch in 4 or 5 days. Though common among "tramps," this knowledge is rare among other American groups. Spradley described several other areas of tramps' cultural knowledge: when to "cop a plea," how to "do a nose-dive," how to avoid "the bulls," and so on.[10] Mainstream observers seldom realize how many practical things homeless people know.

We could multiply such instances. For example, nearly every Native American woman on the Flathead Reservation in Montana knows how to butcher a moose. Few professional-class city-dwelling White women do, but the latter know more about hiring nannies and household help. The point is that these are matters of culture, not of individual knowledge. Researchers need to recognize this difference. Otherwise, they draw inaccurate conclusions from their data.

11. Expert Knowledge

In a sense, much cultural knowledge is also **expert knowledge**—at least to the extent that it gives members of a subculture the ability to survive in their local environment. The Seattle "tramps" whom Spradley interviewed were experts at living on the street, something that not many Americans know how to do. By highlighting "expert knowledge," though, we want to emphasize the fact that not every member of a particular cultural or social group has expertise in all parts of life. Especially in complex societies, certain people know more than others about certain things. Some research projects don't focus on what everyone knows but rather on what the experts know. Thus, we separate these two types of data.

Let's imagine that you want to find out about the interactions that go on between doctors and other medical staff in a hospital operating room. Most Americans know a bit about how hospitals work, but the only operating rooms they've seen were probably on television. Or they might have been operated on as patients, but then they were likely under anesthesia and in no state to observe what was happening. We're clearly not dealing with general cultural knowledge. We have to seek expert knowledge, most likely from medical personnel themselves. Only they can give us the information we seek.

To return to our mass transit example from Chapter 1, only transit experts can tell us what factors transit planners take into account in designing transit systems. Only political decision makers can tell us what factors go into their decisions about what kind of systems to approve. If our research questions call for expert knowledge, then we need to seek out those experts. We can't just ask the next person we pass on the street.

12. Personal and Psychological Traits

The data type of **personal and psychological traits** is found most often in psychology, though there are other fields that use something similar. Psychologists argue that individuals have different inner traits that shape their attitudes, feelings, and behavior. To use a popular example, some people are extraverts: sociable, assertive, emotionally expressive, and even excitable. People who are high in this trait are often outgoing and talkative, while those low in this trait are typically quiet and reserved. This trait is portrayed as part of some people's inner make-up. It isn't a matter of opinion, because believing one is extraverted doesn't make one so. It also isn't a matter of cultural or expert knowledge. Indeed, it isn't knowledge at all. It is a way of being, part of one's personality.

There are hosts of personality theories. Everyone has heard of the Myers-Briggs personality type assessment, but it is far from being the only game in town. One current favorite is the "Big Five" personality dimension scheme.[11] According to this theory, people's personalities vary along five key dimensions: extraversion, agreeableness, conscientiousness, openness, and neuroticism. Pencil-and-paper psychological tests can tell the degree to which a person has or does not have each of these attributes, relative to other people. The tests ask people to respond to 50 or so questions on a five-point scale, ranging from "strongly agree" to "strongly disagree." The pattern of answers is supposed to reveal an inward personality pattern that the test-takers do not themselves know. More exactly, they know it only after taking the test and hearing its interpretation.

Intelligence (as a claimed trait) is another example. Various tests have been devised to measure "g"—a postulated "general intelligence" that is supposed to operate similarly in many parts of life. The Stanford-Binet and the Wechsler IQ tests are the most famous of these tests. They emphasize skill at abstract reasoning, from which they predict such things as success in school and performance at professional jobs. Critics have argued that intelligence involves much more than reasoning, and that these predictions work only because schools and professional jobs reward abstract reasoning more than they reward other kinds of intelligence. They say that musical intelligence, emotional intelligence, kinesthetic intelligence, and other forms of intelligence get fewer rewards, though they are equally important to a well-lived human life.[12] We don't have to take sides in this debate to note that advocates and critics alike are claiming the existence of underlying personal traits. They are simply arguing about the nature of those traits and about what the various tests that measure them are actually uncovering.

That's the point about this data type: It needs to be uncovered. Personal and psychological traits are not a type of knowledge, because these traits do not depend on awareness. They are not matters of personal opinion for the same reason. Nor are they matters of feeling or emotion. We are aware of our knowledge and our feelings, but we have only a vague sense of our traits. (Otherwise, why would we spend time taking tests to find out who we are?) Research projects that seek to discover people's personal and psychological traits thus must use different data collection methods than those that gather attitudes, opinions, knowledge, and other things of which we are aware.

There is one caveat here. Some people claim personal and psychological traits as identities. Think, for example, of how many of your friends claim to be introverts, even if they've never taken a psychological test to measure that trait. The social desirability of different traits varies from one situation to another, so some people are going to claim traits in order to gain social status. That's a fine topic to investigate, but if you do, you're not going to be investigating personal and psychological traits per se; you'll be investigating people's identities.

It's always best to be clear about the type of data you are seeking.

13. Experience as It Presents Itself to Consciousness

Experience as it presents itself to consciousness is a rather tricky data type. In fact, it's the most complicated of the data types, philosophically speaking. To understand it, we have to learn something about the term *experience*. It means something quite different in the research world than it does in ordinary life.

Americans (and quite probably others) are very sloppy with the word *experience*. They talk about movies being "a great experience," they encourage others to "experience this speaker's wisdom," and they refer to difficult encounters by saying, "Well, *that* was an experience." I once interviewed an elderly Presbyterian, who said about her pastor, whom she didn't like: "He said he had a very spiritual experience last week, and I'm sure she was." This is not the kind of experience that I mean.

Philosophically speaking, *experience* took on a technical definition in the early 20th century. Edmund Husserl developed what he called "phenomenology" as a method for separating *raw experience* from the *interpretations of experience* that people typically give.[13] He argued that we first experience things, then attach labels to those experiences. For example, we hear a sound that we cannot at first identify. We focus on it, and then we recognize it: "Oh, that must be an airplane." The sound then fades into the background as "airplane noise."

Examined internally, each of these stages is experienced differently. There is first the pure sound, plus our experience of inner puzzlement. Then there is an experience of realization, followed immediately by labeling. Then we experience the noise fading into the background as our attention moves elsewhere. Phenomenologists explore such processes. They examine experience exactly as it presents itself to our consciousness. They thus hope to learn something about human living.

Of course, things are often more complicated than that. Martin Heidegger, among others, has pointed out that we often experience objects and labels together, inseparably.[14] We do not, for example, first experience a stick of wood with a metal crosspiece on one end and then call it a hammer. We just pick up a hammer to whack a nail. The hammer is "ready-to-hand," to use Heidegger's term for it. We do not even realize that it is metal and wood unless something goes wrong—like the head flying off and breaking a window. Heidegger did, however, see the difference between our shock at seeing the head fly off and our explanation for it. Statements such as "It must have been loose" or "That hammer is getting old" or even "It must have been God's will" are not part of the direct experience. Heidegger argued that we separate experience from interpretation at such moments of failure. Like Husserl, however, he was intent on understanding experience exactly as it presents itself to consciousness.[15]

Because we need to separate types of data as clearly as possible, we'll distinguish between *pure experience as it presents itself to consciousness* and the *later interpretations of it* that people give. **Experience** is what presents itself to us directly, unmediated by ideas, opinions, feelings, or meanings. These ideas, opinions, feelings, or meanings interpret or label that experience; they are thus conceptual in a way that pure experience is not. *Experience* is thus different from *interpretation*. The latter is a belief; the former is not. Experience is a different type of data than the ones we have seen before.

14. Hidden Social Patterns

Men, are you aware that you often interrupt others in conversation but don't like being interrupted? Women, are you comfortable with the fact that you frequently turn statements into questions by raising your voice pitch at the end of them? These are just two of the gender-specific patterns that sociolinguist Deborah Tannen has found among middle-class Americans.[16] Each has its own gender-specific interpretation. To men, for example, a woman's raised-tone question undermines her authority, but to women, it invites further conversation. Tannen argues that men are more likely to be attuned to their position in a dominance hierarchy, while women are more likely to seek connection with others. These are tendencies, to be sure, but considerable research reveals these hidden patterns.

Hidden social patterns are just that: patterns of social behavior that are typically invisible to their participants. They don't think about them; they just do them. Then they are sometimes surprised or upset by the patterns when they are brought to light.

For example, my students routinely underestimate their position in the American class structure. When asked to rank family income on an income distribution scale, they almost universally underestimate by about 20%. They estimate that a family earning $80,000 (two teachers' salaries, for example) is about the middle of the scale. In fact, the 2012 median family income was a shade over $50,000, and an $80,000 income was higher than 70% of families. My students don't feel particularly well off, and they are right about that, but their families are usually doing better than they think.

Hidden social patterns are thus their own data type. They aren't matters of knowledge or opinion, neither personal, nor cultural, nor expert (though experts will often know about them). They differ from acts, behavior, and events because these are all frontstage, to use a theatrical analogy. Hidden social patterns stay backstage, managing the show. We can see their effects, though it takes some effort to do so. They call for their own data collection methods.

This list of data types could go on. I have simply chosen 14 important ones, so that you can understand the differences among them (see Table 3.1). My list includes a lot of data types that interest social scientists, because the social sciences handle a much wider variety of data types than do other scientific disciplines. Natural scientists mainly observe behavior—animal, vegetable, or mineral. Even they, however, must be clear about the kind of data they are seeking.

TABLE 3.1 Fourteen Types of Data
1.   Acts, behavior, and events
2.   Reports of acts, behavior, and events
3.   Economic data
4.   Organizational data
5.   Demographic data
6.   Self-identity
7.   Shallow opinions and attitudes
8.   Deep opinions and attitudes
9.   Personal feelings
10.   Cultural knowledge
11.   Expert knowledge
12.   Personal and psychological traits
13.   Experience as it presents itself to consciousness
14.   Hidden social patterns

> **The Rule: The type of data you want determines the data collection method you use.**

No matter what discipline, the type of data you want is the key element is designing research. After developing a good research question and choosing a logical structure for your project, you need to identify clearly what type of data that question asks you to find. Knowing the type of data tells you what data collection method you can use to gather that data, the data collection site where that type of data is likely to be found, and which data analysis method you should use to interpret the results.

Identifying the type of data you need is thus central to the research process. It is the linchpin that makes good research design possible. Specifically, *the type of data you want determines the data collection method you use.* Chapter 4 will show you how to pick a data collection method.

Review Questions

1. How does your research question tell you what type of data you need?

2. What are the major differences among the data types?

3. Give some examples of each data type and describe a research question that might lead you to seek each type of data.

4. Why is it important to identify the type of data you need before you figure out how you are going to collect it?

The open-access Student Study Site at **study.sagepub.com/spickard** has a variety of useful study tools, including SAGE journal articles, video & web resources, eFlashcards, and quizzes.

Notes

1. C. Kirk Hadaway, Penny Long Marler, and Mark Chaves, "What the Polls Don't Show: A Closer Look at U.S. Church Attendance," *American Sociological Review* 58 (1993): 741–752.

2. Mark Chaves, *American Religion: Contemporary Trends.* Princeton, NJ: Princeton University Press, 2011, pp. 44–45.

3. Stanley Presser and Linda Stinson, "Data Collection Mode and Social Desirability Bias in Self-Reported Religious Attendance," *American Sociological Review* 63 (1998): 137–145.

4. The terms *Hispanic* and *Spanish-surnamed* clearly also include those whose ancestors came to the United States from Spain. Whether it should do so is a matter of considerable debate. See Clara E. Rodriguez, *Changing Race: Latinos, the Census, and the History of Ethnicity.* New York: New York University Press, 2000.

5. See G. Reginald Daniel, *Race and Multiraciality in Brazil and the United States.* State College, PA: Pennsylvania State University Press, 2007.

6. The situation is actually very complicated. As Paul Spickard points out, the American racial system is a social construct, in which some people can choose their race and others have it forced upon them. African slaves, for example, had no choice but to become "Black"—a social category forged in the mid-18th century. Navajo, Iroquois, Cherokee, and so on first became "Indian" by the mid-1800s, then "Native American" in the late 20th century. See Paul Spickard, *Almost All Aliens: Immigration, Race, and Colonialism in American History and Identity.* New York: Routledge, 2007.

7. Americans would say "South Asian," because we use the term "Asian" to refer to people whose ancestors came from East Asia: mainly China, Japan, Korea, Thailand, and Vietnam. That's another peculiarity of identity: People use the same term to mean different things.

8. Arlie Russell Hochschild, *The Managed Heart: The Commercialization of Human Feeling.* Berkeley: University of California Press, 1979.

9. James Spradley, *You Owe Yourself a Drunk: Adaptive Strategies of Urban Nomads.* Boston, MA: Little, Brown, 1970.

10. "Cop a plea" means to plead guilty to a lesser charge, to avoid jail time. "Do a nose-dive" means to get help from a soup kitchen or shelter run by a religious organization, where you have to pray before meals or going to bed. "Bulls" are police officers.

11. See Warren Norman, "Toward an Adequate Taxonomy of Personality Attributes: Replicated Factor Structure in Peer Nomination Personality Ratings," *Journal of Abnormal and Social Psychology* 66 (1963): 574–583; Robert R. McCrae and Paul T. Costa, "Validation of the Five-Factor Model of Personality Across Instruments and Observers," *Journal of Personality and Social Psychology,* 52 (1987): 81–90.

12. Howard Gardner, *Intelligence Reframed: Multiple Intelligences for the 21st Century.* New York: Basic Books, 1999.

13. See, for example, Edmund Husserl, *The Phenomenology of Internal Time-Consciousness.* Bloomington: University of Indiana Press, 1964; original, 1928.

14. Martin Heidegger, *Being and Time.* New York: Harper & Row, 1962; original, 1927.

15. Amedeo Giorgi has developed a rigorous method for using phenomenology as a research tool. See his *The Descriptive Phenomenological Method in Psychology.* Pittsburgh, PA: Duquesne University Press, 2009. I describe his method when we explore how to study experiences in Part II.

16. Deborah Tannen, *You Just Don't Understand: Women and Men in Conversation.* New York: Ballantine Books, 1990.

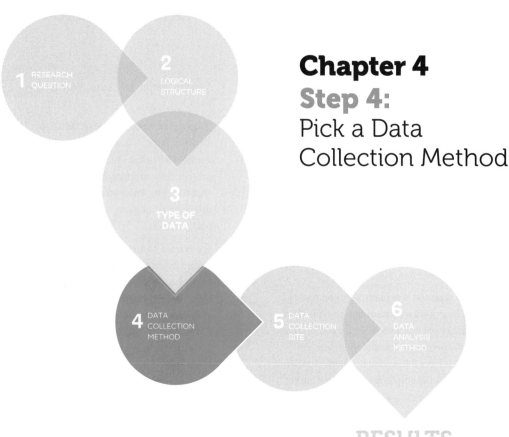

Chapter 4
Step 4:
Pick a Data Collection Method

1 RESEARCH QUESTION

2 LOGICAL STRUCTURE

3 TYPE OF DATA

4 DATA COLLECTION METHOD

5 DATA COLLECTION SITE

6 DATA ANALYSIS METHOD

RESULTS

Now that you know what type of data you want, the next step is easy. You have to pick the right method to collect the data. Not all data collection methods are suitable for all data types. Some work best with one kind; others work best with another.

Table 4.1 summarizes the main possibilities. Here's how to read it:

- The 14 types of data covered in Step 3 are listed across the top, and 12 common data collection methods are listed down the left side.
- Find the type of data you need along the top of the table. Then read down the column until you encounter an X or (X). Follow the row to the left, and you'll find a method you can use to collect the data you need.
- The X means that the method is always able to collect this type of data. The (X) means that it can work in some situations, usually as a by-product of collecting data of another type.

In this chapter, we'll explore several of the common data types to see what data collection methods work best with them. You'll see how these methods work with a few sample research questions, including some of those encountered in Step 1.

STEP **4**

Data Collection Method

TABLE 4.1   How to Pick a Data Collection Method

First, find the type of data you are looking for at the top. Then read down the column underneath the data type. Where you encounter an X, look to the left and note the suggested method. An X in parentheses means that the method can collect this kind of data, though it usually does so as a by-product of collecting one of the other types.

Data Collection Methods		1. Acts, behavior, or events	2. Reports of acts, behavior, or events	3. Economic data	4. Organizational data	5. Demographic data	6. Self-identity	7. Opinions and attitudes (shallow)	8. Opinions and attitudes (deeply held)	9. Personal feelings	10. Cultural knowledge (things everyone knows)	11. Expert knowledge	12. Personal and psychological traits	13. Experience as it presents itself to consciousness	14. Hidden social patterns
A	Public and private records		X	X	X	X						(X)			
B	Detached observation	X													X
C	Ethnography (participant observation)	X	(X)		(X)			(X)	(X)		X	(X)			X
D	In-depth interviews		X		(X)		X	(X)	X	X	X	X	(X)		(X)
E	Surveys/questionnaires		X	(X)	(X)	X	X	X			X	(X)			
F	Phenomenological interviews								(X)					X	
G	Critical incident interviews	X						(X)	(X)		(X)	X			
H	Focus groups							(X)			X	X			
I	Psychological scales and their kin												X		
J	Content analysis										X		(X)		X
K	Discourse (or narrative) analysis										X				X
L	Grounded theory														X

Match Your Method to Your Data

The key to Step 4 is to choose a data collection method that can gather the type of data you need to answer your research question. This should be obvious. If your research question calls for people's opinions, but you've collected their acts or behavior, you're not going to be able to answer the question you posed. Conversely, if you are asking about behavior but collect opinions, your research is going to go astray. That's what Table 4.1 helps you sort out. Let's walk through the first nine columns of that table, to see which data collection methods are best for those nine types of data.

Data Type 1: Acts, Behavior, or Events

I'll start with the Column 1 data type: **acts, behavior, or events**. These are either things that people[1] *do*, or things that *happen to them*. They are not opinions, not beliefs, not ideas about self-identity, or any other such heady stuff. Nor are they a form of knowledge—though knowledge and other heady stuff often generate human behavior. They are, instead, things that happen in the real world. I walk up a flight of stairs: That's an act. I tell you that I've walked up a flight of stairs: That's a *report* of an act, and reports and acts are not the same kind of thing. I think that walking up a flight of stairs is a good thing: That's an opinion or an attitude. Each of these types of data is different, and each calls for a different data collection method.

What method do you use to record acts, behaviors, or events? You have to observe them. You can't simply ask people about what they did, nor can you ask people what they think or feel about such things. Those are other data types. If your research question calls for *acts*, then observation is the only way to go.

If this is clear, revisit Table 4.1 and read down the column to the two Xs in Rows B and C. Looking to the left, you find the Xs are next to two kinds of data collection methods: **detached observation (Row B)** and **ethnography** (also called **participant observation**[2]) **(Row C)**. Both ask the researcher to observe something, but they differ in key ways. Detached observation is just that: You watch, listen to, or perhaps measure whatever it is you are investigating. If you are observing tree sloths, for example, you find some sloths, pull up a chair, and track their activities. Over time, you'll notice that sloths come down from their trees about once a week to defecate, then climb back to their perch. That's when they are the most vulnerable to predators. That's also when you can get hair samples to measure the amount of algae on them. All this is detached observation, because you are not interacting with the sloths. You are just watching.

Natural scientists do this all the time, but social scientists do it too. Let's go back to one of the mass transit topics from Step 1. Let's say that we're investigating traffic jams and we are particularly interested in short-lived "phantom jams." These happen when there's plenty of space on the road but a group of cars gets bunched up anyway.

We could ask the people who were involved in these jams what happened, but that won't tell us what's going on. That's because participants don't really know. Drivers experience such phenomena, but they don't usually understand how they work.

Instead, we're best off observing traffic flow and measuring the collective results of drivers' braking and accelerating to maintain space behind the cars ahead of them. That's what causes these jams.[3] Close observation reveals the large-scale cumulative effects of scores of individual actions—including acts that occur several miles ahead of where the phantom jam happens. Scholars have found that phantom jams flow through freeway traffic like waves in water. Individual drivers' braking and accelerating keeps the waves going.

It took lots of detailed observation to find this pattern. Our research question, in this case, might have been this: "What observable patterns of driver behavior, if any, contribute to the development of phantom jams?" Such a research question calls for detached observation.

Ethnography is a bit different. It combines the direct observation of behavior with the researcher's involvement with the people being observed. Ethnographers watch people do things and ask them to explain what they are doing. An ethnographer studying phantom jams might ride along with drivers, watching when and how they hit the brakes, accelerate, and so forth. She or he would also ask for the driver's explanation of what is going on, why the driver braked or accelerated, and how the driver explained the phantom jam phenomenon. Watching captures what people actually do; asking for the drivers' explanations tells us what they are thinking. Ethnography (participant observation) gathers both types of data, whereas detached observation gathers only the first.

Data Type 2: Reports of Acts, Behavior, or Events

Column 2 involves **reports of acts, behavior, or events**. Sometimes we don't have to watch things. We can ask people what they have done or typically do, and their reports give us the data we need. For example, if we want to learn about commuting patterns, we don't have to watch traffic. Instead, we can ask people to log their driving. This produces a form of **public and private records (Row A)**. Such records can tell us a good deal about individuals' driving patterns. We can learn when they leave home, what roads they take, and so on.

Let's say we want to learn how commuters avoid sitting in rush hour traffic. We can ask people to keep track of their commuting by writing down when they leave work, what route they take, what traffic they encounter, and so on. If enough people are reporting, we can get a pretty good picture of traffic patterns in a given city. We can also learn how people make choices about where and when to drive.

In essence, this is how crowd-sourced traffic apps for smartphones work. Drivers push a button on their phones when they encounter a jam, an accident, construction, and so on, and the app reads their GPS

THINK ABOUT IT

Why do we treat *acts* and *reports of acts* as different types of data?

location and posts the slowdown to a mapping program. Other drivers can see the posts and avoid the area. Such reports aren't perfect. People make mistakes, and sometimes the slowdowns vanish pretty fast. Still, they're usually more up-to-date than the traffic reports on the radio. By the time a radio station's traffic helicopter has called in and the information makes it to the news announcer, the backup has usually been cleared. The point is, reports are often all you need.

Sometimes they aren't, though. At the start of Step 3, we saw what happens when we ask people to report their church attendance: They often inflate their figures. We also learned a way around this, by asking people to keep a log of what they did the previous day. We consult their logs to see what they actually did on Friday, Saturday, or Sunday, depending on which religion they follow. If we don't tell them that we're looking for church attendance, they'll probably report it accurately.

How do you collect reports? Column 2 indicates several ways, marked by four Xs and one (X).

Public records report some kinds of behavior: how many people got married; how many renewed their driver's licenses on time; how many were arrested, jailed, and convicted. Private records report other things: television watching, book sales, sports attendance, and the like. The problem here is access; not all companies that collect information let scholars look at it. Amazon.com, for example, doesn't share sales of its e-readers because it doesn't have to.

In-depth interviews (Row D) do a fine job of collecting certain kinds of reports. Both they and **critical incident interviews (Row G)** let you go into depth with a small number of informants. This gives you lots of details. The difference between the two methods is that critical incident interviews use specific incidents to get people talking about a topic, whereas in-depth interviews are more general. You might, for example, interview traffic engineers about how they manage roadways to keep traffic jams to a minimum. You could ask them general questions, letting them describe how they typically work, or you could ask them about a specific incident that shows the kinds of problems that traffic engineers typically face. To do the latter, for example, you might say, "Let's talk about the worst traffic jam you've ever had to handle. When was it? What, in particular, made it so bad? How did you handle it? What did you and your team do well? What do you wish you had done differently?" These questions focus the interview; they often produce very rich accounts of what happened in a particular time or place. In-depth interviews can produce equally rich accounts, though they do it by other means. (We'll see some examples of each in Part II of this book.)

You could also use a **survey** or **questionnaire (Row E)**. Surveys and questionnaires gather shallower information, but they can gather information from far more people. A short survey may take 15 minutes to complete. That's next to nothing, so you can get a large number of people to tell you about what they've done. An interview, by contrast, frequently takes much longer. This limits the number of people you can interview on the same research budget.

A commuting survey, for example, might ask people what time they left their homes each workday in the previous week, how they got to work, how long it took them, and if they encountered any problems along the way. It can also measure their satisfaction or frustration with their commuting patterns. It just can't measure any of these with much nuance. That's the trade-off. Interviews provide depth at the cost of getting information from fewer people. Surveys provide breadth without nearly as much depth. Both are valuable ways to gather people's reports of their actions.

There's one more option, marked by an (X) in square 2C of Table 4.1. You can use ethnography (participant observation) (Row C) to collect small numbers of reports from individuals while you are observing their social scenes. My own ethnographic observations of a radical Catholic commune, for example, gave me lots of opportunity to ask people how and how long they had been working for social change.[4] I couldn't, however, talk with large numbers of people. That's the problem with ethnographic studies: They are very local. That's why this X has parentheses around it. Yes, you get reports of acts, behavior, and events but as a by-product of collecting another type of data. There are more direct ways to collect reports of acts, behavior, or events, if that's the only data type you need.

Data Types 3, 4, and 5:
Economic, Organizational, and Demographic Data

I'm going to treat the data types 3, 4, and 5 as a unit, because they are all some-what alike. As we saw in Chapter 3, **economic data**, **organizational data**, and **demographic data** are typically reports of behavior or identities that describe the economy, organizations, and populations. We typically find these in the public and private records (Row A) collected and reported by various entities. The U.S. Census Bureau, for example, collects demographic data about the U.S. population. It tells us how many men and women live in different parts of the country and how many have various racial backgrounds, marital statuses (married, single, divorced, widowed), levels of income, housing types, and so on. We can take these data at the national level, the state level, the county level, or the level of the census tract. The latter is the smallest geographic unit for which the Census Bureau provides figures. Tracts aren't all the same size, but each of them is large enough that you can't identify a particular individual or household by looking at the data.

As you learned in Step 3, economic data measure aspects of the economy, whereas organizational data measure attributes of organizations. Economic data, for example, let you compare the levels of employment, business activity, and so on in various cities. School data provide information about numbers of students, numbers of teachers and other employees, spending per pupil, and so on. All of these data report on economic activity, organizational structures, and different population attributes.

Public and private records are a fine way to get all three kinds of information—and more are available to the general public than you might think. Not only do local, state, and national governments collect economic and demographic data, but most large businesses have to report core data about their sales, earnings, numbers of employees, and many other things. You can also use surveys (Row E) to collect economic and organizational data. You can, for example, survey business owners, chambers of commerce, and other groups. I've put parentheses around those two (3E and 4E) to indicate that you have to survey organizational leaders for this information. Ordinary workers don't usually know enough to help you. Surveys also collect good demographic data from individuals. Indeed, the Census Bureau collects most of its data using a series of very broad surveys, which it releases to the public in summary form.

You'll note that I've listed ethnography (Row C) and in-depth interviews (Row D) as ways of getting information about organizations, though I've put parentheses around them (4C and 4D). That's because they are not terribly efficient compared with surveys. These methods are good, however, for uncovering hidden social patterns in organizations (Column 14). Such studies inevitably produce data about the organizations as well. (I'll talk about organizational ethnographies later in this chapter.)

Data Type 6: Self-Identity

Self-identity refers to the set of labels or ideas that people use to identify themselves, subjectively. This is not the same as demographic data: Demographic labels are typically decided by someone in authority, whereas self-identity is decided by each individual. These things are sometimes in conflict.

Until 2000, for example, the U.S. Census Bureau insisted that people identify themselves as White, Black, Native American, or Asian or Pacific Islander. (*Hispanic* was treated as an ethnic group, so Hispanics could be of any race.) My niece and nephew had no place in this schema, because their father is White and their mother is Asian. They had to choose one or another; they could not choose both. This was a case of imposed identity. Starting in 2000, however, individuals were allowed to choose multiple racial identities. This let people describe themselves however they wanted on the census forms.

The census forms are surveys (Row E)—one of the two data collection methods that I've marked as suitable for collecting self-identities. Surveys collect people's self-identities at a relatively shallow level, by asking them to choose from a set of boxes. They are best used for research questions that ask people to sort themselves into preestablished categories. These can be racial and/or ethnic; economic (lower class, working class, middle class, upper class); occupational, depending on how (or whether) people self-identify with their occupations; or based on personality (introvert, extrovert) or on any number of other factors. Surveys work best when people's choices are clear and the distinctions between the identities are common knowledge.

For example, sociologists have known for decades that the division of U.S. society into lower, working, middle, and upper classes doesn't correspond to reality.[5] These terms are common on surveys, however, because most Americans have a rough idea of what they mean. Most people identify themselves as "middle class," with "working class" running second. These are self-identities but at a relatively shallow level.

In-depth interviews (Row D) give people a much wider opportunity to describe who they are and allow them to identify themselves at greater depth. I once carried out an interview study in which I asked long-term social activists about their religious lives.[6] Among other things, I asked them how they identified themselves religiously, and asked what that identity meant to them. The results were extremely rich. They provided long, nuanced discussions about their religious backgrounds, what they liked and didn't like about the religious organizations to which they belonged, and their own sense of religious journey. These data were hard to summarize. They were, however, deep. That's what interviews do. If your research question asks you how people identify themselves in detail, then you should plan an interview study. If your question asks you to collect shallower self-identities, then a survey will do.

Data Types 7 and 8: Shallow and Deeply Held Opinions and Attitudes

The two opinions and attitudes data types have a lot in common. Both are thoughts: things that people carry around in their heads and that orient their behavior. Some people, for example, believe that traffic ebbs and flows at particular times of day, so they adjust their travel accordingly. Other people may believe that traffic is random; they see no point in adjusting their travel times, as it won't make any difference. Still others may think that traffic is always heavy when they're trying to get somewhere fast. There's seldom traffic, they say, when they have lots of time. In effect, they think that the traffic gods are out to get them. (Opinions and attitudes come in all kinds.)

Some opinions and attitudes are relatively shallow and others are relatively deep. Shallow opinions are easily captured quickly; deep ones take more time and effort. We can, for example, ask people if they support mass transit systems and to rank their support as "strong," "moderate," "weak," or "nonexistent." Or we can ask them to rank their support or opposition to a particular transit project on a seven-point scale, ranging from "strongly support" (7) through "neutral" (4) to "strongly opposed" (1). Surveys (Row E) ask such questions. They give us a quick sense of people's shallower views. Unfortunately, they also lack nuance. They don't tell us why people have the views they do.

If you want to know the details about people's opinions or why they hold them, you have to go deeper. You have to use in-depth interviews (Row D). For example, one person might think that mass transit is socialism and not want to pay taxes so that other people have buses or trains to ride. Another might favor some projects and oppose others, especially ones that they think are financial boondoggles that make construction companies rich. Interviewing uncovers such details.

Look at Columns 7 and 8. The only Xs are in Rows D and E, because those data collection methods gather deep and shallow opinions, respectively. There are also a few Xs in parentheses. Ethnography (Row C), in-depth interviews (Row D), critical incident interviews (Row G), and **focus groups (Row H)** let you gather shallow opinions and attitudes while collecting their primary data types. Ethnography (Row C), **phenomenological interviews (Row F)**, and critical incident interviews (Row G) let you gather **deeply held opinions and attitudes** as a by-product of collecting other types of data.

How does this work? Here are two examples. Critical incident interviews can give you both shallow and deep opinions, because people often express such things while they are talking about the incidents that you are asking them to describe. Focus groups give you mainly shallow opinions, because these are group interviews and you often can't get people to speak deeply in a group made up of people they don't know.

You shouldn't choose any of the methods that have Xs in parentheses as your primary data collection methods. They can, however, give you data that supplement what you've learned from the more focused methods.

As a general rule, if you want to gather shallow opinions from lots of people, a **social survey** is the best way to go. If you want to gather deep opinions from a relatively smaller number of people, then an in-depth interview will likely succeed.

Data Type 9: Personal Feelings

Personal feelings are a lot like deeply held opinions and attitudes. In brief, in-depth interviews (Row D) are good data collection methods to use. I've covered those above, so there's nothing new to add here.

Three Examples (that include data types 10–12)

This takes us through the first nine columns of Table 4.1. Rather than continue through all the data types, let's shift gears. This is a book about research design, and it's often easiest to learn something by watching it being done. We'll look at the remaining data types and data collection methods as we explore some concrete research projects.

First, I'll propose some questions related to the research topic we looked at in Step 1: "How does mass transit affect people's everyday lives?" You'll see how opinions, feelings, cultural and expert knowledge, and so on can help you to answer specific research questions on that topic. Then, I'll propose some questions on a new topic: "What kinds of organizations are the best places to work?"

In each case, I'll show you how a research question tells you what type of data you need to collect, and that data type demonstrates what data collection methods are possible. In this way, you'll see how the design process operates.

THINK ABOUT IT
Our research question calls for economic data: How do property values change after mass transit construction?

Example 1: Mass Transit and Property Values

We'll start with one of the research questions encountered in Step 1: "How do property values change after the construction of a mass transit system?" This question calls for economic data (Column 3). We are looking for property values, which are economic in nature. The easiest way to locate those data is through a search of public and private records (Row A). These come in several types.

Certain relevant records—specifically, property sales figures—are typically available to the public. Anyone can find out what houses and buildings sell for. The same is true of another kind of public record: assessments of property values for tax purposes. Which of these records should we use to tell us how property values change?

We should start with property sales figures, as these are typically more accurate ways to gauge true property values. They indicate the amount that people are willing to pay for property. Tax assessments, by contrast, can be distorted in several ways. Some cities undervalue property, and certain tax authorities undervalue property of specific types. In Texas, for example, you can lower your tax assessments on vacant land by keeping a cow on it until a few days before you start building. Developers often start building malls and housing tracts just after assessment time, so they get a year of lower taxes. This makes tax assessments a problematic source of property valuations.

But sales values can also be distorted. Perhaps lots of owners sold their property right before the transit project and very few sold right afterward: Simple supply and demand would push prices lower before and higher after, even if the project itself produced no change. Or perhaps there was a recession that lowered property values about the time the project was completed. That would also throw off the comparison.

The point is, public and private records are useful, but you can never take them at face value. You always have to think through the real causes of the pattern you see. Even so, such records are a good place to start.

Suppose you want to gather the same type of data using another method. You could conduct a survey (Row E) of property values in the relevant neighborhood. You could make appointments with property owners and ask them, hypothetically, the level at which they would be willing to sell their homes. This would give you an idea about how they value their property. This approach could work in an area where there are few property sales; in such places, public records would not reflect current values. In this case, you are asking for information corresponding to reports of acts, behavior, or events (Column 2)—though in this case the acts would be future ones, not ones in the past.

What if you ask property owners a different question? Suppose you ask for their sense of whether property values have risen or declined. This is a decent question, but it doesn't address the research question we asked. People's ideas about things are their opinions, but the question we started with calls for reports of people's potential behavior. Opinions and reports of behavior are different data types, so surveying people about their opinions would be a poor way to answer your research question.

You could, however, change your research question a bit. You could ask, "How do people's impressions of local property values change after the construction of mass transit?" This question asks for people's opinions, so a survey would be appropriate. Note how we let the research question tell us what type of data we need and then we choose a method to find the data.

Here's another research question: "What changes do people report that mass transit has brought to their lives?" The phrase "people *report*" should give you a clue about the data type: You want people's reports of their own behavior.

We've already talked about such reports, though, so let's tweak the question so that it calls for another data type. "What do people think about the changes they have seen since the mass transit system was installed?" This asks us to collect people's *personal opinions*. As we discussed earlier, we can do this at either a deep or a shallow level.

Looking down the personal opinion columns (Columns 7 and 8), we find several methods: in-depth interviews, surveys/questionnaires, critical incident interviews, and focus groups. Each method gets at a slightly different kind of report.

In-depth interviews (Row D) let you talk with people at length. People can tell you quite a lot about their views and experiences in 60 to 90 minutes. You can ask for examples, which can give you an excellent sense of the changes they think mass transit has made. As you'll see in Part II, the main difficulty with interviews is keeping them balanced. You want to give people a chance to express themselves, because you are interested in their unique experiences and ways of seeing things. But you don't want the conversations to wander all over the place. Good interviewing is a learned skill. In Chapter 9, we'll suggest how to do it well.

Another drawback of interviews is that good ones take a lot of time. Only a limited number of people can be interviewed for a single research project. You need to figure out how to get a breadth of opinion while still keeping those opinions deep. Again, we'll take this up in Chapter 9. In the meantime, however, you might want to read "How Many Subjects?" in the "Research Guides and Handouts" section at the end of this book. It provides a strategy for making sure that interview projects gather as broad a range of views as possible, without taking forever to complete.

You might, however, not be interested in collecting complicated data. You might want to focus on just a few of the effects of mass transit, but you want to know how widespread these effects are. For example, you might want to know what percentage of the business owners in mass transit neighborhoods lost money during construction, or what percentage saw their revenues increase as a result of foot traffic around stations. You don't need deep, nuanced accounts; you need a survey or questionnaire (Row E).[7] Specifically, you need to poll a randomly selected sample of your target population, so that you can say with some accuracy what your whole population thinks. We'll talk more about this method in Chapter 8.

> **THINK ABOUT IT**
> What would you ask business owners in order to find out the changes that mass transit has made to their businesses?

One more thing: The survey I've suggested doesn't really answer our whole research question; it focuses on just a part of the picture: business owners' revenue changes around the time of construction. Were you to take this path, you would change your research question to something narrower: "What revenue changes do business owners in the areas surrounding transit stations report during construction and after the project's completion?" This question generates the research I described in the preceding paragraph.

You are, by the way, witnessing something important about the research process. In most cases, you work both forward and backward until you get the research design you need. You choose a question, see what data type it needs, then choose a data collection method, and then go back and change the question slightly to make sure that the question, the data type, and the method all fit together. That's why research design takes time. The steps are interconnected.

There are other possibilities. We could, for example, convene focus groups (Row H) to discuss any of the research questions I've posed in the last few paragraphs. As mentioned earlier, focus groups are small group interviews in which several people are asked for their experiences and views simultaneously. They would be appropriate for our "What changes . . . ?" project, because they would encourage participants to cover a number of issues that they might otherwise forget. We can imagine a group conversation in which one participant says to the rest, "Remember how difficult it was to get across that street before they built the traffic diverter?" and the others chime in with their agreements, disagreements, and similar examples. On the plus side, focus groups give us a sense about how communities, not just individuals, see things. On the minus side, they can be dominated by particularly loud individuals, while quieter people drop into the background. A skilled interviewer has to manage the focus group well. Such groups are better for bringing up ideas than for determining the degree to which they are widespread.

Example 2: Mass Transit and Street Life

Here's another transit-related research question: "What is the observable character of street life in places with and without mass transit hubs?" This question asks about acts, behavior, and events (Column 1)—even though the phrase "observable character" asks us to generalize from the specific acts, behavior, and events themselves. In reviewing Table 4.1, we see two possibilities: detached observation and ethnography. We'll treat the second of these methods later, so let's concentrate on the first for now. How could we use detached observation (Row B) to generate data to answer this research question?

First, we need to choose pairs of places to observe. One location in each pair should be around a transit hub, for example, at a subway stop, a commuter train station, a light-rail loading point, or the like. The other should be a place without such facilities but otherwise as similar as possible to the first location. Our pairs need to match on as many dimensions as possible, such as demographics, the proportion of residences to businesses, social class standing, distance from downtown or other destinations, and so on. Ideally, their only major difference is that one has transit and the other does not. We may not reach that ideal, but we should try. (Using several matched pairs makes it more likely that the differences we find really are caused by the transit facilities.)

Then we need to spend time in each location recording what we see. How many people are there? What kinds of people? What are they doing? What are their patterns? What businesses are there? What kinds of people patronize them? How do they do so? The point is to record as much observable information as possible. We record until we reach what is known as "saturation": until we've pretty much captured the ordinary acts, behaviors, and events that typify each of the places we're observing.

Then we look for patterns. Do particular kinds of people use each neighborhood differently? Do people linger in one type and walk swiftly through the others? How much pedestrian traffic does each see? How new or old are the buildings? Have the transit stations attracted new construction? What can we conclude from the many observations we've made? Good, detailed observations should tell us the characteristic differences between places with transit stops and those without them.

Note that the related research question "Are there any systematic differences in the ways that residents of transit-served and transit-less neighborhoods describe the quality of life in their area?" calls for in-depth interviews (Row D), not observation. The question asks for residents' descriptions of their neighborhoods. That's a different data type than the acts, behavior, and events that you get from observation. In fact, it is *reports* of acts, behavior, and events (Column 2). Interviews are one good way to get such reports, particularly if you want richness and depth. People's descriptions will almost certainly contain ideas, judgments, and so on, simply because the observers are part of the social setting they are trying to describe. That's why you can't treat them as direct observations. If you want to know what actually happens, you have to watch.

Interviews would also be a good way to gauge a related question: "How do people feel about the neighborhood changes that mass transit projects bring?" This question calls for a different data type: personal feelings (Column 9). Interviews are about the only way to get at personal feelings. Critical incident interviews can do this, though probably not for this particular research question, as it asks for general feelings. The point is that you can use various data collection methods to gather a given type of data, just as different data types can share data collection methods. You just have to line them up correctly: The research question determines the data type, and the data type determines the data collection method—not the other way around.

We'll explore two other research questions from our transit project before moving on. First, imagine our topic is "What are the main barriers to constructing mass transit projects?" This topic could produce many different research questions, so let's get more specific: "What are the main barriers that transit experts report encountering in bringing mass transit projects to fruition?" This question asks us to collect **expert knowledge (Column 11).** In reviewing Table 4.1, we find we can interview transit experts (including using a critical incident technique) or we can assemble a focus group made up of these experts. Surveys don't tend to be deep enough, but we might use a survey if we already had a list of potential barriers and wanted to know which ones the experts thought were most significant. We could consult already-written records of such barriers as part of our literature review, though we would likely want more details than such records typically provide. Ethnographers[8] typically collect expert opinion in the course of their studies, though they focus on specific social scenes rather than trying to assemble expertise from widely spread cases. In any case, this research question calls for some kind of interview, either individual or collective.

There is a second kind of knowledge, however. Expert knowledge is known by the few, whereas **cultural knowledge (Column 10)** is known by (nearly) everyone in a particular social milieu. How do we collect common knowledge about mass transit? There are several ways.

We have to start with an appropriate research question. Let's take this one: "What do people in City X know about mass transit?" It doesn't matter whether City X actually has a mass transit system; people will still have ideas about it. We want to know what they are.

There are several ways to collect data about cultural knowledge. Ethnographers collect cultural knowledge by spending long periods of time with residents of a limited social scene, participating in their daily lives. They, however, need scenes that are small enough that they can get to know them well. For the questions "What do people living in the _____ neighborhood in City X know about mass transit?" or "What do the people working at _____ school know about mass transit?," ethnography (Row C) would be a useful data collection method. For larger groups, we could use some of the interview methods mentioned previously. For still larger groups, we might construct a survey, though we would have to know the contours of popular knowledge before doing so. We could ask questions such as this one: "Which of the following statements most closely expresses your views about mass transit?" This would give us a sense of what "everyone" knows and also how widespread this knowledge is among city residents.

Reading down Column 10, we find two other possibilities to help us with our research question: **content analysis (Row J)** and **discourse analysis (Row K)**. These data collection methods also collect cultural knowledge, but they do so in an unusual way.

Both forms of analysis involve locating the implicit cultural assumptions embodied in various kinds of texts. American newspaper articles, for example, have particular ways of presenting stories about social problems. They typically start with an anecdote: what has happened to a particular person whose situation illustrates a more general pattern. Then they describe that pattern, returning to the individual at the end of the article. It's a formula, a genre, a particular narrative style. The fact that it is so ubiquitous tells us something about Americans' cultural assumptions—particularly about the individualism that lies at the culture's heart.[9] A suitable mass-transit research question might ask, "What cultural assumptions about mass transit do we find in the American news media?" Content and discourse analysis would let us find out.

Content analysis is conceptually simple. You collect a set of texts on the relevant topic—in this case, newspaper and television stories about mass transit—and examine them, looking for patterns in the way the topic is portrayed. Once you have identified patterns, you go through the collection methodically, counting the number of

THINK ABOUT IT
What can experts tell us that ordinary people cannot?

instances of each pattern. Scholars have used content analyses to count the number of violent instances in children's television cartoons, to highlight the ways that *National Geographic* magazine portrays various parts of the world, and to trace changing ideas about the nation-state among intellectual publics worldwide.[10]

Discourse analysis is a bit more complex. As developed by Norman Fairclough and others, discourse analysis seeks to reveal the ways in which people's ways of speaking are shaped by systems of social and political power.[11] It focuses not just on the content of texts but also on how those texts are produced and consumed. Cindy Myers, for example, used discourse analysis to show that the term *poverty* meant something different to the editorial writers of the *New York Times* than it did to the editorial writers of the *Wall Street Journal* during a 20-year period stretching from the mid-1980s to the early 2000s.[12] *New York Times* editorials portrayed poverty as powerful and active, as an entity that captures people and mires them, from which they are unable to escape. The *Wall Street Journal* editorials didn't describe poverty; they described poor people. They saw such people as active, often choosing poverty rather than affluence or (if they are government bureaucrats) making others poor with their misguided policies. Neither vision is real exactly, but both have political consequences. The *New York Times*'s way of speaking encourages people to embrace organized solutions to poverty: government programs, charity efforts, and the like. The *Wall Street Journal*'s language encourages people to reject such collective efforts, because the problem lies with individual bad choices and irresponsibility.

That's the point, for Fairclough and others analyzing sociocultural discourses. These discourses are inherently political. Any study of the discourses surrounding mass transit would look at who controls the terms of debate, how they accomplish that control, and how they ensure that alternative ideas are not taken seriously. Analyzing the content of newspapers, television stories, and so on is a key part of that project. But discourse analysts always want to know who benefits from the ways in which people are led to see the world.

Example 3: Best Places to Work

That's enough about mass transit. I'll use another topic to discuss the remaining data collection methods: "What kinds of organizations are the best places to work?"

To refresh your memory, this is a research topic, not a research question. You can tell because it isn't very specific. In fact, it covers a lot of potential research questions. A research question ought to tell us exactly what we're looking for. A research topic does not. We'll need to narrow down this topic, so that we can see how asking for a specific type of data points us toward a data collection method that can deliver it.

As a first step toward narrowing our topic, I'll focus on a subtopic: research on *organizational culture*. Specifically, I'll take the approach developed by Kim Cameron and his associates at the University of Michigan Business School.[13] They developed a system for analyzing organizational culture that has generated lots of empirical research. They found four distinct cultural types:

- *Hierarchies* are structured and rule oriented.
- *Adhocracies* are entrepreneurial and dynamic.
- *Market-oriented* organizations emphasize results and getting the job done.
- *Clan* organizations are personal, familylike, and participatory.

Hierarchies and market-oriented organizations emphasis stability and control; clan organizations and adhocracies emphasize
flexibility. Hierarchies and clan organizations handle everything in-
house; adhocracies and market-oriented organizations outsource as
many things as possible.

THINK ABOUT IT
What is the best
place you've ever
worked? What
made it so
good?

We can use this typology to generate a research question: "What
kinds of people gravitate to these four kinds of organization?" What do
we have to do to answer this question?

First, we need to identify organizations that fit each of these four
patterns. Though Cameron and Quinn are clear that no organization
is homogeneous, we can use a test such as the Organizational Culture
Assessment Instrument (OCAI)[14] to find the organization's central tendency. This questionnaire asks people to rate their organizations on their relative
emphasis on flexibility or control, and their tendency to handle tasks in-house or to
outsource those tasks to others.

As with our pairs of neighborhoods in the mass transit project, we want to make
sure that the organizations are enough alike that we're sure that any differences are
due to organizational culture instead of some other factor. For example, comparing
large organizations with small ones risks mistaking differences of size for differences
of culture. The same is true if we pair new organizations with old, established ones.
As we saw in Step 2, any time we make a comparison, we need to take into account a
whole host of factors.

Once we've found several organizations of each type, our research gets interesting. First, we want to see if these organizations attract different types of people, demographically speaking. Our question becomes, "Are there any demographic differences
between the employees who say they are happy working for the four kinds of organizations?" This question calls for demographic data (Column 5). These are figures
related to people's gender, race, social class standing, education level, marital status,
family type, and other social identities.

Are women happier in clan organizations that are oriented toward people? Do
adhocracies and market-oriented organizations attract hard-charging men? It's pretty
easy to find out. Use public and private records (Row A) to find the relative balances
of men and women at each of the four types of organization (making sure to match
them by industry and the like). Then create a survey (Row E) to ask employees about
their relative happiness. This would let you see whether men are happier in one kind
of work and women in another. (To be clear, I think this won't be the case, certainly
not in any simple manner. Yet it *is* a straightforward research project.)

Next, let's check self-identities (Column 6). An appropriate research question would be: "Do people working in the four types of organizations have systematically different senses of identity? Or are the choices of place to work not a matter of self-identity, but of something else?" This involves finding out how people categorize themselves, as opposed to the way that society categorizes them. These questions can be complex, which often rules out surveys and other data collection methods that don't give people a chance to lay out the nuances of their situations. If you expect this, then in-depth interviews (Row D) are in order. We'll see in Part II how to construct an interview protocol to elicit the information you want.

Finally, we can look for differences in **personal and psychological traits (Column 12)** to see if people with different psychological characteristics fit in better or worse with the four types of organizations. Our research question could be, "Are there any personality differences between the employees who say they are happy [or sad or frustrated] working for the four kinds of organizations?" This research would be similar to the demographic research project, except that we would focus on personality traits rather than on demographics. We would use one or more **psychological scales (Row I)** to measure the particular traits that we think might be relevant.

I can't say which psychological scales we'd use; there are hundreds of them, and I'm not enough of an expert about them to recommend particular ones. If you want to do this kind of research, you'll need to immerse yourself in the psychological literature. My point is that psychological traits are their own data type, and psychological tests are the best method for capturing them. (See Chapter 10 for some examples of how to use them in research.)

Data Type 13: Experience as It Presents Itself to Consciousness

We're going to skip **experience as it presents itself to consciousness (Column 13),** because it doesn't lend itself to research on organizations. It doesn't lend itself to research on mass transit, either, nor on schools. As outlined in Chapter 3, this particular data type is used only in phenomenological investigations. Such studies are detailed and difficult. They involve a particular type of in-depth interviewing that I cover in Chapter 9.[15]

Data Type 14: Hidden Social Patterns

This leaves us with just one data type that we haven't yet covered here: **hidden social patterns (Column 14)**. As noted in Step 3, these are patterns of social behavior that are typically invisible to their participants. This can be as simple as how closely people stand to each other and as complicated as the ways in which some societies hide status differences beneath a veneer of equality.

The problem with hidden patterns is that the participants themselves are seldom aware of them. You can't discover such patterns by interviewing people, nor by surveying them. These methods depend on people having some idea of what is going on; that's not the case when the patterns are unknown.

Looking down Column 14 in Table 4.1, you'll see that I've marked five data collection methods suitable for revealing hidden patterns. The first, detached observation (Row B), is pretty obvious. An outside observer can often see patterns that locals miss. Edward T. Hall made a career out of highlighting hidden behavior patterns in books like *The Hidden Dimension* and *The Silent Language*.[16] He observed people in various cultures, seeing how they stand, gesture, and so on. He then observed cross-cultural interactions, noting which of these body patterns got in the way of communication. This kind of observation isn't apt to take us very far with our topic at hand, though: "What kinds of organizations are the best places to work?"[17]

Ethnography (Row C) can do a much better job with that topic. This method also calls for an outsider to observe social and cultural patterns, but now the observer does not stand outside the social scene. He or she joins in with others, watching and talking to them in order to understand their lives. The term *ethnography* comes from two Greek words that mean "describing peoples." The ethnographer describes societies holistically. She or he spends a long time inhabiting a people's social world and then portrays that world as its members understand it. Simultaneously, she or he locates and describes social patterns of which those people are unaware.

Ethnography integrates two different data types into one data collection method. The first is an analysis of a group's beliefs or worldview: how the group members understand their world, including their place in it. The second is an analysis of the hidden patterns in their shared lives. Both parts are important, though right now we're more interested in the patterns than in people's belief systems. How can ethnography help us with our current project: trying to understand what makes an organization a good place to work?

In one example of *organizational ethnography,* in the late 1960s, John Van Maanen spent a year as an ethnographer with the Philadelphia police force, learning its routines, its tacit rules, and its hidden patterns.[18] Rather than simply observing from the outside, he attended the police academy. He graduated with the other officers, rode on patrol, and protected his patrol partners in dangerous situations. He learned what officers thought about their jobs, the ways they skirted regulations, and the compromises they thought they had to make to keep both themselves and the public safe. His portraits of police life say a lot about what it was like to work in that particular organization at that particular time.

This study speaks to a research question of the form "What are the work patterns, both hidden and conscious, at Organization X at such-and-such a time and in such-and-such a place?" Ethnography does not produce generalizations about what kinds of organizations are good places to work. It does, however, provide deep portraits of particular organizations. This ability to portray nuances and contradictions is without peer among these related data collection methods. It is, however, a very slow method: Good studies seldom take less than a year of fieldwork and sometimes they take much longer.[19]

How else can we investigate such hidden organizational patterns? I previously discussed using content analysis (Row J) and discourse analysis (Row K) to collect cultural knowledge, such as the amount of violence in children's television cartoons and the semiconscious assumptions found in editorials about poverty. Scholars have used these methods to analyze hidden patterns in educational organizations. Liz Morrish, for example, noted the growth in management discourse at British universities and showed how the constant administrative references to "targets," "objectives," "performance indicators," and "mission statements" turn these universities into vehicles for training corporate middle managers and away from their traditional focus on educating citizens.[20] Norman Fairclough examined "marketization" language in university advertisements, showing how various ways of attracting students and faculty to universities signal different power relationships among schools, faculty, alumni, and administrators.[21]

Grounded theory (Row L) is a final way to uncover hidden patterns in social scenes. This data collection method is a bit of an odd duck. Barney Glaser and Anselm Strauss developed it in the 1960s as part of a study of dying hospital patients.[22] They were interested in patient, family, and staff interactions, which sociology at the time provided no good ways of investigating. The research standards of the time called for investigators to make a hypothesis—basically a guess about what was going on—figure out what type of data could test that hypothesis, and then collect the data to see if the hypothesis was right. This assumed that all research ought to be experimental or quasi-experimental, an attitude that we have outgrown. Glaser and Strauss argued that you can't create hypotheses until you have some sense of the situation. Hospital interactions were an understudied topic, and uninformed hypotheses are not very useful.

Instead, Glaser and Strauss entered the wards without preconceived ideas about what they'd find. They noticed things, took notes on them, located possible interaction patterns, and then checked to see whether the patterns were real. They first called this the "constant comparative method" because they were constantly comparing what they thought they were seeing with the data they observed as they investigated further. Later they renamed it "grounded theory," arguing that in such circumstances theory (hypotheses) emerges from a thorough immersion in the data. Low- and middle-range theories don't start with some armchair thinker saying, "This is the way the world works."[23] They begin with people noticing patterns, wondering whether those patterns hold true, and then investigating to find out. Glaser and Strauss argued that grounded theory gave them a rigorous way to do so.

Two points are worth noting. First, Glaser and Strauss developed this method to study human interactions. They based their work specifically on what sociologists call "symbolic interactionism": the study of how human beings cocreate the social patterns through which they structure their ordinary lives. This approach to social life was new in the 1960s, and standard sociological research methods couldn't produce the data it needed. In our schema, these other methods collected the wrong type of data. Grounded theory collects data about hidden patterns of social interaction—exactly what symbolic interactionist studies need.

Second, grounded theory wasn't really new; anthropological ethnographers had been doing much the same thing for nearly a century. They, too, went into the field, looked around, noticed patterns, and then tried to find out if the patterns they noticed were real. Glaser and Strauss gave us a much more rigorous way of doing this, but the result was the same.

In that case, why don't we treat "symbolic interactions" as their own data type? Because they aren't. Such interactions are a type of hidden social pattern. Multiplying data types too far creates confusion, and it's better to stay simple. Any time researchers can say, "Ah! This research question looks for hidden patterns of social interaction," grounded theory is an option. It's a good tool for this.

If ethnography and grounded theory are so similar, why don't we list the latter as a way to collect the other types of data for which we find ethnography useful? The reason is that ethnographers look for several different kinds of hidden patterns, of which interaction patterns are just one. They also look for cultural knowledge. To that end, they consult experts, they conduct deep interviews, and so on—things that grounded theorists avoid. The two methods indeed have similarities, but they are not the same.

Fortunately, organizations have lots of hidden interaction patterns for researchers to explore. Consider this question: "What hidden interaction patterns shape social life in the _____ Department of Corporation Y, and what results do those patterns have, both for corporate functioning and for the people who work there?" Asking this sort of question does not violate the "no preconceptions" rule—at least not fatally. Such research may take a while—all fieldwork does. But grounded theory techniques can help you on your way.

This concludes our tour of data collection methods. Before moving on, I want to reiterate the central point: *The key to choosing a data collection method is to identify the type of data you want to find.* Your research question tells you the type of data you need, and from there you choose a method that will produce data of that type. The idea is simple. Clarity on this point makes for much more successful research.

> **The Rule: The key to choosing a data collection method is to identify the type of data you want to find.**

Research Ethics

Choosing a data collection method has one more complication: It must be ethical. Data collection is not always innocent. Research can harm people, and researchers have an obligation to prevent or minimize that harm. This means more than just avoiding experiments that cause undue pain. It is a matter of making sure that people who participate in research benefit from it as much as possible. At the very least, investigators must make sure that the benefits to society as a whole significantly outweigh the possible harm to any particular research participant. They must also minimize whatever harm that participant suffers. No individual or group of individuals must be hurt just so knowledge can grow.

Research ethics involves the evaluation of the benefits and harms that specific research projects can cause.

Unethical Research

A couple of examples of research gone wrong can help you to understand the importance of research ethics.

Tuskegee Syphilis Study In 1932, the U.S. Public Health Service collaborated with the Tuskegee Institute to study the effects of syphilis on a group of impoverished Alabama sharecroppers.[24] A total of 600 men were enrolled, of whom 399 had contracted syphilis before the study began. Originally planned as a 6- to 9-month study of the disease course, to be followed by treatment, the project became a 40-year study of the disease's progress. Participants were not told of the study's original nature nor of this shift. They were told that the spinal taps to check for neurological effects of the disease were "special free treatment" for "bad blood." They were given free health care for minor ailments and promised free funerals, if they allowed themselves to be autopsied after death. Study participants were not informed of their disease, nor were they given penicillin when it became the standard (and first effective) treatment for syphilis in the 1940s. In some cases, study staff actively prevented participants from getting treatment, though by the 1960s most had received treatment of one sort or another.[25] The program ended in 1972 when a whistleblower leaked details of it to the press. A firestorm of criticism made it the poster child for unethical medical research.

Tearoom Study Not all unethical research is so deadly. In the late 1960s, Laud Humphreys conducted a famous ethnographic study of men who participated in anonymous homosexual sex in public restrooms—"tearooms" in the gay slang of the day. His book, *The Tearoom Trade*, described these covert sexual interactions, which he observed by playing the role of a "watch queen"—someone who observed the sex and also stood on the lookout for police or anyone coming to use the restroom in question.[26] He did not say he was a researcher; in fact, these encounters involved very little talking on anyone's part. As homosexuality was illegal in that era, his research could have jeopardized these men's reputations, family lives, and careers.

There's more. Humphreys knew that these men came from diverse backgrounds and most were not simply gay. Many considered themselves straight, and some 54% were married and middle class. To document this, Humphreys wrote down some of the men's car license plate numbers, located them, and interviewed them many months later in their homes, posing as a health service worker. He did not tell them about his study, nor did he "out" them to their wives, some of whom sat in on his interviews. He also made sure that none of them could be identified from either his book or the dissertation on which it was based. His work contributed to changing the image of homosexual sex in America. It was an early step in reshaping the image of such sex as a victimless "crime."

That, at least, was one positive outcome of the study. More negatively, Humphreys was criticized for potentially endangering his research subjects in an era when homosexuality was more hated and feared. Had word gotten out, some zealous prosecutor might have subpoenaed his field notes and gone after the men for sodomy. His research could have destroyed lives. It would almost certainly have destroyed marriages and careers.

THINK ABOUT IT
What could Humphreys have done to protect his informants? Did he need to deceive them for his project to succeed?

Like the U.S. Public Health Service managers of the Tuskegee Study, Humphreys did not get the consent of his participants before involving them in his research. He protected them at least to the extent that he made it impossible to trace them from his writings, but he did maintain a list of license plates, from which he got the names and addresses for his follow-up interviews. He coded the notes, lists, and interviews and kept them in a safe-deposit box in a different state from the one where he did his research. That's some protection. Would he have gone to jail rather than turn over his notes to a public prosecutor? Rik Scarce did.[27] He was a graduate student studying radical environmentalist groups when one of those groups vandalized a university laboratory. He spent several months in jail for contempt of court for refusing to turn over his field notes.

These cases raise ethical issues, none of which are easy to address. The Tuskegee study attracted the most opprobrium, but Humphreys's study divided the Washington University department where he did his dissertation and has been used as an example of ethically marginal research ever since.

Implementing Ethical Practices

Governments and the research community jointly decided to change this state of affairs. Partly as a result of the Tuskegee and Tearoom studies—and of others, mostly in the medical field—the U.S. Department of Health, Education, and Welfare brought together a group of researchers and ethicists in 1974. Meeting as the National Commission for the Protection of Human Subjects of Biomedical and Behavioral Research, they were tasked with producing a framework for evaluating medical and social science research on human beings. They issued a series of reports, culminating in the **Belmont Report**, which was published in the *Federal Register* in April 1979. That report forms the basis for current regulations controlling research in the United States.

The Belmont Report enshrined three core principles:

1. Research participants must be informed of the research that is being done on them. They must be given adequate information about that research, about the potential dangers it presents, and about any personal benefit they may receive from it. They must neither be bullied into participating nor given any undue enticement that might lead them to disregard their own interests. The basic principle here is **respect for persons**.

2. Investigators must minimize the harm done to participants and minimize the risks that those participants run, both during and after the study. The benefits of the study must significantly outweigh those harms and risks. The basic principle here is **beneficence**.

3. Investigators must ensure that their research procedures are reasonable, non-exploitative, and administered fairly—with particular attention to making sure that they protect vulnerable or less-powerful populations. So, for example, research may not be done on prisoners unless it has a direct connection to the criminal justice or prison system; prisoners cannot be used in research just because they are a handy population. The same is true of people who are hospitalized, the mentally ill, and so on. Similarly, children are a protected class. Both parents and the children themselves must assent to participation. All research on these protected classes must be approved in advance by an independent review board. The basic principle here is **justice**.

These principles have had great influence worldwide. They are now a required part of any U.S. federally funded research; they are also required of any research carried out by organizations that receive U.S. funding of any sort.

Institutional Review Boards

The Belmont Report is the basis for the current system of **Institutional Review Boards (IRBs)**, which must approve all U.S.-based medical and social scientific research using human subjects. All universities have them, as do all public research institutions and most private ones. Other countries have similar requirements, though the details vary from one place to another.

The bottom line is that you have to demonstrate that your research is ethical. You have to show that you aren't hurting anyone by doing it and that you are specifically not endangering vulnerable populations. Or, if you are putting people at risk, you have to show that the value of what you might learn outweighs the potential harm. You also have to minimize those harms. Typically, this involves taking a short training program, thinking through your research carefully, and then writing a clear research proposal for your organization's IRB.

This is actually a good thing. First, it requires you to think through your research more carefully than you might otherwise. IRBs are typically staffed by experienced researchers, who will often catch research flaws that you might have overlooked and will suggest ways to minimize dangers to your participants that might have escaped your attention. Writing a clear research proposal and showing it to experts is always a good thing.

Second, IRB approval may encourage people to participate in your study. Even if you are working with nature or animals, you need people's cooperation. If you can say that your research has passed ethical examination, people are more likely to help you out.

Third, it forces you to confront a key question: "Is my research worth doing?" Usually, the answer is yes, but sometimes it is not. It is far better to discover this early on, before you have sunk too much labor into a project that is not worthwhile.

You'll note that I've been talking about people. That's because human-subjects research calls for special cautions. Animal research does, too, and IRBs have special procedures for dealing with research on animals. The list is long and specifically designed to prevent the abuses common in the recent past. Among other things, the research benefits for animal or human health or for social welfare must significantly outweigh any suffering the research causes. Laboratory animals must be acquired legally, cared for well, and not be subjected to unnecessary harm or pain. Lab studies must have the potential for significant expansions of knowledge, more so when animals must suffer or die as by-products of the investigations. Research on animals in the wild must not interfere with natural animal behavior. Researchers must recognize that their own presence could harm wild populations. The knowledge that studies might gain must help protect or manage the target species; any harm done to individuals must help the species as a whole.

In a sense, these goals are the same as the second and third goals articulated by the Belmont Report for research on human subjects. Research animals are to be treated with both beneficence and justice. The first of these goals minimizes risks to the research subjects; the second ensures reasonable, nonexploitative, and well-thought-out research procedures. Both call for the benefits of additional knowledge to outweigh whatever harm the research causes.

Whether investigating animals or people, researchers have to make sure that their data collection methods do not unduly harm their research subjects. We'll explore how this works in practice at the end of each chapter in Part II. There, we will see how each of the research examples chose to maximize the benefit and minimize the harm it caused.

Review Questions

1. How does knowing the type of data you need help you to choose a data collection method?

2. What are the respective strengths and weaknesses of surveys versus interviews? What kinds of data are best collected by each method?

3. What are the differences between detached observation and participant observation?

4. What are the differences between the kinds of interviews listed in Table 4.1?

5. What are the strengths and weaknesses of the methods that can be used to collect data about hidden social patterns?

6. What role do Institutional Review Boards play in the research process? How can they help your research be better than it might otherwise be?

The open-access Student Study Site at **study.sagepub.com/spickard** has a variety of useful study tools, including SAGE journal articles, video & web resources, eFlashcards, and quizzes.

Notes

1. Or animals or natural systems. The table works for designing both social science and natural science research. Social science research is much more complicated, however, as it involves so many more types of data. Natural scientists design their research using the same six steps. They don't, however, have to take into account such things as what the tigers, atoms, or blood cells think about being research subjects. Social scientists do.

2. Sociologists traditionally used the term "participant observation," and anthropologists use the term "ethnography," though the latter term is now used across several disciplines. Both involve the direct observation of human communities and a personal engagement with the people whom one is observing.

3. Benjamin Seibold, "Traffic Ghost Hunting," *Nautilus Magazine* 3, July 2013.

4. James Spickard, "Ritual, Symbol, and Experience: Understanding Catholic Worker House Masses," *Sociology of Religion* 66 (2005): 337–358; Meredith McGuire and James Spickard, "Narratives of Commitment: Social Activism and Radical Catholic Identity," *Temenos: Studies in Comparative Religion* 37–38 (2003): 131–150.

5. Joseph Bensman and Arthur J. Vidich, *The New American Society: The Revolution of the Middle Class*. Quadrangle, 1971.

6. McGuire and Spickard, "Narratives of Commitment."

7. Most people use the terms *questionnaire* and *survey* interchangeably, though this is not quite correct. A questionnaire is a list of questions you ask people. They are typically short and easy to answer. A survey involves asking that list of questions to a select set of people—either to everyone in a particular group or to a sample that represents the group—so that you can tell what people in that group think. The survey is the process, and the questionnaire is the tool. I'll use the term *survey* from here on.

8. Ethnographers typically spend long periods of time living with groups of people, observing their social lives, shared activities, and habits, and interviewing them about their shared beliefs. Sociologists sometimes call this activity "participant observation." See the explanation at the beginning of this chapter.

9. See, for example, Hervé Varenne, *Americans Together: Structured Diversity in a Midwestern Town*. New York: Teacher's College Press, 1977. Varenne was a French anthropologist who

studied American cultural beliefs about individualism, noting that Americans almost universally thought of themselves as individualistic, despite doing nearly everything together.

10. Kristen Fyfe, *Wolves in Sheep's Clothing: A Content Analysis of Children's Television*, 2006. Retrieved from www.parentstv.org/PTC/publications/reports/childrensstudy/childrensstudy.pdf; Catherine Lutz and Jane Collins, *Reading National Geographic*. University of Chicago Press, 1993; Adrienne Redd, *Fallen Walls and Fallen Towers: The Fate of the Nation in a Global World*. Nimble Books, 2010.

11. See Norman Fairclough, *Analysing Discourse: Textual Analysis for Social Research*. Routledge, 2003; Louise Phillips and Marianne Jørgensen, *Discourse Analysis as Theory and Method*. Sage, 2002.

12. Cindy Myers, "Talking Poverty: Power Arrangements in Poverty Discourse," PhD dissertation, Program in Human and Organizational Development, Fielding Graduate Institute, 2005.

13. See Kim Cameron and Robert Quinn, *Diagnosing and Changing Organizational Culture*, 2nd ed. Jossey-Bass, 2005. This theory resembles one developed years earlier by the anthropologist Mary Douglas. It is best summarized in her book *How Institutions Think*. Syracuse University Press, 1986.

14. Available from www.ocai-online.com.

15. For an extended description, see Amedeo Giorgi's *The Descriptive Phenomenological Method in Psychology*. Duquesne University Press, 2009.

16. Doubleday, 1966, and Doubleday, 1959, respectively.

17. The 2004 film *Kitchen Stories* gives a hilarious image of the pitfalls of detached observation research. I recommend it highly.

18. John Van Maanen, *Pledging the Police: A Study of Selected Aspects of Recruit Socialization in a Large, Urban Police Department*. PhD thesis, University of California at Irvine, 1972. See also John Van Maanen, "The Asshole," pp. 221–238 in P. K. Manning and J. Van Maanen (eds.), *Policing: A View From the Streets*. Random House, 1978. Van Maanen was open about his research project. His informants knew that he was not a regular officer but was interested in studying police culture from the inside.

19. My first ethnographic project—a study of a new Japanese church—took 2 years, with a follow-up a couple of decades later. I spent 13 years on a later project, a study of a network of religious social activists. I did not spend full time in the field, though. See James Spickard, "Globalization and Religious Organizations: Rethinking the Relationship Between Church, Culture, and Market," *International Journal of Politics, Culture, and Society* 18 (2004): 47–63; "Ritual, Symbol, and Experience: Understanding Catholic Worker House Masses," *Sociology of Religion*, 66 (2005): 337–358.

(Continued)

(Continued)

20. Liz Morrish, "A Feminist's Response to the Technologization of Discourse in British Universities," *European Journal of Women's Studies* 7 (2000): 229–238.

21. Norman Fairclough, "Critical Discourse Analysis and the Marketisation of Public Discourse," pp. 130–166 in *Critical Discourse Analysis: The Critical Study of Language*, 2nd ed., Routledge, 2010.

22. Barney G. Glaser and Anselm L. Strauss, *Awareness of Dying*, Aldine, 1965; *The Discovery of Grounded Theory*, Aldine, 1967.

23. On the distinction between middle-range and grand theories in sociology, see Robert K. Merton, "On Sociological Theories of the Middle Range," pp. 39–53 in R. K. Merton, *Social Theory and Social Structure*. Free Press, 1949.

24. James H. Jones, *Bad Blood: The Tuskegee Syphilis Study.* Free Press, 1981.

25. By the end of the study, 128 of the 399 infected men had died of syphilis or related complications, 40 of their wives had been infected, and 19 of their children were born with congenital syphilis.

26. Laud Humphreys, *Tearoom Trade: Impersonal Sex in Public Places.* Duckworth, 1970. I am told that one of the "tearooms" was in the public park across the street from my university office.

27. Peter Monaghan, "Sociologist Is Jailed for Refusing to Testify About Research Subject," *Chronicle of Higher Education,* May 36, 1993, p. 10.

1 RESEARCH QUESTION

2 LOGICAL STRUCTURE

3 TYPE OF DATA

4 DATA COLLECTION METHOD

5 DATA COLLECTION SITE

6 DATA ANALYSIS METHOD

RESULTS

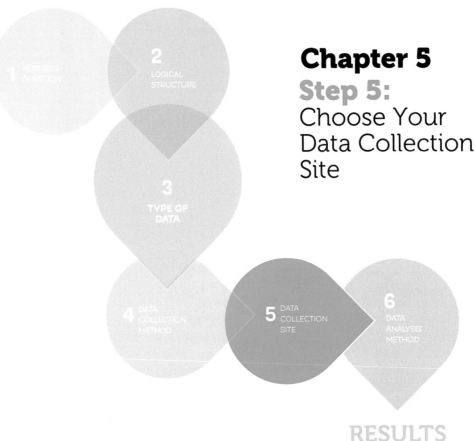

Chapter 5
Step 5:
Choose Your
Data Collection
Site

Okay. You've explored your research topic and developed a good research question. You've chosen a logical structure for your project. You've identified the type of data you need and have chosen an appropriate data collection method. What's next? You need a **data collection site** where you can reasonably expect to find the data you need.

In many cases, choosing a data collection site is not hard. You just ask yourself, "Where am I apt to find the kind of data I'm seeking?" Then you go and look. How you do so depends on the type of data you need. Different types of data call for different kinds of research sites. I can't cover all the possibilities in this chapter, but I can give you some starting points.

Demographic and Economic Data

Let's start with demographic and economic data, typically collected by organizations, governments, and the like. We'll focus on what's called **aggregate data**: data that you might use to compare cities, school districts, churches, companies, or Boy or Girl Scout troops. You could be comparing a pair of these—say Boston and Philadelphia or Troop 15 and Troop 132. Or you could be comparing a large

STEP 5 ▷ Data Collection Site

number of them, such as the 50 U.S. states or the 3,141 U.S. counties. In either case, you want a series of data points from each of your cities, districts, churches, companies, or troops. You use those data to make your comparisons. The data fit whatever interests you: the total population, the median educational level, the number of school dropouts, corporate profitability, regional economic growth or decline, or how fast scouts rise through the ranks. You might want to look for relationships in your data—such as whether the educational level of a region's population affects the region's economic growth. Your research question specifies all of this, which is why crafting a good question is so important.

What data collection site do you use for such investigations? There are really two answers to this question. On one level, your data collection site is whatever group of cities, counties, or organizations you wish to compare. You are, after all, collecting data from those sites or (more likely) using already-existing data collected by others. For example, using census data from Boston and Philadelphia works if the data let you answer your research question clearly. Boston and Philadelphia are thus the data collection sites that you need. The same is true if you are comparing corporate data from Apple and Microsoft, or student success data from the school districts in San Bernardino and Riverside counties, California. In each case, your research question should give you a pretty good indication of which sites will let you come up with useful answers.

On another level, though, whether or not you can answer your research question may depend less on the actual sites you choose than it does on the particular data you have available about them. For example, you can easily find census data from Philadelphia, but the data may not lend themselves to the specific research question you are asking. For instance, they probably won't tell you about neighborhood development along transit corridors. Nor will they tell you about shifts in voting, city politics, and the like. You may need different Philadelphia data to answer these questions—data the Census Bureau does not provide.

Shouldn't you account for this in your research design? Of course—and in fact, you do. The first part of choosing a data collection site for demographic and economic research involves choosing the locations and organizations you are going to compare. The second part, however, involves choosing a dataset that meets your needs. Not just any dataset will do. You have to find data that can answer your research question. Thus,

> For demographic and economic data, specify both:
> - Locations or organizations
> - Datasets

strange as it may sound, the "site" for aggregate data research is often the particular dataset you are using as well as the location where you collected it. You have to account for both.

For the Boston versus Philadelphia example, let's imagine that the local baseball teams collect data about how their fans get to the ballparks. You might be able to answer your transit question by combining these data with census data and then add in rider surveys collected by each city's transit authority. If you can find comparable data from each city, you're home free. Your site is thus the team, census, and transit datasets that you collected for the two cities.

There's another problem. Sometimes, different datasets can paint somewhat different pictures of the location or group you are trying to study. For example, both the Census Bureau and school districts typically collect information on local poverty. Their figures mostly match, but sometimes they don't. That's because they collect the data from somewhat different populations. The Census Bureau collects information from all households, but the schools collect information only from families with children. These might give different results. You need to consider this in your research design.

Here's a second problem: There are always missing data. Even the U.S. government can't interview everyone during its national census. Some people move and others don't return their questionnaires or don't answer their doorbells. Some people are homeless and hard to find. The Census Bureau does a good job, but it estimates that in 2010 it undercounted renters by 1%, African Americans by 2%, and Hispanics by 1.5%, and it missed almost 5% of the Native Americans and Alaskan Natives who were living on reserves or tribal lands.[1]

In any event, you should list as your data collection site both the regional or organizational unit from which your data were collected and the particular data drawn from those units. Your research proposal might say, "I'll answer my research question with data from the Census Bureau's *State and Metropolitan Area Data Book*"[2] or "My data collection site will be California's schools, using data collected by the California Department of Education."[3] That makes clear exactly what you are doing. (Your research proposal will need to justify these choices.)

Fortunately, collecting aggregate data is rather easy—if someone has already done it for you. If, for example, you need aggregate data about California school districts, you don't need to visit every school district in the state. That would be a huge job. Instead, you can download datasets from the California Department of Education website.[4] There, you can find information about school enrollments, graduation rates, school staffing, school performance, and so on. If your project needs this kind of data, then your data collection is very easy. Your general data collection site is California's schools, but each one of those datasets is also a site that helps you answer particular research questions.

The same is true if you need data comparing regions of the United States demographically. The Census Bureau collects information from the whole U.S. population every 10 years, with smaller data collections more frequently. The Census Bureau

makes its datasets public as soon as it has removed anything that might allow someone to identify a particular citizen. Data are thus reported for **census tracts** and
sometimes for **census blocks**, as well as for states, counties, and congressional districts. You can't, however, find census data for individual streets; that might let someone identify your Aunt Millie, which the Census Bureau is forbidden to do. In this
case, your site is both the geographic unit in question and the particular dataset that
contains the information you want.[5]

The situation is a bit harder when you are dealing with private companies. Let's
say you want to compare the employees of Company A with those of Company B. You
don't want to know about individuals; you just want to compare the two companies'
workforces. This information probably isn't public, so you'll have to persuade the two
companies to release the data so that you can use it. They control the site, and you
need to convince them to give you access. This isn't impossible, but they'll almost
certainly want to know how you plan to use their data. They will probably also put
restrictions on what you can do with it. So long as those restrictions don't prevent
you from carrying out your research, this site is appropriate. If their rules prevent you
from answering your research question, then you need to find a different site—that is,
a different pair of companies that are willing to cooperate. Your data collection site is
whatever companies and dataset you ultimately use.

So much for working with data that already exist. Where do you find demographic and other information that no one has collected? That's a much harder matter. If, for example, you are trying to learn what kind of people live in a particular city
neighborhood, you may need to make your own census. You can relatively easily map
the neighborhood's houses, and you can likely find data on property values, tax payments, and home ownership at city hall. More detailed information may require you
to make a door-to-door survey, and then you risk having people refuse to talk with
you. Such research often fails.

In the case of a neighborhood, you can sometimes collect information from a
random sample of houses, buildings, and businesses rather than from the neighborhood as a whole. Consult a statistics book to figure what percentage of the neighborhood you have to survey, so that you have a reasonable chance that your sample
represents the neighborhood as a whole. When someone refuses to participate, you can then replace that person in the sample. So long as there
is no systematic reason for the person's refusal, you are on firm ground.[6]
We'll look more closely at samples later in this chapter.

Where's the site, in this case? On the one hand, your site is the
neighborhood, because that's where you collected your data. Since
you'll be collecting the data yourself, that's probably what you'll list
in your proposal. On the other hand, you'll answer your research question based on whatever dataset you come up with. The only difference
between this dataset and the datasets I've mentioned from schools and
the Census Bureau is size. You can thus treat both the neighborhood
and the dataset as your site here, as well.

THINK ABOUT IT
How would <u>you</u>
solve the problem
of missing
data?

Opinions, Identities, and Reports of Acts at a Shallow Level

What about access to people's opinions and identities? What about their reports of their own actions—not at a deep and personal level but at the level they might be willing to share with a relative stranger? Consider these questions: "Have you, yourself, attended a religious service in the last seven days?" "Do you favor or oppose building a mass transit system in downtown San Antonio?" or "Are you White, African American, Asian American, Latino/Hispanic, Native American, or Other?" These are common survey questions, and surveys easily capture these data types. What data collection sites let you collect **survey data** about such relatively shallow matters?

Populations and Samples

As with aggregate data, there are two connected answers. First, there is the **population** that you are trying to survey. You may want responses from students at your university, residents of a particular city or neighborhood, members of the Lions or Elks Clubs, master chefs, or residents of the United States. These are wildly differently sized groups. Each, however, is a population. The first answer is that your data collection site is the population whose attitudes you seek to measure.

Let's say, for example, that we're trying to measure the differences in viewpoint between the residents of two neighborhoods, one of which has well-functioning mass transit connections and the other of which has none. We want to know whether neighborhood residents support or oppose a sales tax increase to support extending mass transit lines to areas that don't have them. Are there systematic differences in viewpoint between people living in well-served and underserved areas?

Clearly, we're looking for relatively shallow personal opinions, a data type easily captured by surveys. The type of data tells us what data collection method to use. In this case, our research question asks us to compare such opinions between two neighborhoods, so those neighborhoods are the ideal site for our research. Simple, no?

Well, not quite. The problem is that it takes lots of resources to survey an entire population. You need to find people, you need to interview them, and you need to process the results. That's hard enough for small groups but nearly impossible when the groups are large.

Smaller populations are hard to survey, too, unless people are compelled to take part. My university often struggles to get 50% of its faculty to respond to administrators' surveys (with 220 faculty total), in part because those administrators are not allowed to hold up paychecks. That would surely increase participation. The most successful survey ever of this university's 2,400 undergraduates

THINK ABOUT IT
Have you ever tried to get a large number of people to fill out a questionnaire?

reached a response rate of just 40%, and this disproportionally included those who wanted to rescue a valued program. Surveying a whole population is simply hard to do.

The solution, of course, is to survey a **sample** of the population, not the population as a whole. If you choose a small part of the population, then you have a better chance of catching everyone you want. It's a lot easier to survey 3,000, for example, than it is to survey 240 million. That's the number of noninstitutionalized American adults that the **General Social Survey (GSS)** targets every 2 years.[7] A mathematical trick makes this sample large enough, however, to model the attitudes of the full adult American population. This trick tells us how confident we can be that our survey results fall within a given distance from the actual population figure. We call these the **confidence level** and the **margin of error**. The first gives us the odds that our sample results represent the population as a whole. The second tells us the range within which we expect the population result to fall. These two figures depend on the **sample size**. We'll explore this relationship in a moment.

First, an example. Let's say we want to know how many U.S. adults identify themselves as Protestant. In 2012, 44.3% of the GSS sample did so. The margin of error for that survey was ±1.8%, so we can be 95% certain that between 42.5% and 46.1% of American adults are actually Protestants. That's the 44.3% who checked "Protestant" on the survey, plus or minus 1.8%. We have 19:1 odds that the percentage of Americans who are Protestants falls within this range.

There's a caveat, however. Our mathematical trick works only when the survey uses a **random sample**—that is, when every member of the target population has an equal chance of being in the sample. You, Jane Doe, Richard Roe, Molly Moe, and every other member of the population has to have an equal chance of being surveyed. If anyone gets left out, then we don't know our margin of error. That's a serious matter, because it's the margin of error that tells us how close our sample results are to the results we would get, were we to survey the population as a whole. Without equal opportunity, our margin could be ±1%, ±5%, ±20% or more. That makes sampling useless.

It's pretty easy to see why. Let's say we're doing a telephone survey. First off, we'll be talking only to people who own landline telephones, because phone companies are forbidden to give out lists of cell phone numbers. That means we'll catch fewer poor people, as they're less likely to have landlines than are middle-class folks. We'll miss a lot of young people for the same reason; they mostly have cell phones, which we can't reach. Our telephone sample will thus be richer and older than the population at large. Its views are likely to differ from those of the population, too. The problem is, we won't know by how much.

The same is true if we're going door-to-door through a neighborhood. We'll catch some people at home, but who we catch will vary by the time of day. We're less likely to catch working-age people on weekdays, so our sample will have more unemployed and retired folks than the population as a whole. Online surveys are even worse. They eliminate people without easy access to the Internet, people without technical skills, and people unmotivated to answer our questions. As a general rule, online surveys are the weakest kinds of surveys of all.

How do you make sure that your sample accurately reflects your target population? How do you make sure that everyone has an equal chance of being included? It's a three-step process.

First, assign everyone in the population a number. Second, consult a random number table, which is just a list of numbers that has no mathematical order to it.[8] Finally, pick the number of people you need for your sample in the order that their numbers appear on the random list. If your random list starts out "362, 35, 860, 44, 565, 361, . . . ," then the people with these numbers are the first six to get the survey. Continue until you have surveyed the sample you need. That way, everyone has an equal chance to participate.

Sample Size, Margin of Error, and Confidence Level

Now let's talk about the relationships between sample size, margin of error, and confidence level. The number of people you need—your sample size—depends on two things: how close you want your sample's results on an item to approach the population's true value, and how much confidence you need to have that your sample really represents the population at large. Your decisions about these two things together tell you how large a sample to choose.

Let's start with the margin of error, which is how wide a gap you can accept between your sample figures and the true value of the population as a whole. The more error you can accept, the smaller your sample has to be.

For example, the GSS's sample of 3,000 gives the ±1.8% margin of error mentioned earlier. The true population value is close to what the sample provides. From 1973 through 1993, though, the GSS sampled just half that many people. This produced a margin of error of ±2.5%. When 62.5% of the respondents to the 1972 survey said they were Protestants, it meant that the real population figure was between 60% and 65%. That's a larger spread than in 2012, but it's not so large that it makes us doubt the drop in Protestant adherents between the two years. The percentage of Americans who identify themselves as Protestants has clearly fallen, while the percentage identifying as Catholics has stayed fundamentally the same.[9] The number of Americans claiming "No Religion" has soared, however: from 5.1% to 19.7%. Only a seriously small sample would produce a margin of error large enough to cast doubt on those results.

As a second factor, you also get to choose how much confidence you have in your results. This is called the confidence level, a concept that is a bit harder to explain.

Imagine that we want to survey the U.S. adult population. We choose 3,000 people at random and ask them our questions. That's our sample. Then we decide to do it again, so we take another sample. Our random-number table almost certainly will give us a different set of 3,000 people the second time than it did the first. A third sample would almost certainly be different, as would our fourth, fifth, seventeenth, ninety-first, and so on. No two samples would be alike, though each would reflect the attitudes held by the population at large.

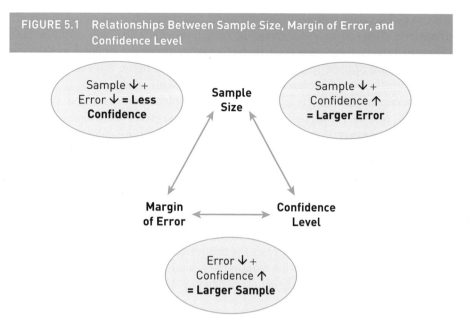

FIGURE 5.1   Relationships Between Sample Size, Margin of Error, and Confidence Level

The problem is, not all of our samples will reflect the population equally well. Just by chance, for example, we could find ourselves with a sample of 3,000 atheists. Or 3,000 gun rights advocates. Or 3,000 fast food aficionados. Or 3,000 college professors. Each of these samples is highly unlikely, because there aren't very many atheists, gun advocates, fast food fans, or professors in the U.S. population. Yet each sample is also possible. Pure randomness will give us a few samples that don't represent the American public very well. Such samples will give us distorted predictions about the general population's views. Each will, however, have the same margin of error: ±1.8%. How can this be?

That's where the confidence level comes in. When we say that a survey has a margin of error of ±1.8% (for example), we mean that 95% of the samples we choose will produce a value that falls within that range. That's a 95% **confidence level**—the smallest level that researchers will typically allow. In 19 times out of 20, the figures we report will reflect the population as a whole, within the margin of error. That's pretty good odds. Still, one sample out of 20 will predict a result outside these boundaries. One time out of 20, our sample results will *not* accurately reflect the population as a whole. The real population figure will be *more* than the margin of error away from the figure our sample produced.

Here's the kicker: *We don't know which sample that will be.* It might be sample #2, or sample #25, or sample #300. We just don't know, and there is no way to find out. Sampling research is therefore always tentative; it always needs to be confirmed by second and third research projects. Only then can you be reasonably sure that your sample gives you a good picture of the population as a whole.

Sample size, margin of error, and confidence level make a triangle (Figure 5.1). If you minimize the margin of error and maximize the level of confidence, then you have to pick a larger sample. If you minimize the sample and maximize the confidence level, then you have to increase the margin of error. And if you minimize both the sample and the margin of error, then the confidence level goes down as well. You can control two of these things, but you can't control all three. You can't have small samples, small errors, and high confidence all at the same time.

Generally, researchers try to draw as large a sample as they can afford. The larger the sample, relative to the population, the more likely it is that the sample reflects the population accurately. If we want to avoid the (admittedly slim) chance of drawing a sample of just atheists, gun advocates, fast food fans, or college professors, doubling the GSS sample size to 6,000 would greatly decrease the odds. Each remaining member of the population would have an equal chance of being in the second 3,000; it's highly unlikely that we'd get 3,000 people from the same small group twice in a row. (It's the same principle as flipping coins. Yes, you can occasionally flip 20 heads in a row, but you're not apt to flip 20 heads in a row twice running.)

Drawing a larger sample increases the confidence level while leaving the margin of error the same. Or it lowers the margin of error while maintaining the same confidence level. Table 5.1 shows the results of drawing various-sized samples of the U.S. adult population of 240 million.

To use an ungrammatical American colloquialism, "You pays your money, and you takes your choice." If you want to be more confident that your sample results reflect the population values, you must either accept more error or use a larger sample. You can't have everything.

TABLE 5.1 Samples of the U.S. Adult Population		
Sample Size	Confidence Level	Margin of Error (confidence interval)
750	95% (19/20)	±3.6%
750	99% (99/100)	±4.7%
1,500	95% (19/20)	±2.5%
1,500	99% (99/100)	±3.3%
3,000	95% (19/20)	±1.8%
3,000	99% (99/100)	±2.4%
6,000	95% (19/20)	±1.3%
6,000	99% (99/100)	±1.7%

Okay, you might be thinking, That's fine for measuring the 240 million U.S. adults. But I only want to measure the 2,400 students at my small university, or the 1,000 students at a medium-sized U.S. high school, or the 400 people who live in a local neighborhood. If a sample of 3,000 gives me 99% confidence that my sample results will be within ±2.4% of the real figure for that huge population, my smaller population won't need much of a sample at all.

Unfortunately, that's not how it works. You have to draw a proportionally larger sample from a small population than you have to draw from a large one. For example, I would have to sample half of my university's students (1,200) to be 95% certain that my survey results are within ±2% of the whole student body's views. A ±3% margin of error needs a sample of 739 at the same confidence level; a ±5% margin of error drops that to 331, but that gives me just 95% confidence that I'm within a 10% spread.[10] That's not very good!

To take the 400-person example, at a 95% confidence level, you'd need a sample of 341 to get a 2% margin of error, 291 to get a 3% margin, and 196 to get a 5% margin. Given how hard it is to make sure your sample is random, you might as well survey the entire population.

Remember, each of your samples must be randomly chosen. Every member of a population must have an equal chance of being chosen. Anything less, and you can't generalize your sample results to the population at large.

Let's return to the place we began: with the question of the data collection site for survey work. As mentioned earlier, this question has two connected answers.

First, all surveys attempt to gauge the opinions, identities, and reports of a target population. Thus, *the population is the data collection site for survey work*. When you use a sample, however, you need a more specific data collection site: *the sample drawn from the population*. The data collection site for the 2012 GSS, for example, is both the U.S. adult, noninstitutionalized, English- and Spanish-speaking population *and* the particular group of people who were sampled to represent them. The data collection site for the 1972 GSS is the same population (minus the monolingual Spanish speakers) *and* the sample drawn that year. As with aggregate data, you need to specify both sites. (If you survey an entire population, of course, there is just one site.)

I've written at length about these first two types of data: aggregate data and survey data, because each lends itself to statistical analysis—which you'll learn more about in Step 6, when we consider how to pick a data analysis method. Some kinds of statistics help you compare organizations, geographic areas, and so on. Others help you analyze survey data. Both raise technical issues that you have to consider early in the research design process. These issues make a difference for the data collection site you choose, so they can't be postponed.

I'll cover the remaining data types more succinctly, because their data collection sites make intuitive sense. You just have to ask yourself the question raised at the beginning of the chapter: "Where am I apt to find the kind of data I'm seeking?"

Observable Behavior

Let's move on to observable behavior: the acts, behaviors, or events we noted in Column 1 of Table 4.1, which linked types of data to appropriate data collection methods. This is the simplest case, because such things happen in places and those places thus become our chosen data collection sites.

Imagine that you want to compare the observable street life in two neighborhoods: one located around a mass transit station and the other located elsewhere, where no mass transit goes. Your research question is "What is the observable character of street life in places with and without mass transit hubs?" The two neighborhoods are your data collection sites. Your task is to observe the two neighborhoods, note what happens in them, and compare. Clear? Well, almost. The main issue is how to choose among the several neighborhoods that have transit stations and among the many more neighborhoods that lack them. On what basis do you decide which ones to include?

Ideally, you want neighborhoods that have a lot in common, so that their only difference is the presence or absence of mass transit. You want their residents' age spread to be about the same, because older people and younger people use streets differently. You are apt to see a different kind of street life where a lot of young people live than where most residents are older. You also want to have a similar mix of businesses. Otherwise, the differences you see may be due to the different businesses, not the transit station. The idea is to find two neighborhoods that are pretty much alike, except for transit, and then see what differences you can observe.

The problem is, having a transit station is probably going to affect a neighborhood's age mix, its business mix, and so on. In fact, it could affect pretty much everything about a neighborhood. How do you know if the neighborhoods differ because of the transit station, or because they've always had different kinds of population?

One solution is to observe a bunch of neighborhoods—ideally those around *all* of a city's transit stations—to see if they have anything in common. Then you compare these to a similar set of neighborhoods that lack stations. If you consistently find younger residents, more businesses, more street life, and so on, then you can generalize. Observing several neighborhoods makes this possible.

THINK ABOUT IT
What do different neighborhoods have in common?

Unfortunately, this approach multiplies research costs. Who is going to do all this observing? Can you afford a team large enough to cover this much area? Probably not, which means either you have to observe in fewer places or you have to observe fewer things. You may, for example, decide to focus on just pedestrians, or just food stores, or just night life. Here, your data collection site is the set of neighborhoods you observe. How you balance the number of neighborhoods against the depth of your observations will influence the specific sites you choose.

Deeply Held Opinions and Attitudes

Where are you apt to find people's deeply held opinions and attitudes—the next type of data on our list? Remember that these data call for interviews (see Table 4.1). That turns your question into "Who am I going to interview?" Your interviewees will be your data collection site—the "place" from which you collect your data.

Let's say you want to interview people about the effects that mass transit has had on their neighborhoods. You want to know what changes people report that mass transit has brought to their lives. You clearly need to pick residents who have lived in their neighborhood long enough to have seen it change. That eliminates younger people, new residents, and specifically those who moved to the area to take advantage of the improved transit opportunities. You can thus interview a subset of the population, and, among that subset, you need to find people who are willing to talk at length with you.

This introduces a problem. How do you locate such people? That's going to depend on the neighborhood. In some neighborhoods, you can advertise. You can put up posters, talk with shopkeepers, ask at neighborhood clubs, churches, barbershops, and hair salons—anywhere people can help you get in touch with potential interviewees. This takes time and effort, but it's doable. The only fundamental barrier may be your own interpersonal skills.

Once you have identified and interviewed a few people, you can ask them who else might have something to say on the issue. Longtime residents have had some years to get to know each other. They may be better placed than others to guide you to more interview subjects. Once you are in their network, you may find enough interviewees with ease. Sociologists call this a **snowball sample** because it gets bigger the longer it keeps rolling. One successful interview leads to another, to another, to another.

The problem, of course, is that most neighborhoods have several networks, not all of which interact with one another. If you gain your first entry through church contacts, for example, you may not be directed toward equally long-standing residents who frequent the local bar. You may inadvertently end up interviewing people with largely similar views. It pays, therefore, to gain entry by as many paths as possible. You want a diversity of views, so you need to reach beyond those whom you encounter first.

How many people do you need to interview? That depends on your project. You need to talk with enough people to make sure that you're getting as wide a variety of opinions as possible. You at least need to catch all the widely shared ones. If you don't, you won't draw correct conclusions.

Here's a rule of thumb: Start by interviewing 25 to 30 people, trying to get as diverse a set of views as possible. Once you've done that, look at the transcripts from the last five people you interviewed and ask yourself if they have told you anything new. If they have not, then interview five more and if *that* group still hasn't told you anything new and important, quit. If they *have* told you new things, keep interviewing. That way, you'll make sure you've captured the major views, without overdoing it. Figure 5.2 (on the next page) illustrates this process.[11]

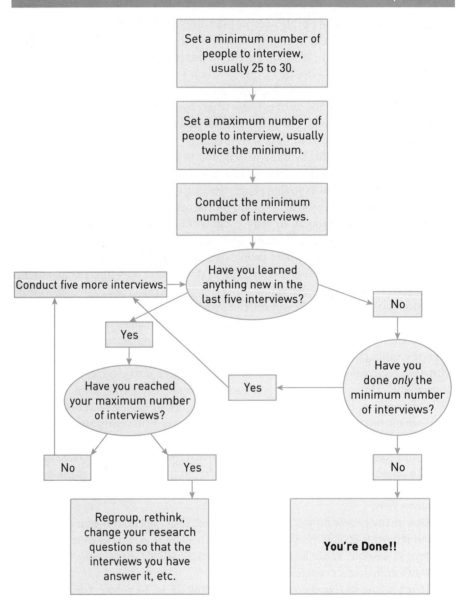

FIGURE 5.2 Interview Rule-of-Thumb Flowchart for Nonrandom Samples

Cultural and Expert Knowledge

Where do you collect cultural and expert knowledge? Cultural knowledge consists of the things that "everybody" knows: how to tie your shoes, what kids ought to learn in kindergarten, the tone of voice to use when speaking to your boss. Expert knowledge is the stuff that true experts know: how to build a particle accelerator, how to bake a prize-winning pizza, how to work with street kids to keep them out of gangs. In one sense, the two types of knowledge are at the opposite ends of the spectrum: Everyone's knowledge is at one end, and things known by only a few are at the other. But to a researcher, both types of knowledge have one essential thing in common: Both can be gathered in the same way.

Clearly, you can gather cultural knowledge and expert knowledge through interviews. I've just covered interviews as data collection sites, so I'll skip doing so again. These two types of knowledge can also be fruitfully collected with focus groups. As discussed in Chapter 4, these are group interviews, in which we ask people questions collectively and record their conversation. By doing so, we get group consensus, or two or three options that everyone in the group thinks are valid. This data collection method is perfect for gathering cultural and expert knowledge. In this case, the data collection site is the focus group.

How do we pull such groups together? The process is a bit like setting up interviews. If, for example, we want to collect the things that everyone knows about how to work at XYZ Corporation, then we get a group of XYZ employees and have them talk about what they have to know in order to work there. We could let the XYZ management organize these groups for us, but then we'd likely get only part of the picture. People are apt to leave out the things that they know management doesn't want said—and that common knowledge is precisely the kind of thing we want to collect. We may, therefore, need to gather employees off-site. Will company politics surface there, too? Probably, but we can likely spot those issues. In either case, we need to be aware of any **biases** our groups happen to demonstrate.

Experts are a bit easier to work with, because they are usually independent of one another and not beholden to a single corporate hierarchy. They also usually recognize each other as experts and may in fact enjoy the chance to share their respective points of view. We still need to be a bit careful whom we recruit, however. The famous architect Frank Lloyd Wright once commented that "an expert is a man who has stopped thinking because 'he knows'."[12] Know-it-alls can ruin a focus group's dynamic and waste everyone's time.

Experts or ordinary people, our data collection site here is the focus group. That's the site where we collect the kind of data—cultural or expert knowledge—that our research question needs.

Hidden Social Patterns

What about hidden social patterns? These are ways of thinking and acting that are so common as to be largely invisible, even to their participants. They include things as mundane as how far people typically stand from one another and as complex as the ways that the members of different cultural groups interpret people's intentions.[13] American preschool teachers, for example, often interpret misbehaving children as bored and thus potentially gifted, whereas Japanese preschool teachers see them as lacking *omoiyari* (empathy). Another hidden social norm is the way American teachers typically intervene more quickly to stop student misbehavior, a practice that Japanese teachers see as excessively adult centered. As the principal of a Japanese preschool put it to Joseph Tobin and his co-researchers, by having to deal with a misbehaving peer themselves, the other children "learn to be more complete human beings."[14]

The data collection site for such investigations ought to be obvious. It is wherever the hidden patterns are to be found. Tobin and his co-researchers compared the cultural and educational patterns they found in three preschools, one in Japan, one in southern China, and a third in Honolulu, Hawaii. Their study showed the different things that members of these three societies thought children should learn. For example, Japanese teachers emphasized interpersonal empathy and developing children's ability to work with a group. Chinese teachers emphasized order and conformity (though the school that Tobin and his colleagues examined was more conservative than most Chinese schools are today). American preschool teachers emphasized individual choice and nurtured children's ability to put their thoughts into words. Each society values these particular skills and so pays special attention to teaching them to its youngest children. These values are, however, largely invisible—at least until the members of one society see what the other two societies think is normal.

In short, research seeking hidden social patterns can take place wherever those patterns can be found.

The Remaining Data Types

I haven't covered all the data types listed in Table 4.1. That's because the remaining data types don't raise any new issues for your choice of a data collection site.

For example, deep personal feelings are much like deep personal opinions: Both call for in-depth interviews. You need to find a set of interviewees who will talk with you at a deep level. These interviewees also need to have something to say about your research topic. Someone who can talk deeply about parenting may not be able to talk deeply about religion. Your data collection site is the set of people whose conversations will help you answer your research question.

Similarly, interview projects that seek accounts of individual experiences are very much like those seeking expert knowledge: Both need people who are expert about whatever it is you are studying. In the one case, you are looking for people who

Other Data Types

- Personal feelings
- Experiences
- Expert knowledge
- Shallow opinions

have undergone similar things: near-death experiences, the experience of speaking in tongues, falls from airplanes—just to name a few of the wilder possibilities. In the other case, you are probably looking for people who know how to do things in the external world: run a corporation, design mass transit systems, and so on. Both types are experts; with one exception, the site-related issues are the same. What's that exception? You can put a bunch of experts in a room and lead them in a focus group, but you can't do that when you want people to describe their individual experiences as they were lived. The latter need the personal attention that only in-depth interviews can bring.

What other data types call for sites like those we have already discussed? Reports of acts, behavior, or events are like opinions and identities: You can collect them at two levels. Shallowly, you use surveys; if you want something deeper, you interview people, so your site involves finding people who can give deep accounts of what happened. Interestingly, measuring personal and psychological traits involves the same kinds of things as survey work. You typically have people fill out questionnaires and then analyze them statistically. You have to pay attention to the differences between populations and samples. There's nothing fundamentally new here.

The point is, choosing a data collection site requires you to find a place or a population where the data you are looking for are apt to be found. That's Step 5 in the six-step approach.

Review Questions

1. What characteristics make a data collection site a good place for gathering the data you need to answer your research question?

2. In what sense is an existing dataset a "site" for research?

3. What is the difference between a sample and a population? Why do you need to know which one you are using?

4. How many people do you need for an interview project? Why? How do you know when you have enough?

5. Where do you go to collect cultural and expert knowledge?

The open-access Student Study Site at **study.sagepub.com/spickard** has a variety of useful study tools, including SAGE journal articles, video & web resources, eFlashcards, and quizzes.

Notes

1. U.S. Census Bureau, "Census Bureau Releases Estimates of Undercount and Overcount in the 2010 Census." Retrieved from http://www.census.gov/newsroom/

(Continued)

(Continued)

releases/archives/2010_census/cb12-95
.html. The U.S. Census Bureau uses some
pretty sophisticated techniques to come
up with these estimates.

2. U.S. Census Bureau, *State and
Metropolitan Area Data Book: 2010.*
Retrieved from http://www.census.gov/
prod/2010pubs/10smadb/2010smadb.pdf

3. California Department of Education, API
Data Files. Retrieved from http://www
.cde.ca.gov/ta/ac/ap/apidatafiles.asp

4. At this writing, the web address is http://
www.cde.ca.gov/ds/. Other states may
have similar resources.

5. Census data from 2010 are available
at http://www.census.gov/2010
census/data/. You can find downloadable
maps of census tracts, blocks, and the
like at http://www.census.gov/geo/
maps-data/.

6. If all the White people refuse to speak
with you, or all the people who live in
the richer-looking houses refuse, then
your sample will not represent the
neighborhood's population. This may
force you to rethink your project from the
beginning.

7. The GSS excludes those under age 18
and also excludes adults who are in jails,
nursing homes, hospitals, and other
"institutionalized" settings. Until 2006,
it excluded people whose English was not
good enough to handle the 90 minutes
it took to conduct the survey interview
(and who had no family member who
could translate for them). Since 2006,
the GSS has included Spanish as a second
interview language. The GSS uses a

very complicated system of sampling to
better reflect its target population. The
resulting data—back to 1973—are posted
for public use at http://gss.norc.org/Get-
The-Data.

8. A list of numbers is random if knowing one
number doesn't let you predict the next,
because there's no pattern. The list "1, 2,
3, 4, . . . " has a pattern; so does "2, 4, 8,
16, . . . " and "4, 7, 5, 8, . . . " and so on.

9. The two margins overlap: 24.9%–29.9%
in 1972, 22.4%–26% in 2012.

10. These numbers come from an online
sample size calculator at http://www
.surveysystem.com/sscalc.htm. Several
free calculators are available. This
particular one has the merit of allowing
truly large population sizes.

11. There is a larger version of this chart in
the "Guides and Handouts" section of
this book, with detailed instructions
about how to use it.

12. Bruce Brooks Pfeiffer, ed., *Frank Lloyd
Wright on Architecture, Nature, and the
Human Spirit: A Collection of Quotations.*
Pomegranate, 2011, p. 48.

13. See Edward Hall, *The Silent Language.*
Doubleday, 1959; *The Hidden Dimension.*
Doubleday, 1966.

14. Joseph Tobin et al., *Preschool in
Three Cultures.* Yale University Press,
1989, p. 30. See also Joseph Tobin et al.,
Preschool in Three Cultures, Revisited.
University of Chicago Press, 2009.
Films to accompany each book are
available from Tobin's website at
http://joetobin.net/videos.html.

1 RESEARCH QUESTION

2 LOGICAL STRUCTURE

3 TYPE OF DATA

4 DATA COLLECTION METHOD

5 DATA COLLECTION SITE

6 DATA ANALYSIS METHOD

RESULTS

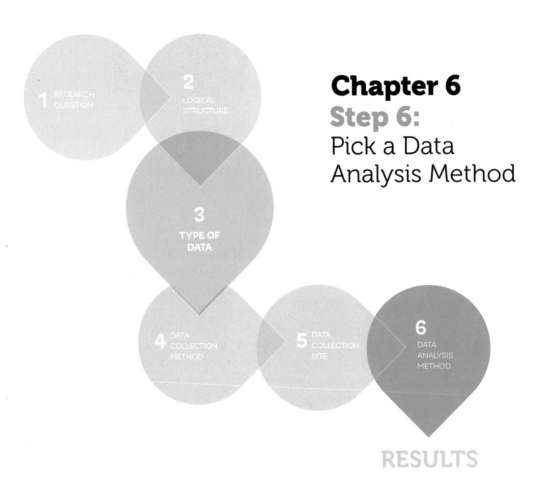

Chapter 6
Step 6:
Pick a Data Analysis Method

W e've covered five of the six steps you need to take when you design a research project. You've crafted a clear research question, chosen a logical structure for your research, identified the type of data you need, picked an appropriate data collection method, and chosen a good data collection method. Now you have to choose an appropriate **data analysis method**.

In this chapter, I'll cover the basic principles of data analysis and then show you some ways to analyze data: first quantitatively and then qualitatively. Remember from the opening chapters that *quantitative* and *qualitative* do *not* refer to different kinds of research: *They are different kinds of data analysis.* Deciding how you will analyze your data is the last step in the process, not the first. We're now at the last step.

This chapter won't be covering all the possible ways to analyze data. There are just too many. We'll cover some in this chapter and more in Part II, where we'll work through several concrete research examples. Whole books, even whole book series, have been written on data analysis techniques. This chapter will, however, give you the basics. Once you're oriented, you can consult those specialty publications as you need them.

Data Analysis Method

STEP **6**

For now, I'll hit the major points and give you enough information to get started. By the end of this chapter, you should know enough to complete your research design and write your research proposal.

Preliminary Questions

Before you decide how to analyze your data, you need to answer three preliminary questions.

First, you need to have a sense of what kind of analysis will answer your research question. This involves figuring out what, exactly, you need your data to tell you. Your research question tells you what kind of data you need, while your logical structure tells you what you need that data to do. Your first step is to think through how to put these together. Phrased as a question: *"What kind of analysis does your research question require?"*

Second, you need to know some basics about your data. Are they **numeric data** (**quantitative data**)—that is, will you have counted something? Or are they **nonnumeric data**—a description in words, pictures, or something else that you can't reduce to numbers? If the data are numeric, what kinds of numbers do you have? In all, there are four main answers to the second preliminary question: *"What form does your data take?"* Most of the time, your data will take one of four forms. If numeric, it will be interval/ratio, ordinal, or categorical; if nonnumeric, it will be qualitative. We'll explore how to work with each of these forms later in this chapter.

The third preliminary question has two related parts: *"What is your unit of observation?"* and *"What is your unit of analysis?"* First, you need to know where your data come from: Did you collect them from individuals, groups, organizations, geographic regions, or something else? Second, you need to know whether you will be analyzing your data by these same units, or by different ones. You can, for example, combine individual-level data together so that they represent groups, organizations, or regions; your unit of observation is then the individual, but your unit of analysis is something larger. Unfortunately, you can't do the reverse. You can't draw conclusions about individuals if your data come from larger units. I'll go into the details in a moment, but you need to identify your units of observation and of analysis. That will let you choose the right data analysis method.

Let's look at these three questions in turn.

What Kind of Analysis Does Your Research Question Require?

You should already have some ideas about the kind of analysis your research question requires, given the importance of the research question in the six-step method. The research question tells you what kind of data you need, and the logical structure you've chosen tells you what you need to do with that data so that you can answer your question. The result is analysis: transforming the data so that it does what you need.

Here's an example. Let's say your research question is "Are parents who volunteer time at their children's elementary schools more supportive, less supportive, or equally supportive of school administrators than are the parents who do not volunteer time?"[1] This asks for parents' opinions, probably relatively shallow ones, because you want to be able to tell easily if they support administrators or not.[2] It also asks for a comparative research logic: You want to find out if parents who volunteer are different from parents who do not.

The terms *more, less,* and *equally* indicate that your comparison is probably quantitative. That is, you'll want to be able to score the level of parent support in some way. Thus, you'll be looking for some sort of quantitative analysis.

You will, of course, have thought all of this through while you were choosing your data collection method. Using a survey both collects shallow opinions and allows for quantitative comparison. If you move through the six-step process correctly, this first preliminary question is not hard to answer.

Other research questions call for other methods of data analysis, but you get the picture.

What Form Does Your Data Take?

Now let's look at the second preliminary question. Data can take any of four different forms. Numeric data can be categorical, ordinal, or interval/ratio; nonnumeric data are qualitative. Each of these forms has to be analyzed differently. The first three are typically called **scales of measurement**, and each calls for specific kinds of **statistical analysis**. Qualitative data call for one or another kind of qualitative analysis.

- **Categorical data** (also called **nominal data**) consist of mutually exclusive, but not ordered, categories, such as men/women, African American/Asian American/Latino/White, yes/no, Northeast/South/Midwest/West, and so on. Each category is different but none ranks above another.
- **Ordinal data** are rank-ordered, but there is no fixed interval between the ranks. For example, "excellent," "good," "fair," and "poor" are clearly ranked, but you can't tell if the distance between "good" and "fair" is larger or smaller than the distance between "fair" and "poor." You can rank the terms, but you can't measure the distance between them.
- **Interval/ratio data** (sometimes called **continuous data**) allow measurement of distance. The distance between 10 and 20 is the same as the distance between 30 and 40. This lets you do more complex mathematics with these data than with the other numeric types. *Interval data* and *ratio data* are a bit

different. Interval data come from scales that have no true zero, such as degrees in Fahrenheit or Celsius. Ratio data have a true zero, such as years of schooling. It makes sense to say that one person has twice as much schooling as another, but it does not make sense to say that an 80-degree (Fahrenheit) day is twice as hot as a 40-degree day. That's because zero on the Fahrenheit scale is arbitrary. It's worth remembering this difference, though interval and ratio data are alike enough that we call them "interval/ratio" data most of the time.

● **Qualitative data** are nonnumeric. They consist of bits of speech, text, visual patterns, and the like—the stuff you get in response to open-ended questions or in the qualitative analysis of visual arts. Statistics don't help you with this kind of data; **thematic analysis** does. We'll encounter some examples later in this chapter.

What does this look like in practice? Let's say that you're collecting *shallow opinions and attitudes,* of the kind that people are willing to share on **social surveys**. You've collected information from a random sample of the residents of a small city. Among your questions were the following, along with the answers that the survey allowed:

1. How many years of school did you attend in total, counting all degrees? (0 to 30)
2. How happy are you with the job the local schools are doing? (very happy, pretty happy, not too happy)
3. Do you support the idea of a tax increase to support our local schools? (yes, no, no opinion)
4. Please tell us why or why not. (open-ended, in up to 50 words)

These four questions illustrate each of the four forms of data.

Question 1 gives you interval/ratio data. Not only is the difference between 4 and 6 years of schooling the same as the difference between 8 and 10 years, but the scale also has a true zero: no schooling at all. Calculations are easy.

Question 2 gives you ordinal data. It has three possible answers, and you can expect that people will rank "very happy" above "pretty happy." You just won't know whether all your respondents think there is the same distance between them. You can, however, count on everyone ranking things in the same way.

Question 3 gives you categorical data, which doesn't allow you to rank responses at all. You can count the yeses, noes, and no opinions, but you can't rank them, nor can you take an average of the three. You can only report how many fall into each category.

Question 4 gives you qualitative data. This gives people the freedom to say things in their own words. Some, for example, may say they don't trust the local schools because of a bad experience with a school principal. Others may say they support the local high school band or football team. In any case, these answers are harder

> **Forms of Data**
>
> ● Interval-ratio
> ● Ordinal
> ● Categorical
> ● Qualitative

to compare than are the numeric forms of data. They are also more nuanced, which is part of their attraction to researchers.

Sometimes you can change one form of data into another. For example, you can turn interval data into ordinal data by sorting years of school into groups. Anyone who reported 1 through 8 years of education would become "grade school only," those reporting 9 to 12 years might become "some high school or HS grad," 13 to 16 years might become "some college or college grad," and more than 16 years might become "grad school." If you do this, you lose the ability to make some calculations, but you gain the ability to compare different educational levels.

It's even easier to treat ordinal data as if it were categorical; you just ignore the rankings. You might, for example, want to compare people who stopped their education at high school with those who attended some form of college. Just treat them as two separate categories. This might help you answer your research question better than hanging on to the rankings would.

Unfortunately, you can't go the other way. You can't change categorical data into ordinal data, nor can you change ordinal data into interval data. Numeric data transform in just one direction.

Can you change qualitative data into quantitative data? That depends on the data themselves. You may be able to sort people's answers by themes and then count the number of times each theme recurs. That turns qualitative data into categories. The categories might not be mutually exclusive, however. People may give two conflicting responses, firmly believing both of them.

The point is, you need to know what form of data you have. *Each of these forms allows you to use certain analytic techniques and forbids you from using others.* That's the central lesson of Step 6.

Now let's consider what types of data come in each of these four forms. Here are some basic rules:

- Economic and demographic data are usually *interval/ratio*. The units from which you collect them (e.g., organizations, states) will be *categorical*, but the data from each unit will be interval or ratio.
- Acts, behavior, and events (or reports of acts, behavior, and events) are *interval* if you count them but *qualitative* if you describe them in words.
- Self-identity is generally *qualitative;* however, you can use a survey to count the number of times people identify themselves in a particular way. When people choose from a predetermined set of possibilities, self-identities are *categorical*, and you can count the number in each category.
- As noted earlier, information collected from surveys—shallow personal opinions, self-identities, and reports of acts or events—can be *interval, ordinal,* or *categorical*. Open-ended answers are qualitative.
- Deep personal opinions, personal feelings, cultural knowledge, expert knowledge, and experience as it presents itself to consciousness are *qualitative*.

- Personal and psychological traits are usually numeric because of the way they are measured. Most often they are captured by scores on psychological tests; these scores are *interval*. A few tests produce *categorical* data.
- The data produced by the search for hidden social patterns varies according to how it is captured. If the patterns are uncovered ethnographically, through nonnumeric observation of behavior, then are they are *qualitative*. If they are uncovered through counting, they are *numeric*.

THINK ABOUT IT
Why is the form that your data takes so important?

These are, of course, rough-and-ready rules. You always need to think through exactly what form your data takes.

What Is Your Unit of Observation? What Is Your Unit of Analysis?

Now let's take up the third preliminary question, about the **unit of observation** and the **unit of analysis**. The first is where you get your data: from individuals, groups, organizations, regions, and so on; the second is how you treat that data in your data analysis. Again, an example will help you to see what's involved.

Let's say you are interested in people's opinions about a mass transit project. For example, you want to know if people support a particular transit development: "Do you or do you not support building a streetcar system that will connect your neighborhood to downtown?" The data type is clear: *opinions*. You ask individuals their opinions and collect what they tell you. Very straightforward. You have, in this case, collected data from individuals. Individuals are your unit of observation, because you are collecting your information from them.

You don't, however, have to analyze these data at the individual level. You could also analyze the data at the neighborhood level, the city level, at the level of various civic organizations, and so on. Each of these analyses would use the same data, collected from individuals, but would work with the data differently. Each of these is a different unit of analysis. What you ultimately do will depend on your research question.

There are several possibilities. First, your research question might ask about what kinds of people favor or oppose the new transit system. For example, are educated people more apt to support mass transit than those with less education? Are car owners more apt to support mass transit, perhaps because having fewer cars on the road makes it easier for them to drive? Here, you would be comparing *individuals*. What combination of personal factors makes one individual support mass transit and another oppose it? *In these cases, the unit of analysis is the same as the unit of observation: It is the individual.*

Or your research question might ask what different groups or classifications of people think about mass transit. Do Republicans think one way and Democrats another? Do members of civic-minded clubs (e.g., Rotary, Elks, Moose) support mass transit or oppose it? In these cases, even though you have collected data from individuals, you want to compare groups. You want to find out if there are systematic differences between them. *Here, the group is the unit of analysis.* Individuals are the *unit of observation,* because you collected information from them, but your research question asks you to compare groups. You combine your individual data to get a group average.

Maybe you want to compare different neighborhoods. Does mass transit have to serve a neighborhood before people will support it? Or are people in some neighborhoods civic minded enough to be willing to tax themselves to benefit their neighbors? *Here, your unit of analysis is the geographic region.* This is different from the group or the individual, even when you base the geographic comparison on individual-level information. As you'll see later in this chapter, the unit of analysis, combined with the data type, tells you which analytic techniques are possible.

Data from the U.S. Census is a good example of how individual data can be used to compare geographic units. The Census Bureau collects data from individuals and households. It doesn't report data in that format, however, at least not right away. That's to protect people's privacy; the government doesn't want anyone to use census data to find data about a specific individual. Instead, the Census Bureau aggregates data into geographic units: census tracts,[3] counties, states, and so on. We can compare these geographic areas with each other. We can compare rates of poverty, percentages of homes with and without indoor plumbing, average commute times for people living in a particular area, and so on. Census data—which generally report behavior, not opinions—can answer a great many research questions. The unit of analysis is the geographic region: the census tract, county, state, and so on. The unit of observation is the individual (or household), but the data are not released in a way that makes individual-level analysis possible.[4]

School researchers similarly collect data on individual children (the unit of observation), which they can then use to compare these children's educational success. If they compare children, the unit of analysis is the individual. If, however, they average those data across classrooms, they can figure out the effect that different teaching methods have on student success, using the classroom as their unit of analysis. Or they can compare schools, using schools as their unit. All these different approaches produce legitimate research.

Without trying to be exhaustive, here are some possible units of analysis that social researchers often use:

- Individuals
- Groups
- Organizations
- Geographic units (census tracts, neighborhoods, towns)
- Social interactions (marriages, friendships, divorces, arrests)
- Artifacts (books, newspapers, movies)

In each case, research compares individuals with individuals, organizations with organizations, interactions with interactions, and so on. It might compare the traits of these units—for example, by comparing the qualities of different marriages and their effect on marital longevity.

> **Things to Decide**
>
> • Kind of analysis
> • Form of data
> • Unit of observation
> • Unit of analysis

This works for all kinds of research. For example, Cindy Myers's project (described in Chapter 4) examined unsigned editorials in the *New York Times* and the *Wall Street Journal* and then compared those two newspapers' ways of imagining poverty. The editorials were her unit of observation, but the newspapers were her unit of analysis. Every researcher needs to know the difference.

This covers our preliminary concerns. Once you have figured out what kind of analysis your research question requires, what form your data take, and what unit of observation and unit of analysis you need, then you can choose an appropriate data analysis method.

In the rest of this chapter, I'll present some ways of working with each of our three forms of numeric data and a couple of ways of working with qualitative data. I'll show what you can do with different data types and what units of analysis each can manage. I'll also show how important it is not to overinterpret your data. Part II of this book covers these topics in more depth. For now, the point is to get you familiar with the basic decisions you have to make.

Working With Numeric Data: Describing

Let's start with numeric data and the simplest thing you can do with it: describe what you've found. There's no point in getting terribly technical about this. Once you've counted things, then you want to report what you've counted. That gives you a quick snapshot of your results.

The New England regional office of the Environmental Protection Agency, for example, has 118 toxic waste sites on its current Long Term/National Priorities List, evenly distributed among the six states in the region. The San Bernardino City Unified School District in California enrolls almost 54,000 students, on whom it spends a per-pupil average of $10,000 each year and for whom it employs about 2,500 teachers. The Ford Motor Company posted a profit of $4.7 billion on its North American automotive operations during the first half of 2013, for an operating margin of 10.7% (about $3,300 per vehicle sold). Such numbers paint a picture of these organizations.[5]

We can do more than just list numbers. Several tools help us see more deeply into our data. Let's start with the notion of **distributions**. These show how the data points are spread out or clumped together.

Figure 6.1 (on the next page) illustrates an example: high school graduation rates from the 50 U.S. states.[6] Each bar shows the number of states with graduation rates of

(a)

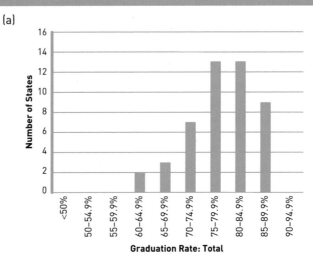

(b)

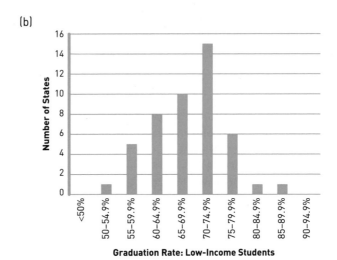

50% to 54.9%, 55% to 59.9%, and so on. The chart on the top shows total graduation rates; the chart on the bottom shows graduation rates for children from low-income families.

These two charts let us describe the distribution of graduation rates across the states. Nevada and New Mexico have the lowest rates, with 62% and 63% rates for all students and 53% and 56% for the economically disadvantaged. Iowa has the highest overall rate at 88%, while South Dakota does the best job with low-income kids at

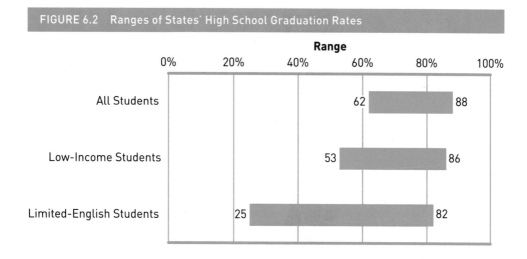

FIGURE 6.2   Ranges of States' High School Graduation Rates

86%. (South Dakota's graduation rate for poor kids is actually a couple of points higher than its overall rate. Are they doing something special?)

The charts also show us that a bit less than half of the states graduate between 75% and 85% of all their students (the two highest bars), and figures for low-income students are about 10% less. A few more states fall below this range than fall above it, especially for low-income students. Such graphs give us a good picture of how values are spread out and how they are bunched up.

We can learn a bit more by digging deeper. First, we want to know the **range** of values for each case (Figure 6.2). Numerically, the overall graduation rate ranges from 62% to 88% and the rate for low-income kids ranges from 53% to 86%. We call this a **measure of dispersion**, because it tells us how widely dispersed the values are. Both of these ranges are narrower than the graduation rates for kids with limited proficiency in English: those range from 25% (Arizona) to 82% (South Dakota and Vermont).

The range for limited English speakers is about twice the size of the overall graduation range. Clearly, states' abilities to graduate students with little English vary a lot more than does their ability to graduate students overall.

Besides **range**, there are several other measures of dispersion, each of which highlights a different aspect of how values spread out. We have the **inter-decile range** and the **inter-quartile range**, which leave 10% and 25% of the values off the top and bottom, respectively. Why would we do that? We use these measures when we have one value that's a whole lot larger or a whole lot smaller than the rest. The full range would deceive us, because that one **outlier** would have so much influence. Ignoring outliers sometimes helps us concentrate on what matters.

Speaking of concentration, where do these values concentrate? Where is their center? We've got measures of dispersion to tell us about the edges, so we've also got **measures of central tendency** to tell us where the middle is. The most famous of

TABLE 6.1 Measures of Central Tendency in U.S. High School Graduation Rates			
	Mean	Median	Mode
All Students	79%	80%	75%-85%
Low-Income Students	69%	70%	70%-75%
Limited English	59%	60%	50%-55%
With Disabilities	58%	59%	55%-60% and 65%-70%

these is the **average**—what researchers and scientists call the **mean**. Add up all the values and divide by the number of cases, and you're set. We've also got the **median**, which is the central number in your collection, by position. Count the numbers from both ends until you meet in the middle, and that's the median. Finally, there's the **mode**. It's the highest bar on the chart—the one with the most cases or the biggest lump, if you want to put it that way. The mean, median, and mode don't always match up, but they sometimes do. They're all pretty useful.

Table 6.1 displays the means, medians, modes for various state-by-state graduation rates. Listing them tells you something about the data.

Take a quick look at the mode for students with disabilities. There are *two* of them! That's because the distribution chart for that graduation rate has camel humps. Only the mode can catch that. It's always a good idea to check.

THINK ABOUT IT
What does the measure of central tendency tell you about your data?

There are, of course, other measures. We often use the **standard deviation** and the **variance** to measure dispersion. Roughly speaking, these are the average deviation from the mean, though that definition hardly does them justice. They are, however, particularly useful for statistical analysis. Unfortunately, that topic is beyond the scope of this book.

All of these measures are good ways to describe your data. They help you see what is going on with the data and also help you to tell its story.

Working With Numeric Data: Comparing

Now let's take up a different task. Let's say that we don't want to just describe the data we've collected. Imagine that we want to compare two groups on the same data. That might be two different organizations, two different neighborhoods, two sets of survey respondents, and so on. Or it might involve a much larger comparison—for example, seeing what factors influence the graduation rates we just described. All of these involve numeric comparisons, but the ways we make these comparisons differ depending on the kinds of numbers we've collected. We have to treat interval/ratio data, ordinal data, and categorical data differently. We'll take a look at each of these in turn.

Interval/Ratio Data

Interval/ratio data come from several sources. First, there are survey data like the "years of education" question discussed earlier. There are also aggregate data collected from groups, organizations, political entities, geographic regions, and the like. This includes such things as the population of each of the 50 U.S. states, the median income of members of the Republican Party, the number of teachers working in each of the school districts in the Los Angeles Basin, the percentage of the population living below the poverty line in each of the 3,141 U.S. counties, and so

FIGURE 6.3   U.S. (a) Suicide Rates and (b) Murder Rates

(a)

Suicides per 100,000

| Highest Suicide Rates | Lowest Suicide Rates |

(b)

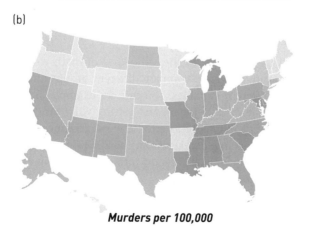

Murders per 100,000

| Highest Murder Rate | Lowest Murder Rate |

on. I'll start by focusing on interval/ratio data that let us compare different groups, organizations, regions, and so on.

How do we analyze these data to answer our research questions? There are several ways. Among the U.S. states, for example, Wyoming and Alaska have the highest suicide rates—just above 23 per 100,000 population. New York and New Jersey are the lowest at about 8 per 100,000.[7] Louisiana has the highest murder rate at 11.2 per 100,000 population, and has been number one at least since 1996. Six states have a murder rate less than one-seventh that high: Hawaii, New Hampshire, Vermont, Rhode Island, Minnesota, and Iowa. They, too, have long had low murder rates.[8] Life expectancy is in the low 80s for core European Union countries, compared with the mid- to high 70s for the new member countries of Eastern Europe and to 79 for the United States.[9] You can learn a lot from such comparisons.

Fortunately, we can do more than just list such figures impressionistically. We can, in fact, measure the degree to which two pieces of data vary together across a collection of groups, organizations, states, and so on. Take a look at the two maps in Figure 6.3 (on the previous page). The one on the top shows the suicide rates for the 50 U.S. states (darker colors have higher rates); the one on the bottom does the same for the murder rate.

Clearly, these two kinds of violence occur in different parts of the country. In general, self-inflicted violence happens more often out West than it does in the East. Violence toward others happens most often across the southern tier of states. This has been the pattern at least since the 1940s. Both suicides and murders are rare, but they clearly have a geographic component. There's something different about the West and the South.

We won't explore that difference here. We'll spend a good deal of time on this in Chapters 7 and 8, where we look at ways to compare aggregate and survey data. There, we'll encounter scatterplots, correlations, and other ways of working with interval/ratio data. We'll see how such comparisons give you clues to the social, political, and demographic factors that may influence such things as suicide and murder rates.

Ordinal and Categorical Data

Except for counting, you can't do the same kind of math with ordinal and categorical data. You can, however, compare different groups and explore the relationships between different variables. You can, for example, find out how people report being treated at work, who reports getting what kind of treatment, and whether one group of people reports better or worse treatment than does another.

Table 6.2 shows an example, taken from the 2012 General Social Survey (GSS). It gives the percentage of people who report "often" or "sometimes" getting negative treatment from their coworkers.

Any of these things could make a workplace an unhappy setting. Fortunately, most people had "rarely" or "never" suffered them. Still, 10% of respondents said they had sometimes or often been joked about and more than 20% had often or sometimes been lied to. This should concern any employer who wants to make her or his company a good place to work.

TABLE 6.2 Sample Responses From the 2012 General Social Survey	
Question	Percentage Responding "Often" or "Sometimes"
Been the object of comments or jokes	10.1%
Been treated rudely	11.7%
Been the subject of rumors	12.1%
Been ignored by others	14.1%
Been lied to	20.8%

Each of these variables is ordinal. "Often" is clearly greater than "sometimes," which is greater than "rarely," which is greater than "never." However, we don't know exactly how often "often" is. Different people have different senses about this. The same is true of "sometimes" and "rarely"; people can easily disagree. Only "never" is completely clear. Moreover, we can't measure the distances between the answers. Is "often" twice as often as "sometimes"? Or three times? Or four? This, too, will vary from person to person.

That's always a problem with ordinal measures. We can calculate the *median* (the value in the middle), but we can't calculate the *mean* (the average). For that, we have to measure the exact distance between our values, and ordinal data don't allow that. All we get is rank-order.

Suppose, however, that we want to see whether two groups of people experience the same amount of harassment. Do men or women experience chillier workplaces? How about Whites and African Americans? Young people and old? Educated people and those with less education?

These are all categorical variables measuring self-identity. To see if one category of people reports more harassment than does another, we construct a table. We put our categories at the top, labeling the columns. We put the possible responses down the side, in rank-order, labeling the rows. Finally, we put the percentage of the people in each category who give each response in the appropriate square, so that the columns add to 100%. We call this a **cross-tabulation**. Table 6.3 (on the next page) is a sample.

Cross-tabulation makes it easy to compare the two categories. All we have to do is look at the columns. We can clearly see when there is a difference.

Here, about the same percentages of men and women report being lied to "often." Men are more apt to report being lied to "sometimes" or "rarely," and women are more likely to report "never" being lied to. There is clearly a pattern here. Before we can interpret it, though, we need to cover a few basics.

THINK ABOUT IT
Why can't we calculate the mean with ordinal data?

First, why do we use percentages rather than the actual number of men and women who report being treated rudely? That's because most surveys don't have the same number of people in each category. This one happened to have a few more men than women answer the question. We have to make sure we're comparing like with like, so we use percentages to make both columns add up to 100. We do the same for the "Totals" column, too. That makes it easy to see which column is lower than the average and which is higher.

Second, why do we put gender at the top? That's because gender is the **independent variable**. By convention, we put the independent variable at the top and the **dependent variable** down the side. This makes sense when you think about what the terms *independent variable* and *dependent variable* mean. The independent variable is the one that we think might cause (or at least influence) the values of the dependent variable. Comparing the columns lets us see if people's gender influences how they are treated.

In this case, we certainly wouldn't expect that being lied to would cause someone to change gender. It is much more likely that men and women would be treated differently *because of* their gender. We put whatever we think is the causal variable at the top, and then we see if it causes a difference between the two columns. In general, if there is a significant difference between the columns, then we say that there is such an influence.

This is the key question: is the difference between the two columns large enough for us to be able to say that men report significantly more instances of lying at work than do women? That's an important issue. Remember that we have a sample here. The General Social Survey interviewed 3,000 men and women, not the entire U.S. population. When does a difference between the columns in a sample become large enough to indicate a systematic difference in the way men and women are treated in the real world?

TABLE 6.3   GSS Responses About Negative Workplace Behaviors, Comparing Men and Women

Have you ever been lied to by coworkers or supervisors?

	Men	Women	Total
Often	2.9%	2.5%	2.7%
Sometimes	20.6%	15.5%	18.1%
Rarely	23.9%	18.6%	21.3%
Never	52.6%	63.4%	58.0%
Total	100.0%	100.0%	100.0%

$\chi^2 = 13.62$; $p = 0.005$; 99.5% conf

That's what the bottom line of the cross-tabulation shows us. It's a mathematical measure of the odds that the difference between the two columns represents a real difference in the wider world.

The first number, marked χ^2, is the **chi-square**. It measures how different the table of responses is from an imaginary table in which there were no differences between the columns. You calculate the table's chi-square, and then you consult a chi-square distribution chart to find out how confident you can be that the difference in the survey sample reflects a real difference in the overall population.[10]

The chi-square distribution chart gives you the second and third numbers: in this table, that's "p = 0.005" and "99.5% conf." These terms refer to the amount of confidence we can have that the difference we see between the columns in our sample reflects a real difference in the population. The two numbers express the same thing in two different ways. The "p" number tells you how likely you are to be wrong if you say that the difference between the columns reflects a difference in the real world. The "conf" number tells you how much confidence you can have that you are right.

The logic is just like our discussion of confidence levels in Chapter 5. A 99.9% confidence level (p = 0.001) tells us that only one sample out of 1,000 with this amount of difference will fail to represent a real difference in our population (1,000 – 999 = 1). A 99.5% confidence level (p = 0.005) tells us that only five samples out of 1,000 with this amount of difference will fail to represent a real difference in our population. That's good enough for most research projects. We can now say that more men than women report being lied to—and we can be very sure we are right.

The GSS asked about some other workplace behaviors, too. Table 6.4 (on the next page) displays men's and women's reports of jokes and rude treatment. Remember that the columns show the percentage of each category giving each answer: 30.7% of men report being joked about at work—three-fifths of those "rarely"—compared with just 20.7% of women; and 13.5% of women report being treated rudely either "often" or "sometimes," compared with 10.1% of men. More men than women report a hostile work environment on the first measure, and more women than men report a hostile environment on the second.

Look at the chi-squares, though. The confidence level for the difference in joking is 99.9% (p = .001), while the confidence level for rude treatment is just 65.7% (p = 0.343). We can certainly say that men report being the butt of jokes and derogatory comments at work more often than do women. We can't, however, say that women report significantly more rude treatment than do men; 65.7% confidence seems like a lot, until you realize that you can be 50% confident that a flipped coin will come up heads. That's just even chance. Social scientists typically insist on at least 95% confidence that they're right (p < 0.05) before they'll claim a result. Medical researchers insist on an even greater confidence level. That's because the stakes of getting things wrong are higher in medicine than in social science. The more damage a wrong result can do, the more you need to be sure that you are right.

TABLE 6.4　GSS Responses About Other Negative Workplace Behaviors, Comparing Men and Women

Have you ever been the target of derogatory comments or jokes at work?	Men	Women	Have you ever been treated in a rude or disrespectful manner at work?	Men	Women
Often	3.0%	2.3%	Often	2.3%	3.4%
Sometimes	9.5%	5.2%	Sometimes	7.8%	10.1%
Rarely	18.2%	13.2%	Rarely	23.9%	23.1%
Never	69.4%	79.2%	Never	66.0%	63.4%
$\chi^2 = 15.38$; $p = 0.001$; 99.9% conf			$\chi^2 = 3.33$; $p = 0.343$; 65.7% conf		

How about the other forms of harassment? Women report being ignored more often than men (95% confidence), but they both report the same amount of rude treatment and rumor-mongering. The percentage of each suffering electronic harassment is extremely small.[11] More men than women report being denied a raise that they thought they deserved (99% confidence). Such findings provide interesting glimpses into the hidden dynamics of the work world.

What do we find for some other categories? A higher percentage of African Americans than Whites answer "often" or "sometimes" to the questions about being ignored (99% confidence), lied to (95% confidence), treated rudely (99.5% confidence), and being denied raises (95% confidence), but there is no difference between the races' reports of rumors, derogatory comments, and jokes.

People with more education report being lied to more often than people who are less well-schooled (99.9% confidence). That may be a result of the kinds of jobs they have, which typically depend on communications and words. They also report more rudeness (99.9% confidence). Less educated people report more derogatory comments and jokes (99.9% confidence). Education makes no difference for rumors. The rest of the variables show no consistent pattern.

Southerners report being ignored, lied to, and the subject of rumors, comments, and jokes more than do respondents from other parts of the country. See how much you can learn from just a few survey questions?

Identifying Cause

Numeric data can tell us something about how two things are related. They have a more difficult time saying whether one thing causes another. You may have heard the famous research mantra "Correlation is not cause." Just because two things are related doesn't necessarily mean a causal connection exists between them. There are several possibilities that we have to keep in mind. We can best see these possibilities with an example. We'll use maps, because they're easy to visualize. Figure 6.4 shows two maps of the 50 U.S. states that look quite similar, though they're not identical. The one on the top shows each state's suicide rate per 100,000 population, while the one on the bottom shows the percentage of the population that moves from one house to another in a given year. Texas is low on suicides but high on residential mobility, whereas the situation is reversed in Utah;

FIGURE 6.4   U.S. (a) Suicide Rates and (b) Residential Mobility

(a)

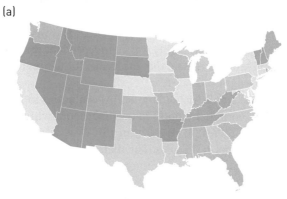

Suicides per 100,000

Highest Suicide Rate   Lowest Suicide Rate

(b)

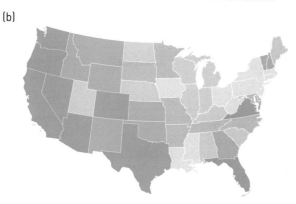

Residential Mobility

Highest Residential Mobility   Lowest Residential Mobility

still, the overall pattern is similar. Both suicides and moving happen more often out West and in Florida.

That doesn't mean, however, that one of these factors necessarily causes the other. Maybe lots of suicides and lots of moving merely happen in the same places.

Take another example: Children from wealthy neighborhoods tend to perform better in schools. Does wealth create good test scores, or do good schools attract wealthy people? Or is something else going on?

The fact that two things happen in the same places doesn't tell us whether there is a causal relationship between them. In fact, there are at least three possibilities.

First, Factor A could cause Factor B. Residential mobility (A) could cause an increased suicide rate (B), not because people who move a lot commit suicide but because places where people move a lot likely have weaker social ties. Strong social ties give depressed people someone to turn to when they are in need. The early sociologist Emile Durkheim proposed this idea in the 1890s,[12] and we can find evidence for it today. In his analysis, social instability was an independent variable and the suicide rate was a dependent variable. He said that the former influences the latter, as A influences B in Figure 6.5.

To use the other example, richer families (A) can afford to hire tutors for their children, so it makes sense that schools in neighborhoods with lots of rich families might have higher test scores (B). Wealth, in this case, would be an independent variable influencing school test scores. But there is another possibility when two things are correlated: Factor B could influence Factor A (Figure 6.6). For example, low test scores (B) in a particular school district could encourage richer parents to move to a district with better scores. That would leave poorer families behind, making the district poorer than it would otherwise be (A). Here, differences in test

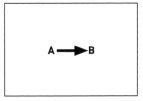

FIGURE 6.5   Factor A Causes Factor B

A � B

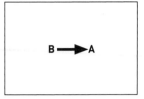

FIGURE 6.6   Factor B Causes Factor A

B ➤ A

FIGURE 6.7   Factors A and B Are Caused by a Third Factor, C

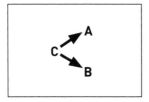

scores create differences in wealth. (In this case, B is the independent variable and A is dependent on it.)

However, this doesn't work in every case; we always have to think through the situation. A high suicide rate (B) is not likely to cause more people to move (A), simply because the number of people committing suicide is so low that it is not likely to drive people away. Most people who change residences don't know anyone who has committed suicide, so they can't be escaping from the memory. In this case, B causing A is very unlikely.

Finally, both Factor A and Factor B could be caused by some third factor—we'll call it Factor C (Figure 6.7). In this case, C is independent and both A and B are dependent. For example, maybe something about particular regions causes both high rates of suicide and high levels of residential mobility. That would create a relationship between residential mobility and the suicide rate, even if neither one directly influenced the other. Similarly, maybe something about particular neighborhoods both attracts wealthy residents and creates good schools, even if there is no direct relationship between the two. In each case, we would have an apparent relationship between A and B, even if the only direct relationships are between C and each of the other two.

We'll see some examples of this in Part II, especially in Chapters 7 and 8. We'll also look at a few other patterns there. For now, it's enough for you to recognize the core logical possibilities. We'll also see that there are various ways of telling which of these patterns is happening in any particular case.

What Statistical Test Should I Use?

Once you've decided whether you are *describing* or *comparing* your numeric data, and you've figured out the relationship between your variables, you can proceed to your data analysis. If you are describing, then you'll want to calculate your variables' distributions, their measures of central tendency, and (if appropriate) their measures of dispersion. If you are comparing, you'll want to use correlations, cross-tabulations, or other more complex options, depending on whether your variables are interval/ratio, ordinal, or categorical. This is not a statistics textbook, so we're not going to go into great detail. Still, you need to know how to make your decision. Figure 6.8 (on the next page) is a decision tree that can help you sort out your options.

FIGURE 6.8   What Statistical Test Should I Use? (A Decision Tree)

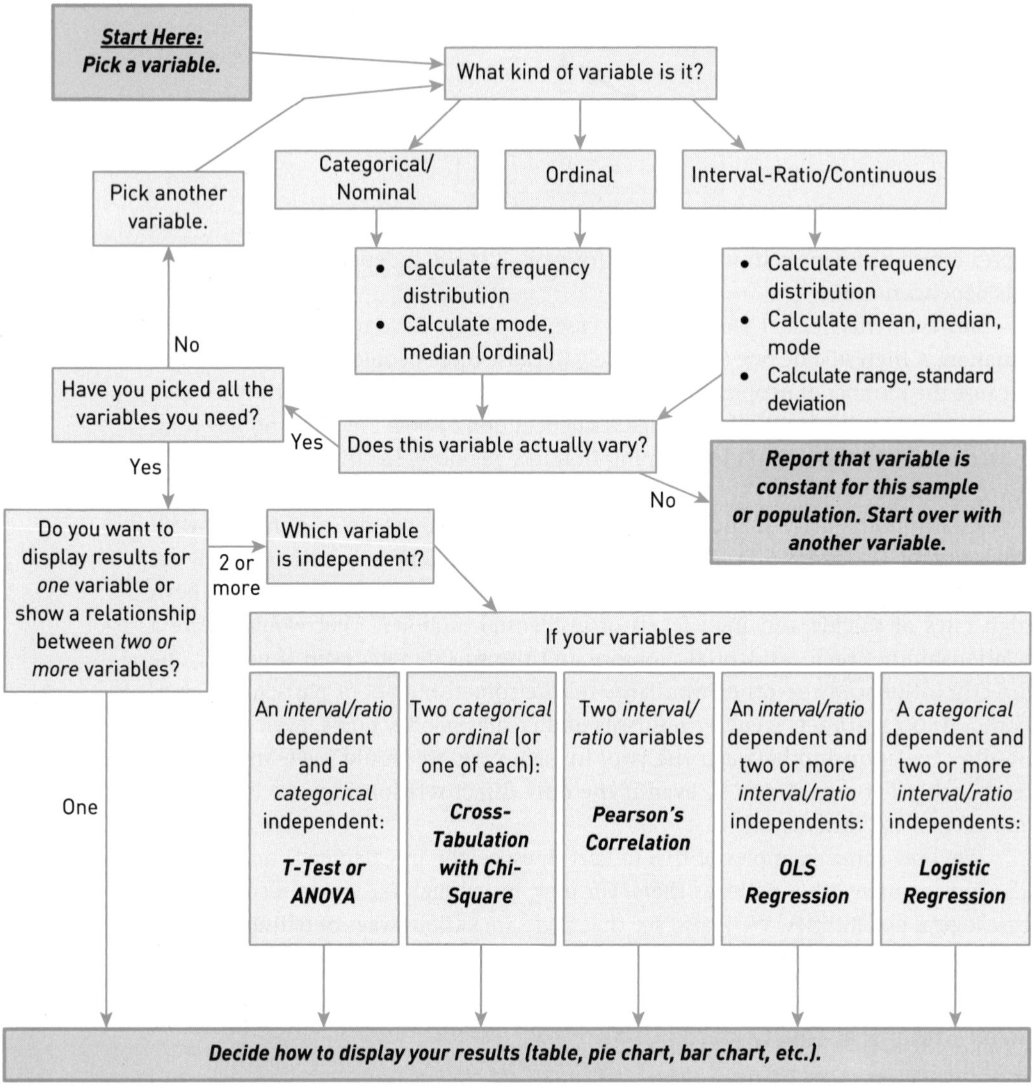

**Start Here:**
**Pick a variable.**

What kind of variable is it?

Pick another variable.

Categorical/ Nominal

Ordinal

Interval-Ratio/Continuous

- Calculate frequency distribution
- Calculate mode, median (ordinal)

- Calculate frequency distribution
- Calculate mean, median, mode
- Calculate range, standard deviation

No

Have you picked all the variables you need?

Yes

Does this variable actually vary?

**Report that variable is constant for this sample or population. Start over with another variable.**

No

Yes

Do you want to display results for _one_ variable or show a relationship between _two or more_ variables?

2 or more

Which variable is independent?

If your variables are

One

An _interval/ratio_ dependent and a _categorical_ independent:

**T-Test or ANOVA**

Two _categorical_ or _ordinal_ (or one of each):

**Cross-Tabulation with Chi-Square**

Two _interval/ ratio_ variables

**Pearson's Correlation**

An _interval/ratio_ dependent and two or more _interval/ratio_ independents:

**OLS Regression**

A _categorical_ dependent and two or more _interval/ratio_ independents:

**Logistic Regression**

**Decide how to display your results (table, pie chart, bar chart, etc.).**

You can find out more about *t-tests* in Chapter 10, where we'll use them to analyze psychological scales; *cross-tabulations* with *chi-squares* in Chapter 8, where we'll use them to analyze survey data; and *correlations* in Chapter 7, where we'll use them to analyze aggregate data. The two kinds of regression analysis (OLS regression and logistic regression) are beyond the scope of this book. They are, however, useful techniques that you may want to learn.

Three Fallacies

There's one more topic to cover before we move on from numeric data. Compared with qualitative data, numeric data are fairly straightforward. You can still get into trouble, though, if you aren't careful in drawing conclusions. Three common fallacies lead far too many quantitative researchers astray: the ecological fallacy, the sampling fallacy, and the significance fallacy. Let's look at each one in a bit more depth.

The Ecological Fallacy The ecological fallacy is relatively simple to describe: The problem arises if you try to apply conclusions that are appropriate for one unit of analysis to a different unit.

For example, the maps in Figure 6.4 show that places where people move a lot have high suicide rates and places where they stay put have low rates. The unit of analysis is the *state*, and the data are the rates of suicide and population mobility at the state level.

The ecological fallacy occurs if you try to claim that *people* who move commit suicide at a higher rate than do people who stay put. That's not what the data say. The data don't tell us anything about individuals; they are about places. Suicide rates and the rates at which people stay in the same home are properties of regions, not of individuals. The flaw is to switch the unit of analysis from *places* to *individuals*.

In fact, lots of people move each year, but very few commit suicide. We have no idea if the particular individuals who move are more or less likely to commit suicide than are those who stay put. All we know is that the states where suicide rates are high are also the states where lots of people shift residence. Maybe all the suicides were people whose friends moved elsewhere. We don't know. We can't say anything about *individuals* when our data are about *places*. The easy way to avoid the ecological fallacy is to keep your unit of analysis firmly in mind.

Even professionals sometimes make this error. There was a lovely exchange of articles published in the journal *Social Forces* about the relationship between the amount of country music on local radio stations and city-by-city suicide rates.

In the first article, Steven Stack and Jim Gundlach argued that places with lots of airtime devoted to country music had higher suicide rates.[13] They didn't specify why this might be the case, but it's easy to imagine. Country music is notorious for being about heartache, lost love, and failed lives. Songs like "All My Ex's Live in Texas," "Old Enough to Know Better," "Will the Circle Be Unbroken," "Rednecks,

THINK ABOUT IT
Can country music really affect city-by-city suicide rates?

with it. Qualitative analysis of my interview material brought to the surface patterns that we could then address.

This is just an example. My point is that your research question will tell you what you need to look for in your qualitative material. Sometimes you need to be respondent centered; sometimes you need to be researcher centered; sometimes you need to be both. Your research question will tell you which way to go.

Coding

So how do you analyze qualitative material? Sometimes you count it, but that turns qualitative data into numeric data, a possibility we'll visit a bit later on. Most often, you code it. **Coding** involves going through interview transcripts, observational records, or field notes, marking similar things with symbols so that you can easily group them together. These marks are called codes. They can be anything you like. They help you remember what things go together.

It works like this. Let's say that you're on a team investigating a much larger organization than the one I described earlier. Imagine that the team has decided to look for gaps in the organization's interpersonal networks—just as I did for the little nonprofit. These networks are the formal and informal connections between people that occur wherever people congregate. You want to know who is and isn't talking with whom. You also want to know how this communication and non-communication affects workplace productivity. It's a team project, and you're collecting lots of information, so you can't just try to keep track of everything in your head, as I was able to do. You have to pool your data and set up a common coding scheme. That way, you can all see what's really going on.

One way to do this—and there are many—would be to ask the interview subjects to describe in detail what they do at work. You could then read the interview transcripts, looking for mentions of other people. Each time Person X appears in an interview account, you would write an "X" next to that mention. Person Y would get a "Y," Person Z would get a "Z," and so on. You could simultaneously code for the kind of interaction—boss-subordinate, team member, nonteam coworker—and also for the medium in which the interaction takes place: face-to-face, at the water cooler, in the lunchroom, by e-mail, and so on.

Once the coding is done (which could take quite a while for a large, multiperson project), you could look for patterns. You might find clusters of people who interact frequently with each other (X-Y-Z, A-B-C-D, J-Q-R) but who have few interactions outside their own groups. This might make organizational sense, if the clusters were each in a separate work unit. But work units might be split. Or bosses and subordinates might seldom talk with one another. Or some interactions might happen only by e-mail and others only around the water cooler. Lots of things are possible.

In fact, broken communication channels often get in the way of workplace productivity. Good bosses know this and work to repair these channels. For example, my father used to pay for his secretary's lunches when she ate with the secretaries from his corporation's other departments. These personal relationships gave her a way to give and get favors across rather high departmental boundaries. All the work units prospered, though this informal network never appeared on any organizational chart. Yet it helped the company run.

This research project's coding stems directly from the research question. Organizational theory tells you that personal networks are important to the workplace. It also tells you that these networks can have gaps. You can, as here, track those gaps by noting which people your interview subjects mention and which they don't mention when they are talking about their daily tasks. Coding is simply the process of writing this down.

TABLE 6.6   Sample Coding Scheme: Factors Making for a Good Place to Work

| | Factors Identified in the Literature | | | | | | | |
| | Aspects of the Job | | | Organizational Structure | | Organizational Culture | | |
	A: Job uses skills?	B: Job provides growth?	C: (etc.)	D: Clear chain of command?	E: Structure aids workflow?	F: Comfort with the style?	G: Stable style?	H: (etc.)
1. Let's start by telling us about your job. What do you do here?	X			X				
2. What aspects of the job appeal to you?	X	X			X	X		
3. Did you expect this when you were hired?	X		X	X				X
4. What attracted you about the company?		X			X	X	X	
5. Did you have any qualms or concerns?		X		X			X	
6. What do you wish you had known then that you know now?	X	X			X			X
7. Tell me about a time when...			X	X			X	
...								

As noted, there are various ways to code. Table 6.6 (on the previous page) is taken from a different research project—on the factors that encourage people to say their organization is "a good place to work."

To make the table, I've listed some actual interview questions down the left-hand column and placed a number of categories across the top. The table is, of course, incomplete. I have presented just enough to let you understand how it works. These categories come from the literature review. Previous research had identified them as factors that affect how people feel about their workplaces. We need to ask about those factors, because we want to get a more nuanced sense than previous research has provided of how they work in real life. We don't, however, want to put our interview subjects to sleep by asking boring questions or making them feel like they're just filling in blanks. We therefore craft a creative, interesting interview—one that (ideally) feels like a lively, insightful conversation. We then code our subjects' responses so that we can answer the questions that previous research has raised. The Xs show which questions we think will produce answers in each category. (Note that the categories mark issues, not specific answers to them. For example, previous research indicates that good places to work have clear chains of command. Any information about that topic, either confirming or denying, goes in Column D.)

Preparing such a table doesn't finish your coding, but it certainly jump-starts it. When the time comes for you to see if people like jobs that give them opportunities for growth, you pull together all the answers to the questions marked relevant to Column B. Here, that's Questions 2, 4, 5, and 6. Many people's answers will speak to this issue, though not all will. This gives you a good start. The point is, planning your interview well can make coding easier.[17]

Internal Versus External Coding

The coding process works for both respondent-centered analysis and researcher-centered analysis. Both ask you to plan your interviews well, but each looks for different things as the post-interview coding continues.

Respondent-centered analysis tries to capture the world as your interview subjects see it. Its coding categories begin with the preliminary codes, but you add codes as your interview subjects bring up topics and points of view that you hadn't thought of. New codes arise from the interview transcripts themselves. They are specifically *not* imposed from without; if they were, then you would not learn much about your respondents' ways of seeing things. That's your point, so you add codes as you need them to understand your respondents better. We call this **internal coding**, and it is typical of respondent-centered projects. The point of internal coding is to help you to understand respondents' ideas as clearly as possible.

Researcher-centered projects, by contrast, favor **external coding**. In that case, the codes originate with the researcher, from previous research, and/or in the researcher's academic discipline. These coding schemes are designed to illuminate unconscious patterns in the text or transcript, typically patterns of which the interview subject is not aware. Also typically, they do not result in a better understanding of the interview subject's personal point of view. That is just not the aim of these projects. Their aim is to help the researcher answer the research question that he or she has posed; in many cases, understanding the worldview and intentions of the research subjects themselves is not part of the picture.

It is absolutely crucial that researchers figure out whether they need internal or external coding schemes, or both, to answer their research questions. Using just an external coding scheme will typically prevent you from understanding interview subjects on their own terms. This is not a problem, if your research question does not ask you to do so. It *is* a problem, however, if you are seeking to describe those interviewees' personal visions. Projects that want to capture the ways that people see and understand their own situations need to use internal codes. Researcher-oriented projects, by contrast, need external codes. Your research question should tell you what's right for you.

I have two more comments before moving on. First, I have used in-depth interview research as examples in this section, in part because this research is popular and in part because it raises the distinction between respondent-centered and researcher-centered projects so clearly. The same issues arise with all other projects that generate qualitative data.

For example, ethnographic field notes must be analyzed qualitatively, so the ethnographer needs to know whether or not she or he is trying to capture a group's way of seeing the world. If so, then internal coding is appropriate. If, however, the ethnographer is trying to understand hidden cultural patterns, then external coding will be the favored choice. That's certainly true if the participants themselves do not see the looked-for patterns.

Behavioral observation also typically requires external coding, but people's reports of their behavior will likely need internal coding. After all, those reports come from the individuals' own points of view. You'll want to know what they intended by their actions, including how they understood them.

Second, internal coding has one distinct advantage over external coding: You can check with your informants to find out if they agree with you. You are, after all, trying to capture their ways of seeing the world. They—and only they—are in a position to tell you whether you are right or wrong. External coding lacks this safety check. No one is in the perfect position to affirm or deny your conclusions. You aren't in such a position, because you may (unknowingly) be using the wrong codes and thus looking at the wrong things. Your research subjects aren't in that position, either, because they are unaware of the patterns that you are seeking. Thus, they can't legitimately affirm or deny their existence. Only your fellow scholars know enough about these patterns to evaluate your conclusions. That is why your literature search is so important: It helps you see how other scholars have analyzed data like yours. As with many things, two (or more) heads are better than one.

This has consequences for your data analysis. We already know that reducing data to numbers strips away much of its information; just think how little we actually know about U.S. federal employees' work lives if we only know that 67%

THINK ABOUT IT
What's the difference between internal and external coding schemes?

of them think their organizations are good places to work and 3 in 10 think that their performance is recognized in a meaningful way.[18] Numeric data are clearly shaped by the data collection process. The same is true of qualitative data. Internal coding fails to pick up patterns that are not part of our research subjects' worldviews; they are thus irretrievably subjective, but they are supposed to be subjective. That's how internal coding schemes are able to interpret those world-views successfully.

However, external coding systems are not objective, either. They simply spring from a different head—the head of the analyst, not the head of the interview subject. This doesn't make them wrong, but it does emphasize the care needed in your analyses and the tentativeness with which you need to draw your conclusions. No system of data analysis captures everything. All systems leave many aspects of life unexplored.

Qualitative Data Analysis (QDA) Software

It is great to live in the computer age. In the old days, you typed up your field notes, interview transcripts, and so on, and then you coded them by hand. When the time came to analyze the data, you made multiple copies of each page, cut out each of the coded passages, and then sorted them in piles on the living room floor. Organized people taped those slips to 3-by-5 or 5-by-8 cards; the rest of us just sorted the slips. We then read through each pile. This gave us a good idea of everything we'd found about a topic. Stories of bad bosses would be in one pile, quotes about what made work most enjoyable would be in another, observations about workplace patterns would be in a third. The same passage could be in several piles; that's why you made multiples.

You just had to hope you finished working before the kids or the cat ran in and scattered everything. If they did, you breathed deeply, smiled, and sorted it all again.

That's now passé. Software programs like NVivo, MAXQDA, Atlas.ti, and QDA Miner allow you to code and sort qualitative data electronically. The process is much the same: You still go through your material and apply codes. But sorting is much easier and safe from kid-cat chaos. You also don't have to make multiple copies; the software does that for you. Read your transcripts and research notes, create your codes, apply them, and push a button. The software creates the "piles" for you. It puts everything with a particular code in a new document, which you can then read onscreen or print out. You can recode things, add new codes, or even change your coding system entirely—all in the middle of your work. The software keeps track and updates your piles automatically.

Figure 6.9 is a screen shot of a sample text, coded using QDA Miner Lite.[19] Text is on the left and colored stripes are on the right (which you can't see in this

FIGURE 6.9   Sample From QDA Miner Lite

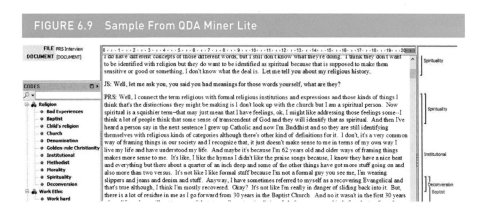

grayscale image). Stripes show the sections marked with particular codes. Codes have different colors, though a well-coded document can have more codes than there are colors available.

You don't depend on the colors, though. All **qualitative data analysis (QDA) software** programs let you put everything with the same code into one document, for easy reading. They also let you tie codes together, so that you can produce documents with closely related material in them. Finally, these programs have expanded beyond text to include pictures, graphs, audio recordings, and so on. They can handle anything that you can code into categories. They also handle multiple categories well.

This is all pretty amazing, but there is one big caveat: *QDA software programs are just fancy ways of piling slips of paper on the living room floor.* You still have to assign codes to things. You still have to make judgments about what goes where. And you still have to see the relationships that result. Yes, these programs can automate some of this, for example, by coding every paragraph that includes a specific set of words. You might set a QDA program to mark a particular code on every paragraph that contains the phrase "good place to work." It works, but you're apt to get a lot of chaff with your wheat, and you will likely leave a lot of wheat on the threshing room floor.[20] You'll still have to read through your material to make sure you've coded what you need.

Nor does QDA software analyze your text for you. It can sometimes show relationships—for example, by pointing out that 60% of the times you've coded something "X" there's a "Y" code less than three paragraphs away. Is that because "X" and "Y" are associated in your data? Or is it because you happened to code things in particular patterns? The machine can't tell you. You still have to make the judgment call.

That's the danger of using software: You might forget that you put the codes there in the first place and think that you've found patterns in the data that are not really there. Still, we used to face the same problem with our piles of slips. At least QDA software keeps us from yelling at the kids and cats.

Warnings

I have, of course, a few warnings for you. Qualitative data analysis must be done carefully. So must numeric data analysis, of course, but most people know that already. The problem with qualitative analysis is that we tend to think it's easier than numeric analysis. It's not. I suggest you keep a few points in mind:

1. "GIGO" (garbage in, garbage out) especially applies to qualitative analysis. Bad data are bad data. If you wrote a poor interview protocol and failed to get your subjects to tell you anything important, no kind of data analysis will save you. I told you in the Introduction about a graduate student who had interviewed ten executive coaches over coffee. He had no research question, so he had worthless data and had to start over.

2. Coding involves judgment and choice. Someone has to create the categories into which you code your data. If you're doing a respondent-centered project, your interview subjects create them. Or you create them, if you're doing a researcher-centered project. Either way, they are a result of someone's informed thinking.

3. QDA software is the electronic equivalent of piling slips of paper on the living room floor. The software makes it easier to keep track of things, but it doesn't do your thinking for you. That's your job.

In short, if anyone ever says to you, "I'm going to throw my qualitative data into NVivo [or MAXQDA, or whatever] and see what categories emerge," run for the hills. Categories *never* just emerge. Think about it. Would you throw a bunch of numbers into a statistics program and expect to get meaningful results? Not likely. Qualitative data analysis is no different on that score.

Review Questions

1. Why are your research question and your logical structure important to your choice of a data analysis method?

2. What are the differences among interval/ratio, ordinal, categorical, and qualitative forms of data?

3. What is a unit of analysis? How is that different from a unit of observation?

4. What three fallacies must you avoid when working with numeric data?

5. What is the difference between respondent-centered analysis and researcher-centered analysis?

6. How do you code qualitative data, so that you can answer your research question? What are the differences between internal and external codes?

7. What three warnings do you have to take into account when analyzing qualitative data?

The open-access Student Study Site at **study.sagepub.com/spickard** has a variety of useful study tools, including SAGE journal articles, video & web resources, eFlashcards, and quizzes.

Summarizing the Six Steps

We've reached the end—not of the book but of the overview of the six basic steps. Every research design has to accomplish six things, which I've described at some length in these pages. I'll explore lots of examples in the rest of this book, but I want to give you one more glimpse at the model:

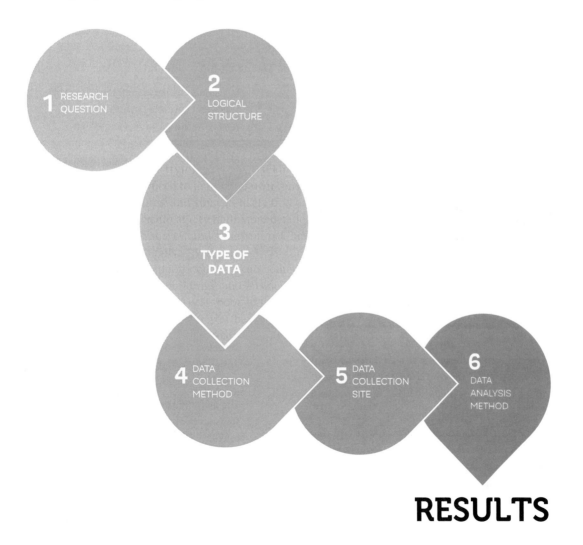

1 RESEARCH QUESTION

2 LOGICAL STRUCTURE

3 TYPE OF DATA

4 DATA COLLECTION METHOD

5 DATA COLLECTION SITE

6 DATA ANALYSIS METHOD

RESULTS

Basic research design consists of six core steps:

1. Develop a good **research question**, identifying the part of a wider topic that you wish to explore.
2. Choose a **logical structure** for your research.
3. Identify the **type of data** you need.
4. Pick a **data collection method**.
5. Choose your **data collection site**, where you expect to find that data.
6. The research question, the type of data, and the data collection method together tell you what **data analysis method** you have to use.

Put it all together, and you can produce good, solid research.

Notes

1. A complete research question would, of course, specify *which* schools you would investigate.

2. Deep opinions are harder to categorize. It can be done, however, with some effort.

3. The U.S. Census Bureau defines census tracts as "small, relatively permanent statistical subdivisions of a county," containing an average of 4,000 inhabitants. The smallest has 1,200 inhabitants; the largest about 8,000.

4. Individual records from the Census of Population and Housing are released 72 years after the census takes place. At this writing, the Census Bureau has just released records from the 1940 Census. Records from the 1950 Census will be released on April 1, 2022.

5. The data in this paragraph were taken from these organizations' websites in July 2013.

6. High school graduation rates for 2010–2011, from the U.S. Department of Education. Available from the Governing States and Localities website, at http://www.governing.com/gov-data/high-school-graduation-rates-by-state.html. Idaho, Kentucky, and Oklahoma did not report figures.

7. 2010 rankings, from the website of the American Association of Suicidology.

8. 2011 figures, from the FBI Unified Crime Reports. See tables at http://www.deathpenaltyinfo.org/murder-rates-nationally-and-state#MRord.

9. World Health Organization, "Life Expectancy at Birth: 1990–2013." Retrieved from http://gamapserver.who.int/gho/interactive_charts/mbd/life_expectancy/atlas.html

10. The math for this is not hard. Any statistics book will show you how to calculate a chi-square, and most will contain a chi-square distribution chart. A quick Internet search for "chi-square calculator" also works.

11. Though only about 5% of men and 5% of women report any electronic harassment, the chi-square does show that there is a statistically significant difference between them. The difference between 4.5% and 5.2% is not, however, worth a hill of beans. This is an example of how something can be statistically significant but *conceptually insignificant*. Put otherwise, the amounts are so small they do not matter.

12. Emile Durkheim, *Suicide: A Study in Sociology*, translated by John Spaulding and George Simpson. New York: Free Press, 1951 (original 1897).

13. Steven Stack and Jim Gundlach, "The Effect of Country Music on Suicide," *Social Forces* 71 (1992): 211–218.

14. These songs were sung or written by, respectively, George Strait, Wade Hayes, the Carter Family, Johnny Russell, Charly McClain, and Don Williams.

15. Edward Maguire and Jeffrey Snipes, "Reassessing the Link Between Country Music and Suicide," *Social Forces* 72 (1994): 1239–1243; Stack and Grundlach, "Country Music and Suicide: Reply to Maguire and Snipes,"

Social Forces 72 (1994): 1245–1248; Gary Mauk et al., "Comments on Stack and Gundlach's 'The Effect of Country Music on Suicide': An 'Achy Breaky Heart' May Not Kill You," *Social Forces* 72 (1994): 1249–1255. Snipes and Maguire, "Country Music, Suicide, and Spuriousness," *Social Forces* 74 (1995): 327–329.

16. The 2012 election archives are at http://fivethirtyeight.blogs.nytimes .com/; newer material is posted at http://fivethirtyeight.com.

17. I have included a longer guide on "How to Write an Interview Protocol" in the "Research Guides and Handouts" section of this book.

18. U.S. Office of Personnel Management, "2012 Federal Employees Viewpoint Survey: Governmentwide Management Report," p 1. Retrieved from http://www.fedview.opm.gov/

19. Available from Provalis Software, http://provalisresearch.com/ products/qualitative-data-analysis-software/

20. Remember the dictum "To err is human; to really foul things up, you need a computer."

1 RESEARCH QUESTION

2 LOGICAL STRUCTURE

3 TYPE OF DATA

4 DATA COLLECTION METHOD

5 DATA COLLECTION SITE

6 DATA ANALYSIS METHOD

RESULTS

COLLECTING AND ANALYZING DIFFERENT TYPES OF DATA

PART II

The end of each chapter contains a section on research ethics. There, I'll high-light the ethical issues that the chapter's examples raise. I'll show how the investigators handled those issues in constructing ethical research. Different data collection methods call for different ethical safeguards. These chapters will give you a good sense of how professional researchers handle these issues.

Chapter 14 is a bit different. It provides an extended example of the efforts to answer a single research question: "How many homeless people are there in the United States?" It explores the history of homeless counts and provides a detailed analysis of several recent efforts. It lets you see how a single research project can combine surveys, censuses, and observations to produce a reasoned estimate of the extent of a social problem. It also shows the strengths and weaknesses of several research techniques.

1 RESEARCH QUESTION

2 LOGICAL STRUCTURE

3 TYPE OF DATA

4 DATA COLLECTION METHOD

5 DATA COLLECTION SITE

6 DATA ANALYSIS METHOD

RESULTS

CHAPTER 7

Comparing: Economic, Demographic, and Organizational Data

		Type of Data			
Comparing Regions and Organizations		**Reports of acts, behavior, or events**	**Economic data**	**Organizational data**	**Demographic data**
Data Collection Method	**Public and private records**	X	X	X	X
	Surveys / questionnaires	X	(X)	(X)	X

This chapter is about comparing. It is specifically about comparing **aggregate data** that have been collected from regions, from organizations, and from schools. Such data describe these things as collectives; they do not describe the individuals who live, work, or study in them. The regions, organizations, and schools in question are the **units of analysis**. Comparing across these units lets us see if there are patterns that might answer whatever research question we are asking.

Most aggregate data consist of reports of acts, behavior, and events. These can include economic data, organizational data, and demographic data, which are specialized forms of such reports.[1] Such data typically come from public and private records and from surveys.

Census data are a good example of aggregate data. The U.S. Census Bureau records what different categories of people live in the United States, where they live, what kinds of houses they live in, what they do for work, and so on. It surveys the population and then releases the results as public records. The U.S. Department of Commerce does a similar job by collecting economic reports from organizations, which it summarizes and releases. Similar aggregate data come from the Internal Revenue Service, the Federal Reserve Board, and other government agencies. Again, these are examples of public records that report acts, behavior, and events. These data are particularly suited for comparing across regional or organizational lines.

Some aggregate data come from direct observations of acts, behavior, and events themselves. For example, researchers on one project visited neighborhoods in Toronto to see how easy it was to walk in them. Public records were not detailed enough, so the investigators had to observe things for themselves. I'll describe that project later in this chapter. For now, just remember that these researchers were observing neighborhoods, not individuals. We'll see how to work with individual-level data in Chapter 8. In this chapter, we'll focus on aggregate data collected from groups of one kind or another.

I'll start with an overview of two kinds of comparison. First, you'll see how to compare a small number of units. Then you'll see some ways to compare larger numbers. I'll use places for my examples. In the second half of the chapter, we'll look at three research examples: one that compares places, one that compares organizations, and one that compares schools.

About Comparing

Aggregate data are well suited for comparing what happens in different places. Sometimes we want to compare just two spots: two neighborhoods, two cities, two states, two countries, and so on. Other times we want to compare a whole bunch of places at once. We'll start by comparing two metropolitan areas; then we'll compare the 50 U.S. states. In each case, you'll get a sense of how such comparisons are done.

Comparing San Antonio and Portland

Let's start by comparing two cities: San Antonio, Texas, and Portland, Oregon. In many ways, they are rather different. San Antonio's population in 2014 was 1,409,019, making it the seventh largest city in the country. Portland's population was 618,012, making it the 29th largest city. However, city boundaries don't define urban areas very well. Urban sprawl, vastly increased populations, and changing politics mean that cities are no longer self-contained units. They are integrally connected to their surrounding suburbs. It thus makes more sense to compare metropolitan areas rather than just cities.

To make this easier, the U.S. Office of Management and Budget has identified 381 metropolitan statistical areas (MSAs) across the nation. The San Antonio–New Braunfels MSA has a population of 2,328,652, making it the 25th largest in the nation; the Portland-Vancouver-Hillsboro MSA has a population of 2,348,247, putting it at 24th. These two MSAs are nearly the same size.

Why, then, are the actual city populations so different? San Antonio has aggressively incorporated its suburbs into the city, to expand its tax base. Portland has not. Thus more of Portland's MSA is outside the city limits.

Table 7.1 (on the next page) compares the San Antonio and Portland MSAs on some relevant dimensions:[2]

TABLE 7.1 Comparison of San Antonio and Portland MSAs		
	San Antonio MSA	**Portland MSA**
Total Population (2014)	2,328,652	2,348,247
Increase since 2010	186,134	122,236
From net births less deaths	64,490	49,662
From net in-migration	114,872	70,835
Core city population	1,409,019	618,012
Age		
Median age (2013)	34.2 years	37.5 years
Age 17 and younger (2010)	26.9%	23.7%
Age 65 and older (2010)	11.0%	11.3%
Ethnicity (2010)		
White non-Hispanic	36.1%	75.4%
Black	6.2%	2.9%
Hispanic	54.1%	10.9%
Asian/Pacific Islander	1.5%	6.2%
Native American	0.8%	0.9%
Income (2010)		
Median household income	$40,764	$53,078
Per-capita income	$18,713	$27,451
Households in poverty (2012)	17.3%	14.0%
Residential segregation by income (rich and poor live in separate areas: 1 = high segregation, 0 = low)	0.700	0.264
Population paying more than 30% of income in rent (2013)	48.4%	51.6%
Commute-Related Characteristics		
Number of commuters	825,000	932,000
Average commute time (city only)	23 minutes	24 minutes

	San Antonio MSA	Portland MSA
Commute ≥ 60 minutes	4.4%	5.4%
Use public transit (2012)	3.3%	11.9%
Carpool (2012)	11.4%	8.8%
Congested travel (% of peak time)	63%	68%
Dollar loss per person to peak commuting traffic congestion	$787	$937
Excess CO_2 per peak commuter	323 lbs.	415 lbs.
Air Quality Index ("good" days in 2014)	219	282

What can Table 7.1 tell us about these two metropolitan areas? Here are some highlights:

- San Antonio is growing faster, despite Portland's reputation as a magnet for millennials.
- San Antonio is also younger, largely as a result of having a higher percentage of children rather than from having a lower percentage of old people.
- San Antonio is far more ethnically diverse than Portland. Like much of the Northwest, Portland has fewer African Americans but more Asians than other parts of the country. San Antonio has far more Hispanics; in fact, it is in many ways a Latino city: 42.5% of the city's population and 36.2% of residents of the MSA speak predominately Spanish and many more are bilingual. The corresponding figure for Portland's MSA is 8.1%.
- San Antonio is poorer. It has greater income inequality. It has *much* greater income segregation; indeed, it has been called the most economically segregated large MSA in the country.[3] Portland is the second-to-least segregated major MSA by income.
- Both MSAs have about the same percentage of renters spending more than 30% of their income on housing. That's because housing is more expensive in Portland, at least for people at the bottom of the income pyramid.
- Portland has more commuters: About 40% of its MSA population commutes, as opposed to 35% of San Antonio's. Average commuting times are about equal, as are the percentages of commuters who have to travel an hour or more to work.
- A lot more Portlanders use public transportation, and a greater number of its center-city residents walk to work (I didn't show these figures). This

THINK ABOUT IT

Why are Portland and San Antonio so different?

reflects its better mass transit system, though that system has clearly not gotten everyone out of their cars.

● Portland's traffic congestion is a bit worse, and its commuters waste more time and gas in traffic.

● Portlanders also produce more pounds of carbon commuting. Fortunately, Portland's rain washes much of its particulate and ozone pollution out of the atmosphere.

● The Environmental Protection Agency records more "good" air quality days for Portland than it does for San Antonio, though the total of days with "good" and "moderate" air quality is about the same.

We could go on. There are lots of ways to compare cities, and these are just some of them. Demographic data, economic data, and data about transportation, air quality, and so on paint a picture of the two places. We could easily paint other pictures, as well.

All these data are aggregate data from public sources. They let us describe various aspects of the MSAs. Those of you who live in San Antonio or Portland might have had a general idea of the patterns but probably didn't know the specifics. I know the two places reasonably well, but even I learned quite a bit from putting the table together. That's research. In this case, the research process was pretty simple. That's true of much research using data collected by others. The main issue is figuring out just what the data mean.

Comparing the 50 U.S. States

Rather than continuing to compare data about just two places, however, let's compare a whole bunch of them. For this exercise, we'll look at some aggregate data from the 50 U.S. states. We'll look specifically at two of the data points we collected when we looked at San Antonio and Portland: commute times and high rents. First we'll look at the data, and then we'll see if we can explain the patterns we find.

We'll start with a table, as before, but this time we have 50 cases to compare. Table 7.2 shows the states with the highest and lowest percentages with long commutes, and those states' figures for the percentage paying high rents. Clearly, this

TABLE 7.2	Comparison of Populations in Eight States								
	New York	New Jersey	Maryland	Illinois	...	Kansas	Iowa	Nebraska	South Dakota
Percentage With Long Commute	16.6	13.9	13.9	11.7	...	3.5	3.5	3.5	3.5
Percentage Paying High Rent	53.2	54.3	52.	52.6	...	45.5	45.8	44.9	41.6

FIGURE 7.1	Maps of (a) Long Commutes and (b) High Rents

(a)

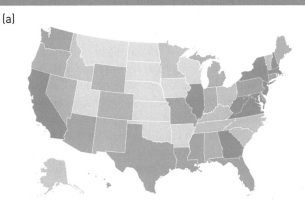

Working Commutes of 60 Minutes or More

Most Commutes	Fewest Commutes

(b)

Renters Spending More Than 30% on Housing

Most High Rents	Fewest High Rents

table is much harder to read than Table 7.1. It's pretty easy to compare two cases, but comparing 50 is a lot harder. What can we do to make it easier?

Let's try mapping the variables. Figure 7.1a shows the percentage of a state's working population who have to commute 60 minutes or more to work. Figure 7.1b shows the percentage of a state's renters who spend 30% or more of their income on housing.

As with the maps we saw in Chapter 6, the dark-colored states have the highest percentages and the light-colored states have the lowest. How alike do the maps look? Are places with long commutes also places with high rents?

It would certainly make sense if they were. Here's the logic: High urban rents encourage people to move to the edge of town, where they face longer commutes. At the same time, long commutes push up in-town rents, as richer people are willing to pay more rent so that they can spend less time commuting. There's a plausible case for a relationship.

In fact, the relationship *seems* to work out. Most of the top 20 states on the commuting map are in the top 20 on the high rent map as well. At the other end of the spectrum, the Great Plains states are low on both measures, as are Montana, Arkansas, Wisconsin, and Utah. These places have short commutes and also have low rent-to-income ratios. Is this enough to demonstrate that these commutes and rents are related?

Unfortunately, no. "Seems" isn't good enough for real research. We need a better way of comparing such figures. Fortunately, we have one: It's called a **correlation coefficient**. It gives us a number that measures how alike these two maps are. To understand it, we have to learn something about correlations.

About Correlations

A **correlation** measures the degree to which one set of numbers is related to another set of numbers from the same population: a group of states, a group of cities, a group of organizations, and so on. For example, 16.6% of New Yorkers commute more than an hour to work, and 13.9% of New Jerseyans spend that amount of time in transit. Similarly, 53.2% of New York renters and 54.3% of New Jersey renters spend more than 30% of their income on housing. Rather than put all the states on a table, let's put them on a graph. Specifically, we'll make a two-dimensional graph, with the percentage of the working population having a long commute on the y-axis and the percentage of renters with high rents on the x-axis (Figure 7.2). We'll put a dot for each state at the point where that state's values fall on each axis. We call this a **scatterplot**. Each dot represents one state, plotted on the two axes.

There's something interesting going on here. As you can see, the dots form a bit of a cloud, angling up from the lower left corner to the upper right. See the dots at the lower left corner? Those states have low values on both measures. The states closer to the upper right corner have high values on both. The upper left and lower right corners are empty. That's where you'd find states that are high on one value and low on the other—but there aren't any, so you don't find anything there. With a few exceptions, the farther right you go on the graph, the higher the dots are.

This tells you something. Specifically, it tells you that states where few workers have long commutes also tend to be states where few renters have high rents. States where a higher percentage of renters spend more than 30% of their income on housing tend to be states with long commutes. This is a pattern. Yes, there is variation: The dots form a cloud, not a straight line. Yet it is at least a tendency.

You can make money off this, if you can find someone foolish enough to bet against you. Bet them that if they tell you the percentage of long commutes in two different states, you can tell them which of these states has the higher percentage of renters with high rents. You'll lose sometimes, but not very often. That's what the graph indicates: Long commutes and high rents tend to happen in the same places.

FIGURE 7.2   Scatterplot of Commute Times Versus High Rents

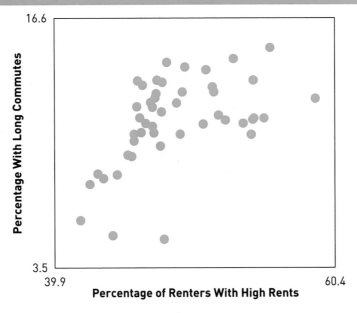

What would the graph have to look like to let you win the bet every time? In that case, the states would need to line up in the same order on both measures. New York, which is highest on commute times, would have to be highest on rents. (It's number 1 on the commute measure but number 14 on the rent measure.) South Dakota, with the lowest percentage of long commutes, would also have to be lowest on high rents. (It's currently 48th on the latter, above North Dakota and Wyoming). The scatterplot in Figure 7.3 (on the next page) shows what you'd get if every state were in the same order on both.

The pattern is easy to see: It's a straight line. New York is on the upper right; South Dakota, Nebraska, Iowa, and a few others are at the lower left. There's nothing at all in the upper left and lower right corners. This particular line goes at a 45-degree angle, because that's how I've drawn the x and y scales. I could draw the scales differently, but the states would still line up. If the data lined up like this, you'd win any bet anyone would make with you.

This is what we call a perfect **positive correlation**. If we know a state's value on one variable, then we know the state's value on the other—perfectly. Such correlations are rare in real life, but they show you the limits of possibility.

Let's go back to our original scatterplot. I've modified it in Figure 7.4 (on the next page) by drawing a line across it, from the lower left to the upper right. This isn't just any old line, but a special line that comes as close as possible as a straight line can to going through all the points. Yes, I know that's impossible. Still, we can draw a line, measure the vertical distance between that line and each point, square that distance (to get rid of any minus signs), and then add up the resulting numbers. I've drawn the line for which that sum is the smallest.

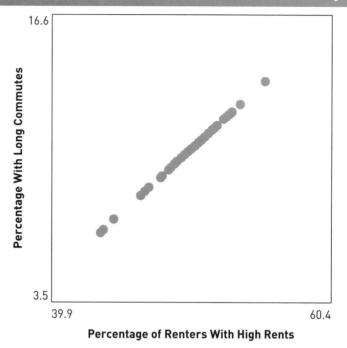

FIGURE 7.3   Imagined Perfect Correlation: Commute Times Versus High Rents

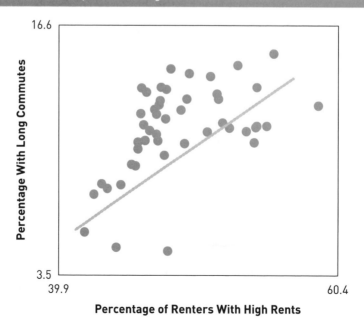

FIGURE 7.4   Scatterplot With a Regression Line

Because we've squared the vertical distance, this is sometimes called the *least-squares line*. More often, It's called the **regression line**. Finding it helps us calculate the **correlation coefficient**. Specifically, it lets us calculate the most common such coefficient, the **Pearson's r**.[4] This measures the degree to which the dots coalesce around the regression line. It comes in several varieties: *perfect, strong, moderate, weak, none*. The Pearson's r gives us a number that tells us which of these varieties we have and, thus, the relationship between the two variables we are examining.

Here's how it works. If the correlation is *perfect*, the dots are all on the line—as in the scatterplot in Figure 7.3. The Pearson's r is equal to +1.0. That indicates a perfect positive correlation.

More often, you'll see a scatterplot that looks like one of the ones in Figure 7.5. Each one shows a relationship between two variables, but of different strengths. The leftmost shows a *strong* but not perfect relationship between the two variables; in that case, the dots are near the line but not all on it. If the relationship is *moderate,* then the dots are spread more widely, but you can still see a pattern. If the relationship is *weak,* then the dots are spread even more widely but a pattern is still there. A weak correlation doesn't mean that the relationship isn't important. It just means that the correlation is not as significant as a strong or moderate correlation would be. *No correlation* means that the dots are so scattered that there is no relationship at all between the variables.

If 1.0 is a **perfect correlation**, then what numbers should we see for strong, moderate, weak, and no correlations? The exact values depend on the number of states, cities, or organizations you are comparing. For the 50 states, anything above 0.50 is a strong correlation. Moderate correlations run from 0.35 to 0.49. Weak correlations run from 0.25 to 0.34. Anything between 0.25 and 0 is uncorrelated. That means there is no relationship between the two variables.

Those values apply when you have 50 cases; more or fewer have different values.[5] Fortunately, most statistical software tells you how strong a correlation is, without you having to memorize lots of values. Typically, software uses three stars to indicate a strong correlation, two stars to indicate a moderate one, and one star to indicate a weak one. No stars means no correlation at all.

FIGURE 7.5   Types of Positive Correlation

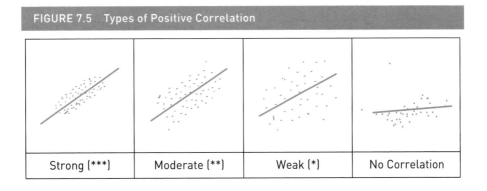

| Strong (***) | Moderate (**) | Weak (*) | No Correlation |

So, how closely related are long commutes and high rents—the two variables that we mapped earlier? The Pearson's *r* between them is 0.44. That means they are *moderately* related. Where one is high, so is the other—but not as strongly as would be the case if the Pearson's *r* were 0.60. It is, however, more than a weak correlation. A weak correlation would be anything from 0.25 to 0.34. For all of these values, we can say that the two things we are measuring happen in more or less the same places.

However, remember the mantra from Chapter 6: *Correlation is not cause*. Just because two things happen in the same places doesn't mean that one of them causes another. They could, for example, both be consequences of some other factor that you haven't examined. Or the chain might extend through several variables. I suggest that you review the possibilities outlined in Figure 6.5 to Figure 6.7 (pages 132-133).

This raises a question, however. If correlation can't prove causality, why bother? Is finding correlations just a waste of time? Not at all! Here are two things that correlations let us do.

First, they help us describe our data better. If our data show a correlation between two factors, then we can take a closer look at how those factors might operate in real life. Do high rents cause people to move to the suburbs, thus increasing their commute time? That's probably the case in many European cities, where slums exist outside the city centers rather than in the city cores. Paris's *banlieues* trap French poor people and immigrants in poverty, away from the centers of tourism and power. It may not be the case in the United States, where richer people tend to live farther away from work so that they can live more spacious lives. Here, the search may be for larger housing, not lower rents. These are guesses, but they warrant empirical investigation. The correlation we see in our aggregate data for the 50 states clues us in that something is going on.

Second, the *lack* of a correlation between two measures can throw doubt on a claim that those measures are related. If, for example, the Pearson's *r* had been 0.10, then we would have concluded that there is no relationship between the percentage of the population having a long commute and the percentage of renters paying more than 30% of its income on housing. That's what "no correlation" means: There is no direct relationship between the measures. There may be an indirect one, but testing for that involves regression analysis—an advanced statistical technique that is beyond the scope of this book. At any rate, finding no correlation between two measures gives you *prima facie* evidence that there is no relationship between them.

One last point about correlation: What is a *negative* correlation? So far, our correlations have been positive, but they can be negative, as well.

Let's imagine that we have shifted our y-axis, so that it measures the percentage of the population having a commute *shorter* than 60 minutes (Figure 7.6). No surprise. This just turns the previous scatterplot upside down (Figure 7.4). The regression line also turns upside down, and the Pearson's *r* becomes –0.44. How do we interpret this?

It's easy. Now we're talking about short commutes, not long ones. Whereas long commutes were positively correlated with high rents, short commutes are negatively correlated with them. In this case, places with lots of high rents relative to income

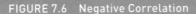

FIGURE 7.6   Negative Correlation

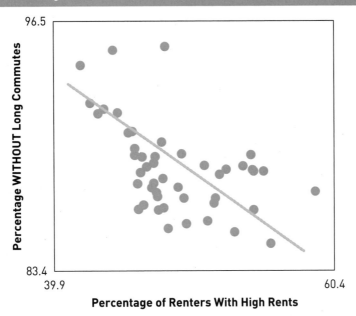

Percentage of Renters With High Rents

have fewer short commutes and places with low numbers of high rents have more of them. A **negative correlation** means that where one value is high, the other is low. Like positive correlations, negative correlations come in *perfect*, *strong*, *moderate*, and *weak* forms (Figure 7.7).

To generalize,

- A positive correlation means that values on the two variables track one another: Where one is high, so is the other; where one is low, the other follows suit.
- A negative correlation means that the values move in opposite directions: high on one means low on the other and vice versa.

FIGURE 7.7   Types of Negative Correlation

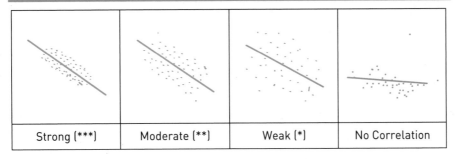

THINK ABOUT IT

No correlation means there is no relationship. How is this different from a negative correlation? From a weak correlation?

What's the takeaway here? When is a correlation coefficient useful?

It's simple. If you're comparing just two things—regions, organizations, or whatever—you're pretty much limited to describing them with the aggregate data that you've collected. Table 7.1 is a good example. We were able to tell a lot about the similarities and differences between San Antonio and Portland, just by looking at the numbers. We weren't, however, able to see any wider patterns. For that, we needed a larger dataset—one containing more than just two cases.

That's why we turned to the 50 U.S. states. I chose the states because they are easy to map, and maps are a good visual way to introduce ideas. They're certainly easier to read than long tables. Yet we still need a way to identify the patterns.

That's where a correlation coefficient comes in—and it's just *one* of many ways to calculate relationships. You'll learn about others in a statistics class. For designing research, you just need to know that using aggregate data lets you compare regions (and other things).

In fact, it's pretty easy to discover patterns in aggregate data. You can compare two or more places, organizations, schools, or whatever in order to see their similarities and differences. You can also find relationships when you have a large number of cases. Both make for very interesting research.

Three Examples

Now that you've got the concepts, let's look at three examples. Each focuses on a different kind of comparison.

Comparing Places: Do Walkable Neighborhoods Improve Health?

This example comes from Toronto, Canada, where Richard Glazier and his team investigated the qualities of neighborhoods that made them walkable.[6] They argued that neighborhood design affects people's transportation choices. Prior research showed that urban areas with high population densities, interesting places to walk, and nearby stores encourage residents to reduce their car use. Low-density areas with few nearby stores and fewer places to walk make people more dependent on cars. This could contribute to increased obesity.

Their project asked two *research questions:*

● Do these associations between neighborhood characteristics and higher rates of walking hold up across Toronto's neighborhoods, as they have in other cities?

● Are health issues related to lack of exercise also associated with various aspects of these neighborhoods—and if so, which ones?

The researchers used a *correlational logical structure,* because they wanted to see if associations existed between neighborhood design, transportation choices, and health factors. The team needed to collect *reports of acts and behavior, demographic data,* and *economic data.* These were the *types of data* relevant to this study.

To gather the data, researchers focused on *public records* and on *observations* of various neighborhoods. They collected records about population density, housing types, car ownership, and so on from Statistics Canada, which runs the Canadian census. They got these measures for each one of Toronto's 10,180 dissemination blocks (DBs)—the smallest geographic units for which census population and dwelling data were available. These blocks were the *data collection sites* that the study compared. The team then gathered data about DB residents' health, transportation use, and so on from various sources—creating aggregate data by assigning individual results to the DBs using postal codes.

For their *data analysis method,* they constructed a "walkability index" and assigned each DB to one of five walkability levels. Rather than use a Pearson's correlation (which doesn't work well with only five levels), they created ratios between the values for the least walkable areas (Q1) and the most walkable (Q5). With all their aggregate data in hand, they then examined transportation use, health outcomes, and so on, comparing the least walkable areas with the most.

Here's what they found for the relationship between neighborhood walkability and transportation use:

> As compared with individuals in the most walkable areas, those living in areas with the lowest walkability owned almost twice as many vehicles (Q1:Q5 ratio = 1.80), were almost twice as likely to travel by automobile (Q1:Q5 ratio = 1.75), were almost half as likely to use public transportation (Q1:Q5 ratio = 0.58), and were roughly one third as likely to walk or bicycle (Q1:Q5 ratio = 0.32). (p. 4)

These findings supported the results of previous research. A neighborhood with fewer attractive destinations within walking distance was associated with more automobile use, less use of public transportation, and less walking overall. These relationships were strong—the equivalent of a strong Pearson's correlation.

On the health front, individuals in the least walkable areas were a third more likely to be obese (Q1:Q5 ratio = 1.34) and a third more likely to be diabetic (Q1:Q5 ratio = 1.33). These relationships were strong, too.

In line with their article title—"Density, Destinations or Both"—the research team then separated out two aspects of the walkability index. The first was the neighborhood's population density and the presence of stores and services within easy walking distance. These often go together, but not always. Some of Toronto's neighborhoods are relatively high density but lack services. Many of these are what the U.S. Department of Agriculture (USDA) would call "food deserts": neighborhoods in which there is little access to supermarkets, grocery stores, and other sources of healthy food. The USDA argues that "the lack of access contributes to a poor diet and can lead to higher levels of obesity and other diet-related diseases, such as diabetes and heart disease."[7]

They compared the low-density areas that had walkable destinations against the low-density areas that lacked them. They also compared the high-density areas that had walkable destinations against the high-density areas that lacked them. These areas were the *units of analysis*. In these comparisons, the research team found that all of the low-density areas had greater car use, less use of public transportation, and less walking than the high-density areas—even if they were (relatively) high in walkable destinations. At the other end of the scale, however,

> within the highest quintile of residential density, the average number of daily walking and cycling trips per person was more than twice as high in the areas that also had the highest number of destinations as compared to the areas with the lowest number of destinations (0.34 vs. 0.14 trips per person). (p. 4)

The high-density/high-destination neighborhoods also had significantly less car use, significantly more use of public transportation, and significantly less diabetes than did equally dense neighborhoods with fewer shops and services within walking distance. The lack of walkable destinations had no effect on residents' weight, however.

What can we take away from this study? First, it supports the notion that having compact neighborhoods with stores and shops within walking distance reduces car use and improves health. Second, it is a fine example of how you can compare regions (in this case, neighborhoods) using aggregate data.

Table 7.3 matches Glazer's research design to the six-step method developed in Part I of this book.

Comparing Organizations: Does Treating Employees Well Increase Company Performance?

Now let's shift our focus to organizations. How can we use aggregate data to compare organizations with one another? In this example, organizations are our unit of analysis. A team led by Ingrid Smithey Fulmer investigated the relationship between a company's good treatment of its employees and its financial success.[8] They noted that nearly everyone wants "a great place to work." They also noted that the popular literature assumes that happy, motivated workers will bring a company financial success. However, there had been relatively little empirical testing of this relationship. This raised the following *research question:* "Does treating employees well improve a company's bottom line?" That's what they set out to investigate.

TABLE 7.3   Summary of Glazier et al.'s Study of Walkable Neighborhoods in Toronto

1. Research Questions	(a)	Are Toronto's urban neighborhoods associated with more walking and less car use than its more suburban areas?
	(b)	Are obesity and diabetes more common in neighborhoods where people walk less?
2. Logical Structure	Correlational	
3. Type of Data	Reports of acts and behavior, demographic data, economic data	
4. Data Collection Method	Collected public records: census data, housing and business records, health data, transportation data	
5. Data Collection Site	Toronto's 10,180 census dissemination blocks	
6. Data Analysis Method	Compare ratios of lowest to highest walkability values for each of the variables being examined	
	Unit of analysis: *areas*	

Fulmer's research team decided to explore this question using a group of companies on *Fortune* magazine's 1998 list of "The 100 Best Companies to Work for in America," written by Robert Levering and Milton Moskowitz.[9] The research team broke their project into three parts. They first tried to find out whether companies included on the 1998 list maintained positive employee attitudes over time, or were just one-year wonders. Second, they measured whether companies included on the 100 Best list exhibited better economic performance over time than did similar companies that treated their employees only averagely. Finally, they tried to determine if positive financial performance could be traced to better employee relations, or whether it might stem from other factors.

These questions called for *correlational research:* The team wanted to see if treating employees well was associated with better financial performance. They also called for the analysis of three *types of data*. One was *economic data* from the various companies. The team gathered these data from *public records*. To understand the other two types of data, we need to know something about the *Fortune* magazine list.

The idea for the list was developed by Levering and Moskowitz in a 1993 book that ended up being a best seller.[10] That book measured companies on how well they treated their employees, based on a review of company practices. This was based on organizational data submitted by the target companies. The 1998 update in *Fortune* added to this a direct *survey* of employee satisfaction—data summarizing employees' opinions and attitudes about their work. Levering and Moskowitz's team distributed a survey to 225 randomly selected employees at each of the 161 participating companies. The survey was returned directly to Levering and Moskowitz, to encourage honest employee responses.

The survey consisted of a 55-item Great Place to Work Trust Index, developed by Levering and Moskowitz's consulting group.[11] Fifty-eight percent of the targeted employees completed the 1998 survey, which produced a total of more than 20,000 completed forms. Of the 175 points that a company could earn on the "Great Places" ranking, 100 came from the Trust Index and 20 additional points came from handwritten comments solicited from the same employees on the survey form. The remaining 55 points came from Levering and Moskowitz's evaluation of the company's response to a 29-page company-level questionnaire about personnel practices. Thus, the bulk of a company's ranking came from its employees. Some, however, came from that company's own self-report.

The total ranking system was thus a combination of two data types. One was *employee attitudes* of the kind that can be captured on surveys—that is, relatively shallow opinions and attitudes. The other was the companies' *organizational data*. Leveling and Moskowitz gathered these data from the survey participants and from the company reports, respectively.

Levering and Moskowitz analyzed these data to produce the *Fortune* magazine article. Their method was (and is) proprietary and thus not available to outsiders. Fulmer et al.'s article, however, describes it in reasonable detail. The Great Place to Work consulting group has used such data to create 100 Best rankings ever since.

The full list of 100 companies was not suitable for the research question that Fulmer and her colleagues sought to ask. For example, it included some nonprofit organizations, for which financial success is irrelevant. It also had some privately held companies, which do not have to report financial figures. The research team took the article's 100 Best list and narrowed it so that it included just profit-seeking, publicly traded enterprises. Then they eliminated companies working in the financial sector—banks, brokerage firms, and the like—because that sector is so unlike the other parts of the economy that comparisons would be misleading. The result was a subset of 50 companies from the 100 Best list that were appropriate for answering the team's research question. That became one of the two groups that Fulmer and her colleagues sought to compare.

THINK ABOUT IT
Why do you have to make sure that the Best 100 list measures what it claims to measure?

The other group was a matched set of companies that were similar to the 50 from the 100 Best list in size, industry, and operating income. These companies had not appeared on any *Fortune* 100 Best list, up to and including the list published in 2001.[12] Had this been an experiment, we could have called this a control group, but this research used a comparative, not an experimental, logical structure. The point was to have a group of companies that matched, as closely as possible, those chosen from the 1998 *Fortune* list. That focused the differences between the two groups on the company's personnel relations. That was the point of the project. These two groups were the project's *data collection site.*

The next step was to validate the claim that the 100 Best list actually contained companies with exemplary employee relations. There would be little point in doing this research, if there were a problem with Levering and Moskowitz's choices. The research team gained access to a set of six questions that had been administered to employees at the time of the Trust Index survey but that had not been part of the index itself. These ranged from questions about whether employees felt they were given opportunities to participate in decisions to whether they would like to be working for the company one year and five years in the future. The companies' ranks on these items correlated strongly with their ranks on the 100 Best list, suggesting that the list reflected the companies' positive personnel relations. This, plus some other tests, convinced the research team that the companies on the list had much higher than average employee satisfaction. Compared with the average company, they were, in fact, good places to work.

So, let's return to the team's research question—Do positive personnel policies improve a company's bottom line?—and to the three subquestions into which the team broke its *data analysis.*

First, "Do companies included on the 1998 list maintain positive employee attitudes over time?" Though the team was not able to examine the Trust Index survey's raw data itself, it was able to get access to subsequent years of the questions about whether employees would like to continue working for their companies. The team took the average score on this question for each of two years for each company. This gave them two measures. The correlation between these two measures for the entire set of companies (not just their target 50) was 0.65. This is extremely strong. Moreover, they estimated that, for their 50 companies, the variation between the two years was just 3%. They concluded that, yes, companies with positive personnel relations do maintain them over time.

Now for the second subquestion: "Do the 50 companies on the list exhibit better economic performance over time than the set of 50 matched companies that the team chose as a comparison group?" For this, they compared the two groups' performance on two economic measures. First, what was their multiple-year return-on-assets (ROA)? This measures how much net income a company is able to generate from its accumulated assets.[13] Second, what was their multiple-year stock performance, counting both dividends and stock market gains or losses? ROA measures the financial success of the company itself. The stock performance measures the return to the company's owners.

The team calculated these figures for the six years from 1995 to 2000. As a group, the 50 target companies came in ahead of the matched group for all six years. The differences were small in 1995 and 1996, large in 1997 and 1998, and small-to-moderate in 1999 and 2000. The target 50's market performance was lower than the matched group in 1995 but higher in all subsequent years. Thus, both the comparison based on internal accounting and the comparison based on stock performance suggest that companies that treat their employees well perform better financially than do companies whose employee treatment is average.

The research team was not able to answer the third of their three subquestions: the question of causality. They could not determine whether the positive financial performance could be traced to better employee relations, or whether it had a different cause. True, the target 50 companies and the matched 50 companies differed mainly on their employee relations (excellent for the first, average for the second). That, plus the former's better performance makes a *prima facie* case for a causal relationship. But it is still correlational because correlation is not cause. However, they did demonstrate a strong association between companies that treat their employees well and those companies' financial performance.

As we did in the preceding section, let's summarize this study in terms of the six-step method (Table 7.4).

TABLE 7.4   Summary of Fulmer et al.'s Great Place to Work Study

1. Research Question	Do positive personnel policies improve a company's bottom line?
2. Logical Structure	Correlational
3. Type of Data	Shallow opinions, economic data
4. Data Collection Method	Collected survey data, company reports, financial and stock market data
5. Data Collection Site	50 of the 100 "best places to work" plus a matched set of ordinary corporations
6. Data Analysis Method	Compare employee attitudes between the two groups of companies; compare financial performance between the groups

Comparing Schools: Do Charter Schools Improve Student Test Scores?

Let's look at one last piece of comparative research. This one compared charter schools with regular public schools in Michigan. Charter schools are public schools that have been taken over by private groups, with the promise of doing a better job. They use public funds but are freed from some of the usual regulations and procedures. This is supposed to let them experiment. They try new things and see what works; ideally, other schools will learn from their experiences. The question is, do they work?

In 1992, there were just two charter schools in the United States, both in St. Paul, Minnesota. Twenty years later, there were more than 6,000. That's about 6% of all public schools in the country. About 4% of public school students are enrolled in charters, an indication that the average charter school is smaller than the average regular school. There is, however, no such thing as an "average" school, except mathematically. Charters were intended to be wildly diverse. That's what experimenting means.

The National Center for Education Statistics reported that 7% of all public school students in California were in charter schools in 2011–2012. That's a lot of kids, though it's not the highest percentage. The District of Columbia figure was 39%; Arizona came in second at 13%. As in regular public schools, the percentage of children from poverty-level families and from minority families enrolled in charter schools has increased with time.

The question is, do charter schools improve education for the students who attend them? There have been many efforts to answer this question. Eric Bettinger's effort, published in 2004, is neither the most recent nor the most extensive project.[14] It is, however, a good example of the kind of comparative research covered in this chapter.

Bettinger estimated the effect of charter schools both on students attending them and on students at neighboring public schools. Using school-level data from Michigan's standardized testing program, he found that "test scores of charter school students did not improve, and may actually have declined, relative to those of public school students." He also checked to see whether the existence of charter schools improved the schools near them—as would be the case if charter school competition were to spur innovation in the regular schools, as had been imagined. He did not find these effects, either.

How did he design and carry out his project? We'll start by identifying his *research questions*. First, he asked: "Do Michigan's charter schools improve student performance on state standardized tests, compared to non-charter schools operating within 5 miles of the charters?" Note how specific this question is. It tells us which charter schools Bettinger studied (Michigan's), what measure of performance he used (standardized tests), and his comparison group (regular public schools within a 5-mile radius of the charters). Such specificity makes research design much easier. The reason for comparing schools near one another, by the way, was to compare like with like. Charter and public schools from the same area draw students from similar economic, demographic, and family backgrounds. That eliminates some possible sources of variation that might muddy the research waters.

Bettinger's second question inherited its key terms from the first. It was this: "Does the presence of nearby charter schools have any impact on student test scores at neighboring public schools?" As Bettinger pointed out, two kinds of impacts might be possible. First, if charter schools draw away students who are doing poorly in public schools (as Bettinger showed was the case), then the public school scores ought to increase—even if they are not doing a better job. Take away a school's low performers, and the average scores for those remaining will rise automatically. If, however, the public schools react to charter competition as proponents claim they should—by improving—then their students' scores should rise even more. In either case, one should expect to see their scores change.

This project was a *natural experiment*. It used school-level test data to compare two groups of schools—charter schools and nearby regular public schools—to see if the charter process had any effect on children's education. The *unit of analysis* was the school, not the individual student. That's because Michigan reports its scores by school, not by individual. Moreover, it administers its standardized tests to fourth and seventh graders, so different students take the tests each year. Thus no individual-level analysis is possible.

The closest data type on our list is *behavior*. The tests measured whether the students could demonstrate knowledge and skill in reading and math. It did not rely on their reports of whether they could read or calculate, nor did it measure their opinions about their own knowledge. Instead, the tests asked them to complete tasks that demonstrated what they knew. The test results thus amount to *detached observations*. As each school's test results are matters of public record, Bettinger's *data collection method* was to collect records from the Michigan Department of Education. He then *analyzed* these data, both descriptively and statistically. It is pretty easy to see our six steps in Bettinger's research design.

There are, of course, some interesting details. For example, Bettinger wanted to see whether charter schools' scores improved between the 1996–1997, 1997–1998,

TABLE 7.5 Test Scores in Charter Schools and Public Schools in Michigan						
Fourth Grade MEAP Test	**Charter Schools Established in 1996–1997 School Year**			**Public Schools Within 5 Miles of Charter Schools in 1996–1997**		
	October 1996 Test	April 1998 Test	April 1999 Test	October 1996 Test	April 1998 Test	April 1999 Test
Math Scores						
% satisfactory	34.2	54.2	49.0	56.3	70.0	66.3
% moderate	22.7	24.9	24.7	21.3	19.3	19.3
% low	43.1	21.0	26.3	22.4	10.7	14.4
Reading Scores						
% satisfactory	34.9	39.8	40.8	47.1	55.3	53.0
% moderate	28.4	33.9	30.5	28.5	26.4	27.8
% low	36.7	26.3	28.8	24.4	18.3	19.1
Number of Schools	33	32	31	552	546	546

and 1998–1999 school years. Each of his charter schools began operation in the 1996–1997 school year, so that year served as a baseline. He chose to begin with that year because the Michigan standardized tests in 1996–1997 took place at the beginning of the school year, not the end. This let him treat that year's scores as a pretest and the next year's score as a posttest. This contributed to the natural experiment. Because the 1996–1997 figures measured student achievement in their regular schools, later years could measure whatever effect the charter school had.

Indeed, Bettinger did see an effect. Table 7.5 shows the fourth-grade scores on math and reading. It lists the percentages of students at each school scoring "satisfactory," "moderate," and "low" on each test.

Take a good look at this table. First, compare the charter school scores on the October 1996 test with the public school scores for that same year. The charter school scores are significantly lower than are the public school ones. A smaller percentage of charter students score "satisfactory" on math and reading and a higher percentage score "low" on each measure. What does this mean?

This doesn't mean that the charter schools are doing badly. These schools had been open at most a month and a half, so they could not reasonably have had much influence on their students. The lower 1996 scores simply show that charter schools attracted lower-performing students. The more important question is, did the difference in scores between the first and second and the second and third years show any progress?

On the face of things, yes. Let's look at just the percentage of "satisfactory" scores, which we'd hope to raise, and the percentage of "low" scores, which we'd hope to lower. I've put the improvements and slippages in Table 7.6.

TABLE 7.6	Test Score Changes in Charter Schools and Public Schools in Michigan			
	Charter Schools		Public Schools	
Fourth Grade MEAP Test	Change From 1996 to 1998	Change From 1998 to 1999	Change From 1996 to 1998	Change From 1998 to 1999
Math: % satisfactory	**+20.0**	−5.2	+13.7	**−3.7**
Math: % low	**−22.1**	+5.3	−11.7	**+3.7**
Reading: % satisfactory	−4.9	**+1.0**	**+8.2**	−2.0
Reading: % low	**−10.4**	+2.5	−6.1	**+0.8**

Note: Better-performing schools are indicated in boldface type.

Clearly, the charter schools had more improvement in math than did the regular schools in the first year between the 1996 and 1998 tests. Both sets of schools raised their percentages of students who tested "satisfactory" and lowered their percentage who tested "low," but the charter school change was larger. Reading scores were more complex. Regular schools made more progress with "satisfactory" students, whereas charter schools had more success among those who originally scored "low." The math jump was larger in all cases, however. Charter schools seemed to be doing something right. Yes, their fourth graders still performed less well than did the fourth graders in regular public schools, but there was more improvement overall, especially in math.

The change between 1998 and 1999, however, was more worrisome. Both sets of schools slid back on almost all measures. The charter schools slid more on three of the four measures and advanced on one, but the numbers are small. That probably means that their students were doing about the same as they had in the previous year. Public school students also did not advance, though they still had higher test scores and the charter school students were no longer catching up.

Wait a minute! Didn't Bettinger find that "test scores of charter school students do not improve, and may actually decline, relative to those of public school students"? Don't the first year's results show just the opposite? How can he make that claim?

Notice that Bettinger had to account for another factor: the difference in student populations between the charter and public schools. If charter schools and public schools had different kinds of students, then the charter schools' success in the first year might have been a result of that difference, not of the charter schools' quality *per se*.

What kinds of differences might these be? Bettinger had already eliminated the effect of neighborhood, by comparing charter schools against public schools within a 5-mile radius. This controlled for some potential differences. Yet we already know that the charter schools attracted underperforming students, so we know that they didn't serve exactly the same student population as did their comparison group. What other aspects of the population might have been involved?

It turns out that there were consistent demographic differences between Michigan's charter schools and the public schools near them—at least during this time period. First, charter schools attracted more White students and public schools attracted more African Americans. Second, charter schools attracted fewer Hispanic students of whatever race.[15] Third, charter schools attracted relatively fewer students who were eligible for free or reduced-price lunches (a measure of family poverty). Charter schools did attract African Americans, Hispanics, and students from poor families, but they attracted non-Hispanic Whites and the non-poor in greater proportions.

THINK ABOUT IT
Why might the demographic differences between the schools matter?

What happens when we correct for these differences?

Quite a lot, it turns out. Bettinger used a rather complex form of **regression analysis** to control for these demographic differences. This analysis compared the progress of White non-Hispanic charter students against White non-Hispanic public school students, African American charter school students against African American public school students, and so on. The details are beyond the scope of this book, but the net result was that the charter schools' relative performance declined. After comparing like to like, the charter schools' math advantage was cut in half and its reading deficit was doubled. That is why Bettinger drew his conclusions. Once he accounted for racial differences, the charter schools had about the same improvement in "satisfactory" math scores as did the public schools, but less improvement in "satisfactory" reading scores, at least among fourth graders.[16]

How about Bettinger's second research question: "Does the presence of nearby charter schools have any impact on student test scores at neighboring public schools?" The raw data would indicate yes, because of the large bump in public school math and reading scores between 1996 and 1998. This, however, can't possibly be due to competition: The charter schools had just been founded, so they could not have forced change on their public counterparts. It is more likely that part of this bump comes from lower-performing students leaving the public schools. The rest is unexplained. Bettinger used some further complex analysis to show that charter school influence was highly unlikely.

Why, then, was there also a bump in charter school math scores between 1996 and 1998? Bettinger suggests (but does not demonstrate) that this may be a result of parents choosing to send their low-performing students to charter schools in the first place. He cites several scholars who have demonstrated that workers tend to join job-training programs after a sudden dip in earnings. This dip leads them to seek a remedy, but their improvement during training is often just a matter of them returning to the same level that they had previously attained. Bettinger could not demonstrate this with school-level data; he would have needed individual test records to make that claim. Yet the argument is plausible. Imagine yourself as a parent of a child who has done okay in school so far but suddenly is struggling. If you have the resources for it, wouldn't you seek extra aid? This may explain why a higher percentage of charter school students are White, non-Hispanic, and non-poor. These people typically have more resources that make it easier for them to shift their children to new schools.

That, however, is something for future research to decide. Bettinger simply showed that in Michigan for these years (1996–1999), enrollment in charter schools had little or no effect on student test scores, relative to scores at the public schools in the same areas. His natural experiment was made possible by two factors. First, a number of charter schools began operation in the 1996–1997 school year. Second, the standardized state testing took place in October that year; this gave Bettinger a good measure of student skills before the charter schools could make a difference. He compared these beginning scores with those attained after one and two years. He also compared charter schools with nearby public schools. Such complex comparisons make for rich research.

Table 7.7 shows how the six-step method applies to this research project.

TABLE 7.7   Summary of Bettinger's Charter Schools Study

1. Research Questions	(a) Do Michigan's charter schools improve student performance on state exams, compared with nearby non-charter schools?
	(b) Does the presence of nearby charter schools have any impact on student test scores at neighboring public schools?
2. Logical Structure	Comparative/natural experiment
3. Type of Data	Test scores
4. Data Collection Method	Collected percentages of fourth-grade students at satisfactory, moderate, and low levels in each school
5. Data Collection Site	Public schools in Michigan
6. Data Analysis Method	Compare score improvements after students have been attending charter schools, controlling for demographic differences

Research Ethics

Let's shift gears now and talk about research ethics. What ethical issues does each of these research examples raise? These issues can arise on two levels.

First, there is the level of the Institutional Review Board (in the United States) and the Research Ethics Board (in Canada). These boards review research to make sure that it protects human subjects from harm. All subjects need to give informed consent for their research participation and need to know the purpose of the research in which they are asked to participate. Researchers need to ensure that the research does not harm the participants. This is especially true for research on people who are especially vulnerable: children, prisoners, sick people, pregnant women, and some others. Even nonvulnerable people deserve protection, however.

The second level generalizes this protection but at the level of research results, not data collection. It, too, stems from the three core values identified by the 1978 Belmont Report on the treatment of human research subjects: respect for persons, beneficence, and justice. This level asks who benefits most from the results of this research. Even though the research itself does not harm participants, what will be the social consequence of the knowledge produced? Does this knowledge primarily benefit elites? Or does it benefit people like those providing the data? In the former case, will this knowledge enable elites to increase their wealth and power vis-à-vis ordinary people? Or will it create a more equal society than the one we have now? Researchers have to think about such issues and need to be ready with ethical answers. The principles of respect for persons, beneficence, and justice operate at this level, too.

Let's walk through this chapter's research examples with these two levels in mind. The first few examples involve publicly available aggregate data. Table 7.1, for example, contains information from the U.S. Census Bureau, Brookings Institution, Texas A&M Transportation Institute, and a few other sources. The data come mostly from decennial census reports, the Census Bureau's yearly American Community Surveys, and reports that businesses and cities submit to the U.S. Department of Commerce and to other government agencies. The rest of the data come from secondary analysis of the data, such as Richard Florida's analysis of residential segregation.[17] None of the data allow for the identification of any individuals or companies. That protects them from any direct harm. That's why IRBs (in the United States) routinely grant waivers to projects that use publicly available aggregate data. I assume that Canada's Research Ethics Boards do the same.

That takes care of the first ethical level: No human subjects can be harmed by this kind of research, because it is impossible to identify people as individuals. The second level is a bit more complex. Does the mere existence of such data potentially harm people? Do aggregate data make it harder or easier to create programs that benefit those with relatively less social and economic power?

In theory, this could go either way. The issue is the use to which such data are put. The comparison between Portland and San Antonio, for example, could lead companies to build new factories in Portland, which might increase poverty in San Antonio. Or the data could lead the U.S. Department of Housing and Urban Development to build more affordable housing units in San Antonio because social inequality is greater there. Put otherwise, second-level ethics are not part of the research but are part of the business and political decisions that might result from it. That's not something that investigators can control.

However, we get a different picture if we turn things around. Imagine that the Census Bureau did not produce the American Community Survey, from which so much of these data come. Who would benefit? The American political gadfly Ralph Nader had an opinion about that. Writing in the 1980s, he pointed to consequences of the Reagan administration's decision to collect less economic data from major corporations:

> This administration does not want to know what corporations do; it has stopped collecting much data about the large oil companies. It has stopped collecting data about the line of business reporting by conglomerates. Referring to across-the-board cuts in federal statistics gathering services, University of Chicago Dean William Kruskal wrote: "When a vessel is in stormy seas, it is foolhardy to cut corners on radar, navigational equipment, good maps, and ample, well-trained crews." Coupled with not wanting to know, the government has defined as trade secrets whatever information companies want withheld from the public, even though it is supplied to the government for particular proceedings affecting the public.[18]

THINK ABOUT IT
How would you protect less-powerful people in your research?

One does not have to be a political radical to see how not collecting important social and economic data could favor the powerful and prevent less powerful people from bettering their lot.

The Toronto neighborhood comparison also used aggregate data: census records, housing data, and so on. The researchers also, however, collected data from individuals: health data, information about individuals' transit use, and the like. They collected these data from individuals, but they aggregated it to match the dissemination blocks by which the census and housing data were reported.

Here, the onus was not on Statistics Canada to protect individual informants; the researchers had to do it themselves. I have not examined their Research Ethics Board filings, but I suspect that they took simple precautions to prevent anyone from tracing their data back to the individuals who supplied it. Typically, this includes giving people code numbers, making sure that the codes and not their names appear on their data forms, and keeping any list that contains both names and codes in a locked cabinet or encrypted in a password-protected file on a computer hard drive. IRBs, at least, typically ask that the data be destroyed after a few years. Sometimes they ask only that the sheets with names and codes be shredded. That, plus the aggregation, keeps any individual participant from harm.

These cases raise no new second-level issues. In fact, publishing the results of such research informs everyone of what has been discovered. That should, in theory, give both elites and common people equal access.

Levering and Moskowitz's Great Place to Work project also used a survey, along with publicly available information about the companies they compared and those companies' responses to a 29-page questionnaire. The survey asked employees to rank their companies' personnel practices. Had Levering and Moskowitz relied on the companies to collect those surveys, they could have endangered the employees. You can imagine how a company might respond to a worker's criticizing workplace life. To avoid this, they had the employees send their forms to the researchers directly. They also distributed the forms at random, so that the companies did not know exactly who got them. And they refused to tell the companies which employees had responded and which had not. All this kept the employees safe from retribution.

Finally, Bettinger's research on the effects of charter schools used only aggregate, publicly available data to analyze school and student performance. These data were reported at the school level, not at the individual level, so no issues about protecting human subjects arose. He furthermore reported the data in such a way that no individual school could be identified. He did this for intellectual reasons, not for ethical ones. It did, however, add a layer of protection.

This is a common pattern in comparative research. Publicly available aggregate data typically raises no ethical issues. Surveys of individuals do, but there are usually ways to protect those individuals. Reporting aggregate patterns aids that process.

This completes our discussion of how to compare regions and organizations using aggregate-level data. In Chapter 8, we'll look at some ways to compare individuals.

Review Questions

1. Why do aggregate data—whether economic, demographic, or organizational—lend themselves to comparing regions and organizations?

2. What are the differences between comparing a few regions or organizations and comparing many of them?

3. How do you use a correlation coefficient to measure the relationship between two variables, when you are comparing many regions or organizations?

4. What other ways of comparing regions, groups, and organizations did you encounter in this chapter?

5. What issues do you have to keep in mind as you design research that investigates regional and organizational differences?

6. What ethical issues does such research raise?

The open-access Student Study Site at study.sagepub.com/spickard has a variety of useful study tools, including SAGE journal articles, video & web resources, eFlashcards, and quizzes.

Notes

1. See Chapter 3 to remind yourself of how these types of data are related.

2. Data are from the U.S. Census Bureau, Brookings Institution, Atlantic/Citilab, Texas A&M Transportation Institute, DiversityData.org, USA.com, and the Environmental Protection Agency.

3. Richard Florida, "The U.S. Cities With the Highest Levels of Income Segregation," Atlantic/Citilab, April 2014. Retrieved from http://www.citylab.com/work/2014/03/us-cities-highest-levels-income-segregation/8632/

4. The full name is the Pearson product-moment coefficient of correlation. It was invented by Karl Pearson in 1896, based on prior work by Francis Galton.

5. The fewer units you compare, the higher the values have to be to reach each strength level. The more units, the lower the values can be. When comparing two variables for a dataset containing just 25 units, for example, you would need an r greater than 0.70 to have a strong correlation. On the high end, for the dataset of the 3,143 U.S. counties, an r value above 0.15 counts as strong.

(Continued)

(Continued)

6. Richard H. Glazier et al., "Density, Destinations or Both? A Comparison of Measures of Walkability in Relation to Transportation Behaviors, Obesity and Diabetes in Toronto, Canada," *PLOS One*, January 14, 2014.

7. U.S. Department of Agriculture, "Food Deserts." Retrieved from http://usda.gov

8. Ingrid Smithey Fulmer et al., "Are the 100 Best Better? An Empirical Investigation of the Relationship Between Being a 'Great Place to Work' and Firm Performance," *Personnel Psychology* 56 (2003): 965–992.

9. Robert Levering and Milton Moskowitz, "The 100 Best Companies to Work for in America," *Fortune,* January 12, 1998, pp. 84–95.

10. Robert Levering and Milton Moskowitz, *The 100 Best Companies to Work for in America*. Doubleday, 1993.

11. Their consulting group's website is www .greatplacetowork.com.

12. Robert Levering and Milton Moskowitz, "The 100 Best Companies to Work for in America," *Fortune,* January 8, 2001, pp. 148–168.

13. Return-on-equity (ROE) is a related measure of financial success, but it adds the extra income that corporate borrowing can produce. Return-on-assets (ROA) is a better measure of stable financial performance.

14. Eric P. Bettinger, "The Effect of Charter Schools on Charter Students and Public Schools," *Economics of Education Review* 24 (2005): 133–147.

15. The Census Bureau (and thus school authorities) treat *Hispanic* as an ethnic category, not a racial one.

16. The charter schools were marginally more successful at moving "low" scores to "moderate," though they were not significantly better than the public schools at this task.

17. Florida, "The U.S. Cities With the Highest Levels of Income Segregation."

18. Ralph Nader, "The Megacorporate World of Ronald Reagan (1984)," *The Ralph Nader Reader*. Seven Stories Press, 2000, p. 89.

1 RESEARCH QUESTION

2 LOGICAL STRUCTURE

3 TYPE OF DATA

4 DATA COLLECTION METHOD

5 DATA COLLECTION SITE

6 DATA ANALYSIS METHOD

RESULTS

CHAPTER 8

Surveying: Shallow Opinions, Identities, and Reports of Acts

	Surveying	Type of Data			
		Reports of acts, behavior, or events	Self-identity	Opinions and attitudes (shallow)	Cultural knowledge
Data Collection Method	Surveys/questionnaires	X	X	X	X

M any research projects ask people questions. Most of these projects fall into one of two categories. If we want to question a lot of people and don't need much depth from any of them, we use a survey. If, however, we want depth and are willing to settle for talking to fewer folks, we use interviews. Interviews let us pay attention to the details of each person's ideas. Surveys skim the surface. Each approach has advantages and disadvantages.

This chapter and the next will focus on these different ways to ask people questions. Chapter 8 covers surveys and Chapter 9 covers interviews. I've separated the discussion of these data collection methods because they are looking for different types of data. Surveys get shallow information from a lot of people; interviews get deep information from just a few. You choose, based on what your research question demands.

What can you do with surveys? Several things.

First, you can see how widespread something is in a population. How many of the people you surveyed have college educations? How many didn't graduate from high school? How many voted Republican in the last election? How many voted Democratic? Such things *describe* a population. Surveys are a very good way to do this.

Second, you can use surveys to compare two or more parts of that population, such as two or more groups or categories of people. Do college-educated people have different political opinions from high school dropouts? Are men or women more likely to favor capital punishment? You can learn a lot by comparing on whatever dimensions your data allow.

Finally, surveys can be used for correlational research. They let you see if certain attitudes and behaviors tend to go together in individuals. Do people who describe themselves as politically conservative also describe themselves as favoring universal college education? Are self-described religious people more inclined to report helping others than are those who say they are not religious?

This makes surveys very useful tools.

Three Reminders

Let's remember three things about surveys and **survey data** before we begin.

Reminder 1: Surveys usually produce quantitative data. That's because they ask the same questions to a lot of people, and those questions are easy to answer. We can thus count how many people give what kinds of answers. Counting makes a study quantitative. Moreover, if we survey a **random sample** of a population (see Chapter 5), we can draw conclusions about the population as a whole. We can do this only if the sample is large enough and if every member of the population has an equal chance of being part of it. Well-designed large-scale surveys make sure of this, so researchers can tell exactly how close their results must be to the population as a whole.

Reminder 2: Survey data typically take one of three different forms. These are **interval/ratio data**, **ordinal data**, or **categorical data**, which we covered in Chapter 6.

You get interval/ratio data when you ask people to give a numeric answer that is precise enough that you can do complex math with it. Age is one example; number of years of schooling is another. You can figure the average for either—a sign that you've got interval/ratio data on your hands.

You get ordinal data when you have people rank things in order, without asking them for strict measurements. "Are you very happy, pretty happy, or not so happy?" Everyone agrees how to rank these, but one person's "very happy" is another person's "pretty happy." That makes taking an average useless. You can, however, count how many people give each answer.

Categorical data come from unranked categories: male/female, yes/no, White/Black/Asian, and so on. Surveys collect such data easily, but no one would imagine doing more than counting them. None of them have an inherent order. We can, however, count how many of our survey respondents choose each category.

*Reminder 3: There is a difference between a **unit of observation** and a **unit of analysis**.* The unit of observation is whatever unit produces your data. For most surveys, that means the individual. The **General Social Survey (GSS)**, for example, polls about 3,000 noninstitutionalized U.S. adults every even-numbered year. It asks each person several hundred questions, such as age, sex, number of children, political leanings, attitudes on current social issues, and—yes—whether they are "very happy," "pretty happy," or "not so happy." The GSS collects data from individuals, so that is its unit of observation.

That's not the same as its unit of analysis, however. You can explore GSS results by seeing how many people answer a question in a particular way. Here, you are describing a population, and so your unit of analysis is the population. Or you can compare how two categories of people answer that question, in which case your unit of analysis is the category. For example, comparing the average education of Catholics, Protestants, Jews, Muslims, and Hindus uses religion as the unit of analysis—even though the unit of observation remains the individual.

Here's the point: *You can draw conclusions only about the unit of analysis that you use.* If you know that the average Protestant has 12.55 years of schooling, you can't tell how much education any individual Protestant has. You can't jump from one unit of analysis to another. That's why you need to keep the unit of analysis straight. Doing so steers you away from false conclusions.

Two Examples

When most people think about surveys, they imagine survey takers with clipboards, asking people about their opinions and behaviors. They imagine census workers going house-to-house, telephone pollsters calling us after dinner, and the public issue surveys we get in the mail. They read about survey results in their newspapers or hear about them on television: "Survey finds U.S. schools ramping up safety measures." "Survey: fewer homeless people on Augusta's streets." "Survey finds most patients are positive about their hospital care."[1] Though newspapers and television reports don't present many details, most people value this information. They know that good public policy depends on us knowing how safe our schools are, how many homeless people live on our streets, and whether hospitals are meeting people's needs. Surveys are a good way to collect such information.

Studying School Safety

Take that first headline, about school safety. This comes from a nationwide survey of school principals that asked about safety and discipline issues during the 2013–2014 school year.[2] Sponsored by the National Center for Educational Statistics (NCES), this is but one of several dozen school surveys that track various aspects of school life. Surveying schools lets researchers see what is going on in them. Repeating such surveys lets investigators see how schools change from one decade to the next.

The survey headline comes from one of the report's main findings: that more and more schools are developing programs to respond to and control in-school violence. Of schools in the 2013–2014 survey, 75% reported having closed-circuit security cameras, as opposed to 61% four years earlier. In the 2013–2014 survey, 82% reported having an electronic parent-notification system (versus 63% four years earlier). More schools allowed students to carry cell phones and texting devices than did so previously—in part, I suspect, because of the positive role that such devices played in major school crises in the past. Clearly, schools nationwide continue to respond to incidents such as the shootings at Sandy Hook Elementary School (2012) and Marysville Pilchuck High School (2014).

The latest NCES survey also reports fewer incidents of school violence than five years earlier, though there is no way to show that the various new safety measures had any role in this change. The percentage of public schools reporting at least one violent incident dropped from 74% to 65%. The percentage of schools reporting a serious violent crime dropped from 16% to 13%; the rate of violence fell from 25 per 1,000 students to 16 per 1,000. That's progress by any reckoning.

That's not all that fell. Figure 8.1 compares the percentage of schools reporting various student disciplinary problems in the 2009–2010 and 2013–2014 surveys. Student bullying is clearly the largest problem: About a quarter of the schools reported weekly incidents in 2009–2010 and about a sixth of the schools reported such problems in 2013–2104. Racial, sexual, and gender harassment are present but less widespread. All of these problems now occur less frequently than they did in the recent past.

You now know more about this NCES study than was reported in any of the news stories I read while writing these paragraphs. Newspapers reported at most three of these findings; television stations typically reported one or two. You have to read the report's executive summary to get the main findings. You have to read the whole

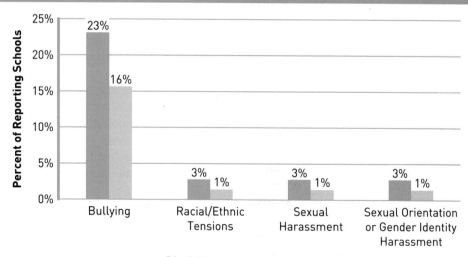

FIGURE 8.1   Percentage of Schools Reporting Various Disciplinary Problems (NCES, 2009–2010 and 2013–2014)

report to get the details. Yet we can learn a lot more from this study than just what its authors found.

How, for example, was this survey carried out? Who got the questionnaires? How many were returned? Who filled them out? Do they cover the entire 2013–2014 school year? Such details can make the difference between a survey that describes U.S. schools accurately and one that does not. Let's explore a few of these issues.

Taking a Sample We'll start with the survey population. There are 84,200 elementary, middle, and high schools in the NCES database. This includes both regular and charter schools, but it does not include alternative schools, technical schools, preschools, and kindergartens. That's a lot of schools—and it would take a lot of paper, a lot of stamps, and a lot of staff time to survey all of them. The NCES doesn't have the budget to do that, and they've got a lot of surveys to run. So they took a legitimate shortcut: They surveyed a **representative sample** of those 84,200 schools: They chose 1,600 schools, shaping their sample to reflect all the schools in the United States as accurately as possible.

We covered the basics of sampling in Chapter 5, and I won't repeat the details here. The core idea is that a sample works if every school in the NCES database has an equal chance of being chosen. If that's the case, then the laws of probability tell us exactly how likely it is that the particular sample of schools we've chosen represents the country's schools as a whole.

In this case, a sample of 1,600 schools means that you can be 95% confident that the actual figures you report are accurate within a ±2.4% margin of error. For this survey, that means we can be 95% confident that the actual percentage of schools experiencing weekly bullying incidents in 2013–2014 is no higher than 18.1% and no lower than 13.3%. That's significantly lower than the 2008–2009 range: 25.5% to 20.7%. We can be almost positive that bullying decreased over those five years.

The NCES study went one step further, however. There are lots of different schools in the United States: big ones, small ones, rich ones, poor ones, urban, suburban, and rural ones, and so on, plus schools at the elementary, middle, and high school levels. A normal **random sample** would give each of the 84,200 schools an equal chance to receive a survey. That's great, but the sample might—just by chance— be all elementary schools, or all small schools, or urban ones, or small ones. Samples frequently don't match the full diversity of the population from which they are drawn. That makes it very hard to get a sense of what is really going on.

THINK ABOUT IT
Why does using a random sample make survey research more accurate?

How do we keep the randomness, so that we can know how accurate our sample is, while still highlighting the sample's diversity? That's a key issue for much survey research. Fortunately, survey experts have figured out some ways to do it.

In this case, the NCES project used a **stratified random sample** to make sure the survey captured the diversity of the U.S. school system. First, the researchers took the random sample. That ensured they would

TABLE 8.1	Composition of NCES Sample			
	Number in Sample	Percentage of Sample	Number in NCES Database	Percentage of NCES Database
Elementary	460	34%	49,700	59%
Middle	410	30%	16,100	19%
High	490	36%	18,400	22%

know how accurate their overall results were. Then they checked to see how many schools in that sample were elementary schools, middle schools, and high schools (Table 8.1).

Clearly, high and middle schools were overrepresented in this sample. Schools at those two levels between them constitute just 41% of the schools in the NCES database (19% + 22%), but they made up 66% of the sample. Similarly, 59% of the country's schools are elementary schools, but they were only 34% of the sample. That's not a very good match. It will lead us to underestimate what happens in elementary schools and overestimate what happens in middle and high schools.

To fix this problem, we have to adjust the numbers. We do this by weighting each school in the sample, so that each elementary school counts more and each middle and high school counts less. This doesn't change the survey's accuracy, but it does let us compare the schools at the three levels. It aligns the figures at each level more closely with real life.

In the end, the NCES team decided to count each elementary school in the sample as 59/34ths (1.74) of a school (the percentage in the database divided by the percentage in the sample). They counted each middle school as 19/30ths (0.63) and each high school as 22/36ths (0.61). By doing this, they made sure that the low proportion of elementary schools in the sample didn't underestimate the discipline problems at that level. The report didn't give the raw data, but Table 8.2 (on the next page) shows what it might have looked like.[3]

The left-hand column of that table shows the total number of disciplinary incidents reported by the schools at each level on the 2013–2014 survey. The middle column shows the weighting factors. There were fewer incidents at the elementary level, but elementary schools were only 41% of the sample, when they should have been 59%. As you can see, the weighting adjusts the number of incidents to overcome the fact that elementary schools are underrepresented.

Had the sample's percentages at each school level matched the population, there would have been 409 incidents from elementary schools, 411 from middle schools, and 434 from high schools. That tells us that about a third of the country's disciplinary cases happen at each of these three levels. The weighted figures let us make an accurate comparison—without losing the randomness that guarantees the survey's accuracy.

TABLE 8.2 Weighting of NCES Data			
	Number of Incidents Reported	Weight (converted to decimals)	Weighted Number of Incidents
Elementary	235	1.74	409
Middle	653	0.63	411
High	712	0.61	434

We have to be careful, though, lest we misinterpret this result. We can't conclude that each elementary school has as many disciplinary problems as does each middle school or each high school. Remember, there are three times as many elementary schools as there are schools at each of the other two levels. *This means that similar numbers of incidents (in the weighted sample) translates to a third as many incidents per elementary school.* Individual elementary schools have many fewer disciplinary problems than do individual middle and high schools. Only the aggregate figures are similar.

The team did the same calculation for each of the other dimensions of difference: rich/poor, urban/suburban/rural, and so on. This let them adjust the sample along these dimensions of difference.

The actual procedure was a great deal more complicated, of course, but you get the picture. Stratifying your sample and then weighting the results can make a survey better represent the whole population. As the choice of individual schools is still random, this doesn't stop you from using your sample to draw conclusions about schools overall.

Getting People to Respond What else do we need to know about this project? Well, who got the questionnaires, who filled them out, and how many of them were returned? These are important issues. You can't get accurate survey results unless you ask people who have the information you want. You can't draw conclusions from your survey unless you have a high response rate. In this case, the NCES team asked school principals for the information and asked that the surveys "be completed by the person most knowledgeable about safety and discipline at the school." Often that was the principal, but sometimes a vice principal knew the answers better.

How did the NCES ensure a high response rate? First, they offered two ways of submitting data. The local expert could complete the three-page forms on paper, or she or he could do so online. That made returning the forms easier. Second, the NCES team followed up with those who didn't respond, which produced some more submissions. Finally, the team called to talk with the stragglers and collected their data by telephone. In the end, the team got good answers from 85% of the schools surveyed. Twenty-five of the surveyed schools turned out to have been closed or were otherwise ineligible, which raised the response rate to 86%. That's very good for studies of this type.

The team had one further trick in its bag. Surveys have to be random. That's why you can generalize the results from a sample of schools to the population of all schools in the country. Randomness works, though, only if there is no systematic reason why some schools didn't fill out the questionnaire.

Did the nonresponders have so many disciplinary problems that they were ashamed to admit it? Were they so understaffed that no one had time to fill out the forms? Whatever the reason, the result would be a sample that unintentionally excluded schools with specific characteristics. That would make generalizing from the sample to all schools impossible.

How can we find out if our nonresponders are of a particular type? The answer is rather simple: We test to see if there is any systematic difference between those who respond early and those who respond late. If there is, then we can assume that those that did not respond at all are probably more like the late responders than they are like the early responders. That indicates a systematically biased sample. If, however, the late responders and the early responders are alike, then there is not apt to be any bias present.

In this case, there was no potential **bias**. The NCES team compared the results from the schools that responded on their own with the results from those that had to be reminded to turn in their forms. These two groups of schools were equally distributed in terms of size, resources, community setting, number and type of disciplinary problems, and so on. This makes it unlikely that the schools that failed to respond did so for any unified reasons. That is, their reasons were random, not patterned. This meant that the sample was random as well.

One last question: When were the surveys filled out? They were sent out in February 2014 and were returned later that spring. Telephone follow-ups started in March and ended by June. This means that some of the schools reported data for just part of the school year and late filers reported it for the whole year. Does this make any difference to the results?

Probably not. Schools that reported security cameras, telephone response systems, and so on probably didn't take them out after completing the survey, so those figures are most likely accurate. For schools that reported bullying every week through February, it's possible that the bullying could have stopped, but that's not likely. The real reason for running the survey early, though, was to make it match the 2008–2009 survey, which had been run over those same months. One of the points of the NCES project was to compare schools across various years. You can do that only if you do things the same way each time.

Table 8.3 (on the next page) lines up our six-step process with the NCES research project.

TABLE 8.3 Summary of the NCES's Safety and Discipline Survey	
1. Research Questions	(a) What measures do U.S. schools report having taken to ensure student safety? (b) How many and what kind of disciplinary situations do U.S. schools report?
2. Logical Structure	Descriptive
3. Type of Data	Reports of acts
4. Data Collection Method	Survey of school principals
5. Data Collection Site	Representative sample of U.S. schools
6. Data Analysis Method	Summarize responses, compare with previous surveys
	Unit of analysis: *schools*

Kids' Attitudes Toward Reading

Let's look at another survey, this time of grade-school students' attitudes toward reading. The NCES study took the school as both its unit of observation and its unit of analysis. For this example, our *unit of observation* will be individual students and our *unit of analysis* will be categories of students (e.g., boys/girls, able/average/ low readers). We'll see what shapes students' expressed enjoyment of reading, both reading for school and reading for pleasure. We'll also see how the investigators were able to ask very young students about their interest in reading by matching their survey questions to those students' intellectual and emotional levels. All survey research has to do this kind of matching. Working with 6- to 11-year-olds merely presents an extra challenge.

Let's get some background on this issue. What do we mean by "attitudes toward reading"? Schools teach kids to read. Some kids like reading and others don't, but nearly all of them learn to read at an early age. Some of them keep with it, turning into lifelong readers. Others grow up to read sporadically. The latter are not so much *il*literate as *a*literate: They can read, but they don't do it much. They usually choose to do other things.

Interestingly, most children start out liking to read, but that liking declines with time. Scholars suspect that as children grow older, they have more choices of things to do: sports, movies, cell phones, you name it. The more options, the harder it is for books to hold kids' attention. Michael McKenna, Dennis Kear, and Randolph Ellsworth—the leaders of the project we'll be examining—noted that this is true both for skilled readers and for those who don't read as well.[4] Both good and poor readers show less interest in reading as they move through the elementary grades. McKenna and coauthors cited evidence from several studies that confirmed this change.

What other things might shape kids' attitudes toward reading? What about gender? Girls typically like to read more than boys do, though that's only on average;

there are always exceptions. What, however, is the exact mechanism? There's probably no gene for liking reading on the X and Y chromosomes, but there are social expectations. Maybe girls are expected to like reading and boys aren't. We know that kids often live up to social expectations. Or do girls like to read not from social expectations but because they are better students. We know that better students like reading more than weaker students do. Are we really measuring ability here and not gender?

Ethnicity could similarly affect kids' attitudes. African American and Latino children may live up to parents' and teachers' expectations that they won't like reading as much as White children do. But these kids also do worse in school. Is kids' liking to read shaped by their school success, by adults' expectations, or both? Very few studies have investigated these matters.

Finally, different ways of teaching reading may affect how much kids enjoy reading in later years. McKenna and his coauthors noted that lots of people have opinions about this question, but there was very little good empirical research on it.

Specifically, at the time of their research (the early 1990s), few studies compared the results of the two main teaching techniques then in common use. One used basal readers: special books written specifically to teach reading. The *Dick and Jane* series used in the mid-1950s is a particularly famous example. Passages such as, "See Spot. See Spot run. Run, Spot, run." and "Oh, see. Oh, see Jane. Funny, funny Jane." were near cultural icons of that era. The second approach, often called whole language, had students read actual literary works. These were aimed at children's interests, but they skipped the dumbed-down prose and the artificially compressed vocabulary that made *Dick and Jane* so famous. My own first-grade favorite was Gelett Burgess's *The Goops and How to Be Them*. It struck me as being far more interesting than Dick and Jane's "adventures." Still, I was a good reader, so what did I know?

The point is, several things could be shaping kids' attitudes toward reading. Older kids might choose to read less because they have more choice of things to do than when they were littler. Weaker students might grow to dislike reading because they were frustrated in school. Gender expectations might play a part. So might people's expectations that minority kids would dislike reading more than Whites. Different ways of teaching reading might play a role. How can we sort out which of these are really the case?

Tracking the Six Steps That's precisely what McKenna and his colleagues set out to do. They laid out three *research questions* that they wanted to answer. In their words:

1. What are the overall developmental trends in recreational and academic reading attitude across the elementary grades?
2. What is the developmental relationship between recreational and academic reading, on the one hand, and (a) reading ability, (b) gender, and (c) ethnicity?
3. What effects on reading can be ascribed to the use of basal reading materials?

Let's decode their language a bit, so that we can be clear about what they were asking. Their first question asked whether older children are, in fact, less interested in reading than are those in the lower elementary grades. That's what the authors meant by "developmental trends." They could have asked the question more simply, but they wanted to find patterns of all types, not just whether grade-school students' interest in reading declines. Perhaps older students aren't more negative about reading; maybe they're more positive. Perhaps the drop (if there is one) is only in the fifth or sixth grade. Phrasing the question more generally let them look for such things. In any case, their question is a "what" question. It asks them to discover the trends. Its *logical structure* is descriptive: The authors wanted to find out what the patterns are.

The second question also calls for description. It asks whether there are any patterns that connect reading preference to reading ability, gender, and/or ethnicity. Do better students like to read more or less than weaker students? Does girls' interest in reading drop as they get older? Is their drop greater or less than the drop for boys?

The second question also asks whether these patterns are different for recreational reading than for school reading. Perhaps girls keep liking to read at home but grow to dislike reading at school. The researchers would like to find out. These, too, are "what" questions. It takes a descriptive project to answer them.

The third question is a bit different: It asks about causes. The researchers didn't just want to know if the kids' attitudes toward reading are different, depending on whether their schools taught them using basal readers or using whole-language texts. More than that, they wanted to know if the learning method shapes the attitudes themselves. Does the teaching technique affect the extent to which kids retain an interest in reading?

The key words from the research question are "what effects . . . can be ascribed." It takes a causal logical structure to answer this question. Mere description will not do.

We've identified the first two steps of the design process. Now for the third: what *type of data* can answer these questions?

McKenna and his colleagues were looking for attitudes. Specifically, they were looking for children's reports of their own attitudes. Attitudes are somewhat like opinions, though with a bit more emotional overtone. The investigators weren't asking children for deep personal feelings, however. They just wanted them to report how much they liked reading. The closest data type from our list in Step 4 is *shallow opinions and attitudes*. Research that seeks personal feelings, by contrast, typically wants to tap deeper feelings than McKenna and his colleagues needed.

What kind of *data collection method* works best for collecting children's attitudes at this level? Take another look at Table 4.1 on page 69. Scanning down column 7, you can eliminate participant observation and in-depth interviews. These methods collect shallow opinions as a by-product of seeing deeper matters. That leaves *surveys, critical incident*

THINK ABOUT IT
What's the difference between describing something and looking for its causes?

interviews, and *focus groups*. Surveys work for this kind of research and have the benefit of being easy and suitable for collecting data from large numbers of people. Critical incident interviews and focus groups work only for small-scale research and are too complicated to use with young children. Children need easy-to-answer, noninvasive questions. Surveys collect this kind of data very well.

What survey questions did the researchers ask? First, they asked teachers for the demographic information they wanted for each student. This included the students' grade level, the teachers' estimates of the students' reading ability (high, medium, low), the students' gender and ethnicity, and how much their classes used basal readers.

Second, they had each student fill out an Elementary Reading Attitude Survey (ERAS). This survey asked students 20 questions about how much they liked reading. Ten questions were about reading for pleasure, for example, "How do you feel when you read a book on a rainy Saturday?" "How do you feel when you read a book in school during free time?" and "How do you feel about reading for fun at home?" The other 10 questions were about reading for school: "How do you feel about reading in school?" "How do you feel when it's time for reading class?" and "How do you feel when the teacher asks you a question about what you read?" Each question was followed by four images of Garfield, the famous cartoon character, in moods that ranged from ecstatic to angry. Kids were asked to circle the picture that most matched how they felt.

This proved to be an easy method of collecting data. Kids filled out the surveys in class, with the teacher giving instructions and answering whatever questions the kids had. Teachers made sure that the students knew there was no wrong answer. "Feelings are your own," they said. "However you feel is perfectly all right." The project collected surveys from 18,185 children from 229 schools in 95 school districts. That's a big survey, but it was relatively easy to carry out.

Why such a big *data collection site*? There are two reasons. First, surveys are particularly good at collecting relatively limited data from a large number of people—just what a project on kids' attitudes toward reading needs. Most previous research on this topic had been small-scale. McKenna and his colleagues wanted to find national patterns, not just ones from a particular area. McKenna was based in Georgia and had done research on student attitudes there. It was, he thought, time to see if the local patterns were also true nationwide.

Second, the research team wanted to be able to separate out several factors at once. They wanted to know how attitudes change across the elementary grades for students of different reading abilities. They wanted to see how boys and girls differ. They wanted to see if there are differences among Whites, African Americans, and Latinos. Finally, they wanted to see if the way schools teach reading makes any difference.

That's four variables, each of which potentially interacts with the others. That's because kids can be described by each of the four factors, not just one. Fred, for example, is male, White, reads poorly, and was taught using the whole-language method. Ginny is female, African American, reads well, and was also taught using whole language.

Darcy is female, White, reads well, and was taught using a basal reader. You get the idea. The only way to measure the influence of four variables at once is to have a really big survey. That's what McKenna and his colleagues set out to do.

I won't go into the full details; you can look up the study and read it yourself. The researchers made sure that their sample of children matched the national figures for gender (within 1%) and ethnicity (within 3%). Of the school districts they selected, 4 were in isolated rural areas, 33 were in small communities, 38 were in medium-sized communities, and 20 were in large communities. They took more schools from the latter two groups, so that they could match national distributions. The only shortfall was large metropolitan districts. Although districts in Baltimore, Pittsburgh, and Salt Lake City participated, New York, Chicago, and Los Angeles did not. This could throw off their data. Ideally, a follow-up study could see if the patterns they found nationwide held true for these areas.

What did they find? To answer that, we must look at their *data analysis method*. We needn't go into great detail, but we do need to understand something about how they drew their conclusions from the data they collected.

For each of the more than 18,000 students, they had seven pieces of data, summarized in Table 8.4. The first five are relatively straightforward, but the other two deserve some attention.

TABLE 8.4 Data Collected in McKenna et al.'s Study	
DATA	**VALUES**
Grade Level	1st to 6th
Reading Level	High
	Medium
	Low
Gender	Male
	Female
Ethnicity	White
	African American
	Latino
Reliance on Basal Readers	Heavy
	Some
	None
Attitude Score for Recreational Reading	10 to 40
Attitude Score for School Reading	10 to 40

When the investigators scored the students' attitudes toward each kind of reading, they counted 4 points for each ecstatic Garfield, 3 points for each smiling Garfield, 2 points for each frowning Garfield, and 1 point for each angry Garfield. Someone circling all ecstatic Garfields on the recreational reading survey, for example, would get 40 points on the recreational scale. Someone circling all angry Garfields would get 10. Most kids got something in between. This produced two scales, one for recreational reading and one for school reading. Each scale ran from 10 to 40, with a midpoint at 25. Kids who were indifferent to reading scored in the mid-20s. Those who liked reading scored above that. Those who disliked reading scored below it.

Results The results were interesting, though I won't go into detail. There was a clear, steady drop in kids' attitudes toward both school and recreational reading between first and sixth grades. First graders liked reading a lot; their scores were at or near the smiling Garfield on the ERAS survey. For sixth graders, the average score for academic reading was a bit better than a frown. Sixth graders were significantly more positive than that about recreational reading, though their attitude toward that, too, was lower than for first graders.

This pattern held true for students regardless of reading ability. High, medium, and low readers all liked reading less in sixth grade than in first. The decline was steeper for school reading than for recreational reading, though students with higher reading skills maintained more interest in recreational reading across the grades. Girls were more interested in reading than were boys. The ethnic groups' results were mixed: White sixth graders were a bit more interested in recreational reading than were African Americans and Latinos, whereas African Americans were more interested in school reading than were Whites.

The degree to which teachers used basal readers did not seem to make much difference. Sixth-grade reading interest was lower than first-grade interest both for those who used basal readers heavily and for those who did not. Despite some people's worries, reading the modern equivalents of *Dick and Jane* did not kill kids' wish to read. McKenna and his colleagues did not find that either reading system had any significant effects on student attitudes.

Did this study accomplish its objectives? Let's go back to the three research questions, to see if the survey was able to answer them.

The answer to the first question is clear: The study showed that kids' interest in reading dropped steadily between first and sixth grades. It dropped about half as much for recreational reading as it did for school reading, but it dropped for both. We now know that the earlier, local findings are also true for schools nationwide.

The answer to the second question is also clear: Reading skills, gender, and ethnicity somewhat affected the shape of the drop in interest, though they did not reverse it for any of these student categories.

The answer to the third question is a bit less clear. On a descriptive level, the extent that teachers used one or another reading system did not seem to matter much

TABLE 8.5	Summary of McKenna et al.'s National Attitudes Toward Reading Survey
1. Research Questions	(a) How does student interest in reading change across the elementary grades? (b) Is this affected by reading ability? By gender? By ethnicity? (c) What effects can be ascribed to the use of basal reading materials?
2. Logical Structure	Descriptive (mostly), with the hope of finding a causal relationship with basal readers
3. Type of Data	Students' self-reported opinions and attitudes
4. Data Collection Method	Survey of more than 18,000 students in first through sixth grades
5. Data Collection Site	Chosen from a representative sample of U.S. schools
6. Data Analysis Method	Summarize responses; find differences between various student categories
	Unit of analysis: *population subgroups* (categories of students)

to students' loss of interest. Remember, though, that this question was not just descriptive but also causal. The authors wanted to know what effects could be ascribed to the use of basal readers. That's a harder question, to which this research does not give a satisfactory answer.

The problem is, the teachers were asked how much they used basal readers in the current year, not how much the students had been exposed to them in the past. A sixth-grade student might have used basal readers for several years but now be in a non-basal-reader class. It turns out, this wasn't a good measure of basal reader use. As a result, McKenna and his colleagues couldn't make any causal claims.

In reality, I think that McKenna and his colleagues did the best they could. They reported—accurately—that they found no effect of the reading program on kids' reading interest, and they also reported the flaws in the data. You can't ask for more than that. Table 8.5 summarizes this research, using our six-step method.

In all, this is a good example of what survey research can accomplish. The last part of this discussion also brings us to our next topic: how we can analyze survey data.

Survey Data Analysis

The two research projects described in this chapter illustrate the issues related to the use of surveys as a data collection method. Each of them had to identify the target population (of schools or students), choose a representative sample of that population, design a survey that was easy for the people in that sample to answer, and find ways to encourage them to respond. Each of these examples had a different combination of problems. School principals are busy folks, so the NCES survey had to find creative ways to get them to respond. Grade-school students can't read complicated sentences, so McKenna and his team designed a cartoon-based answer sheet that all of the respondents could understand.

Such data collection issues come up in every survey project. They're always part of the picture. Once the data are collected, though, we have to analyze it. This section describes several ways to do so. I've organized them by the form of data involved: interval/ratio, ordinal, and categorical. Each form calls for different data analysis methods.

Analyzing Interval/Ratio Survey Results

We'll start with *interval/ratio data*—the same sort of data we saw in Chapter 7, when we were comparing places and organizations. Remember that we compared San Antonio and Portland by listing such things as population size, age and ethnic composition, median income levels, average commute times, and so on. These are all interval/ratio data. These numbers have equal intervals, true zeros, and all the other things that make it possible to work with them mathematically. San Antonio's median household income, for example, was $40,764 and Portland's was $53,078. Simple math tells us that Portlanders' median income is 30.2% larger than median incomes in San Antonio. Ordinal and categorical data don't let you do that; interval/ratio data do.

Chapter 7 also introduced you to correlations as a way of locating the relationships between two interval/ratio variables. We saw, for example, that high rents relative to incomes are correlated with long commutes. More exactly, places where a high percentage of people pay more than 30% of their incomes for rent are also places where high percentages of people have long commutes to work. The two things don't always go together, though. The Pearson's *r* is 0.44, which indicates only a moderate correlation when working with 50 cases (the U.S. states). This means that there are other factors involved. We can, however, say that there is a moderate relationship between the variables, and a moderate relationship is, indeed, a connection. If we know the percentage of people who have to pay high rent, then we can predict the percentage of the population with long commutes—and we'll be reasonably close much of the time.

We can also use correlations with surveys that collect interval/ratio data. Such data are more common in surveys of organizations than they are in surveys of individuals. Schools, for example, will report both average class size and scores on achievement tests. We can correlate these data very easily. A 1997 nationwide correlation study of Israeli elementary school classes, for example, found that small classes were strongly associated with high average test scores in fifth-grade classes, moderately associated with high average scores in fourth-grade classes, and only barely associated with average scores in third-grade classes. (This study took the average class score as its unit of observation and its unit of analysis.)[5]

Unlike surveys of organizations, surveys of individuals often don't collect interval/ratio data. That's partly because people are often more comfortable sharing some things by ranges rather than by exact numbers. Americans typically don't like to tell people their incomes, so most surveys ask people to choose a range of income (under $20,000; $20,000–$29,999; $30,000–$39,999; and so on). That produces an ordinal variable, because we don't know where in the range each person's income falls.

In survey research, the two most common interval/ratio variables are *age* and *years of schooling*. The General Social Survey (GSS) collects both, and we can learn something from their correlation. Table 8.6 shows the correlation between age (18–89 years) and highest year of school completed (0–20) for U.S. adults surveyed over the past four decades.

TABLE 8.6	Correlation Between Age and Highest Year of School Completed (GSS, 1974–2014)				
	Survey Year				
	1974	1984	1994	2004	2014
Pearson's *r*	−0.33	−0.23	−0.20	−0.07	0.00
Number of People	1,475	1,465	2,980[6]	2,802	2,528

It's pretty easy to see the pattern. First, the Pearson's *r*'s are negative for each year except 2014, which means that older people in the earlier surveys have less schooling. Second, that number moves steadily toward zero as we move through the decades. There is a much lower correlation between age and schooling now than there was 40 years ago.

This makes sense. A higher percentage of young people attend college now, partly because it is much harder to get jobs with just a high school education. We saw the same pattern a generation and a half ago, but at a lower educational level. More people finished high school in the 1950s than had done so in the 1930s. Each generation got more education as we moved through the decades, and the less educated older generations died off. Now, for the first time, the new generation is not more educated than its parents. The connection between age and level of education has disappeared.

It's easy to tell that there is no correlation for 2014, but which of the other correlations are strong, moderate, and weak? Remember that the correlation value alone doesn't tell you how closely two things are connected. The larger the number of cases, the smaller the Pearson's *r* can be and still indicate a significant relationship. In fact, the 1974, 1984, and 1994 correlations are all strong ones. The 2004 correlation is moderate. Except for 2006, there's been no correlation between age and years of education since.

I think you see the pattern. Interval/ratio survey data are no different from interval/ratio aggregate data. You can figure correlation coefficients, run regression analyses, and use other complicated mathematical techniques with either type. You can't, however, do this with ordinal or categorical data—the kind of data that most surveys produce. We have to handle these forms of data differently.

Analyzing Ordinal and Categorical Data

As noted in Chapter 6, ordinal and categorical data have a lot in common. They result from questions to which people can give discreet answers. For example, instead of asking for peoples' ages, we can ask them to check which age range they're part of: "18–30," "31–45," "46–60," and so on. Instead of asking how many years of school someone completed, we can ask them to choose from the following categories: "not HS grad," "HS grad," "some college," "college grad," "postgraduate degree." These are both *ordinal variables,* because the answers come in a strict order. A high school graduate has more education than someone who didn't graduate. Someone who has attended college without graduating has more education still. A college graduate has yet more education, and someone with a postgraduate degree has the most of all. Think "order," and you'll remember what *ordinal* means.

Categorical variables are like ordinal variables in that one has to check one box and not others. They are unlike ordinal variables in that those boxes have no inherent order. There is no order to "male" or "female"; nor to "yes" or "no"; nor to "Protestant," "Catholic," "Jew," or "Other"; nor to "Democrat," "Republican," or "Independent." These are separate categories, which could appear in any order.

How do you analyze ordinal and categorical data? We spent some time in Chapter 6 doing just that. We learned how to report the distribution of a single ordinal or categorical variable and also how to cross-tabulate two variables to show their relationship. Here, I'll give you an example as a reminder. Let's see what the GSS has to say about education. The GSS surveys about 3,000 U.S. adults every two years. That sample is large enough to represent the entire population.

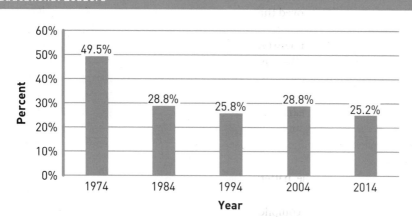

FIGURE 8.2   Population Reporting a Great Deal of Confidence in Educational Leaders

The GSS ask its respondents how much confidence they have in the people running their major social institutions. Here's the question for education: "As far as the people running education are concerned, would you say you have a great deal of confidence, only some confidence, or hardly any confidence in them?"

This is an ordinal variable. It ranks confidence, but it doesn't measure it mathematically. We can, however, count the number of people giving each answer. Figure 8.2 (on the previous page) shows the percentage who replied "a great deal of confidence" for five surveys stretching back to 1974.

You can see the pattern: a rather precipitous drop in the 10 years after 1974, with the figure staying level at about a quarter of the population since then. This graph describes the data. It does not explain it, because it doesn't show us any other relationships.

Let's ask a different question: "Do different types of people have different levels of confidence?" We can find out by showing the figures for each. Take a look at the two cross-tabulations in Table 8.7, which combines the values for all five of these years. The one on the left compares men and women, and the one on the right compares Whites and African Americans. We get to see if men's confidence differs from women's and if Whites' confidence differs from African Americans'.

The bottom row is important, as we saw in Chapter 6. To review, the chi-square statistic (χ^2) tells us whether the difference we see between the columns in our survey sample reflects a real difference in the population as a whole. The chi-square produces a p value, which is the chance that there is no difference. If the p value is less than 0.05 (5%), then we can confirm that there *is* a difference in the population. (The "conf" stands for "confidence": how confident we can be that there is a difference. Not all disciplines use this figure, but enough do that it is worth reporting.)

As you can see, there's not much difference between men and women. There is only a 10% chance that the difference we see between these columns represents a real difference in the U.S. population. A coin flip has a 50% chance of coming up heads, so there's less than a coin-toss chance that men and women are different. In fact,

TABLE 8.7   GSS Responses About Confidence in the Education System, Comparing Men and Women, and Whites and African Americans

How much confidence do you have in the people running education? (1974, 1984, 1994, 2004, 2014)

	Men	Women		Whites	African Americans
A great deal	32.0%	31.0%	A great deal	29.6%	42.1%
Some	53.7%	54.4%	Some	55.3%	47.1%
Hardly any	14.3%	14.6%	Hardly any	15.1%	10.8%
	$\chi^2 = 0.235$; p = 0.889; 10.1% conf			$\chi^2 = 35.5$; p < 0.000; 99.99% conf	

men and women have pretty much the same attitudes about the people running our educational institutions.

African Americans, however, have significantly more confidence in educational leaders than do Whites. Their chi-square is much higher, which gives us a lower p value and greater than 99% confidence that the difference between these columns represents a real difference in the U.S. population.

That's an important finding. If we hadn't divided our data into racial groups, we wouldn't have discovered this pattern. That's the point of using cross-tabulations. They help us identify systematic attitudinal differences between different categories of people. We could, by the way, have done this for each of the five years surveyed. We would have gotten the same answer each time. You are welcome to do this analysis yourself, as the GSS is available for public use online.[7]

Let's take a different survey question, also from the GSS and also about education. This time we'll focus on just one year—1985—when that survey asked people what they thought kids ought to learn in high school. Let's see what kinds of people give what kinds of answers.

We'll start with an overview: topics that some, but not all, adult Americans think high school students should learn. The questions read: "How important is it that schools teach _____ to 15-year-olds?" Topics included "reading, writing, and mathematics" (3Rs); "history, literature, and the arts" (Hist/Arts); "science and technology" (Sci/Tech); "job training"; "sex education"; "respect for authority"; "discipline and order"; and "concern for others." The first five are formal school subjects; the last three are attitudes. Respondents could choose for each from "essential," "very important," "fairly important," "not very important," or "not needed" (Table 8.8).

TABLE 8.8   GSS Responses About the Importance of Teaching Various School Subjects

How important is it that schools teach _____ to 15-year-olds?

	3Rs	Hist/ Arts	Sci/ Tech	Job Training	Sex Education	Respect	Discipline	Concern
Essential	89.7%	37.9%	41.0%	41.3%	16.8%	48.2%	47.7%	25.7%
Very Important	9.0%	33.4%	37.1%	35.9%	29.5%	32.8%	35.6%	32.8%
Fairly Important	0.6%	23.7%	19.2%	16.9%	34.3%	15.1%	13.6%	29.4%
Not Very Important	0.0%	4.6%	2.8%	4.4%	11.0%	2.6%	2.0%	7.6%
Not Needed	0.7%	0.5%	0.0%	1.5%	8.4%	1.4%	1.1%	4.5%

TABLE 8.9 GSS Responses About the Importance of Sex Education, Comparing Across Political Preferences and Races

How important ... sex education?

	Democrat	Republican	Independent	White	African American	Other
Essential	21.8%	10.7%	14.4%	16.0%	39.3%	18.4%
Very Important	29.8%	24.5%	28.1%	29.4%	11.4%	58.3%
Fairly Important	34.2%	27.8%	40.5%	35.2%	26.4%	18.4%
Not Very Important	10.5%	26.1%	9.0%	11.7%	9.3%	0.0%
Not Needed	3.7%	10.8%	8.0%	7.7%	13.5%	4.9%

$\chi^2 = 21.49$; $p = 0.006$; conf $= 99.4\%$ $\chi^2 = 69.2$; $p < 0.001$; conf $> 99.9\%$

Clearly, American adults think that some lessons are more important than others. Reading, writing, and math top the list of valued subjects, followed by science and technology, job training, and the liberal arts. Sex education has the lowest support. Nearly half say that respect for authority and discipline are "extremely important," while only a quarter say the same about concern for others. Most people think all these lessons are worthwhile. "Sex education" and "concern for others" are the most frequent to be named "not very important" or "not needed," but those answers are still in the minority: 80.6% and 87.9%, respectively, say they are at least fairly important.

The more interesting question, though, is whether different kinds of people have different judgments about what should be taught. We would expect so, but it's always worth seeing what's actually going on. That's what research is all about!

Table 8.9 shows what people think about teaching sex education to 15-year-olds. The left part of the table divides people according to their preferred political party. The right part divides them by race. The table shows some very interesting patterns.

First, we see that the columns are not at all alike. Democrats, Republicans, and Independents have very different attitudes toward sex education. So do Whites, African Americans, and those of other races (which are lumped together in this chart)[8].

Briefly, Democrats are much more supportive of schools teaching 15-year-olds about sex. Republicans are the least supportive, and those choosing neither major party fall somewhere in between. Far fewer Whites than Blacks think that sex education is "essential," but fewer also think that it is "not needed." African Americans are more divided on the subject. However, over three quarters of the members of other races think that sex education in high schools is either "essential" or "very important."

TABLE 8.10	GSS Responses About the Importance of Teaching Science and Technology, Comparing Across Three Religious Tendencies			
How important ... science and technology?				
	Fundamentalist	Moderate	Liberal	Total
Essential	41.0%	44.3%	39.1%	41.0%
Very Important	36.3%	35.1%	37.4%	37.1%
Fairly Important	21.2%	17.7%	18.9%	19.2%
Not Very Important	1.5%	2.9%	4.6%	2.8%
$\chi^2 = 4.06$; $p = 0.669$; conf $= 33.1\%$				

Take a look at the chi-square, the p value, and the confidence level at the bottom of the table. We can be 99.4% certain that Democrats, Republicans, and Independents have different attitudes about the importance of teaching sex education. We can be over 99.9% certain that Whites, African Americans, and the members of other races (grouped together) have different attitudes as well.

Now let's look at something that many people will find surprising. Table 8.10 shows how important various kinds of religious people think it is for high schools to teach science and technology. I've divided the religious people according to whether they consider their religious views to be "fundamentalist," "moderate," or "liberal." I've included only the "essential," "very important," "fairly important," and "not very important" rows. No one answered "not needed," so I've left out that one.

Clearly, there's not much difference between these columns. The percentages of fundamentalists, moderates, and liberals giving each answer are pretty much the same. Moreover, the chi-square calculation below the table confirms this. It tells us that there is only a 33% chance that the small differences between the columns that we see in the GSS sample reflect real differences in the population as a whole. That's less than a coin flip. We can say with confidence that the degree of religious fundamentalism or liberalism makes no difference to people's sense of the importance of teaching science to 15-year-olds.

It seems that the popular belief that religious fundamentalists are prejudiced against science is a myth! Some individuals may be, but most are not. Self-described fundamentalists are on the whole indistinguishable from religious moderates and religious liberals in their support for science instruction.[9]

What is the bottom line? There are two. First, you need to know what form your survey data take: categorical, ordinal, or interval/ratio. Second, you need to choose the analytic tool that best works with that kind of data. We've covered two possibilities in this chapter:

- For interval/ratio data, you can calculate means, ranges, and correlations.
- For ordinal and categorical data, you can create distributions and cross-tabulations.

I'll cover a third possibility in Chapter 10: how to work with interval/ratio and categorical data simultaneously. I'll also talk there about how to use control variables. These tools can be used with surveys, but they are best treated in the context of analyzing data collected from scales.

Practical Matters

There remain three practical matters to discuss in this chapter. First, I need to say a few words about questionnaire construction. Second, I need to remind you of some issues with sampling. Finally, I need to bring up some special issues raised by conducting surveys online.

Creating Your Questionnaire

How do you draft a questionnaire? The process seems easy: Just write clear questions that ask people for the information you want. That's a simple concept but one that is very hard to put into practice. Here are some potential problems:

- *Everyone has to be able to understand your questions in the same way.* The word *quite,* for example, is equivalent to the word *very* in American English and to the word *fairly* in British English. An American millennial might use the word *awesome* where an Australian would use the word *ripper.* Examples are legion. Researchers have to make sure that everyone interprets their survey questions in the same way.
- *A complete set of response options is needed for each survey question.* You can't, for example, ask people to mark their age-group and limit their choices to 0–17, 18–30, 31–40, 51–60, and 61+. What is the 45-year-old to do?
- *Respondents should check only one answer, unless you want them to check more.* If you ask for age using the categories 0–18, 18–30, 30–40, 40–50, 50–60, and 60+, you'll get two answers from the 18-, 30-, 40-, 50-, and 60-year-olds.
- *Questions should not encourage biased answers.* The question "How was your sociology class last semester?" needs to offer more options than "pretty good," "very good," "fantastic," and "extraordinary." This ordinal variable includes only the top half of the scale. What if your respondent thought the class bombed?
- *Questions should ask for only one thing at a time.* Asking "What is the cheapest and best cell phone service?" causes problems for someone who thinks that the cheapest service is not necessarily the best. Split up such questions, so that you get the information you want.

Here are a few things you should be sure to do:

- *Focus your questions on the survey topic.* This helps people understand what you are asking.
- *Ask people about things they know about.* Ask dog trainers about training dogs, teachers about teaching, and chefs about cooking. You can expand this when you are asking about matters of general interest. You can, for example, ask chefs about politics, but you probably can't ask politicians about being a chef. Target your questionnaire to the people who can give you the information you need.
- *Include a "Don't Know" or "No Opinion" option where appropriate.* Even people with expertise sometimes have no opinion about some part of a topic. You want to know what percentage of your population thinks they don't know enough to respond.
- *Phrase your questions simply and positively.* Asking teachers to agree or disagree with the statement that "small-group exercises are useful" is better than asking them to agree or disagree that "small-group exercises should not be abolished." The first is easy to understand; the second is not.
- *Organize your questions into a natural flow.* Usually, you'll want to put questions on a single topic together, so that your respondents can see the connection between them. This helps people finish the survey without getting bored, confused, or angry.
- *Test your survey.* Test it on the kind of people you will be targeting. Ask them whether they found any questions confusing, difficult, or ambiguous. Then test again until you get everything right.

I won't go on. Whole books have been written about questionnaire construction, and there is no point in replicating that information here. Building a good questionnaire isn't rocket science, but it is a learned skill. It's worth taking some time to do it right.

Sampling (Again)

We covered sampling basics in Chapter 5. Here, I just want to remind you of what you need to do to make sampling work.

The short answer is that you need to use a random sample: one that makes sure that every member of your population has an equal chance to get into the sample. If you do this, and your sample is large enough, then you can draw conclusions about the population as a whole based solely on your sample results.

The GSS, for example, uses an extremely well-designed random sampling system. If 54% of its 3,000 respondents answer one of its questions yes and 46% answer that question no, then you can be 95% confident that between 55.8% and 52.2% of the U.S. adult population as a whole would answer yes and between 47.8% and 44.2% would answer no. That's a margin of error of 1.8%.

To survey my university's 2,400 students with similar accuracy, I would need to include 1,326 of them in my sample. That's too many, so I would most likely increase my margin of error to 3%, which would drop my sample size to 739. Increasing the margin of error even further to 5% would drop my sample size to 331. A 5% margin of error, though, would mean that I could no longer be 95% certain that the yes-no ratio of 54%–46% indicates a real difference in the student population. The yes range would be 5 percentage points on either side of 54% (59%–49%) and the no range also would be 5 points on either side of 46% (51%–41%). These ranges overlap. I could no longer say that the yeses outnumbered the noes among students as a whole.

Remember the relationship between level of sample size, margin of error, and confidence level, which we encountered in Chapter 5 (Figure 8.3).

Also remember: Sampling works only when you choose your respondents randomly. Standing outside the student cafeteria and surveying every fifth person would not produce a random sample. It would poll only those students who ate their meals there. Moreover, it would sample only those who used the main entrance. That would be a very poor way to survey the student body.

Surveying Online

These issues with sampling become terribly relevant when you try to collect survey data online. Done poorly, a Web survey is even worse than standing outside the student cafeteria. At least at the cafeteria, you know where you are and who is coming and going. On the Web, you have no idea who is filling out your survey.

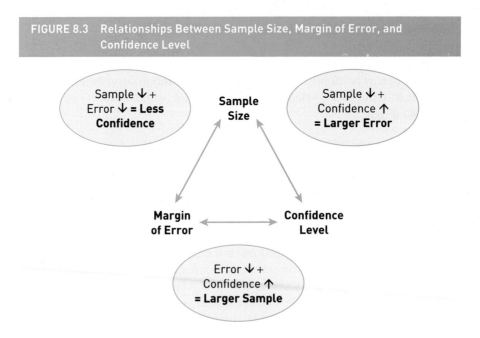

FIGURE 8.3   Relationships Between Sample Size, Margin of Error, and Confidence Level

You know the joke: "On the Internet, nobody knows you're a dog."[10] Maybe dogs don't fill out Internet surveys, but survey bots do. These are robot programs that crawl the Web, locating and filling in surveys that they encounter. Ever wonder why those online news sites report such weird results about what their readers are saying? Mostly, their surveys aren't completed by readers. They're completed by automated software designed to ruin real data collection.

Some bots aren't totally automatic. As of this writing, for example, the Chrome browser extension JunkFill randomly inserts junk answers into forms its users encounter while Web surfing. It's an aggressive response to website owners' attempts to collect and sell data from their visitors. The program's author writes, "Most web forms . . . are long and annoying. People would just give junk responses anyway. JunkFill only facilitates the process."[11]

This makes online surveys much less useful than we once hoped. You have to work around such issues, if you are to get good data. Fortunately, that's possible with proper planning. Here's a short list of rules:

- *Don't just release your survey into the wild.* Use a professional, protected website that gives one-time access only to those people to whom you have given a specific link. This prevents dogs, bots, trolls, and multiple survey entries from messing up your results.
- *Construct your sample offline, and then ask the sample members if they would be willing to participate.* If they say yes, then send them a link to the survey site. If they say no, then choose the next person on your randomized list. Once they've gotten the link, you'll get a report from the site operator showing who has completed the survey and who has not. You can then send out reminders to increase your response rate.
- *Pay attention to your user interface.* You want the survey to seem simple, to be easy to use, and to have eye appeal. Make your survey pages short and easy to read. That keeps people going.
- *Make sure you have some way to show people how much of the survey is left to do.* This keeps them from leaving the survey when they realize that the "10-minute survey" they've been promised will take them three times that long. The Web makes people impatient. Web surveys have to be shorter than other kinds.
- *Don't ask intrusive questions.* I can't count the number of surveys I've abandoned because they asked for information that I wouldn't want to give out on the Web. Most people have been scammed too often to trust websites with much. They'll quit the moment they think you're after too much.

Beyond these tips, you'll want to make sure that your respondents know as much as possible about your project. You need them to see its importance and to want to participate. Experienced Web users are both impatient and skittish.

Inexperienced users can get lost in complexities. You want both types to finish the survey. Otherwise, your data won't be of much use.

I could go on. There are, however, an increasing number of books on the subject, plus guides put out by most of the survey hosting sites.[12] I've introduced you to the principles; you can find details there.

Research Ethics

What ethical issues arise in survey research? The same principles apply to survey research as to all other kinds:

- Everyone you survey needs to give informed consent before participating.
- Participants need to know the purpose of the research and how its results will be used.
- You need to make sure that participants cannot be harmed by participating.
- You need to take special care when surveying vulnerable populations: children, prisoners, sick people, pregnant women, and the like.

Applying these principles in practice, however, depends on your answers to three interlocking questions. First, are you creating a new survey that is specifically tailored to your own research, or are you using a survey that someone else has developed? Second, are you collecting data yourself, or will you use data that someone has already collected? Third, if you are collecting your own data, what specific population do you wish to poll?

No matter how you answer these questions, your project will always need Institutional Review Board approval. Your answers will, however, shape the safeguards you have to put in place.

Put briefly, if you create your own survey, you will need to make sure that the questions you ask do not potentially harm your survey participants. This is more than just a matter of getting their informed consent to answering them. You actively have to protect people from harm. There are several common ways to do this. For example, you can make sure that participants' names are not on their answer sheets and that the list of their names is kept separate both from those sheets and also from their contact information. You can put code numbers on each, but you need to keep the lists separate from each other and the codes secure. Usually that means under lock and key or on a password-protected computer in an encrypted file. This prevents anyone from tracing specific answers back to specific people or to those people's addresses. It prevents anyone from knowing exactly whom you surveyed.

Here's another consideration: You need to make sure that your questions are appropriate to your research objectives. To use an extreme example, you do not want to ask people about weird sexual practices on a survey about nutrition. That question is irrelevant to your project, and it has the potential of getting your participants in trouble. For some people, it could even produce a psychological response—for example, if a research participant had been sexually abused. It's okay to ask about traumas if that is your research topic (though you will have to raise the questions gently and make it clear that participants can leave your study if they feel uncomfortable). There's no point in asking such questions unless that's your topic of investigation.

Moreover, asking such irrelevant questions will likely raise people's suspicions about the true point of your research. They may cease trusting you and withdraw—which they have the right to do at any time. This results in a skewed sample, because the people who remain in the sample will be systematically different from those who do not. How? They will be willing to answer irrelevant and possibly offensive questions. Only some people will do that, and they may not be typical of your target population. This makes it hard for you to draw conclusions about that population as a whole.

This is generally less of a problem with surveys that have been developed previously. The questions on the General Social Survey (GSS), for example, are very well tested and do not cause this kind of problem. You can use such questions in your own work, though your IRB will want to review them. Point out that you are using established questions, show their relevance to your research topic, and you will be on the right track.

If you are collecting your own data, you need to get informed consent from participants and need to tell them about your project's purpose. You also need to let them know exactly how you will protect their privacy, who will see the data, how the data will be reported, and so on. This is more than just politeness. It lets them decide whether or not to take part.

There is a side benefit to doing all of this, by the way: It encourages people to participate in your project. People like to be part of projects that they think are worthwhile. If you show your participants that they will be part of a great project, and that you will protect them from any possible harm for doing so, then they are more apt to join in. People like to do good things for others. That's the kind of active participation you want.

Of course, this is not an issue if you use an existing survey for which someone else has already collected the data and passed IRB authorization. That's the case with the GSS. If you use such data for your project, you do not need to take extra steps to protect any research subjects. The National Opinion Research Center (which runs the GSS) has already done so. You don't know who answered their questionnaires, and you will not be able to find out. Nor can you identify individuals from the dataset you analyze. You thus cannot harm the survey participants. You'll simply tell your IRB that you are using previously collected data, from which it is impossible to identify individuals. Protection accomplished!

For other surveys, the level of protection depends on who is being polled. Consider this chapter's examples. The NCES and McKenna and colleagues created their own questionnaires and collected their own data. This meant they had to pay attention both to their survey instruments and to their target populations.

THINK ABOUT IT
What information would you like me to protect?

The NCES safety survey polled school principals, who do not need special protection. Not only are they not a protected class, but they were reporting facts from their workplaces rather than their own personal attitudes. Keeping track of these facts is part of their jobs. Participating in the survey cannot do them any harm. Moreover, the research reported aggregate data for U.S. schools as a whole, not data for individual schools. Thus, no schools can get in trouble for not having specific safety measures in place.

McKenna and colleagues' reading survey polled schoolchildren, who *are* a protected population—though some kinds of educational research can get expedited IRB approval. Such surveys always need special scrutiny. Clearly, though, the questions on this survey were not invasive, and circling cartoon Garfields did the children no harm. To further protect individual children, the classroom teachers removed students' names from the data before sending them in. The final research reports drew conclusions about categories of children (e.g., boys/girls, high/low readers, ethnic groups), not about individuals. This was sufficient protection.

As you can see, survey research is complicated. It is also a valuable research technique. The key point to remember is the type of data you are seeking. Surveys are best used for asking questions that can be answered quickly and are easily understood by all kinds of people. They are thus ideal for collecting people's shallow opinions and attitudes, for collecting relatively superficial identities, and for collecting quick reports of acts.

Review Questions

1. What types of data can you collect with surveys?

2. Why are surveys useful for collecting data from large numbers of people?

3. What is a random sample? Why does survey research need to use random samples, if it is to draw conclusions about a population as a whole?

4. What are the differences between interval/ratio data, ordinal data, and categorical data? What kinds of data analysis do you use for each?

5. What are some effective ways of protecting survey participants?

The open-access Student Study Site at study.sagepub.com/spickard has a variety of useful study tools, including SAGE journal articles, video & web resources, eFlashcards, and quizzes.

Notes

1. These three survey reports were released on May 21, 2015, while I was writing this chapter. Their sources are the National Center for Educational Statistics, "Public School Safety and Discipline"; Augusta, Georgia, Continuum of Care, "Annual Homeless Count"; and Quality Care Commission (UK), "Annual Survey of Hospital Care."

2. National Center for Educational Statistics, "Public School Safety and Discipline, 2013–2014." Retrieved from http://nces.ed.gov/pubs2015/2015051.pdf

3. I've used fictional data to illustrate how weighting works. The NCES report didn't include the raw figures.

4. Michael C. McKenna et al., "Children's Attitudes Toward Reading: A National Survey," *Reading Research Quarterly* 30 (1995): 934–956.

5. Joshua D. Angrist and Victor Lavy, "Using Maimonides' Rule to Estimate the Effect of Class Size on Student Achievement," *NBER Working Paper* #5888, 1997. Retrieved from http://www.nber.org/papers/w5888.pdf

6. In 1994, the GSS shifted from surveying about 1,500 people every year to surveying about 3,000 people every two years.

7. These and other data are available through the University of California's Survey Data Archive (http://sda.berkeley.edu/archive.htm). The archive includes software to analyze results online.

8. These are mostly Asians, along with a few Native Americans and Pacific Islanders. As on the U.S. Census, the GSS considers Latinos an ethnic group, not a race.

9. Elaine Howard Ecklund made this point in her study of scientists at elite American universities. Her book *Science vs. Religion: What Scientists Really Think* (Oxford, 2010) is well worth reading. It is a fine piece of well-designed survey and interview research.

10. This phrase began as the caption of a 1993 *New Yorker* cartoon by Peter Steiner. It has since become an Internet meme.

11. Quote taken from the JunkFill page in the Chrome web store. The author adds, "JunkFill is [also] a decent tool for testing your own annoying web forms :)."

12. See, for example, Jelke Bethlehem and Silvia Biffignandi, *Handbook of Web Surveys*. Wiley, 2011. Survey hosting sites include SurveyMonkey.com and SnapSurveys.com.

CHAPTER 9

Interviewing: Deep Talk to Gather Several Types of Data

	Type of Data						
Talking With People	Reports of acts, behavior, or events	Self-identity	Opinions and attitudes (deeply held)	Personal feelings	Cultural knowledge	Expert knowledge	Experience as it presents itself to consciousness
In-depth interviews	X	X	X	X	X	X	
Phenomenological interviews			(X)				X
Critical incident interviews	X		(X)		(X)	X	
Focus groups			(X)		X	X	

(Row label, left side: Data Collection Method)

As you learned in Chapter 8, surveys are a good way to collect people's relatively shallow opinions, identities, and reports of behavior. They scratch the surface, but they let you collect data from large numbers of people.

What do you do, though, if you want something deeper: things that are too complex to be captured by check-the-box or single-word responses?

Perhaps you want to learn the details about something that has happened to people. Maybe you want a deep understanding of people's attitudes toward life. Maybe you want a detailed account of what everyone in a particular social setting knows—what we call "common cultural knowledge." Maybe you want to learn what experts think about a given topic, and we all know that experts' views are far too detailed for surveys to be of much help. Or perhaps you want people to tell you about things they have experienced—not just their thoughts but their sense perceptions, their feelings, and what those experiences felt like from the inside.

These kinds of data ask you to go beneath the surface. You aren't going for shallow stuff; you are interested in nuance. You want more than a quick summary—and certainly more than people can report on a survey instrument. That means you have to talk with them at some length. An in-depth interview will meet your needs.

There are several types of interviews, each of which collects a different kind of data. **Hermeneutic interviews** let you collect reports of acts, behavior, or events at a deep level—far more than you can collect through a social survey. They also let you gather details about people's deeply held opinions and attitudes. **Expert interviews** collect the views of experts: people with special knowledge about a topic who can provide detailed information. **Phenomenological interviews** collect detailed accounts of people's experiences. None of these things can be captured by asking people multiple-choice questions or whether they agree or disagree with simple phrases. These types of data call for in-depth conversations.

Interviews can capture other things as well, such as people's deep-level *self-identities*, their deep *personal feelings*, and their *cultural knowledge*. The first two of these are personal, while the last consists of things that everyone in a particular social scene knows. The interview techniques are similar, though each type of data puts its own spin on the interview process. The data analysis techniques are similar, too. So are the ethical issues that interview research raises.

Hermeneutic Interviews

First, let's look at interviews designed to collect people's deep accounts of events and actions, and also their deeply held opinions and attitudes toward life. Specialists call these *hermeneutic interviews*, after Hermes, the Greek messenger god. Just as Hermes helped the gods understand one another, hermeneutic interviews help interviewers understand the people they are interviewing. The term became popular in the late 19th century as a means of understanding Biblical texts by placing oneself in the shoes of the people who wrote them. Hermeneutic interviewing involves speaking, not texts, but it has the same aim: to tease out what the world looks like to one's conversation partner. The point is to understand, and then reexpress, other people's individual ways of seeing the world.[1]

These interviews have a common structure. Interviewers ask people to talk about events, actions, opinions, or attitudes. This produces words, which the interviewer takes in and tries to understand. Then the interviewer summarizes what she or he has heard, producing an interpretation. The interviewer then shares that interpretation with the interviewee, to see if it is right. Interviewees typically correct such interpretations, adding details and nuance. This produces more words, which the interviewer tries to understand, reinterprets, and feeds back to the interviewee again. Ideally, this goes on until the interviewee says, "Yes, you have understood me." Then the investigator is ready to write up a summary of what she or he has learned.

This process is known as the **hermeneutic circle** (Figure 9.1, on the next page). Let's see this in action.

FIGURE 9.1   The Hermeneutic Circle

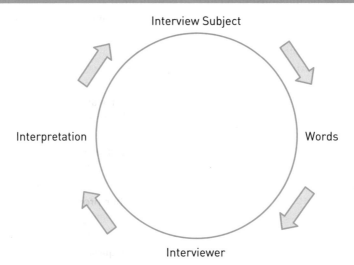

Interview Subject

Interpretation

Words

Interviewer

An Example: "Motherloss"

In 2000, sociologist Lynn Davidman published an interview study of 60 middle-aged men and women whose mothers had died when the interviewees were in their early teens.[2] Davidman was interested in three aspects of these people's lives. First, she wanted to hear their accounts of their loss: how it happened, their families' and relatives' responses, and what sense her interviewees made of those events at the time. Second, she wanted to get the interviewees' stories about the effects of their mothers' deaths on their subsequent lives. How did their loss affect their adult sense of self? Were they able to construct a coherent biography and restore a sense of having a "normal" life? If so, how did they do it? What did they now (at the time of the interview) see as the effects of having suffered such a traumatic event as young teens? Third, she wanted to uncover the cultural patterns that shaped both the families' responses to loss and the interviewees' later efforts to come to terms with not having a "normal" childhood. In-depth interviews gave her the right kind of data. Her book identified several common paths by which both the families and the interviewees responded to their early loss.

Six Steps How did Davidman structure her study? Like all good researchers, she first focused the list of issues she wanted to investigate. This helped her design her investigation. Here are her *research questions:*

1. What do the men and women describe as the events leading up to and following their mothers' deaths?
2. What do these people say are the lingering effects of their mothers' deaths on their subsequent lives? To what extent do they report having been able

to construct coherent life stories, and what life stories do they actually relate?

3. What is the relationship between these men's and women's narratives and the standard cultural narratives of the time (late 1950s/early 1960s) about the effect of parental death on families?

Crafting these questions was Step 1 of Davidman's research design process. The questions make it pretty clear that her project was a descriptive one. The questions called for her to describe what her interviewees told her. They also asked her to describe the relationship between her interviewees' narratives and the cultural patterns that historians, anthropologists, and scholars of family life have identified as being typical of their generation and era. The questions did not ask about cause, nor did they call for correlations, case studies, longitudinal research, and so on. Step 2, then, was to identify her project's *logical structure* as descriptive research.

The research questions similarly identified the *types of data* that Davidman needed. Take a close look at the language of her three questions. The first question—"What do the men and women . . . describe . . . ?"—asks for a *report of events*. The second question—"What do these people say . . . ?"—asks for their *deeply held opinions and attitudes*. So do the questions about their life stories. These data types are the first and third shown in the grid at the beginning of the chapter.

The third research question asks about something else. It asks about the relationships between these men's and women's stories and the cultural knowledge about family disruption that was common when these interviewees' mothers died. This *cultural knowledge* is the fifth data type in the grid at the beginning of the chapter. It calls for a bit of explanation.

Most societies have a set of common cultural beliefs about death and about family disruption. Those beliefs vary from society to society. They can also change between eras and between generations. Some societies and eras accept early death as normal (though it is never welcome). Other societies and eras see it as extremely abnormal and not to be talked about. All see it as posing particular problems for the remaining family members, though those problems are imagined to be different from place to place and time to time.

Davidman drew on extensive anthropological and historical research to identify the beliefs about parental death and family disruption that were common in the United States in the 1950s and early 1960s. This was the era of the Baby Boom: the largest birth cohort in American history. Boomers grew up in an era of relative prosperity, one in which an expanding middle class created a new suburbanism centered on stay-at-home moms and working dads. Popular entertainment celebrated this family structure. Television shows like *Leave It to Beaver* and the popular Disney movies portrayed two-parent, one-worker families as the norm. Death seldom intervened on television or in the movies, and when it did, it was sanitized. Dogs might die and be mourned (as in the film *Old Yeller*), but people seldom did, at least not those with whom viewers would identify.

Davidman noted two aspects of this cultural pattern. First, death was not talked about, nor were illnesses. She wrote about her own experience with this, as she was never told about her own mother's cancer until after her mother's death, and then none of her relatives helped her process her feelings. Second, the common culture imagined that families that suffered a parent's death were faced with one of two problems. If the father died, the issue was money: Who was going to support the family? If the mother died, money wasn't the problem but emotions were. Women were imagined to be the emotional center of family life. Who would keep the family on an even emotional keel? That gender-divided age could not conceive of emotionally strong men and breadwinning women. Cultural knowledge ran a different way.

Davidman's third research question was designed to see how her informants dealt with this situation. Did their families' experiences correspond to the common cultural expectations? What influence did such cultural beliefs have?

All three of Davidman's research questions called for in-depth accounts. Surveys could not produce that depth; in-depth interviews were the only way to go. Step 3 thus led directly to Step 4: the choice of in-depth interviews as a *data collection method.*

Step 5—the choice of a *data collection site*—was reasonably simple. Davidman's target population was men and women of the Baby Boom generation whose mothers had died when the interviewees were between the ages of 11 and 15. She advertised in several East Coast magazines for people willing to participate. From those who responded, she chose 30 men and 30 women. (Among other things, she wanted to see whether men's and women's experiences and stories were different.)

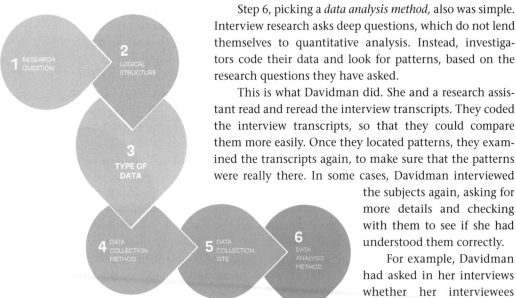

Step 6, picking a *data analysis method,* also was simple. Interview research asks deep questions, which do not lend themselves to quantitative analysis. Instead, investigators code their data and look for patterns, based on the research questions they have asked.

This is what Davidman did. She and a research assistant read and reread the interview transcripts. They coded the interview transcripts, so that they could compare them more easily. Once they located patterns, they examined the transcripts again, to make sure that the patterns were really there. In some cases, Davidman interviewed the subjects again, asking for more details and checking with them to see if she had understood them correctly.

For example, Davidman had asked in her interviews whether her interviewees had any rituals to honor their mothers, and she found that most of them said no.

Realizing later that the word *rituals* might have misled them, she got back in contact and asked whether they had any special ways of remembering their mothers: a piece of clothing, a set of photos, and so on. Nearly all of them had some special object or means of remembrance. Moreover, they treated these objects or activities as if they were sacred. One man, for example, smoked a cigarette at his mother's grave each year. He did not see this as ritual, but he did find it very meaningful. Davidman's commitment to the hermeneutic process helped her understand her interviewees more deeply.

That's the point. Hermeneutic interviewing aims to capture the world as our interview subjects see it. It is particularly appropriate when we want to collect our interviewees' deeply held beliefs, ideas, reports, impressions, and views.

Results What did Davidman learn from her study? She found not one pattern but several. First, she found that few of her families talked about the mother's death and those that did so talked about it only briefly. This was particularly true of fathers, who (in that era) were not expected to bare their negative or unhappy emotions, particularly around children. Her interviewees reported that their families had followed the dominant cultural pattern.

Second, she found that many fathers remarried quickly or otherwise found female relatives to take the absent mother's place. This was particularly true of the professional-class men. They hoped that someone else would reestablish the family's emotional center. Bringing in a mother replacement, of course, caused its own problems. Some children cast her as the "evil stepmother," blaming her for the consequences of their mothers' deaths. Others embraced her, particularly if the mother herself had not been very nurturing.

A few working-class families followed another pattern: They assigned the "mother" role to the eldest daughter, who became chief cook, child care worker, and emotional support for the other family members. These women recounted their sacrifices, though they were generally positive about their family outcomes. Their stories show the differences that social class brings.

Davidman described several other patterns in her interviewees' stories: in the treatment of death and grief, in the ways that families tried to reconstitute themselves, and in their varied responses to the cultural pressures of that era. Her book described her interviewees' feelings about their experiences, both positive and negative. In all, it is a rich read.

How to Write an Interview Protocol

Davidman included a list of her interview questions as an appendix to her book—her **interview protocol**, to use professional jargon. This was a great gift for budding researchers. Readers can see what she asked and in what order. They can learn how she structured her conversations. Interviewing is a skill, and there is no one-size-fits-all approach. Having good models like hers helps you learn the ropes.

That said, there are some general guidelines that make interviews go well. Good interviewers plan their interviews carefully, making sure they gather the information needed to meet their research objectives. They write good questions and they put their questions in a coherent order, so that the interview flows like a good conversation: smoothly and easily. They make sure that the interviewees know in advance what they will be asked, so that they will be comfortable giving complete answers. They make sure that the interviewees know that they can decline to answer some questions, if they choose, or even withdraw from the study, if they change their minds about participating. And they find ways to record things accurately. The sections that follow provide some details about each of these guidelines.

Structuring Your Interview My first paid research job was at an unnamed East Coast university, where I was an assistant on a project evaluating two drug-treatment programs. I was not in charge of the research, but it taught me a lot about what not to do. The main problem was that the project director had no idea what we were supposed to be looking for. We were directed to interview people who had drug addictions, but we weren't given any advice about what to ask them. So we asked a lot of questions, most of which gave us little or no real sense of those people's lives. The project failed because it didn't start where it should have, with a *central research question.*

That's where all interview research begins. Following Tom Wengraf, who has written a helpful book about interviewing,[3] we'll call this central research question a *CRQ.* Figure 9.2 sets this question at the center of our process.

For Davidman, this CRQ was "How do the men and women interviewed report wrestling with the aftermaths of their mothers' early deaths, in the context of a culture that failed to talk frankly with children about death and that saw mothers as the emotional centers of their families?" (This CRQ combines her three research

---

FIGURE 9.2 Structuring Your Interview: Central Research Question (CRQ)

CRQ

Source: Tom Wengraf: Qualitative Research Interviewing (Sage, 2001)

---

questions into a single overarching question—at the cost of making it considerably less readable.)

Next, we consult the scholarly literature. What questions does that literature tell us that we have to answer, if we are to answer this CRQ? These become the actual research questions. In Davidman's case, we have already seen three of them. We need the interviewees' reports of what happened around the time of their mothers' deaths; we need the interviewees' reports of the lingering effects of those events on their subsequent lives; and we need to ask the interviewees about whether their families tabooed talk about the death and reconstituted the family's emotional center—and if so, how. Wengraf calls such questions *theory-based questions* or *TQs.* Answering them makes answering the CRQ possible (Figure 9.3).

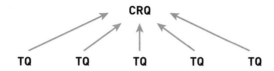

FIGURE 9.3   Structuring Your Interview: Theory-Based Questions (TQs)

Source: Tom Wengraf: Qualitative Research Interviewing (Sage, 2001)

You can layer these questions, of course. For example, the literature on the 1950s and 1960s predicts several ways in which a family can create mother-substitutes. We've mentioned two: a quick remarriage and a daughter stepping into the mother role. Besides these, some families have aunts who take over child care. Others bring in a grandmother. In still others, the kids move in with grandma and the father devotes himself to work. In a few, the father even takes on the mother role, becoming a "Mommy-Daddy" to the kids, nurturing the family as well as supporting it financially. Suitable TQs will help sort out which of these is happening. They will also help you create *interview questions (IQs)* that provide the needed details.

That's the next step, of course: to craft the actual questions that you'll be asking (Figure 9.4). Theory-based questions are too general, too all-encompassing, and frequently couched in such academic jargon that ordinary people have a hard time answering them. It would not be a good idea, for example, for Davidman to have asked her interviewees, "Did your family taboo talking about your mother's illness and death, because of the American cultural reluctance to admit that death is a part of life?" That question might elicit a "Could you repeat that?" or a "Huh? What's that supposed to mean?" or at best something that sounds like an answer but doesn't really tell you much. People need to understand clearly what they are being asked, if they are to give you the details you need.

The trick is to break down the TQs into smaller parts, so that people can answer them easily. "How did your mother die?" "How did you hear about it?" If

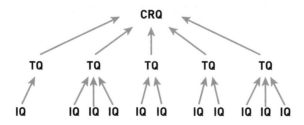

FIGURE 9.4   Structuring Your Interview: Interview Questions (IQs)

Source: Tom Wengraf: Qualitative Research Interviewing (Sage, 2001)

she was ill, "When did you learn that she was sick?" and "Did anyone tell you what was the matter with her?" Small questions like these, suitably combined, let you answer the more abstract questions that you are investigating. Figure 9.4 illustrates the process.

The interviewees' answers to the IQs should, collectively, answer one or more of the TQs. The answers to the TQs, taken collectively, should answer the CRQ. You work downward to create your interview protocol, and then you work upward to let your interviews answer your research question. It's very straightforward, so long as you plan what you are going to do.

Writing Good Questions What makes a question good for interviewing? Three characteristics stand out:

1. *Ask clear questions.* Your interviewees have to know what you are talking about, and they have to see quickly how to respond. They don't have to know the whole answer—at least not right away. But they have to see how to start. You can always guide them deeper, but you can't do that unless you ask them clear questions. If they're confused, your interview stalls, both of you get uncomfortable, and you don't end up learning anything. Clear questions get people going. Fuzzy or incoherent ones kill conversations.

2. *Ask somewhat open-ended questions.* In-depth interviews want details, and you get those details only if people keep talking. You have to ask questions that are easy to start but deep enough to get the details you need. You don't want people to finish too quickly. It helps to have follow-ups ready, too. They let you dive deeper.

3. *Ask for examples.* The question "Can you tell me about a time when . . . ?" usually elicits depth. So does "What would you do if . . . ?" These questions call for stories, and stories let people give concrete answers. They also let you ask follow-up questions that draw forth subtleties. That's the key to in-depth interviewing: capturing the nuances that survey research misses.

I won't say more here because there are lots of books on how to write good interview questions. Wengraf's *Qualitative Research Interviewing* covers this topic well. You can also consult studies like Davidman's, to see what master interviewers do, or you can look at how other scholars have constructed interviews on your research topic. Not everyone publishes a full interview protocol, but you can often find specific questions in the text. If you find a question that seems perfect, use it. Scholarship is all about building on what others have done before.

Making It Flow Now that you have your questions, you have to make the interview flow. In addition to being logical and clear, interviews also need to engage your informants. Asking a long string of rather specific questions seldom does this. Nor does it typically encourage informants to give you more than you asked for—the rich detail that enlivens their accounts and deepens your understanding of them.

Fortunately, this is relatively simple to do. You take the list of interview questions (IQs) and rearrange them so that they create an interesting conversation. Typically, you start with something simple that's easy for your interviewees to answer, for example, "Tell me how old you are." You can then follow up with "How old were you when your mother died?" "What do you remember about that time of life?" "What kind of kid were you?" and "What were your favorite things?" Such questions set people at ease, so they are comfortable talking with you before you ask them for the hard stuff. Then they're ready and committed by the time you get to the main topic. Figure 9.5 illustrates a good pattern to follow.

You first get your interviewee talking and then you ask some harder questions—ones that make your conversation partner think. After a bit of depth, you back off. This keeps the interview from being a long slog. Then you dive into the deepest part of your conversation, which is often the most personal. Finally, you end the interview with a series of relatively easy questions. This brings both of you back to ordinary life.

Getting this right takes practice. Davidman does it well. In fact, she is one of the best interviewers I have ever known. She got that way by practicing, and you should, too. Use your CRQ and your TQs to create the IQs that you want to ask. Shape those interview questions so that they make a good conversation. Then practice on your friends. Get their feedback, modify the protocol, and practice again. Sooner or later, you'll develop the skills you need.

One last hint: Listen carefully to what your interviewees tell you. Nothing stops an interview faster than when people think that you don't really care about what they have to say. If you're tired or distracted, put off the interview until you can focus. You need to be completely involved with the people you interview. That's the only way to get rich data.

FIGURE 9.5   Sample Flow for Interview Questions

A few harder questions

Deepest conversation

Slow opening

Relax a bit

Easy end

Informed Consent Interview studies demand informed consent. This means that your interviewees need to know in advance what your study is about, what you will ask them, how you will use what they tell you, and how you will protect their privacy. This is a basic principle of research ethics. You must ensure that people's participation does not harm them in any way. They also have to be able to withdraw from the study at any time—even after the interview is over. They need to be the judge of whether or not they participate.

The only exception to such full disclosure is if you have to deceive your research participants in order to collect the information you need. This is extremely rare in interview research. In that case, you have to convince your Institutional Review Board that the knowledge you gain outweighs the cost of your deception. If your IRB approves, it will usually require that you debrief your participants after the study. It will sometimes require that you allow them to rescind their consent. You will certainly have to take extra steps to make sure that their privacy is protected, even if doing so inconveniences you. Anything else would violate your intellectual duty.

What do such informed consent documents look like? They typically have several parts. Besides the list of questions, you have to provide a summary of your project that lists its purpose, your target audience, how you will draw conclusions from your data, and the form in which you intend to publish those results.

You need to tell your interviewees whether they will remain anonymous and, if so, how you intend to protect their anonymity. Most researchers assign code letters to each interviewee and store the identifying particulars in a locked file separately from the interview transcripts. Some also ask the interviewees to choose a pseudonym for use in any publications. In the United States, researchers typically agree to destroy the raw interviews after a certain date, as well as to destroy all means of identifying the individuals who have been interviewed. This might be two or five years after the project closes.

You also need to identify any potential risks to the study participants. You don't need to get paranoid about this; space aliens will not likely beam up your data for their interstellar amusement. However, some research topics may trigger traumatic memories, unresolved psychological issues, and the like. If that happens, let your participants know that you can give them a list of counselors to see (at their expense), and remind them that they can decide to withdraw from the study at any time.

This has happened to me. When it has, I've torn the pages out of my notebook and handed them to the interviewee and have done the same with the tape that I was using to record the interview. That's harder with digital equipment, but it's easy to show someone that you've erased his or her file.

To Tape or Not to Tape? This brings us to the final issue: Should you tape your interviews? Or should you just take paper-and-pencil notes? Both work, though a balancing act is involved. The decision depends on the interview topic, and it pits your concern for your interviewees' privacy against your concern for recording their views accurately. Interviewees want to feel safe. They also want you to get their information right. I often give people the choice. I use tape as the default but ask them if they would mind if I tape the interview or if they would rather I just took notes about it. Most people choose tape but a few do not. I follow their wishes.

Sometimes you absolutely do not want to tape your interviews. That's when you are collecting rather simple information and you especially need to protect your informants. For example, some years ago one of my classes was asked to interview a set of homeless people in my university town. Homeless people are not a formally protected population, as are children, prisoners, hospital patients, pregnant women, and a few others. They are, however, extremely vulnerable. We not only didn't tape them; we also didn't put any names, pseudonyms, or the like on the interview notes. We interviewed them in teams (two students for each), and the teams debriefed afterward to make sure they had the data written down correctly. Our IRB agreed that even having the participants sign an informed consent document could cause them trouble, so it allowed verbal permission, heard by both team members. This is an extreme case, but the results ultimately helped our local homeless people far more than the data collection process endangered them.

If you do tape, you will have to transcribe the interviews before you analyze them. Here's a trick to make this easy. Get yourself some voice recognition software and train it so that it can type out whatever you tell it. Then play your tape, using an earbud or headphones so that the computer mic can't pick up what the tape is saying. Listen to the tape and speak the words into your computer. The software will recognize your voice and record what you are saying.

This isn't hard. It may, however, take a few interviews before it flows smoothly. It's worthwhile on three counts. First, you don't have to pay someone to transcribe the tapes for you. That's always helpful to your research budget. Second, you have to review the tapes anyway, so this gets two things done at the same time. Third, you can also add in clarifying comments where needed ("Open bracket. She was referring to her ex-husband. Close bracket.") The result is an accurate set of transcribed interviews that you know well.

Coding Your Data

Once you've transcribed your interviews, you can code your data. We covered this in Chapter 6, so I won't say a lot about it now. As I noted there, having a good interview protocol gives you a head start on your coding. You know which of your interview questions will help you answer your theory-based questions—the questions that you drew from the scholarly literature. Put the actual questions you asked people on the left side of a table and the TQs and IQs across the top. Then mark an "X" to show which of the questions that you asked will help you answer the TQ/IQ combinations. I showed you how to do this in Chapter 6. Table 9.1 (next page) is similar to Table 6.6, with the TQs and IQs marked. This table was drawn from an interview study about good places to work.

Once you've built your table, the next step is to go through your transcripts with your IQs, TQs, and CRQs in mind. Write down any words or phrases that you think summarize some aspect of your data. For example, for Row 1, Column A, in

TABLE 9.1   Sample Coding Scheme: Factors Making for a Good Place to Work (With TQs and IQs Identified)

Actual Questions	Factors Identified in the Literature							
	Aspects of the Job (TQ)			Organizational Structure (TQ)		Organizational Culture (TQ)		
	A: Job uses skills? (IQ)	B: Job provides growth? (IQ)	C: (etc.) (IQ)	D: Clear chain of command? (IQ)	E: Structure aids workflow? (IQ)	F: Comfort with the style? (IQ)	G: Stable style? (IQ)	H: (etc.) (IQ)
1. Let's start by telling us about your job. What do you do here?	X			X				
2. What aspects of the job appeal to you?	X	X			X	X		
3. Did you expect this when you were hired?	X		X	X				X
4. What attracted you about the company?		X			X	X	X	
5. Did you have any qualms or concerns?		X		X			X	
6. What do you wish you had known then?	X	X			X			X
...								

Table 9.1 you might be interested in the kinds of skills a particular job demands. You might want to track different kinds of skills, for example, "thinking skills," "manual skills," "interpersonal skills," and so on. Row 4, Column B, might draw forth "personal growth," "skill growth," "intellectual growth," "interpersonal growth," and the like. Other boxes on that row might produce "good work team," "predictability," and so on.

You would also want to list other things that make jobs attractive: "salary," "opportunity for advancement," "better position," "less stress," and whatever else you can think of. These terms become your starting codes:

- thinking skills
- manual skills
- interpersonal skills
- . . .

- personal growth
- skill growth
- intellectual growth
- interpersonal growth
- . . .

- good work team
- predictability
- salary
- advancement
- less stress
- . . .

Examine your transcripts, marking paragraphs that contain something connected to these concepts. You might, for example, find a paragraph that talks about "thinking skills," "personal growth," and "opportunities for advancement." Mark that paragraph with all three codes. It's pretty easy to do this with a word processor by adding those terms as comments to the text. Or you can use qualitative data analysis (QDA) software such as NVivo, MAXQDA, QDA Miner, or the like. Each of these programs lets you apply codes to paragraphs or to portions of text, and then you can retrieve all the texts that have the same coding. You could, for example, retrieve all the segments of all of your interviews in which your informants refer to intellectual growth. That lets you look for commonalities.

There are two important things to realize about such coding. First, coding and retrieval are no substitutes for thought. As I said in Chapter 6, I've heard people claim that they plan to "code the transcripts and see what categories emerge." Categories never *emerge* from the data by themselves! You coded the data, so you put the categories there. What emerges (or doesn't) is a set of relationships between the categories, which you notice only after you've collected all of the paragraphs that you've coded alike.

Let's say, for example, that you are looking over all of those paragraphs that you've coded "intellectual growth" and you find that most of them also contain codes for "less stress." Interesting! Is there some relationship between people wanting intellectual growth in a job and also wanting less stress? Go back and read those paragraphs to see if you can tease out what's really going on.

The codes make it easier for you to see such patterns. It's then up to you to identify them. Saying "I'll code the transcripts and see what categories emerge" makes no more sense than does saying "I'll throw these numbers into a statistics program and see what it tells me." Coding, QDA software, and statistical software don't produce research results on their own. You have to produce those results. Computer programs are just tools.

Second, qualitative coding doesn't need software to work well. As mentioned in Chapter 6, QDA software is merely a mechanized version of the pre-computer process that involved copying transcripts, cutting them into paragraphs, and sorting them into piles on the living room floor. The software sorts pieces of interviews according to codes that you've inserted, letting you see all the paragraphs with a single code in one place. Learning to code and to use QDA software makes interview analysis much easier. It helps you understand what your interviewees are telling you.

Interviews With Experts

Hermeneutic interviews get at people's deeply held opinions and attitudes, along with their detailed reports of events and actions. These tend to be personal, and they don't typically produce technical accounts of things like how to fly an airplane, how to manage a sewage treatment facility, or how to intervene in a medical crisis. Instead, they usually focus on individuals: those individuals' views, their personal reactions to things that have happened to them, and the like.

What if you don't want that individuality? What if you want technical accounts? Maybe you need to collect pilots' accounts of a particular mechanical failure? Maybe you want to debrief longtime sewage plant technicians so that you can train their replacements when they retire. These people are experts, and you want their expert knowledge. How does interviewing experts differ from interviewing ordinary people?

In some ways, there isn't much difference. Most steps of the process are the same. You still have to review other research on the topic, so that you'll know what topics to bring up. You still have to create an interview protocol and then turn that protocol into questions that maintain your interviewees' interest in the conversation. You also have make sure that you've understood what your interviewees are telling you. All of these steps are important, but reviewing previous research is especially important when you interview experts. Most experts don't like to waste their time educating you about things that you can find out on your own, so they aren't apt to cooperate well if they think you are unprepared. To use a school analogy, you have to do your homework. Otherwise, experts won't think your research is worthwhile.

Assuming that you've prepared, interviewing experts one-on-one is a lot like the hermeneutic interviewing that I just described. The topic differs, but the structure of the interview does not.

Interviewing experts does, however, open up two new possibilities. The first involves detailed interviews with experts about critical incidents in their work. The second involves interviewing several experts at once, in focus groups. We'll look at these possibilities in turn.

THINK ABOUT IT

When is it better to interview experts instead of interviewing ordinary people?

Critical Incident Interviews

Let's start with an example. In 1981, Christy Dachelet and her colleagues published a study of clinical nurse training based on a series of interviews with the program's preceptors.[4] These are the doctors and nurses who supervise nurse education. They were asked to identify the elements of an educational program at the University of Rochester Medical School that contributed the most and the least to nurse training. They were experts. Moreover, they were committed to improving the program rather than just defending it. They were thus the right people to ask about what was and wasn't working.

Wait a minute! Why not ask the students? Shouldn't they know what's going right and wrong? Not really. Students know what they like and don't like, but they don't have enough experience to tell which parts of a training program will be the most valuable. Long-term teachers do. Yes, students' views provide useful data, but they do not present a full picture. They provide evidence that, together with the experts' accounts, can generate solutions.

The key part of Dachelet's research was that she and her colleagues didn't just ask the experts for their opinions; they asked them to describe critical incidents that demonstrated what did and didn't help the students learn. They asked for detailed descriptions, with the experts' judgments of what went right and wrong.

For example, one supervisor described a particularly hectic day in the clinic, during which a beginning student was asked to help a patient who had a complex set of medical problems. That student was the only person available, but she was inexperienced and so was not able to identify exactly what care the patient needed. This critical incident highlighted the need to match patients to student skills. It also highlighted the need for more staffing on days when the clinic had a large number of patients to serve. Accounts such as this one identified several areas where the clinic needed better organization.

The critical incident technique was originally described by John Flanagan, based on his experiences working with the U.S. Air Force during World War II.[5] Flanagan and some colleagues were asked to help solve several key problems facing the armed forces. They sought, for example, to identify the specific factors that led pilots to flunk out of flight school. They examined pilots' reports of botched bombing raids to see what went wrong and how raid procedures could be improved. In all these cases, they asked experts to identify the critical elements that produced these outcomes. By comparing a large number of expert responses, they could identify common problems across a large number of cases. This let them make concrete changes that produced solutions.

Dachelet and her colleagues did this for nursing education. They asked the student nurses' supervisors to give them examples of successful and unsuccessful training efforts. This let them identify factors that hindered student learning as well as those that helped it. Among their recommendations for change, they identified the following:

> The high patient "no show" rate, the large portion of patients inappropriate to the student learner, . . . the demands placed on preceptors' time and energy, and the problems with the scheduling system were substantiated through the incidents reported.[6]

The key part of the critical incident technique is that it asks experts on a topic to describe particular cases in detail. This makes their recommendations specific. It also prevents them from retreating to generalizations that might not be accurate.

Collecting stories about specific incidents lets the interviewer draw conclusions across cases, without negating the experts' expertise. It makes good use of that expertise to draw practical conclusions.

Focus Groups

Focus groups are a bit different. They are essentially group interviews that focus on a particular problem or issue, designed to combine several perspectives and generate good conversations. They work best when the participants are evenly matched. They all have expertise to share, they all are willing to speak up, and they all are willing to listen to each other rather than try to impose their own views. The ideal group size is five to eight participants. That's small enough so that everyone can talk but large enough so that no one dominates. The researcher usually facilitates the conversation. She or he makes sure that the group stays on track and that everyone's expertise is heard.

How does this work? Quite smoothly, so long as you have prepared well for the experience. For example, Robin Cash, a former graduate student of mine, used focus groups to identify the memorable techniques used by her college coach to promote what Cash called "an organic model of coaching."[7] She put together several focus groups of women who had studied with Eleanor Snell, who coached at Ursinus College from 1931 to 1972. She generated multigenerational conversations about Snell's coaching techniques, aims, and effectiveness. Another former student, Lydia Forsythe, used focus groups as part of a project to develop training techniques to cut down on surgical errors in hospitals. The focus groups helped her identify the key spots at which things go wrong. She then developed a simulation exercise that improved surgery team awareness.[8] I used focus groups in a 1995 study of an Episcopal congregation in San Antonio, Texas. I was profiling that congregation for the Spiritual Vital Episcopal Congregations Project, which wanted to see what congregations deemed "spiritually vital" by their bishops had in common.[9] The project found few commonalities between the congregations, but I used focus groups organized through the San Antonio church's neighborhood worship groups to see how widespread were the attitudes I was getting from my individual interviewees. The conversations were quite rich, and they helped me identify the key ways in which this particular congregation maintained its vitality.

Facilitating focus groups is a learned skill, as is one-on-one interviewing. Both take practice, but they demand a different kind of attention. One-on-one interviews involve keeping one person talking and on track. Focus groups require that you attend to those who are not talking as much as to those who are, that you draw out the former and keep the latter from dominating, and that you encourage conversation among the participants while managing the conversation so that it remains productive. Not every researcher can do this off the bat. You may wish to work with a co-investigator or even hire a facilitator, depending on your project. You can, however, gather a lot of good data from focus group conversations.

Phenomenological Interviews

Phenomenological interviews collect a very different kind of data. They do not collect people's ideas, opinions, or attitudes. They do not provide expert knowledge in the way I have just described. They do not report on external events. Instead, they report on individuals' experiences *as that experience presents itself to their consciousness*. To understand what this means, you have to understand something about phenomenology.

Phenomenology stems from the work of the German philosopher Edmund Husserl.[10] He argued for a radical shift in perspective—one that placed human experience at the center of philosophical investigation. By setting aside ("bracketing") our thoughts about things, he argued, we can open ourselves to pure experiencing. This does not allow us to experience the world objectively. He followed Immanuel Kant in arguing that direct knowledge of the world is not possible. Yet we can be objective toward our own subjective experiences by separating them from the ideas we have about them. Bracketing away those ideas lets us see our subjective experience directly. Phenomenological interviews are designed to capture the subjective experiences of others by separating them from the ideas in which people typically wrap them.

An Example

Here's one account of pure experience, taken from the work of psychologist Susan Blackmore. It captures the difference between someone sitting at a desk in ordinary consciousness and sitting in meditation. At the desk:

> My [experience] of reality consists of self and the world—well divided from each other. "I" consist of a stable body image with arms and legs. . . . "I" have plans for future actions (I must tidy up) and wishes that things were different (I wish I could concentrate harder). . . . The world around consists of the room, the sounds outside; the birds (Oh there are some birds singing. Don't they sound nice? I wonder what sort of birds they are . . . .); children [playing] (I wish they'd be quiet), the radio (I hate the noise).[11]

Note the combination of elements that make up this experience. "Self" and "world" are relatively distinct, though both are built of thought, memory, and sensation. The experienced "I" combines sensations, thoughts, plans, and self-images. The experienced "world" combines sensations, concepts (e.g., birds and their kinds), and judgments (hating the radio). "Self" and "world" intertwine in this experience, in that "I" am always reacting to the "world"—both positively and negatively. "I" experience myself as distinct from the "world," but I am not free of it; each involves the other, continuously. This is part of what we mean when we say that someone experiences the world in a "normal" way.

Now see me meditating:

> I am still. The birds are singing outside, there are sounds of children play-
> ing a long way away, and a distant radio. The muddle on my desk and the
> room full of things are filled with stillness. There is me sitting. The sounds
> are full of silence. I hear a woodlouse crawl across the floor.[12]

Here there is much less going on. My experience of my "self" is less elaborate
and contains no thoughts. I sense, rather than think, my stillness. My experience
of the "world" is also sensory; it remains free of concepts and judgments. Both
exist on the same level. I sense myself, I sense the world—but I somehow remain
objective to them. Depending on the depth of my meditation, I may not separate
them at all.

In meditation, Blackmore says, my normal experiences of "I" and "world" cease
to exist. My attention is focused in such a way that different experiences emerge. In
her words, in meditation

THINK ABOUT IT
How are these
two experiences
different?

> "I" am as much the sounds as the hearer of the sounds because
> I have not constructed the [brain] model which distinguishes
> them. . . . In a different meditative state, I may not even hear the
> sounds of birds, or at least not label them birds, or even sounds,
> though I do not block them out either. The early processing in the
> system may be just the same, but never leads to a complex high
> level [separation].[13]

Blackmore's example gives you a clear picture of the kind of data
that phenomenological interviewing seeks.

How Is It Done?

How do we do this, in practice? Psychologists Amedeo and Barbro Giorgi have developed a clear outline of how to use phenomenological interviewing in empirical
research.[14] They outline four separate steps:

1. *Locate and interview a number of informants who have shared a particular experience.* These interviewees might have experienced a particular kind of meditation,
as in Blackmore's example. Or they might have learned how to engage in a specific
kind of physical activity, as with David Sudnow's exploration of the phenomenology of playing jazz piano.[15] The topic depends on your research question. Though
philosophical phenomenology depended on introspection, social-scientific phenomenology calls for interviewing several informants. This avoids **bias**, but it also
lets you identify which aspects of the experiences are crucial and which are not.
Individual introspection does not do as well.

2. *Help your informants focus on exactly how this experience presented itself to their consciousness, leaving aside what they (or you) think was "really" happening.* To take a trivial example, I can describe how I experience holding my morning cup of coffee, and my interviewer can help me delve into how that experience presents itself to my consciousness, without either one of us worrying about whether the coffee or my cup actually exists. Beyond the warmth of the porcelain, its heft in my hands, there is the slip of warm liquid down my throat, the slight but growing buzz as the caffeine enters my system, and so on. I can describe this without ever postulating that I, the cup, or the coffee are "real." The goal is to describe pure experiencing.

3. *Compare and analyze the accounts you have collected, in order to identify the basic structures of the experience.* This is harder than it seems, because you need to have good enough interview material to determine which features of the experience are peculiar to a single person and which are shared by everyone. You have to read beneath each person's account to find the patterns that it represents. Some accounts will have extra material in them; other accounts may use idiosyncratic language while still exhibiting a common structure. You must decide which elements are central and which are not, and you must be able to justify this decision by reference to your data.

4. *Redescribe or summarize the experience, boiling it down to its basic shared structures.* The point is to capture the shared aspects of people's subjective experiences objectively. That way, you can grasp the shape of that experience, without buying into the particular ideas or interpretations that any particular individuals make of it. (Those ideas are interesting, but they are not what phenomenological interviewing is trying to gather.)

The point is to describe the experience so that a "native" can recognize it, without taking on board any of those natives' particular interpretations of what is going on. The description must be "experience-near," though you are not limited to using just the informants' own words.

Throughout this process, you must be alert to the possibility that you are dealing with two or more different phenomena rather than with a single one. For example, as Roger Walsh pointed out, psychologists long equated shamanic spirit-flight with schizophrenia because they never examined the experiences closely enough to see their clear differences.[16] His phenomenological interviews with native Balinese and Basque shamans, plus interviews with Westerners who were trained by shamans from various traditions, clearly showed the differences. They also distinguished both shamanism and schizophrenia from various Buddhist and yogic meditation states.

Walsh nowhere said what is "really" happening in any of these states of consciousness. He did not reduce schizophrenia to brain-wave malfunction, nor did he claim that the shaman "really" leaves her or his body during a trance. His phenomenological exercise focused on mapping and comparing the basic structures of the various experiences he reviewed. That is the point of phenomenological investigations: to chart people's subjective experiences as objectively as possible.

Other Types of Data

Interviews can collect other types of data as well. These do not, however, raise new issues of technique, beyond those we have already met. Cultural interviewing, for example, collects people's reports of the things that everyone knows in a particular cultural scene. Anthropologists use this kind of interviewing to understand those scenes. Rather than concern themselves with individuals' personal views, or with raw experiences, they collect common knowledge: what people know that makes daily life possible. Most American 18-year-olds, for example, know how to drive. Their age-mates in several others societies lack that skill, though they have skills that American young people lack. How many young Americans know how to butcher a moose? Or catch one, for that matter. "What everyone knows" varies from place to place.

Cultural interviewing, however, is just like hermeneutic interviewing. You ask questions, get answers, check to make sure that you have understood those answers, modify them if you have not, and so on. You do this when you want to understand someone's self-identity or deep personal feelings. Yes, each type of interviewing gathers a different type of data, but the interview process is very similar. I don't need to walk through all the options. You already know enough to design interview research unaided.

How Many Subjects?

An important question remains: How many people do you need to interview for a particular project? The short answer is that you need to interview new people until you cease getting new answers. You want to collect all the possible patterns that are out there—at least the major ones—but you don't know how many those are. You interview until you keep hearing the same things over and over.

How many is that? Here's my rule of thumb:

1. *Pick a minimum number of interviews,* one that seems sensible to you, given your topic, time, and resources, and the type of data you're seeking. I've never seen a hermeneutic interview project that could get by with fewer than 25 interviewees. Expert interviewing needs fewer, as does phenomenological interviewing. That's because expert opinion and reports of direct experience are more focused than are deeply held opinions and attitudes. At any rate, pick a starting number.

2. *Set a maximum number of interviews,* usually twice the minimum number you've just set. This should be high enough to collect a lot of information but low enough that you won't spend the rest of your life on this project.

3. *Identify interviewees.* Make sure you are casting a wide net and collect interviews from as many different types of people as makes sense for your project. If you're interviewing Americans about prayer, for example, you want to make sure that you have Catholics, Baptists, Mainline Protestants, Pentecostals, Jews, and a few others in your pool. They all have different

prayer-lives, and you need the variety.[17] Make sure to choose interviewees who will expand your horizons, not narrow them.

4. *Carry out those interviews.* Conduct the full number of interviews that you decided at the beginning. Once they're done, look back at the last five interviews you conducted. Did you learn anything new from them? If so, keep interviewing. If not, interview five more and look back again. If you *still* didn't find anything new, then you're done.

Repeat this process until you've ceased getting new information. To make this process clear, let's revisit the flowchart on interviewing that appeared in Chapter 5 (Figure 9.6).

FIGURE 9.6   Interview Rule-of-Thumb Flowchart for Nonrandom Samples

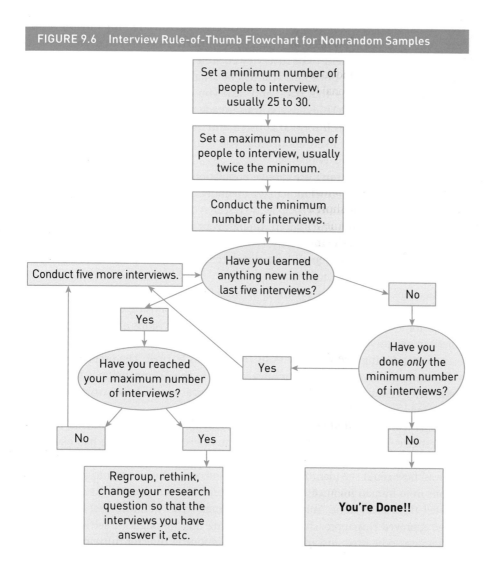

What if you reach the maximum number of interviews that you set and you are still getting new information? That's a judgment call. If you are only finding differences of detail, not of substance, then you probably have enough interviews already. You can quit collecting and start analyzing your data. If, however, each interview brings significant new knowledge, then you are probably asking too broad a research question. You can either keep collecting data or quit and see what research question your current data let you answer. The choice depends on how long you want your project to take.

Research Ethics

We have already reviewed most of the ethical issues involved in the interview process. You know that you need to protect your interviewees and that you need to get their informed consent to be interviewed. You know that you need to describe the interview topic, the questions you will be asking them, how you will use their data, how you will store that data, and how you plan to make sure that no one will use the information they give you to invade their privacy. We covered these topics in the sections on informed consent and on taping, earlier in this chapter. We haven't, however, talked about how you'll find interview subjects, and this process also raises ethical concerns.

You know that you can't use captive populations as research subjects: prisoners, hospitalized people, the institutionalized mentally ill, and so on. They are not independent enough to refuse to participate, so research on them is generally banned. The same is true for research on children, though your IRB can approve that research if you protect those children adequately. (We covered this topic in Chapter 5, and it will be covered thoroughly in the ethics training that your IRB requires of you before it will review your research proposal.)

There are, however, other dangers as well. Imagine this scenario, taken from a real research proposal: Many large corporations send promising employees overseas to work for a while, so as to gain experience in other divisions of the company. An American executive may be posted to France, for example. She may return a couple of years later, bringing back the new skills that she has learned. The problem is, many such employees have a hard time reintegrating into their company once they return home. They've lost touch with their cohort, few local people know what skills they have gained, and they typically feel underappreciated.

Some years ago, Carol Sommerfield, one of my former graduate students, decided to investigate this phenomenon. She wanted to interview people who had been sent abroad, but who then felt underused and underappreciated on their return. The problem was, how could she identify such people. She originally planned to solicit nominations from human resources directors at Fortune 500 companies, asking for people who felt themselves to be "subjectively underemployed." I and the rest of her committee approved this approach, without realizing that we might be setting up those interviewees to be fired. Just imagine a human resources director thinking about the company's recently returned employees and looking for one who is dissatisfied. Guess who would get the axe. Our university's IRB flagged this and asked the student to come up with another means of identifying research participants.

The student ultimately solved the problem by advertising in New York City–area newspapers and magazines that she hoped her target population might read. That worked, and she collected enough interviews to complete her project. She wrote a fine dissertation.[18] Her original strategy, however, might have harmed her informants. I'm embarrassed to say that I did not think this through at the time. Fortunately, our school's IRB did think it through, and it helped her take corrective action. IRBs can be very useful in the research process. They can be among your research project's best friends.

Review Questions

1. What different types of data can you gather with interviews?

2. What is the hermeneutic circle? How does it ensure that you capture your interviewees' ideas accurately?

3. When might you want to interview experts?

4. How does phenomenological interviewing differ from interviewing to collect people's deeply held opinions and attitudes?

5. What are some things to remember when you are constructing your interview protocol?

6. What ethical considerations do interview researchers have to keep in mind?

The open-access Student Study Site at **study.sagepub.com/spickard** has a variety of useful study tools, including SAGE journal articles, video & web resources, eFlashcards, and quizzes.

Notes

1. Wilhelm Dilthey (1833–1911), the most prominent hermeneutic philosopher, distinguished the natural sciences' search for laws from the humanities' search for understanding. Social sciences can go either way.

2. Lynn Davidman, *Motherloss*. University of California Press, 2000.

3. Tom Wengraf, *Qualitative Research Interviewing*. Sage, 2001. A handout summarizing this approach appears in the "Research Guides and

(Continued)

(Continued)

    Handouts" section at the back of this book.

4. Christy Z. Dachelet et al., "The Critical Incident Technique Applied to the Evaluation of the Clinical Practicum Setting," *Journal of Nursing Education* 20 (1981): 15–31.

5. John C. Flanagan, "The Critical Incident Technique," *Psychological Bulletin* 51 (1954): 327–358.

6. Dachelet et al., "Critical Incident Technique," 28.

7. See Robin G. Cash, "A Coach's Way: A Life-Affirming Organic Model Created in Sport," *Women in Sports & Physical Activity Journal* 15 (2006): 56–73.

8. Lydia Forsythe, "Action Research, Simulation, Team Communication, and Bringing the Tacit Into Voice," *Simulation in Healthcare* 4 (2009): 143–148.

9. Nancy T. Ammerman and Adair Lummis, "Spiritually Vital Episcopal Congregations: Final Report to the Trinity Church Grants Board, New York City," Hartford Seminary, 1996.

10. See, especially, Edmund Husserl, "Pure Phenomenology, Its Method and Its Field of Investigation," Inaugural Lecture at the University of Freiburg, 1917, translated by R. W. Jordon, in *Husserl: Shorter Works*, edited by P. McCormick and F. Elliston. University of Notre Dame Press, 1981.

11. Susan Blackmore, "Who Am I? Changing Models of Reality in Meditation," pp. 71–85 in *Beyond Therapy: The Impact of Eastern Religions on Psychological Theory and Practice*, edited by Guy Claxton. Wisdom Publications, 1996, p. 83.

12. Ibid.

13. Ibid., p. 84.

14. Amedeo P. Giorgi and Barbro M. Giorgi, "The Descriptive Phenomenological Psychological Method," pp. 243–273 in *Qualitative Research in Psychology*, edited by P. M. Camic et al. American Psychological Association, 2003.

15. David Sudnow, *Ways of the Hand*. Harper & Row, 1978.

16. Roger Walsh, "Phenomenological Mapping: A Method for Describing and Comparing States of Consciousness," *Journal of Transpersonal Psychology* 27 (1995): 25–56.

17. In fact, there is so much variety *within* each of these religions that you would be better off exploring just one of them. Otherwise, you could be interviewing for the rest of your life.

18. Carol Sommerfield, *Where's the Ticker Tape Parade? Subjective Underemployment in Repatriated Employees*. PhD dissertation, Fielding Graduate University, 2006.

1 RESEARCH QUESTION

2 LOGICAL STRUCTURE

3 TYPE OF DATA

4 DATA COLLECTION METHOD

5 DATA COLLECTION SITE

6 DATA ANALYSIS METHOD

RESULTS

CHAPTER 10

Scales: Looking for Underlying Traits

	Type of Data	
		Personal and psychological traits
	Scales	
Data Collection Method	**Psychological scales and their kin**	X

hapter 8 focused on social surveys as a way of asking people about things they already know. These include their personal opinions and attitudes, their demographic and political identities, and their reports about what they have done or seen. This chapter focuses on a different kind of survey—scales that collect information about people's **personal and psychological traits**. Unlike opinion surveys, these scales probe beneath the surface, while still asking easy-to-answer questions. They use the answers to measure internal factors that shape people's lives.

These deep characteristics are different from the deeply held opinions and attitudes and the reflections on experiences that we explored in Chapter 9. To put it a bit oddly, they aren't things that people know; they are things that people typically *don't* know. Who among your friends can tell you where they fall on the "Big Five" personality scales? Who can tell you they are an "INTP," unless they've taken the Myers-Briggs personality assessment (and remembered their results)? **Psychological scales** like these work by combining people's answers to easy questions into a measurement of whatever personal or psychological trait they are trying to uncover. This is not a matter of tapping preexisting knowledge. It is a matter of inferring some aspect of a person's life by how that person responds to a set of simple questions.

For example, a personality test doesn't ask you whether or not you identify yourself as an extravert. Instead, it asks you to rank how comfortable you are at large parties, talking in front of groups, and so on. It then locates you on a personality scale based on how you respond. An IQ test doesn't ask you if you are intelligent; it asks you to solve problems and then deduces your intelligence from your answers. These are both surveys, but they are not the kind of surveys we saw in Chapter 8. By looking beneath the surface, they find qualities that people may not even know they have.

In short, personal and psychological traits are a different type of data from shallow opinions, identities, and reports of actions. They are also different from deeply held ones. They thus call for a different method of data collection.

We'll start this chapter by examining a research project that used a particular set of these scales: the Ryff Scales of Psychological Well-Being. These scales measure how people feel about various aspects of their lives. We'll take a look at how such scales are constructed—a process called factor analysis. This process uses people's answers to create a set of simple questions to measure the strength of one or another underlying trait. Then we'll see how the scales were used in a project studying the effects of college education.

That done, I'll show you how to use scales to compare groups. Scale scores are interval/ratio data, whereas groups are categories. Comparing group scores uses t-tests and one of several kinds of analysis of variance. These are new kinds of quantitative analysis for us that use categorical and interval/ratio data together. In previous chapters, we met kinds of analysis that used them separately.

We'll end the chapter with some reflections on the ethics of using scales as a data collection method.

Scales of Psychological Well-Being

Most people want to feel good about life. We want friendship with others, a sense of purpose, and comfort with ourselves. Most Americans, at least, also want some personal independence, a sense that they have a say in what happens to them, and a feeling of progress. These preferences may not be universal, but they are widespread. They are also not always what we get, when we assess how our lives have turned out.

How do we measure a person's sense of well-being? We can ask directly, but we may not get very helpful answers. We've already seen the General Social Survey's attempt at this: "Taken all together, how would you say things are these days: Would you say that you are very happy, pretty happy, or not too happy?" (31.6% answered "very happy," 55.9% answered "pretty happy," and 12.5% answered "not too happy" over the more than 40 years that the survey's been run). That's a pretty shallow measure. Surely someone can do better.

Carol Ryff and her associates have tried.[1] They have constructed a set of Scales of Psychological Well-Being, designed to measure six dimensions of people's sense of life accomplishment. The dimensions are as follows:

- *Autonomy:* A sense of autonomy in thought and action
- *Environmental Mastery:* The ability to manage complex environments to suit personal needs and values
- *Personal Growth:* A sense of growth and development as a person
- *Positive Relationships With Others:* The establishment of quality interpersonal ties
- *Purpose in Life:* The pursuit of meaningful goals and a sense of purpose
- *Self-Acceptance:* The ability to be comfortable with oneself as one is.

Ryff chose these dimensions after a thorough examination of existing research in the areas of mental health, self-actualization, optimal functioning, maturity, and the developmental life span. In her view, this literature clustered around not a single measure of well-being, but the six that I have just listed. Each can be expressed as a scale, on which a person could have a high or a low score. For example, someone who scores high on the self-acceptance dimension

> possesses a positive attitude toward the self; acknowledges and accepts multiple aspects of self, including good and bad qualities; feels positive about past life. [A] low scorer feels dissatisfied with self; is disappointed with what has occurred with past life; is troubled about certain personal qualities; wishes to be different than what he or she is.[2]

Each of the other five dimensions can similarly be described. Someone who scores high on the personal growth dimension "has a feeling of continued development," whereas someone who scores low "has a sense of personal stagnation." Someone scoring high on the environmental mastery dimension "has a sense of mastery and competence in managing" her or his life situation, whereas someone scoring low "has difficulty managing everyday affairs." Each dimension has two ends, with a continuum in between. The idea is to ask people questions that will let you place them on that continuum. Asking the right questions lets you score them on each of the six scales.

Let's look at an example, to see how this works. Figure 10.1 is a list of 10 questions taken from Ryff's survey. The full version contains 84 questions that measure the six different aspects of well-being—14 questions for each. A shorter version uses 54 of these questions to provide a quicker, but more approximate, set of scores. These 10 questions are typical of this kind of research. They are easy to answer, yet they give us quite a bit of insight into a person's psychological makeup.

FIGURE 10.1   Ten Questions About Psychological Well-Being

1. I am not afraid to voice my opinions, even when they are opposed to the opinions of most people.
2. In general, I feel I am in charge of the situation in which I live.
3. Most people see me as loving and affectionate.
4. I am not interested in activities that will expand my horizons.
5. I live one day at a time and really don't think about the future.
6. When I look at the story of my life, I am pleased with how things have turned out.
7. Maintaining close relationships has been difficult and frustrating for me.
8. My decisions are not usually influenced by what everyone else is doing.
9. I am good at juggling my time so that I can fit everything in that needs to be done.
10. I don't want to try new ways of doing things—my life is fine the way it is.

Here's how it works. Respondents answer these questions on a scale from 1 to 6, with "1" meaning that the statement does not describe them at all and "6" meaning that it describes them very well. There are no right or wrong answers, just different ones.

For example, a person might answer "5" on the first question, meaning that he or she agrees with the statement "I am not afraid to voice my opinions. . . ." That person might answer "3" to the second question, meaning that she or he disagrees slightly with the statement "I feel I am in charge of the situation in which I live." He or she might answer "6" to question 3, strongly agreeing that "most people see me as loving and affectionate."

What do these questions tell us about psychological well-being? To figure this out, take a look at the following three pairs of questions: 1 and 8; 2 and 9; and 3 and 7. What does each pair have in common?

Clearly, questions 1 and 8 both have to do with personal autonomy. "I am not afraid to voice my opinions, even when they are opposed to the opinions of most people" and "My decisions are not usually influenced by what everyone else is doing" both proclaim that one is willing to go against the crowd. Each covers a different aspect of this trait: the first cites opinions and the second cites decisions, which are not quite the same thing. Yet both assert one's autonomy vis-à-vis others. A person who thinks of herself as autonomous will answer "5" or "6" on both. A person who is easily swayed by others will answer "1" or "2."

Questions 2 and 9 are similarly close. "In general, I feel I am in charge of the situation in which I live" and "I am good at juggling my time so that I can fit everything in that needs to be done" both express the sense that one has mastered one's environment. People who feel competent at managing their lives will answer "5" or "6"; people who think that life runs them rather than the other way around will answer "1" or "2"; and people who are between these extremes will answer "3" or "4." You get the picture.

However, what's up with questions 3 and 7? The first says, "Most people see me as loving and affectionate" and the second says, "Maintaining close relationships has been difficult and frustrating for me." These aren't alike. They are more opposites. What's happening here?

They are, indeed, opposites, but they are still measuring the same thing: relationships with others. This is Ryff's Positive Relationships Scale, so she scores question 7 in reverse. A "strongly disagree" on question 7 ("difficult and frustrating") is much like a "strongly agree" on question 3 ("loving and affectionate"). Both measure positive relationships. A "5" becomes a "2," a "4" becomes a "3," and so on. Reversing the scores makes the two questions match. They are just different ways of measuring related things.

That's the point of creating a scale. Having people see you as loving and affectionate is related to the ability to maintain close relationships, but the two are not identical. Just as the willingness to stick by one's *opinions* and the willingness to stick by one's *decisions* are different aspects of personal autonomy, having others think of you as affectionate and being able to maintain close relationships are different aspects of having positive relationships with others. Each one captures a piece of a psychological trait that no single question can capture completely.

Figure 10.2 lists nine questions that make up Ryff's Positive Relationships Scale on the 54-item version of her test. This scale measures the extent to which respondents have satisfying, trusting relationships with other people. The statements with "RS" after them are reverse-scored: a "6" counts as a "1," a "5" as a "2," and so on. The rest are scored directly.

Try it out! Decide how much you would agree or disagree with each statement, using the scoring system that appears below the list. Then add up the scores (after proper reversing), average them, and see how you score on Ryff's measure of ability to form close personal ties.

What score did you get? Does it match your image of yourself? It should, because you're the one giving the answers. Yet, the result is a lot deeper than you'd get if you asked just one question on a typical survey. Each question gets at an aspect of the underlying trait it seeks.

These items are like arrows, shot at a target that we cannot see directly. Each one hits in a slightly different place, but those hits all tell us something about the target's shape. That's how psychological tests work. They combine answers to a series of easy-to-answer questions to tell us something about the personal traits that shape the respondent's life. Add up the answers, and you get a scale. Different people will get different scores on that scale. It tells us something about their personal lives.

FIGURE 10.2   Positive Relationships With Others Scale

1. Most people see me as loving and affectionate.
2. Maintaining close relationships has been difficult and frustrating for me. (RS)
3. I often feel lonely because I have few close friends with whom to share my concerns. (RS)
4. I enjoy personal and mutual conversations with family members or friends.
5. I don't have many people who want to listen when I need to talk. (RS)
6. It seems to me that most other people have more friends than I do. (RS)
7. People would describe me as a giving person, willing to share my time with others.
8. I have not experienced many warm and trusting relationships with others. (RS)
9. I know that I can trust my friends, and they know that they can trust me.

Do you:

1	2	3	4	5	6
strongly disagree	disagree somewhat	slightly disagree	slightly agree	agree somewhat	strongly agree

Creating Scales

How do you create good scales? First, you have to use simple questions or statements, which everyone will interpret in the same way. That's nothing new. You had to do that with opinion surveys, and it's exactly the same process. You test your items on lots of people, and see if everyone has the same understanding. That's what Ryff and her colleagues did. They made sure that everyone understood the statements "Most people see me as loving and affectionate" in the same way. There were some limitations, as they tested their statements only on English-speaking, middle-class adults over the age of 25. You would have to retest the items if you wanted to use them for other populations.

Second, you have to be sure that the questions or statements are all getting at the same trait. They've got to measure one thing, not two (or more) different things. That's a matter of making sure that one's arrows are all aimed at the same place. It involves generating a lot of items, testing them on people, and seeing which ones seem to be getting the same kinds of answers. You weed out the ones that don't fit and keep the ones that do. Pretty soon, you've got a set of questions that all aim in the same direction.

Let's take statements 1 and 9 from Ryff's Positive Relationships Scale as an example: "Most people see me as loving and affectionate" and "I know that I can trust my friends, and they know that they can trust me." If these statements measure the same trait, then people who score high on one of them will score high on the other. People who score low on one of them will score low on the other. People who score in the middle on one will score in the middle on the others. Graphing the scores in two dimensions illustrates this (Figure 10.3)

This looks familiar, doesn't it? It's a scatterplot—a diagram that we saw in Chapter 7. Each dot represents an individual, located at the intersection of that individual's answers on the two items. The diagonal line is the regression line; that's the straight line

FIGURE 10.3   Scatterplot of Two Statements From Ryff's Positive Relationships With Others Scale

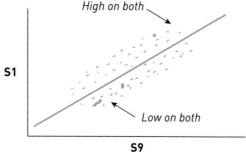

- Autonomy
- Environmental mastery
- Personal growth
- Positive relations with others
- Purpose in life
- Self-acceptance

that comes as close as possible to going through all the dots. When dots cluster closely around that line—as they do here—it means that the two statements are correlated. High scores on one predict high scores on the other; lows predict lows. It works the same way for item scores as it did when we were comparing values for the 50 U.S. states.

To return to our arrow-and-target analogy, these two questions are both hitting the same target. Their high correlation shows that they both measure aspects of the same psychological trait. It turns out that all nine statements on Ryff's Positive Relationships Scale are strongly correlated with each other. That's why she chose them, from among the 80 items that she tested for that scale. She didn't use a Pearson's *r*; she used a technique called **factor analysis**. It's the same idea, though. This technique lets her see the relationships between multiple questions at the same time. Statements that measure the same trait will be highly correlated with each other. Statements that are not so correlated will most likely be measuring something else. Ryff ran a factor analysis of her 80 statements, keeping the 20 that fit most closely and throwing out the rest. In the end, those 20 items scored 0.91 on a scale of 0 (no correlation) to 1 (complete correlation).[3] Her full, 20-item Positive Relationships Scale is aimed at a single target.

Ryff created the other five scales in the same way: She reduced 80 statements for each to the 20 that were the most closely related. She then put the 120 remaining questions in one batch and ran a factor analysis on that, to see if the whole set of questions tapped six separate factors (dimensions) of well-being. It did. Factor analysis is a complex technique but a powerful one. It tells you which arrows are hitting which target.

There was one more step. Ryff still had a total of 120 statements—six scales of 20 statements each. That's too many to use in practical research. People get tired filling out long forms.

Ryff returned to her six scales and chose 14 of the 20 items on each—a total of 84. The 14-item scales correlated with the 20-item scales almost perfectly: $r = 0.97$ through $r = 0.99$. Ryff and Keyes's analysis of the 84-item version showed that all six scales were distinct but related. As they put it, "The model that best fit the data was one of six primary factors joined together by a single higher order factor."[4]

That higher-order factor is "psychological well-being." The six scales each measured an aspect of that overall term. Together, Ryff and Keyes argued that the six scales give us a comprehensive picture of that illusive target. They wrote that "other frequently used indicators [such as] positive and negative affect, [and] life satisfaction . . . neglect key aspects of positive functioning emphasized in theories of health and well-being."[5] In short, Ryff and her colleagues argued that their scale does a better job than these other measures.

Using the Scales

How have investigators used Ryff's scales for empirical research? They have done so in various ways. For example, a few years ago, I used three of the scales in a small project to evaluate a pregnancy literacy program for low-income Latinas. We wanted to see whether the program helped the women feel more confident in their interactions with medical staff, and we wanted to examine this at a deeper level than just asking them how confident they felt. (We did that, too.) We hoped that Ryff's Autonomy, Environmental Mastery, and Self-Acceptance Scales would give us useful evidence.[6]

A much bigger project was the Wabash National Study of Liberal Arts Education. It examined how and how much college students change over four years of higher learning. It was run with three cohorts—2006–2010, 2007–2011, and 2008–2012—at as many as 49 colleges and universities.[7] Students at each university completed an array of surveys and tests at three points during their college careers. The first was when they arrived on campus for their first fall semester. The second was at the end of their first school year. The third was at the end of their fourth year, when many of them were ready for graduation. The study used the Ryff scales to find out whether students increased their sense of autonomy, environmental mastery, and so on over their four years. Higher education is supposed to improve such things. Does it?

Unfortunately, the results were mixed. We can focus on the 2006–2010 cohort as an example. As with the later cohorts, students took several surveys in the fall of their first year. One collected demographic information and some information about the students' high schools. Another surveyed students about their life goals, academic orientations, values, and so on. The rest were scales, designed to tap underlying traits. These included a scale measuring how much people enjoy difficult thinking, a leadership scale, a scale measuring acceptance of diversity, plus several others. These formed a baseline: a "before" test, to see how much change the students' college experience made.

At the end of their first and fourth years, students retook all these scales plus the life goals survey; this gave the investigators "after" scores to compare. Students then took two surveys—opinion surveys, not scales—to report how much they had engaged in college activities during their four years.

In short, this was a causal research design, but not an experimental one. Students took the tests, experienced a year of college, and then retook the tests. Three years later, they took the tests again. At least some of the changes should be attributable to their college experiences, though some simply result from growing older. The two opinion surveys provided information about what aspects of the college experience might be making a difference. Figure 10.4 (on the next page) illustrates the logical structure.

That's the logic. What did they find? In early fall 2006, 4,501 students from 19 different institutions completed the surveys. At the end of the following spring, 3,081 of those students returned to complete the surveys again. That's a pretty significant drop, but many schools lose students during the first year. More than 3,000 participants is still a pretty good number. Those students increased their moral reasoning scores by about 10% and their critical thinking scores by about 1%. The first is commendable, the second less so. These were, however, the highest increases on any of the scales.

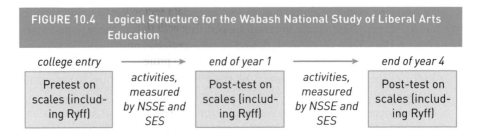

FIGURE 10.4   Logical Structure for the Wabash National Study of Liberal Arts Education

For this cohort, the first college year did not see much improvement. Indeed, student scores declined significantly on five of the six subsections of the life goals and academic orientation survey. As the study authors reported:

> We observed a . . . consistent decline in students' academic motivation and their interest in academic subject matter, community involvement, and professional success. We found these declines to be especially trouble-some because these attitudes and values may shape the extent to which students engage with subsequent college work.[8]

At the one-year mark, the student scores on the Ryff test were unchanged. On average, students neither gained nor lost a sense of psychological well-being on the scales that the test measures.

The pattern after four years was a good deal more positive.[9] Students reported an increased sense of autonomy, environmental mastery, and the four other aspects of well-being that the Ryff scales measured. The increase was small: about a third of a point on the six-point scale. Yet it was definite.

These results are, however, averages. They combine the results for students of all types, who had all kinds of college experiences. Did any college experiences produce better outcomes? The answer is yes. Certain types of teaching improved students' Ryff scores as well as scores on several of the other study measures.

THINK ABOUT IT
How has college changed *you*?

Specifically, students who reported having high-quality interactions with faculty saw significant increases on all the Ryff scales. The same is true of students who reported that their faculty challenged them and had high expectations of their work. Having these two experiences, plus a few others, left students with a greater sense of autonomy, environmental mastery, and so on. Students who did not report such experiences, by contrast, scored lower on the Ryff scales than did the rest.

The study found the same pattern with several of the other scales. Good faculty interactions significantly increased student scores on academic motivation and on political and social involvement; high standards and expectations increased scores on those scales and also student orientation to professional success.

The lesson to college faculty from the Wabash data seems clear. *According to this study, faculty should interact positively and intellectually with their students, should maintain high academic standards, and should have high expectations of student work.* Do so, and not only will students increase their academic and professional motivation; they will also leave college with a significantly higher sense of psychological well-being than they had when they entered. That's music to any teaching professor's ears.

Table 10.1 summarizes the six-step process for the Wabash study.

So, what limitations might the Ryff scales have? One issue is that Ryff's questions were pretested on middle-class American adults, aged 25 and up. That is the population that Ryff polled when choosing her questions. That is the population whose answers came back with such high correlations that Ryff could be sure that she was tapping deep-seated psychological traits, not just random personal attitudes. That is a key aspect of scale construction: Different social and cultural groups can interpret questions differently. A set of questions that works for one population may not work (or work as well) with another.

The authors of the Wabash study thought that the stretch from middle-class American adults to American college students was not too large. They were probably right. You could test that, by rerunning the factor analysis on this new population, to see the extent to which the nine questions that make up each of the six scales are correlated.

This is what other scholars have done, in developing new Ryff questionnaires to be used in other countries. Dirk van Dierendonck and his colleagues, for example, developed a Spanish version of the questionnaire to be used in Spain and Colombia.[10] They used confirmatory factor analysis to show that this questionnaire captured the six scales of psychological well-being in two different linguistic and cultural milieus.

TABLE 10.1 Summary of the Wabash National Study of Liberal Arts Education	
1. Research Question	What changes does a liberal arts education make in students' scores on several scales, including Ryff's Scales of Psychological Well-Being?
2. Logical Structure	Causal (but not experimental), using before and after testing of students' traits and attitudes
3. Type of Data	Underlying psychological and attitudinal traits, as measured by several scales
4. Data Collection Method	Three surveys of students: as they start college, after the first year, and after the fourth year
5. Data Collection Site	Students at 19–49 participating schools
6. Data Analysis Method	Calculate measures of central tendency and dispersion on each scale, both before and after; compare to find difference
	Unit of analysis: *student population as a whole and various subgroups*

Those populations were, however, still from the educated middle class. My own attempt to use a modification of van Dierendonck's Spanish version with marginally educated, low-income Latinas in the United States failed in part because the women could not understand how to interpret a reverse-scored question. It appears that decoding these questions is a culturally learned skill. Educated middle-class people have no trouble with this. People who lack formal schooling do.

Even changing the reverse-scored items into positive ones didn't work: The factor analysis showed that the scale items did not correlate with each other. It seems that social class and schooling make a big difference in how people respond to this test. In the end, we could not use Ryff's scales for measuring traits with our population.

My negative experience does not undermine the utility of Ryff's scales for measuring psychological well-being. It just shows that scales developed for one population may not work for another. This makes sense. We saw in Chapter 8 that survey questions have to be clear and easy to understand by anyone who is part of the survey's target population. Scales are the same. People have to understand clearly what is being asked and must know how to respond without thinking too much about it. That's how scales can delve beneath the surface. The whole idea is to learn something about people's personal and psychological traits from their responses to simple questions or statements. That's a worthy goal.

Analyzing Scale Research

How do we analyze the data we gather using scales? As with all data analysis, we start by asking about the data's form. Is it *interval/ratio, ordinal, categorical,* or *qualitative*? Scales are interval/ratio. This tells us what kind of analysis we can do.

We covered several possibilities in Chapter 7. We can, for example, describe the scores we get from our respondents. That's what the Wabash study did. Average scores dropped slightly by the end of the students' first year but rose about a third of a point by graduation. That's not enough to raise a "slightly disagree" to a "slightly agree" or a "slightly agree" to an "agree somewhat"—that would take a full-point jump. It shows, however, that a liberal arts college education does increase a student's psychological well-being, on average. An average measures a variable's central tendency, and the central tendency is slightly up.

The Wabash study summary report did not include the range, inter-decile range, variance, or standard deviation, all of which are measures of dispersion. These, too, are ways of describing interval/ratio data. They work for all scales, not just Ryff's.

Could we compare Ryff's scales with other interval/ratio variables? It makes sense to do so. George Kaplan and his colleagues did this using data from a 29-year longitudinal study of residents of Alameda County, California.[11] They compared the income levels of study participants with their scores on a shortened version of Ryff's six scales. They also compared scale scores with participants' income growth or decline and the source of that income: regular income (salary, investments) or public benefits (unemployment, welfare, disability).

They found strong positive correlations between income and all of the scales except autonomy. They also found strong correlations between these four scales and income growth. People who reported higher incomes and higher income growth also reported a greater sense of purpose in life, self-acceptance, personal growth, and environmental mastery. People who reported lower incomes and lower income growth (or even decline) scored themselves lower on each of these scales.

FIGURE 10.5   Scatterplot of Income Versus Ryff Scores

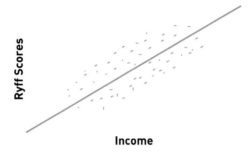

Ryff Scores

Income

I can't show you an exact scatterplot of these figures, but it would look very much like Figure 10.5. Economic success and psychological well-being predict each other. If you know that someone's score is high (or low) on one of these measures, you can be very sure it will be high (or low) on the other.

T-Tests and Analysis of Variance

This brings us to a final data analysis technique—one that expands our tool kit significantly. Correlations let us see relationships between two interval/ratio variables (e.g., income and Ryff scores, income and education, Ryff scores and education). What if we want to compare the interval/ratio scores of two different categories of people? What if we want to see whether men or women have a greater sense of psychological well-being? What if we want to compare the incomes of Whites and African Americans? What about the life satisfaction of college graduates versus the life satisfaction of those who never made it past high school? Yes, we can compare their average scores, but can we do more? Can we somehow compare the whole range of values that we find for one group on an interval/ratio variable with the whole range of values that we find for another? Can we analyze interval/ratio and categorical data together? The short answer is yes. It's pretty simple to do this with a **t-test**. It's an old technique, invented by an early-20th-century brewer to compare batches of beer.[12] It works well for comparing two groups on any interval/ratio scale.

Let's imagine that we've got two school districts: District A and District B. These districts serve two different populations in a major city. District A serves the city's central area, which is inhabited mostly by poor people. District B serves the northern suburbs, whose inhabitants are mostly from the middle and professional classes. We want to see how these districts are doing at educating their respective populations. We'll compare student scores on a standardized test, to see if there are any differences.

Take a look at the graphs in Figure 10.6.[13] They compare the two districts' scores on the 5th-grade test, the 8th-grade test, and the 12th-grade test. In these districts, that's the end of elementary school, middle school, and high school. How do the two districts compare?

First, we need to know what the three graphs represent. They each compare two figures. The first figure—the line across the middle of each vertical bar—is the average score for all the children who took that particular exam. We call this the **mean score**—or average, in everyday language. T-tests compare mean scores for two groups, to see if they are significantly different from one another. The vertical bars themselves represent the scores' **standard deviation**. That measures the degree to which a districts' scores vary around the mean. This is an important measure of dispersion, as 68% of values fall within one standard deviation on either side of the mean. The t-test compares those, too. The t-test thus uses a **measure of central tendency** (the mean) and a **measure of dispersion** (the standard deviation) to tell whether the two districts' score patterns are similar or different. I won't go into the math. You can find the formula in any statistics book, in far more detail than I can provide here. For design purposes, you just need to know that you can use a t-test to compare two groups on any interval measure. That's the point of the graphs.

What do those graphs tell us? On the left, we have the fifth-grade scores, and it's pretty clear that District A's scores are higher than District B's. In this case, the t-test tells us that we can be confident that the scores are higher. How confident? I don't show it here, but the **confidence level** happens to be 99% (p = 0.01). T-tests always give you a confidence level. Though the math is different, this means the same thing it did when we talked about levels of confidence with cross-tabulations and chi-squares. Fifth graders are doing a better job on standardized tests in District A than in District B.

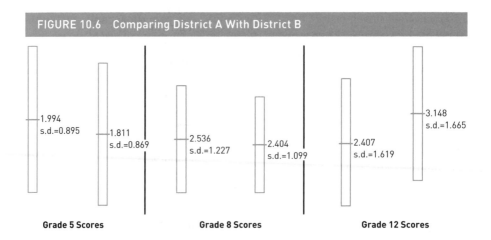

FIGURE 10.6   Comparing District A With District B

1.994
s.d.=0.895

1.811
s.d.=0.869

2.536
s.d.=1.227

2.404
s.d.=1.099

2.407
s.d.=1.619

3.148
s.d.=1.665

Grade 5 Scores   Grade 8 Scores   Grade 12 Scores

On the right side, we have the opposite result. District B's 12th graders have higher scores, and the t-test also gives us that verdict at the 99% confidence level. (Again, I don't show the confidence level here; all statistical software reports it, however.)

Finally, in the middle we have the 8th-grade results. These are a lot closer: The District A mean is 2.536 versus District B's mean of 2.404. The standard deviations are also similar: 1.227 versus 1.099. In this case, the t-test tells us that the difference between the districts' 8th-grade scores is *not* significant. In fact, it is only a 60% confidence level (p = 0.4), which is below the 95% that social science research usually requires.[14] In fact, that's pretty close to a 50% confidence level—the same as a coin flip. There's really no difference here.

THINK ABOUT IT
How might you have used the t-test in the Wabash study to see if there was a difference between the effect of college in women's and men's well-being scores?

You see how this works. It's really very simple to set up and fairly simple to interpret. That's why the t-test is so useful. It's a particularly powerful way to analyze how different two groups are on an interval/ratio variable.

What happens if you have more than two groups? You use an extension of the t-test called an **analysis of variance**. Typically known as **ANOVA**, this tool lets you compare interval/ratio scores across three or more groups, organizations, or categories.[15]

Why do we need these techniques? You can't do correlations using categorical variables, so you can't use that statistical test to compare two school districts. Cross-tabulations with chi-squares won't work with interval/ratio variables. The t-test and its siblings let you compare interval/ratio variables across two or more groups.

Control Variables

Let's add one more wrinkle. What if you want to compare interval/ratio scores across *two* categorical variables simultaneously? For example, we know that, on average, college graduates have more prestigious occupations than do those who completed only high school. We also know that Whites, on average, have more prestigious occupations than do African Americans, largely as a result of generations of racial discrimination. Do both racial discrimination and unequal educations contribute *separately* to unequal occupational prestige, as in Option 1, diagrammed in Figure 10.7 (on the next page)? Or does racial discrimination produce unequal educational opportunity, which in turn creates unequal prestige, as in Option 2? Or does racial discrimination create both unequal educational opportunity and unequal prestige, separately, as in Option 3?

In Option 1, both the greater educational attainment of college graduates and the social privileges accorded to Whites give the two groups advantages in getting more prestigious jobs. In Option 2, Whites' privileges give them more access to education; that, in turn, gets them the higher status jobs. Here, racial status differences work only indirectly. In Option 3, Whites' privileges give them both more educational opportunity and more prestigious jobs, but these privileges do so separately; education has no direct result for occupational prestige itself. How can we tell which option describes American society?

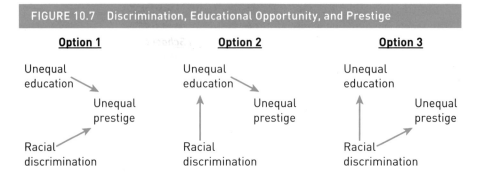

FIGURE 10.7   Discrimination, Educational Opportunity, and Prestige

We do this by using **control variables**. Basically, a control variable lets us split a population into parts—in this case Whites versus African Americans and those who completed only high school versus those who graduated from college. We run our analysis as usual, but we do it on the parts separately. This tells us if the relationship we see in the whole population is also present in the subgroups.

For prestige, we'll use the NORC Occupational Prestige Scale, along with data from the combined General Social Surveys from 2000 to 2014. The scale was constructed in the late 1980s by a team at the National Opinion Research Center. Based on earlier research by Paul Siegel,[16] this scale ranks occupations according to their relative prestige in the eyes of the American public. It takes into account such factors as the degree of education required to hold the job, the amount of leadership necessary, the social importance the job holds in others' eyes, and so on. It is a complex scale. It is also very well tested and widely used to rank occupations.

This is not the same kind of scale as the Ryff Scales of Psychological Well-Being. That's because those scales measure something internal to the person (autonomy, self-acceptance, environmental mastery, and so on), whereas the Occupational Prestige Scale measures something external. The latter, however, is an excellent vehicle for understanding control variables. As an interval/ratio scale, running from 1 to 100, it lets us see how to use control variables with t-tests in a particularly clear way. We'll start with the t-tests between occupational prestige and our two categorical variables: race (White vs. African American) and education level (college vs. high school).

As shown in Figure 10.8, Whites and college graduates have higher average occupational prestige than do African Americans and those with at most a high school education. The line across the middle of each box marks the average or mean for each, and I've labeled the values. The boxes show the standard deviations. The scores for Whites and Blacks are closer together than are the scores for high school grads versus college grads. Those scores are also more widely dispersed. You know that because the boxes are longer. Generally speaking, the two races are more widely dispersed across the occupational spectrum than are either of the educational groups.

This is the pattern in the population as a whole. The figure covers people from both racial groups and from all levels of education. Now we have to divide those groups. That way, we can see whether the educational pattern that works for everyone

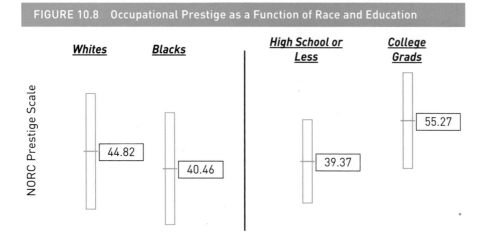

FIGURE 10.8   Occupational Prestige as a Function of Race and Education

also holds true for both of the races. Then, we'll see whether the racial pattern holds true for each level of education. That's what control variables are all about: controlling the influence of one variable so that you can measure the influence of another.

The answer is yes. Education makes a great difference to occupational prestige for both Whites and African Americans. In both charts shown in Figure 10.9, p < 0.001. That means that there is less than one chance in 1,000 that the difference we see in this sample is not found in the population as a whole. In fact, the numbers for both Whites and Blacks are nearly identical. No matter what their race, those with at most a high school education have, on average, jobs that score in the high 30s on the prestige scale. Those who have graduated from college have jobs that average about 55 on the prestige scale. The standard deviations are also nearly identical. Education determines occupational prestige for both African Americans and Whites.

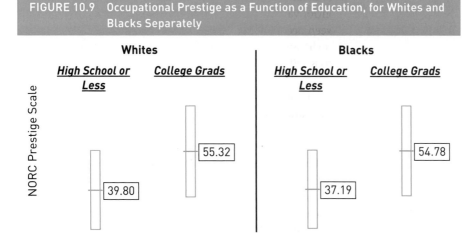

FIGURE 10.9   Occupational Prestige as a Function of Education, for Whites and Blacks Separately

FIGURE 10.10   Occupational Prestige as a Function of Race, for the Two Educational Levels Separately

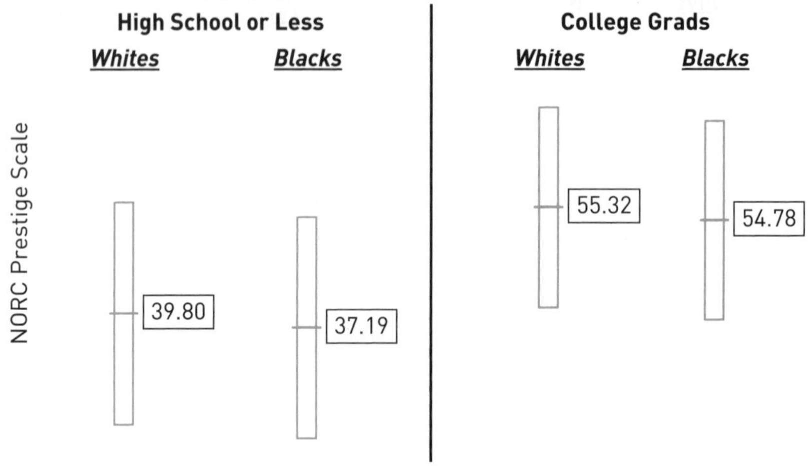

High School or Less

Whites   *Blacks*

College Grads

Whites   *Blacks*

NORC Prestige Scale

55.32

54.78

39.80

37.19

Now let's separate those who graduated at most from high school from those who graduated from college (Figure 10.10). The left-hand chart includes only the former. The right-hand chart included only the latter. This way, we'll get to see whether race makes a difference, too.

Interesting! African Americans and Whites are almost identical on both diagrams. The difference for those with at most a high school education is less than 2 points on the prestige scale. It's less than 1 point for college grads. Race doesn't seem to make much difference, once we separate the two educational levels. What's going on here?

Let's take a look again at the options we laid out earlier. Option 1 says that both unequal education and racial discrimination are connected with unequal occupational prestige (Figure 10.11). By separating the two factors, we discovered that unequal education is, in fact, connected but that race is not. The bottom arrow in the figure is thus incorrect. Option 1 cannot be true.

FIGURE 10.11   Option 1 Disproved

Option 1

Unequal education

Unequal prestige

Racial discrimination

Option 3 says that unequal education is *not* connected with unequal occupational prestige, but we now know this is false (Figure 10.12). It also says that race *is* connected with unequal prestige, once we have calculated the relationship for race and education separately. This is also false. The absence of an arrow between education and occupational prestige is incorrect. So is the presence of an arrow between race and prestige. (We'll return to the arrow between race and education shortly.)

FIGURE 10.12   Option 3 Disproved

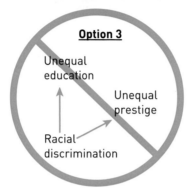

This leaves us with Option 2. That option says that unequal education is connected with unequal occupational prestige. It also says that race is connected with unequal education. We now know that the first of these is true. What about the second?

To find out, we have to use a cross-tabulation. That's because both race and education are *categorical* variables. A correlation requires two interval/ratio variables; a t-test requires one interval/ratio variable and one categorical variable. Two categorical variables call for a cross-tabulation, with a chi-square to check to see whether the educational difference between the races is important (Table 10.2).

TABLE 10.2   Cross-Tabulation: Race and Education

	White	Black
High School or Less	69.2%	83.7%
College Graduate	30.8%	16.3%

$\chi^2 = 58.39$; $p < 0.001$; conf $> 99.9\%$

There's no question about it. A much higher percentage of African Americans than Whites have at most a high school education, and a much higher percentage of Whites than African Americans have a college degree. And $p < 0.001$ and conf $> 99.9\%$, so we can be very confident that our sample represents the population as a whole.

This means that the upward arrow in Options 2 and 3 is correct. Race does influence educational inequality. Option 2 is the only option that fits all of our findings. Our cross-tabulation has confirmed the upward arrow from race to unequal education. Figure 10.9 confirms the arrow from education to occupational prestige. Figure 10.10 confirms the *lack* of an arrow connecting prestige and race directly. Thus racial discrimination produces unequal occupational prestige, but it does so indirectly: by means of differential access to education (Figure 10.13).

FIGURE 10.13   Option 2 Proved

Option 2

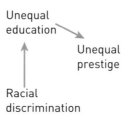

African Americans have long had less access to education than have Whites. It used to be legal school segregation. Now it is unequal access to good schools, unequal financing of schools in African American communities, and restricted access to the resources needed to attend college.[17] The recent growth of college costs and the increasing loan burden for students of all races makes access even harder. The result is diminished access to prestigious jobs.

You see how this works. We started by knowing that inequalities of both race and education were related to unequal occupational prestige. Now we know the exact path of influence. That's what control variables can do for you: They can help you sort out the relationships among several variables.

The kind of control variable that I've just described is but one variety. It works when you have one interval/ratio and multiple categorical variables. You can do something similar with cross-tabulations, when you are working with three or more categorical variables. Multiple regression lets you work with multiple interval/ratio variables. Logistic regression lets you work with a combination of interval/ratio and categorical variables. Other statistical tools give you options for ordinal variables in combination with any of these.

That's why it's so important for you to know the kind of data you have. You need to choose the analytic tool that works best with categorical, ordinal, or interval/ratio data. Between Chapters 6 to 8 and this one, we've now covered a broad range of possibilities:

- For interval/ratio data, you can calculate *means, ranges,* and *correlations.*
- For ordinal and categorical data, you can create *distributions* and *cross-tabulations.*

- For interval/ratio and ordinal/categorical data together, you can use *t-tests* and their extensions.

There are, of course, other possibilities, but these are the simple ones. All of these tools help you analyze your results more deeply.

Research Ethics

Like all research, projects that use scales raise ethical issues. Most of these issues, however, are exactly the same as those raised by surveys. You need to get informed consent, participants need to know the purpose of the research and how its results will be used, you need to make sure that the research subjects cannot be harmed by participating, and you need to take special care when surveying vulnerable populations (e.g., children, prisoners, sick people, pregnant women). You could do worse than reread the section on "Research Ethics" in Chapter 8. That section covers most of what you need to know.

Scales do raise an ethical issue that does not affect other surveys. It's a bit unusual, and it's not an ethical problem for which Institutional Review Boards can provide much help. That's because it has less to do with data collection than it does with the very information that scales are trying to collect. Scales are designed to bring to the surface personal and psychological traits. What are the consequences of bringing such hidden things into the open? I'll present two aspects of this issue very briefly.

First, there is the question of the traits themselves. As you know by now, these traits don't sit at the surface, nor do people automatically know that they have them. Few people know their IQ score with any level of accuracy. More know (or claim to know) their Myers-Briggs personality type. I'll bet, though, that few of you had ever heard of Ryff's scales before reading this chapter. That doesn't mean these traits don't exist. But it does mean that there is no easy way to ensure that they do. Couldn't we just ask you a bunch of questions and make up some bogus characteristic? People do. Just look at all those Facebook quizzes that purport to tell you things about yourself that you hadn't imagined. What's your color? Which Disney royalty are you? Which Greek philosopher are you? Which Star Trek character, famous TV dog, and so on? These are fun entertainment but not exactly science. Trait research demands extensive testing and a well-functioning baloney detector. Even such famous traits as "emotional intelligence" have come in for criticism.[18] Telling people that they score X, Y, or Z on a test for a possibly nonexistent trait does not do science any favors. Nor does it do research participants any favors—especially if they alter their lives because of what they have been told.

This is an ethical problem, best solved by making sure that the trait you are measuring is well grounded in reputable science. Ryff grounded her work in existing literature on well-being, but even her scale has been questioned. Garrett J. Kafka and Albert Kozma's reanalysis of Ryff's scales, for example, produced three separate factors, not six, and those three factors were not, they wrote, reducible to one higher-order measure.[19] Other scholars have come to other conclusions, so the point is not that Ryff's scales are inaccurate. The point is, you need to test your scales thoroughly to make sure that they are measuring what they claim. Scholars call this **construct validity**. This is the idea that any scale should be measuring something real.

The second ethical issue is related. It has to do with the consequence for people's lives of knowing that they possess one or another personal or psychological trait. What difference does this knowledge make? How does it change people's behavior?

I'll use myself as an example. I'm a college professor. You have to be something of an introvert to earn a PhD, because that task requires long months spent in near-isolation, pursuing odd references in musty libraries and reading old tomes that may not have been opened for years. This is not a communal activity. My ability to enjoy this solitude, even to draw strength from it, was an entry ticket into my career. Introverts do well at this. Early on, I tested high on the introvert side of an introversion/extraversion scale. That made sense to me, so I claimed the identity.

But once I started teaching, I had to learn how to deal with crowds. This calls for a different set of skills. You have to be able to handle crowds, remember names, give entertaining lectures to large classes, and interact with other professors, many of whom are used to being the brightest person in the room and are willing to let you know that you don't measure up. Extraverts do rather well in these situations. They know how to read other people, and they also get energy from doing so. Introverts don't. They either learn the skills or learn how to avoid such encounters.

I learned the skills. I can now do a really good imitation of an extravert. That's how I explain my teaching ability.

Notice something: I've taken on an identity ("introvert") and created an explanation for my success ("imitation of an extravert") that fits that identity. I've shaped my sense of self around the results of a psychological test taken long ago.

This isn't unusual. Most people shape their lives around their identities, as they understand them. Men often (not always) try to be "manly," however that is defined in their sociocultural milieu. Women often (not always) try to be "womanly," also in whatever form they have learned it from those around them. For me, one of the joys of living in the 21st-century United States is that we have a much more fluid sense of these gender identities than was the case when I was growing up.

Here's my point: Any scale that measures personal or psychological traits risks shaping the lives of the people who take it. How would you feel, were you to get a low score on Ryff's Autonomy Scale? In theory, there's no "right" score on this scale, just as there is no "right" score on the others. In contemporary America, though, autonomy is highly valued. People like to be independent. They like to have positive relationships with others. They like to have a sense of control over their environments. From

THINK ABOUT IT
How would you handle this ethical issue, if you were the researcher?

every side, they hear that people should have meaningful goals, should grow and develop, and should accept themselves.

How do you think study participants would feel, were they to learn that they scored low on each of these traits? How will they feel, when they discover that they score low on psychological well-being?

That's the ethical issue. Are you, as a researcher, going to give people their scores on the Scales of Psychological Well-Being—at the risk that they might shape their identities around what our society tells them is failure? Or are you not going to tell them but merely use the scores to investigate what factors create greater senses of autonomy, positive relationships with others, and the rest? I'm not sure there's a right answer to this, but it is a question that must be asked.

In any case, my own presumed introversion turned out well. Not only is introversion not badly stigmatized; it turns out that I'm not an introvert after all. I took another test a few years ago, to see if there had been any change. Either there was, or the original test was poorly designed. I came out right in the middle, with a balanced mixture of extravert and introvert strengths. Several other tests gave me the same answer. I no longer see myself as so one-sided. Thinking about it, I probably never was. Just like others, I was too quick to let a single test score define me. It has been a good lesson, learning to avoid that error.

Review Questions

1. What do we mean when we say that something is a personal or psychological trait?

2. How can you investigate such traits, recognizing that people themselves may not realize the traits they possess?

3. How do you construct a scale to measure personal or psychological traits? How might you use one in your research?

4. How did the Wabash study use these traits? What results did it find?

5. What kind of data do scales produce? What kinds of data analysis can you use with them?

6. What new ethical issues must researchers consider in research that uses psychological scales?

The open-access Student Study Site at **study.sagepub.com/spickard** has a variety of useful study tools, including SAGE journal articles, video & web resources, eFlashcards, and quizzes.

Notes

1. See Carol D. Ryff, "Happiness Is Everything, or Is It? Explorations on the Meaning of Psychological Well-Being," *Journal of Personality and Social Psychology* 57 (1989): 1069–1081; Carol D. Ryff and Corey Lee M. Keyes, "The Structure of Psychological Well-Being Revisited," *Journal of Personality and Social Psychology* 69 (1995): 719–727.

2. Tricia A. Seifert: "The Ryff Scales of Psychological Well-Being," Wabash Study Center of Inquiry, 2005. Retrieved from http://www.liberalarts.wabash.edu/ryff-scales/

3. Factor analysis uses the term *internal consistency* rather than *correlation,* but it's the same idea. Factor analysis simply lets you see the relationships between several measures at a time instead of just two.

4. Ryff and Keyes, "The Structure of Psychological Well-Being Revisited," p. 724.

5. Ibid., p. 719.

6. Susan Auger et al., "Participatory Group Prenatal Education Using Photonovels: Evaluation of a Lay Health Educator Model With Low-Income Latinas," *Journal for Participatory Medicine* 7 (December 2015).

7. Wabash National Study website, http://www.liberalarts.wabash.edu/study-overview/.

8. Wabash National Study of Liberal Arts Education, "Overview of Findings From the First Year." Retrieved from http://static1.1.sqspcdn.com/static /f/333946/3612649/1247854258370/ Overview_of_Findings_from_the_First_ Year_web_07.17.09.pdf, p. 3.

9. Wabash National Study of Liberal Arts Education, "How Do Students Change Over Four Years of College?" Retrieved from http://static1.1.sqspcdn.com/ static/f/333946/10418206/ 1296073333 850/4-year-change-summary-website.pdf

10. Dirk van Dierendonck et al., "Ryff's Six-Factor Model of Psychological Well-Being, a Spanish Exploration," *Social Indicators Research* 87 (2008): 473–479.

11. George Kaplan et al., "Socioeconomic Determinants of Psychological Well-Being: The Role of Income, Income Change, and Income Sources Over 29 Years," *Annals of Epidemiology* 18 (2008): 531–537. The study was based on a 1965 representative sample of 6,928 county residents, as many as possible of whom were surveyed in 1974, 1983, and 1994; 1,127 were surveyed in all four years.

12. The full name of the test is "Student's t." William Sealy Gossett, a chemist, invented it to aid his work at the Guinness Brewery in Dublin, Ireland. Company policy forbade employees from publishing their work, so he used the pseudonym "Student."

13. I have chosen to invent these data so that I can show you the possibilities. Districts that serve middle- and professional-class families typically score higher on such tests than districts that serve

poorer families. This may have nothing to do with the quality of their teaching, but using real data wouldn't let us show contrary cases.

14. Medical research usually requires a much higher level of confidence than that, because the risk of being wrong is so much greater. You'll need to consult a statistics text for details.

15. There are other extensions as well (e.g., MANOVA, Kruskal-Wallis test, Wilcoxon rank-sums test).

16. Paul M. Siegel, *Prestige in the American Occupational Structure*. University of Chicago, 1971.

17. See Jonathan Kozol, *Savage Inequalities: Children in America's Schools*. Harper, 1991; Ta-Nehisi Coates, "The Case for Reparations," *The Atlantic* (June 2014).

18. Jeffrey M. Conte, "A Review and Critique of Emotional Intelligence Measures," *Journal of Organizational Behavior* 26 (2005): 433–440.

19. Garrett J. Kafka and Albert Kozma, "The Construct Validity of Ryff's Scales of Psychological Well-Being (SPWB) and Their Relationship to Measures of Subjective Well-Being," *Social Indicators Research* 52 (2002):171–190.

CHAPTER 11

Recording Behavior: Acts and Reports of Acts

Type of Data		
Recording Behavior	**Acts, behavior, or events**	**Reports of acts, behavior, or events**
Public and private records		X
Detached observation	X	
Ethnography (participant observation)	X	(X)
In-depth interviews		X
Surveys/questionnaires		X
Critical incident interviews		X

(left margin: Data Collection Method)

magine walking down a street in a medium-sized city. You don't live there. In fact, this is your first visit. What do you see? Buildings, storefronts, cars and trams, and perhaps pedestrian areas with sidewalk cafés. Lots of people strolling? Or just a few? Office workers on lunch break? Or panhandlers on the corner? Upscale or downscale businesses, or perhaps both? Signs saying "For Lease," or marks of prosperity? You can learn a lot just by observing what's around you. You see people doing things, and you see the city they've built. You just need to understand what they have to tell you

Take the downtown of my college city at 11 a.m. on a weekday. The core area is six blocks long and almost as wide. Most of the buildings are two or three stories high, with a few taller, but the stores are all at ground level, and there aren't obvious offices on the upper floors. Some of the older brick buildings sport painted ads for soaps and household cleaners of the kind common before the 1930s. They are clearly nostalgia pieces. Other buildings have newly painted murals depicting the city's imagined agricultural past.

The main street is one-way, a single wide lane with cars angle-parked on both sides. Every 40 feet, you see trash bins nestled in wrought-iron containers that match the faux-antique streetlights. Large trees shade the sidewalks. The street is lined with stores, and there is a plaza-like park with a few benches.

The downtown businesses are a mixed lot. The core downtown has at least six jewelry stores, four high-end restaurants, a few mid-priced eateries, two optometrists plus an upscale eyeglass store, nine banks, and a very nice children's bookstore. It seems rather ritzy.

But no one is shopping here on this weekday morning. You see two thrift stores, one of them advertising "estate sales" (clearly not from high-end estates). You find several discount clothiers and a few vacant stores on the connector street. Looking more closely, you see "For Lease" signs in several second-story windows. You see peeling paint and (in the distance) a few homeless people walking the other way. You start counting the hair and nail salons, finding 17 within a few blocks' radius. Not high end ones, either. They serve the poorer classes.

Is this area upscale or downscale? It seems both. The main street with its neat brick sidewalks, big trees, antique streetlights and trash cans, nostalgic paintings, banks, and high-end restaurants tells us what the city leaders want. They see a prosperous and genteel place where the "right people" can do their business. That's their imagined tradition. Look carefully or move a block away from the center, and this carefully tended picture begins to fray.

In fact, this is not an overall prosperous place. It is two cities, hiding as one. One caters to the professional classes—the south-siders, whose larger and older homes make them seem more numerous than they are. The other serves the north-siders: working-class people with service industry jobs, just getting by. Business is bad for both, but especially for the upscale places that the city leaders favor.

All this from walking the streets at 11 a.m., noticing what people are doing and not doing, and what is and isn't there. This is what observational research is all about.

Watching People

Now imagine this. You're at a business meeting, with colleagues you know reasonably well. You all break for coffee and stand around chatting. You are talking with two coworkers about your weekend plans. It's relaxed. You are all enjoying the conversation. Can you visualize this? Good. Now answer a few questions:

- How far are you standing from the coworkers? How directly are you facing them? Does this vary with your topic of conversation? How?
- Does gender matter? Would you be standing differently, if your coworkers were female and you were male—or vice versa? How about if all three of you were male? All three female? How does gender affect conversational position?
- What if one of them were your boss? Same conversation, same relaxed tone, just a status difference. What would be different in how you stand?

This is a perfect opportunity for an observational study.

In the mid-1960s, Edward T. Hall published a book based on two decades of systematic observations of how people in various societies use space.[1] In it he distinguished four zones, each with different spatial norms. In the "public zone," people stand far from each other—in the United States, between 12 and 25 feet. This is the distance granted to public speakers, to professors in lecture classes, and to politicians who hold high office. These people can approach others, but those others are not supposed to approach them. This reflects a status difference. Only people of equal status can be on the same stage.

"Social distance" is closer—5 to 10 feet in the United States. This is the distance you stand from strangers, if that's possible. Interactions with store clerks are at the near end of this range; most people move to the far end when not interacting. There are exceptions: elevators, movie theaters, and lines among them. Here, though, there are special rules. Everyone faces front in elevators, for example, and looks into the distance rather than viewing anyone directly. This maintains a fictional social distance when the actual distance is impossible to achieve.

"Personal distance" and "intimate distance" are closer still—2 to 5 feet and 0 to 2 feet, respectively, for most Americans. Your imagined break-time conversation is probably in the former category, perhaps closer to 5 feet with the boss present or in mixed-gender conversation. In the United States, a group of all women will stand closer than a group of all men. The men will also typically not face each other directly. American men become uncomfortable standing too close to one another. They maintain a clear line between personal distance and intimacy.

Hall pointed out that these four zones are present in all cultures, but the actual distance involved varies widely. For example, personal distance in Arab culture verges on what Americans think is intimate. Business colleagues stand a mere foot from each other, close enough to smell each other's breath. This is a sign of honesty and cordial dealing. Americans think it is pushy, but Arab business folk think that Americans stand too far away and find them distant and cold. Different ways of using space can easily produce misunderstanding and ill will.

Watching Gender Speech

Gender also matters. Sociolinguist Deborah Tannen has conducted many observations of men and women in conversation and has identified several ways in which they use speech differently. Though there is considerable overlap, she found that a higher proportion of men's speech is "report-talk": talk designed to convey information. A higher proportion of women's speech, by contrast, is "rapport-talk": talk designed to produce connection. Both men and women use both styles, but the balance is different. To the extent that they use language differently, men and women can easily misunderstand one another. Their two patterns amount to a culturally learned difference in ways of speaking.

Tannen argued that boys learn in childhood to maintain relationships primarily through their activities, so conversation for adult males becomes a contest.[2] A man is an individual in a hierarchical social order "in which he [is] either one-up or one-down."[3] Girls, by contrast, are socialized as children to believe that "talk is the glue that holds relationships together."[4] As adults, women have conversations that are "negotiations for closeness in which people try to seek and give confirmation and support, and to reach consensus."[5] Boys do this, too, just as girls convey information. Yet Tannen's research with children showed that, on balance, their styles differ.

In one study, for example, Tannen analyzed videotapes in which 2nd-, 6th-, and 10th-grade same-sex best friends talked to each other for 20 minutes in an experimental setting.[6] She then coded those conversations, using John Gumperz's framework for cross-cultural communication.[7] This is essentially a list of strategies that conversation partners use to keep a conversation going. Tannen wrote that

> the girls exhibit minimal or no difficulty finding something to talk about, and they talk about a small number of topics, all related to troubles. There is more concern among the girls with avoidance of anger and disagreement. The boys exhibit more discomfort with the situation. The . . . younger boys produce small amounts of talk about a great number of topics. The 10th-grade boys talk about highly personal topics, but each develops his own topic and minimizes the other's.[8]

Tannen concluded that "these differences in ways of creating involvement can account for frustrations in cross-gender conversations."[9] Neither gender is at fault; they just use language differently.

Both Hall and Tannen wrote popular books on their respective topics. They also received the criticism typically addressed at scholars who do so. (Calling a scholar's work "journalistic" is a common term of abuse.) Hall seldom published his individual studies. Tannen has published not just popular books but also a large number of journal articles and scholarly book chapters—more than 100 as of early 2016. Her work is harder to dismiss. It is also easier to map onto our six-step system.

Take the study mentioned above. The *research question* was "What differences can we observe in the conversational strategies of best-friend pairs of boys and girls at three different ages?" This is a descriptive *logical structure,* because it asked Tannen to observe pairs of kids talking and describe what she saw. Her *type of data* was behavior, and her *data collection method* was detached observation. Her *data collection site* was the laboratory or school where the taping occurred, and her *data analysis method* involved coding the data according to Gumperz's qualitative scheme and then looking for distinct patterns. The research design was extremely straightforward.

That is often true of observational studies. If you can observe behavior, you can analyze it.

Collecting Self-Reports

What do you do, though, if you can't observe? Lots of things go on behind closed doors; we all know that. Some things don't even need doors to hide them. You can't observe people's dreams, for example, nor where homeless people sleep, nor how often people forget to tip restaurant wait staff, nor what people are thinking about at different times of day. At least you can't do this consistently. If you want such information, you need people to report it to you. There are several ways to get such reports. I'll start with two common ones.

First, you can use **social surveys** to ask people what they have done. We learned at the beginning of Chapter 3 that various polling organizations routinely ask Americans if they have attended a religious service in the past week. About 40% tell the Gallup and Pew pollsters that they have, and the figure for the General Social Survey is a few percentage points lower. This is much higher than religious attendance in most other countries. Interestingly, it is also higher than the few cases in which people have conducted systematic counts.[10] Many Americans apparently feel that they should be attending church more than they do, and this inflates the figures.

Another reporting strategy often works better: time diaries. These are daily diaries that people fill out, listing the previous day's activities and the time they spent on them. Tuesday's entry reports on Monday, Wednesday's on Tuesday, and so on. Diaries are more expensive to collect than surveys, and they require more commitment from the participants. But they are nearly contemporaneous records. Moreover, they don't highlight any single activity, so people are not apt to inflate or deflate the time they spent on them. We cited a diary study in Chapter 3 that found that just 29% of Americans actually attended some sort of religious service.[11] This is more accurate than the 40% that pollsters' direct questions elicited.

A Variation: The Beeper Studies

Reed Larson and Mihaly Csikszentmihalyi brought the time diaries technique into the electronic age. In an early study, they gave participants electronic pagers, which signaled them according to a random schedule, once every 2 hours between 8 a.m. and 10 p.m. for a week.[12] The signal was a cue to complete a self-report questionnaire that asked what they were doing at that specific moment in time.

"Participants might be driving a car, eating supper, or watching television. When the pager signals, they are to complete a report if it is at all possible."[13] The researchers learned about activities but also about feelings, boredom or anxiety, and what people thought about during a typical day.

They later used this technique with a random sample of high school students.[14] Perhaps unsurprisingly, the study found that teens spent more time watching television than they did studying. They were also unhappier when they were alone, though they cheered up when they got together with friends and also when they were engaged in any engrossing activity. The reports included occasions of drug use, fights with parents, and sexual intercourse, which the authors argued speaks to the technique's ability to capture adolescent experience accurately.

THINK ABOUT IT
Would you be willing to write down what you are doing at six random times during the day? How could researchers entice you to participate?

Larson and Csikszentmihalyi called their technique "the experience sampling method." Its main problem is the time commitment it takes on the part of the participants. But it collects better data than do written diaries and much better data than after-the-fact surveys. It is one of the better ways of collecting people's reports of their own behavior.

Watching Animals

Animal researchers can't rely on reports; they have to observe things. At least so far, even chimps and dolphins can't tell us what they have been doing. We have to watch them if we want to find out anything at all. Field biologists know how to do this. They have to find the animals and then get them accustomed enough to people that they let the researchers observe them without getting them so accustomed that they change what they are doing. This is a hard balance to reach. Each species is different, so there is no single rule that works for them all.

I'll give you three examples of animal observation research. These will show you what's possible and what's difficult about animal observations.

Watching Chimps

The first example is well known: Jane Goodall's work with wild chimpanzees (*Pan troglodytes*) in the Gombe Stream National Park in Western Tanzania.[15] Goodall began observing chimps in 1960, before much was known about their family structure, their intelligence, or even their diet. She would locate chimp groups in the park, sit as near to them as they would allow, and quietly take notes on their behavior. She learned to identify individuals and noted that they had distinct personalities. At the time, this was a revolutionary insight. It also attracted criticism. She was accused of anthropomorphizing the chimps, because she referred to them by names rather than by numbers. Numbering them was supposed to maintain researcher objectivity.

Goodall did, however, take thorough notes on the chimps' behavior and trained her research assistants to do so as well. By the late 1960s, assistants were checking forms that listed such things as aggressive displays (tipping the head, flapping hands in the air, swaying branches, throwing objects, and charging), tool use (using twigs to collect termites, making leaf-sponges to sop up water), interpersonal contact (various kinds of grooming, patting, hugging, leaning, touching chins), and communication (greeting hoot, pant-hoot, alarm, excited food grunt).[16] These records helped Goodall identify patterns in chimp behavior that ultimately convinced other investigators of the complexity of chimpanzee social life.

One of Goodall's most significant discoveries came early in her work, when she observed an older male chimp, "David Greybeard," using stems of grass to pull termites out of a nest. He inserted the stem, wriggled it around, then removed it covered with termites, which he ate. She later observed him and another chimp stripping leaves off twigs to do the same kind of termite "fishing." This was more than tool use;

it was tool creation. At the time, animal researchers thought that tool making was a purely human practice. Now they realize that several nonhuman species do it, too.[17]

Goodall also discovered that chimps hunt and eat smaller primates, sometimes hunting them in groups and then sharing the meat. She even observed chimp intra-group warfare. During a four-year period in the mid-1970s, one chimp band at Gombe wiped out another. Goodall was herself surprised by this, as she had previously thought that "Gombe chimpanzees were, for the most part, rather nicer than human beings."[18] She expressed shock that chimps, like humans, have a dark side to their nature. Critics argued that the war may well have been instigated by Goodall's practice of feeding the local band, which they suspected was defending its access to these resources.[19] Goodall replied, however, that the band that was attacked had its own food elsewhere and was, moreover, not moving in on the Gombe group's territory. Research by others has since shown that chimpanzee warfare is rare but not likely driven by human interference.[20]

Goodall's observational study of chimpanzees has been extremely influential, but it is not different in kind from other animal observation research. The *research question* is almost always "What do these animals do?" The *logical structure* is descriptive. The *type of data* is behavior, and the *data collection method* is observation. The *data collection site* is wherever the animals can be found. The *data analysis method* varies, depending on the tools available. Goodall herself depended on qualitative coding and the charting of behavior patterns.

That charting was very well done. Joseph Feldblum and his colleagues recently used social network analysis software to reanalyze Goodall's notes. They were able to trace the origins of the mid-1970s "Gombe War" to a split in the Gombe friendship patterns several years earlier.[21] When the prime group leader died, the group split in two. One side later wiped out the other. Being able to trace this pattern 30 years after the fact is a testimony to how thorough Goodall's observations were.

Ravens and Elephant-Shrews

Not all animal observation projects take this much time. Some are much simpler. They can be important, however, especially when they help preserve endangered species. Field biologist Wendy McIntyre completed one such study for the U.S. Fish and Wildlife Service.[22] It was designed to find a new habitat for the endangered desert tortoise (*Gopherus agassizii*). Found only in the Mohave and Sonoran Deserts of the American Southwest, this tortoise has been losing ground for decades. As the human population grows, they are threatened by everything from powerlines and pipelines to off-road bikes and dune buggies. They are also threatened by the U.S. military. The U.S. Army uses much of the California desert for target practice, bombing ranges, and war games. McIntyre was asked to evaluate some land outside the military reserves, to see whether tortoises could be moved there successfully.

Her first step was to survey the territory, to see what other wildlife was already inhabiting it. Of particular concern were common ravens (*Corvus corax*). They prey on juvenile tortoises, flipping them over and attacking their softer undersides. Predation is not so bad in territory the tortoises know well, because they dig burrows, which the ravens cannot enter. Moving them to new territory, however, spells danger if there are ravens around. McIntyre had to figure out where the ravens were most likely to be. She could then recommend that the tortoises be released elsewhere.

Her strategy was to map the proposed release area, to see where ravens congregate. She and several assistants divided the area into several-acre sections and then counted the ravens they found there in various seasons and at various times of day. They mapped the results, overlaying them on a map of local roads, powerlines, and so on. Figure 11.1 is a reproduction of her map. It shows clearly that the ravens hang out in areas where they can scavenge food waste from passing travelers. McIntyre recommended that the military avoid releasing tortoises near these sites.

This was a classic short-term animal observation project, designed to solve a specific problem in wildlife conservation. Unlike Goodall's project, it didn't provide new knowledge about the target species. It did, however, document the ravens' habitual locations, which helped authorities decide which areas to avoid in their tortoise rescue project.

FIGURE 11.1   McIntyre's Raven Map

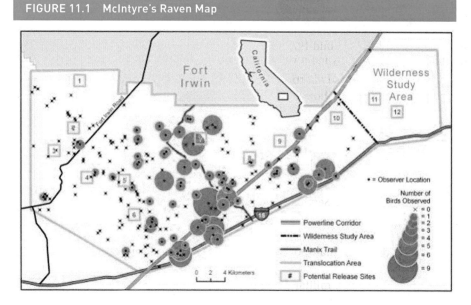

Source: Blodwyn M. McIntyre: "Raven Nest Mapping for Management Plan and Threats Assessment for the Desert Tortoise," Contract No. 814405m053. Report to the U.S. Fish and Wildlife Service, 2006

What If They Hide?

Let's turn to a third observational study—this one of an animal that is hard to find. Wild chimpanzees often avoid humans, but the researchers can at least hear them. Biologists who study giant elephant-shrews (*Rhynchocyon* sp.) can spend a long time in their habitat without seeing hide nor hair of them. How do you observe an animal that stays hidden?

Elephant-shrews are small, long-nosed, scaly-tailed mammals that live in the undisturbed lowland and mountain woodlands of eastern Africa. The "giant" variety are up to 10 inches long. They forage in the leaf litter for beetles, termites, other insects, and centipedes, which they uncover with their noses and scoop up with their long tongues. They form monogamous pairs, each of which establishes its own several-acre territory. Habitat damage is their greatest enemy.

Why aren't they seen? There are several reasons. First, they live in relatively deep woods, so they have lots of places to hide. Second, they are not very social and do not congregate. It is much easier for solitary animals to hide than for groups to do so. Third, they are well camouflaged and adept at hiding; they can freeze and can scarcely be seen. Fourth, if discovered, they are quick and can dash away from threats. Some species even clear trails through the fallen leaves so that they can run to safety quickly. Finally, they make their nests in rock crevices, beneath tree roots, and in holes of their own making. They maintain as many as 10 of these nests across their territory. This ensures that a hiding place is never far away.

Stephanie Coster and David Ribble wanted to estimate the number of black-and-rufus elephant-shrews in the Chome Forest Reserve in Tanzania.[23] That forest is dense enough to make finding and counting the shrews impossible. Moreover, parts of the forest are subject to illegal logging, which ruins shrew habitat. How could they figure out how many shrews this forest is currently supporting? How could they determine the extent to which logging depressed shrew numbers?

They decided to locate shrew nests and then extrapolate from that figure to an estimate of the shrew population. Rather than search the whole forest, they searched a representative portion of it. They chose 12 strips to search, each one 300 meters long and 5 meters wide. They set these strips a half kilometer apart along an existing trail. They then counted the number of nests in the strips. At each nest, they measured the amount of forest cover. This gave them a sense of how different amounts of cover affected shrew populations.

Nests, of course, are not shrews, but at least you can find them. They used previous research on other giant shrew populations to get a shrew-to-nest ratio. Using this method, they discovered that the Chome forest has a much lower density of black-and-rufus elephant-shrews per square kilometer than do other forests in that region. This might be due to illegal logging, to the presence of a nearby village, or to some other factor. Or, perhaps, the Chome shrews had a much different shrew-to-nest ratio there than did the shrews in other areas. That's not likely, however. In any case, they did not need to count actual shrews to estimate the size of their population.

Such creativity is common in animal research. It is also used for investigating humans. For example, Chapter 14 explores some of the ways that researchers have attempted to count homeless people. They, too, are hard to count, because they often hide to avoid authorities. Fortunately, we can hire homeless people to help us find other street people, and the homeless people we do find can tell us where they spent the last several nights. They might have been on the streets, in hotels, in cars, in shelters, or elsewhere. Being able to use reports of acts to supplement our observations helps tremendously. Animal researchers are not so lucky.

THINK ABOUT IT
How can you draw conclusions about animal behavior when the animals are so shy that you can't observe them directly?

Now let's turn to another kind of observation: experiments.

Experiments

At their simplest, experiments work by dividing test subjects into two groups, only one of which is exposed to the test conditions. The other group serves as a control. Both groups have the same experiences, except that the test subjects experience the condition that is being tested and the control group does not. Investigators observe the differing results. If the groups' results are significantly different, then the investigators conclude that the test condition had an effect.

This structure works for experiments on the physical world. It also works for experiments on plants, animals, and people. I, personally, am most interested in people, and experiments that are done properly can tell us things about people that we otherwise would not know. Specifically, experiments let us manipulate people's surroundings in precise ways. We then observe whether those manipulations make a difference in people's behavior.

The only difference between experiments and other kinds of observational studies is this manipulation. They give us a precise knowledge of the factors that shape behavior, but at a cost. Almost all experiments require a laboratory setting. They thus may tell us less than we'd like about human behavior in the real world.

Experiments About Stereotype Threat

We'll start with a justifiably famous example. Social psychologist Claude Steele has spent much of his career investigating what he calls "stereotype threat." This is the threat that people of stigmatized groups feel when they are doing something that their group is not expected to do well. Steele argued that mere knowledge of the stereotype can be distracting enough to hurt an individual's performance. African American students, for example, are aware that people of their race are frequently thought incapable of serious intellectual work. Steele wanted to find out whether this awareness hurt their performance.

Together with Joshua Aronson, Steele designed a set of four experiments to test his hypothesis.[24] Their first study was typical of the method they used. First, they randomly assigned 114 White and African American elite university students to one of three test conditions. All took the same 30-minute test, containing questions from the verbal section of the Graduate Record Exam that would be difficult for any undergraduate to answer well.

- One group was told that this was a test of verbal ability, designed to measure their strengths and weaknesses. This was the experimental group, as the notice that the test measured ability should activate the African Americans' stereotype threat.
- A second group was told that it was *not* a test of personal ability, but an effort to improve the investigators' understanding of student verbal learning. This was the control group, as there is no reason for students to think that their own ability is being measured.
- The third group was also told that the test was not examining their personal ability, but that it was designed to provide "even highly verbal people with a mental challenge." This was a second control group, designed to see if diverting attention away from race would have any effect.

Once the test was over, the students were asked three sets of questions about their experience. First, they were asked 18 questions about their sense of academic competence and self-worth. These were rated on a scale from 1 to 5, low to high. Then they were asked 12 questions about their experiences during the test. These included questions about distracting thoughts (e.g., "I wondered what the experimenter would think about me." "I thought about how poorly I was doing."), also rated from 1 (never) to 5 (very often). Finally, they were asked to rate the test's difficulty and their own estimate of their final score. These became additional independent variables, along with the test-takers' race and gender. The test scores themselves were the dependent variable.

In fact, the experimental group confirmed the effect that stereotype threat had on the African American participants. Their scores were significantly lower than White students' scores, after controlling for their differing academic skills as measured by SAT scores. This was not the case with the control group. The third group's scores, however, were also split by race. Apparently, White students increased their efforts, though Black students did not.

To sort out this anomaly, Steele and Aronson set up three further experiments. Study 2 used a revised test and left out the "mental challenge" group, focusing only on the experimental and control groups. It added an anxiety questionnaire to the after-test surveys, and it also used computer terminals in place of paper and pencils. This let the investigators track mouse movements, hesitations, and other signs of nervousness. Study 3 used three groups but began the test with an 80-item word-completion exercise that included 12 words that called racial stereotypes to mind:

__ __ C E (race), __ __ O R (poor), __ __ A C K (black), and so on. It also included seven words that suggested poor academic performance: __ __ M B (dumb), F L __ __ __ __ (flunk), etc. Study 4 repeated Study 2, except that it asked the experimental group members to list their race on a demographic questionnaire at the start of the exam. This primed them to think about race before the event. The control group was not asked to provide this information.

In general, all four studies showed that stereotype threat makes a difference to test performance. Each provided that threat in a different form. For example, the researchers found that Black students who thought the test measured intelligence were more likely to complete word fragments with relevant negative stereotypes (e.g., "__ __ M B" with "dumb" rather than "numb"; "__ __ C E" with "race" rather than "face"). Each study showed a difference between the races as well as between experimental and control groups. The final two studies, which overtly primed African American students to think about race, depressed their performance even more than did the studies described as tests of individual ability. Steele and Aronson conclude:

> What this experiment shows is that mere cognitive availability of the racial stereotype is enough to depress Black participants' intellectual performance, and that this is so even when the test is presented as not diagnostic of intelligence.[25]

Stereotypes become a self-fulfilling prophecy.[26]

Experiments About Discrimination

Steele and Aronson's study is only one of many experiments designed to see how race works in America. Many social experiments have been designed to measure American racial discrimination.

Marianne Bertrand and Sendhil Mullainathan, for example, sent thousands of résumés to potential employers, identical in everything except the applicants' first names.[27] Those with stereotypically "Black" names, such as Jamal and Lakisha, received far fewer callbacks than did those with stereotypically "White" names, such as Brendan, Emily, and Greg. This indicates that many prospective employers do respond to racial differences in first names. They systematically prefer to hire people they think are White over those they think are Black.

Devah Pager, Bruce Western, and Bart Bonikowski did a similar experiment, but they went beyond mere résumés. They sent actual people to apply for entry-level low-wage jobs, after training them to be as alike as possible in their behavior.[28] Not only were Black applicants half as likely as equally qualified Whites to receive a callback or job offer, but Black and Latino applicants with no arrest records also fared no better than White applicants just released from prison. This, too, demonstrates discrimination.

Such experiments are relatively easy to design. Like all experiments, they compare two groups that differ as little as possible from one another. In these studies, the relevant topic is race; all other differences are minimized. Both groups receive the same treatment, and the results are compared. Most such experiments, though not all, show that Americans treat people from different races differently. Most White Americans are surprised that this is the case.

In a separate article, Sendhil Mullainathan argued that these experiments do not demonstrate conscious bigotry. He distinguished between two kinds of thinking, which he labeled "fast" and "slow." "Slow" thinking weighs matters carefully. It looks at all sides of an issue before coming to judgment. This thinking does not discriminate, because it is aware of possible **bias** and guards against it. It is, however, deliberate; it is not suited to making quick decisions, such as which résumés are interesting enough to ask their owners for an interview. That is the job of "fast" thinking:

> Our snap judgments rely on all the associations we have—from fictional television shows to news reports. They use stereotypes, both the accurate and the inaccurate, both those we would want to use and ones we find repulsive.[29]

Employers have to make snap judgments about whom to consider further, whether sorting through résumés or conducting screening interviews. That calls for fast thinking, which leads them to discriminate—whether or not they actually want to. Mullainathan recommended that employers arrange their interviews more consciously, slowing them down so that they can make a considered decision. This would do more than lower levels of employment discrimination. It would also give employers a larger pool of potentially good workers.

Rules for Experiments

Designing experiments is not terribly difficult. Here are some basic rules:

1. *Be very clear about what you are trying to test.* Experiments work best when you vary just one factor at a time. If that isn't possible, then use more than one control group, each of which controls a single factor. For example, Bertrand and Mullainathan's résumé experiment varied only first names. Steele and Aronson used multiple control groups.
2. *Design your intervention carefully so that it varies exactly what you intend.* Check to be sure that it does not affect your outcomes in unexpected ways. For example, Steele and Aronson ran multiple experiments to account for possible interfering factors.
3. *Select a large enough sample so that your results are not affected by just one or a few individuals.* For example, Bertrand and Mullainathan sent out thousands of résumés testing potential discrimination.

4. *Consider measuring both groups before and after your intervention, if that's possible.* This can help you identify whether there are prior differences between your experimental group and your control group. It can also let you measure individual progress; this is very helpful if you are trying to evaluate a medical treatment, an educational technique, or the like. For example, Susan Auger's study of a pregnancy literacy program for low-income Latinas used a pretest/posttest design to evaluate how much knowledge the women had gained.[30] A simple posttest would not have taken into account the women's prior knowledge differences.

5. *Monitor your experiment carefully.* Watch for unexpected factors that might alter the outcome. For example, Auger found that staff at one of the two clinic sites gave study participants inaccurate medical information. That affected their answers on the posttest.

6. *Review all your data at the end, to make sure that there were no unexpected differences between your experimental and your control groups.* If there were, either run the experiment again or report the differences in your conclusions.

Following these rules will make your research conclusions more secure.

Research Ethics

Different kinds of observational studies raise different ethical questions. All require Institutional Review Board approval, but some studies easily pass ethical scrutiny whereas others do not. The primary principle is the same for all: *Do not harm your research participants.* The nature of potential harm depends on the particular kind of observations you make and on what other information you gather.

In general, observing people's behavior in public raises few ethical issues. If the behavior is public, the actors know that it is public, and you do not collect identifying information about them, then you are neither invading their privacy nor endangering them by your mere observations. Few IRBs will limit your activity. The same is true of observing animals, either in captivity or in their natural habitats. So long as you do not interfere with their activities—such as by frightening them, interfering with their feeding, or significantly altering their behavior—your research is apt to be approved. In neither case are you interfering with or harming them as a result of activities that they would be engaged in already.

An exception would be for a study of officially protected populations (children, prisoners, or hospital patients), vulnerable people (homeless people), or rare animals. For example, a local police department asked my university to approve a study that would have fitted 20 local homeless people with GPS trackers, to find the routes they take in their daily wanderings through our city. They would do so with the individuals' permission. They planned to use the results to locate services (such as restrooms) in places where homeless people would use them. Our IRB did not approve the research. Even though the department's leadership designed this research to help the homeless, a future, more punitive leadership might use it to harass them. Goodwill on the researcher's part is not enough to avoid such a project's ethical pitfalls.

I described another questionable observational study in Chapter 4: Laud Humphreys's study of impersonal male sex in public places.[31] Humphreys observed anonymous sexual encounters in public restrooms, at a time and place where such sex was illegal. After discovering the patterns of behavior, he took down the men's license plate numbers and then showed up on their doorsteps six months later to interview them. Despite storing his data in a locked bank vault in another state and thoroughly disguising the men in his writings, he endangered people without their permission. A zealous prosecutor could have subpoenaed Humphreys's records and ruined the men's lives and reputations.

Animals don't have to worry about prosecutors, but animal researchers do have to be careful that they observe those animals in a way that does not significantly alter their behavior. For example, whale researchers have to be careful that their observations do not interfere with whale migration or feeding.[32] Commercial whale-watching boats do, indeed, cause whales to stop feeding and move away, though some research suggests that the impact on individual whales is small enough not to be worrisome.[33] Still, researchers do not want to add to whale stress. Among other things, it makes their observations less typical of whales' natural behavior.

Experiments raise parallel concerns. Studies like Bertrand and Mullainathan's résumé experiment are unproblematic: They responded to hundreds of public job ads, observing which applicant names produced callbacks and which did not. This endangers no one and violates no one's privacy. At the other end of the spectrum, the infamous Nazi experiments on concentration camp prisoners caused considerable pain, disfigurement, and death.[34] They are one of the reasons that research on animals and humans now needs IRB approval.

The current gray area involves studies that need to mislead their participants in order to be effective. Steele and Aronson's experiments, for example, would not have been able to test for stereotype threat if the participants had known in advance what was going on. Both the control group and the experimental group needed to be ignorant of the project's real aims. It was the only way that the researchers could get accurate data.

Typically, investigators do two things when they propose such experiments. First, they get IRB approval for the deception—and also IRB advice about how to mitigate its effects (which in this case were not very severe). Second, they usually debrief the participants afterward, so that they know what is really going on. In Steele and Aronson's case, they could not debrief the students immediately. Had word gotten into the student community about this project's real intent, then follow-up research would have been impossible. Thus, Steele and Aronson waited until the project was over and scheduled for publication before telling the research participants what it was all about. This seemed to them, and to the IRB, to be a reasonable compromise. And it was.

Review Questions

1. What kinds of research questions lend themselves to observational studies? When is observation the best choice for a data collection method?

2. When do you need to use self-reports instead of detached observation? What precautions do you have to take to ensure that you are getting accurate data?

3. What kinds of things can you learn by observing animals? What are some indirect ways that you can study animal behavior?

4. Under what circumstances do social and natural scientists use experiments as a way to gauge behavior? What are some of the advantages and drawbacks?

5. What special ethical issues do observational studies raise?

The open-access Student Study Site at **study.sagepub.com/spickard** has a variety of useful study tools, including SAGE journal articles, video & web resources, eFlashcards, and quizzes.

Notes

1. Edward T. Hall, *The Hidden Dimension*. Doubleday, 1966.

2. Deborah Tannen, *You Just Don't Understand: Men and Women in Conversation*. Harper-Collins, 1990.

3. Ibid., p. 24.

4. Ibid., p. 85.

5. Ibid., p. 25.

6. Deborah Tannen, "Gender Differences in Topical Coherence: Creating Involvement in Best Friends' Talk," *Discourse Processes* 13 (1990): 73–90.

7. John Gumperz, *Discourse Strategies*. Cambridge University Press, 1982.

8. Tannen, "Gender Differences in Topical Coherence," p. 73.

9. Ibid.

10. C. Kirk Hadaway, Penny Long Marler, and Mark Chaves, "What the Polls Don't Show: A Closer Look at U.S. Church Attendance," *American Sociological Review* 58 (1993): 741–752.

11. Stanley Presser and Linda Stinson, "Data Collection Mode and Social Desirability Bias in Self-Reported Religious

(Continued)

(Continued)

Attendance," *American Sociological Review* 63 (1998): 137–145.

12. Reed Larson and Mihaly Csikszentmihalyi, "The Experience Sampling Method," *New Directions for Methodology of Social and Behavioral Science* 15 (1983): 41–56.

13. Ibid., p. 43.

14. Mihaly Csikszentmihalyi et al., "The Ecology of Adolescent Experience," *Journal of Youth and Adolescence* 6 (1977): 281–294.

15. For the best overview, see Jane Goodall, *The Chimpanzees of Gombe: Patterns of Behavior.* Belknap Press, 1986.

16. My wife worked as Goodall's assistant for a few months in 1968. I was amused to hear her later refer to our daughter's early vocalizations as "excited food grunts." They were identical to what she had observed with chimps in the field.

17. See, for example, G. R. Hunt, "Manufacture and Use of Hook-Tools by New Caledonian Crows," *Nature* 379 (1996): 249–251.

18. Jane Goodall, *Through a Window: My Thirty Years With the Chimpanzees of Gombe.* Houghton Mifflin Harcourt, 2010, p. 128.

19. Margaret Power, *The Egalitarians—Human and Chimpanzee: An Anthropological View of Social Organization.* Cambridge University Press, 1991.

20. Michael Wilson et al., "Lethal Aggression in Pan Is Better Explained by Adaptive Strategies Than Human Impacts," *Nature* 513 (2014): 414.

21. Joseph Feldblum et al., "Politics by Other Means: Social Networks, Community Identification, and the 'Four Years' War' in the Chimpanzees of Gombe National Park, Tanzania." Podium presentation at the 2014 American Association of Physical Anthropologists meeting, Calgary, Ontario, April 12.

22. Blodwyn M. McIntyre, "Raven Nest Mapping for Management Plan and Threats Assessment for the Desert Tortoise," Contract No. 814405m053. Report to the U.S. Fish and Wildlife Service, 2006.

23. This is the least known of the three giant elephant-shrew species. Stephanie Coster and David O. Ribble, "Density and Cover Preferences of Black-and-Rufous Elephant-Shrews (Rhynchocyon petersi) in Chome Forest Reserve, Tanzania," *Belgian Journal of Zoology* 135 (Suppl., 2005): 175–177.

24. Claude Steele and Joshua Aronson, "Stereotype Threat and the Intellectual Performance of African-Americans," *Journal of Personality and Social Psychology* 69 (1995): 787–811.

25. Ibid., p. 808.

26. Steele and Aronson's findings are considerably more complex than I can present here. Steele has also studied stereotype threats to women studying math and science. See S. J. Spencer, C. Steele, et al., "Stereotype Threat and Women's

Math Performance," *Journal of Experimental Social Psychology* 35 (1999): 4–28.

27. Marianne Bertrand and Sendhil Mullainathan: "Are Emily and Greg More Employable Than Lakisha and Jamal? A Field Experiment on Labor Market Discrimination," National Bureau of Economic Research Working Paper #9873, July 2003. Retrieved from http://www.nber.org/papers/w9873.pdf

28. Devah Pager et al., "Discrimination in a Low-Wage Labor Market: A Field Experiment," *American Sociological Review* 74 (2009): 777–799.

29. Sendhil Mullainathan, "Racial Bias, Even When We Have Good Intentions," *New York Times*, January 3, 2015, BU6. Retrieved from http://www.nytimes.com/2015/01/04/upshot/the-measuring-sticks-of-racial-bias-.html

30. Susan Auger et al., "Participatory Group Prenatal Education Using Photonovels: Evaluation of a Lay Health Educator Model With Low-Income Latinas," *Journal of Participatory Medicine* (December 2015).

31. Laud Humphreys, *Tearoom Trade: Impersonal Sex in Public Places.* Duckworth, 1970.

32. Lei Lani Steele et al., "Activity Budgets and Diving Behavior of Gray Whales (*Eschrichtius robustus*) in Feeding Grounds off Coastal British Columbia," *Marine Mammal Science* 24 (2008): 462–478.

33. Fredrik Christiansen and David Lusseau, "Linking Behavior to Vital Rates to Measure the Effects of Non-lethal Disturbance on Wildlife," *Conservation Letters* 8 (2015): 424–431.

34. The experiments included tests of the effects of hypothermia, of various pharmaceuticals, and of the effects of low atmospheric pressure. See the article "Nazi Medical Experiments" in the online *Holocaust Encyclopedia*. Retrieved from http://www.ushmm.org/wlc/en/article.php?ModuleId=10005168

CHAPTER 12

Finding Hidden Social Patterns: In Life, Texts, and Popular Culture

Type of Data		Hidden social patterns
Finding Hidden Patterns		
Detached observation		X
Ethnography (participant observation)		X
Content analysis		X
Discourse (or narrative) analysis		X
Grounded theory		X

Data Collection Method

C hapter 11 discussed how to learn things by observing people, animals, and the natural world. With people, observation lets us discover personal and social patterns. With animals, we observe behavior, some of it social. Natural phenomena are not social but are ripe for observation just the same.

The present chapter focuses on humans. We'll look at various ways to collect data about hidden social patterns. *Detached observation* is one such method, because it can reveal patterns of human behavior of which the participants are unaware. We covered it in Chapter 11, so we won't cover it here. We'll address *participant observation* in Chapter 13. Otherwise known as *ethnography,* it is a complex data collection method that needs its own treatment. We'll leave the related *grounded theory* method to that chapter as well.

That leaves us with two data collection methods that focus directly on finding hidden social patterns: **content analysis** and **discourse analysis** (or **narrative analysis**).They are related, in that both analyze texts, discourses, and artifacts of popular culture to discover social patterns hidden below the surface. They are the topic of this chapter. We'll see lots of examples, because that's the best way to learn how these methods work.

About Hidden Patterns

What is a hidden social pattern? Simply put, it is a pattern of behavior of which people are typically unaware. Edward T. Hall's research on body language and the distance that people stand or sit from one another is a good example.[1] As we saw in Chapter 11, young American men stand a bit farther from each other than do young American women and are less comfortable than women standing face-to-face. They also prefer to leave a seat between themselves and other men in movie theaters, if possible. These behaviors are largely unconscious, though easily revealed by observation.

Other such patterns abound. For example, Joseph Tobin and his team studied the cultural differences between Japanese, Chinese, and American preschools.[2] They used video to identify the behavioral habits that teachers tried to instill in their students. On seeing this video, my American students often remark that they never realized they had been socialized to be such talkers! Chinese and Japanese preschoolers speak quite well, but their teachers do not insist on individualized verbal performances to anywhere near the extent that American teachers do: "Can you tell me in words what this looks like?" "Can you use your words instead of hitting?" Students recognize the pattern once they see it, but it was hidden previously.

Some hidden patterns are less benign. For example, Monika Goyal and her colleagues found that a significantly lower percentage of African American children with severely painful appendicitis received opium-based pain medication than did White children (12% versus 34%).[3] This suggests a bias against African American children, though not necessarily racial animosity. Emergency room personnel may think that African American children do not feel pain as strongly as do Whites, or they may think that opium-based medications are more likely to lead to addiction in African American children. In any event, fewer African American children receive the pain relief they need. Other studies of racial discrepancies have uncovered differences in traffic law enforcement,[4] treatment of sellers on eBay,[5] treatment of job applicants,[6] and politicians' willingness to respond to constituents,[7] among other matters.[8] Though these patterns are no surprise to those who study race relations, they are not generally acknowledged. They can cause considerable concern when brought to light.

A recent controversy illustrates this point. To many people's dismay, only White actors were nominated for the 2016 Academy Awards (Oscars) for acting. No actors of color were nominated the previous year, either. In both years, the Twitterverse exploded with the hashtag #OscarsSoWhite, columnists fumed and defended, and the Academy of Motion Picture Arts and Sciences vowed to diversify its voting membership. The pattern was obvious. All one had to do was count. Zero nominations in the four acting categories, despite several stellar performances by Black actors that had been recognized by other award organizations.

The full data were even more disturbing. It turns out that the acting category was the second most diverse of the Oscar competition. Take a look at Figure 12.1.[9] On the one hand, the Oscar nominations for movies that appeared from 2006 to 2015 (which includes the 2016 nominees) were less lily white than ever before. On the other hand, they still did not approach the actual percentage of African Americans in the U.S. population. Thus the outcry.

Figure 12.1a shows considerable progress in the acting category, but Figure 12.1b shows something noticed less frequently. Many more Blacks have been nominated for acting Oscars than for any category besides songwriting. Only 1% of nominations in other categories have gone to Black artists. It would seem that Academy voters buy the stereotype that African Americans are good at music and can occasionally be showcased for acting, but are not world class at much else. Given Hollywood's liberal

FIGURE 12.1   Oscar Nominations of African Americans: (a) Acting Category, 1936–2015; (b) Selected Categories, 2006–2015

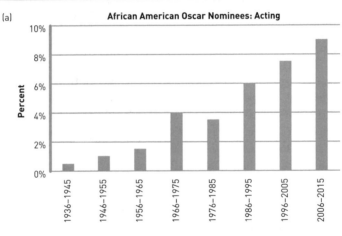

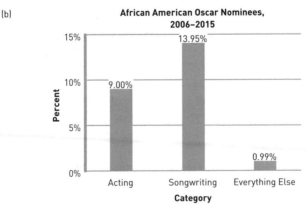

political leanings, this could well be unconscious **bias**, yet it is bias just the same. What does this example tell us about research?

First, it tells us that finding hidden patterns can be relatively straightforward. You notice a pattern, locate some data that let you test whether that pattern is true, and then compile your results. It's not rocket science.

Second, the example tells us that we need to look at lots of data, rather than just a bit of it. Yes, the 2015 and 2016 Oscar nominations for best actor, best actress, best supporting actor, and best supporting actress fit the #OscarsSoWhite hashtag. The 10-year total, however, was not so bad. In fact, it represented a steady increase in the percentage of African American nominations in that category, when viewed over the past 80 years.

However, the dearth of nominations in all but the acting and songwriting categories tells us something else. Between 2006 and 2015, just one African American was nominated for costume design, one for sound editing, and one for each of the two documentary categories. There were no nominations for cinematography, score, original screenplay, editing, and so on. Even if the picture for actors is not as bad as touted, #OscarsSoWhite makes an accurate point about the Academy Awards as a whole. As African American actor Chris Rock wrote, "It's a White industry. It just is."[10] He was not surprised that so few awards go to non-White movie artists. Neither should we be.

This is an example of content analysis. This data collection method examines the contents of some aspect of texts, discourses, or popular culture. Many examples of the technique, including this one, count the number of times that a particular event, incident, or theme occurs. They then compare that number to what would be the case if no hidden social pattern was operating. Other examples don't count things but instead use qualitative techniques to reveal patterns. We'll see some of each in the pages that follow. In either case, content analysis is a particularly powerful tool to probe beneath the surface of social life.

Analyzing Texts

Our Hollywood example analyzed the patterns by which people are honored for their work in the film industry. This is one form of content analysis, but there are others. Many content analyses work with texts. They reveal patterns that are hidden in the texts as written.

Adrienne Redd, for example, examined 555 unsigned editorials and letters to the editor in three of the world's most prominent newspapers: the *New York Times*, the *Jamaican Daily Gleaner*, and the *Times of India*.[11] Reading their comments on several world crises since World War II, she examined the ways in which writers described the nation-state. She looked at the terms they used, their metaphors, and their conclusions about the role that the nation-state must play in world events. Contrary to the predictions of several contemporary political scientists, she saw no signs of a decline in the reliance on nation-states as key building blocks of the international political order. She concluded that those predictions were premature.

As described in earlier chapters, Cindy Myers carried out a similar project, reading 20 years of editorials in the *New York Times* and the *Wall Street Journal*—respectively, the major national-level left-center and right-center newspapers in the United States.[12] Myers looked at the ways these two newspapers wrote about poverty. The two papers were quite different. As we'll see in the next part of this chapter, *Times* editorial writers portrayed poverty as a natural force, whereas *Journal* writers portrayed people as active, often choosing poverty rather than affluence. These two papers' differing ideas about poverty can be easily found in their prose.

These two investigators used a similar method:

1. Each collected a large series of texts that contained material relevant to the research question.
2. Each developed a coding system that identified specific aspects of those texts that related to that question.
3. Each coded the texts and then examined the codes, looking for patterns that might answer the research question.
4. Finally, each drew forth a complex answer, showing the hidden patterns that textual analysis revealed.

These four steps typify all content analysis research.

Dreams as Texts

Not all content analysis "texts" are written down. Some are elicited in the research process and others are nontextual cultural products. Let's look at a study that subjects dreams to textual analysis.

In 2002, Kelly Bulkeley published an analysis of the relationship between dream imagery and political outlook.[13] From a set of more than 400 dreams collected from college undergraduates, she chose 56 reported by respondents who had decidedly Republican or Democratic political allegiances. She chose that number because only 14 of the males had Republican leanings; she then took 14 people at random from among each of the three remaining groups: Democratic males, Republican females, and Democratic females. She deliberately chose people who were on the two ends of the political spectrum, to see if there were any differences in their dream imagery. Leaving out people in the middle should make those differences easier to see.

These dreams constituted the "large series of texts" required in the first step of content analysis. Bulkeley wanted to see if there were any differences in dream imagery between the four sets of students. She chose the Hall/Van de Castle system of dream analysis, which focuses on imagery rather than on other dream elements.[14] This system treats dreams as plays or stories, in which there are casts of characters, settings, objects, social interactions, activities, emotions, successes and failures, good fortune and bad fortune, and so on. Not all dreams will have all of these elements, but the coding scheme lets the investigator see rather quickly the similarities and differences between the dreams being examined. This was the second step of content analysis.

Next, Bulkeley trained herself and two assistants to code the dreams. They coded the dreams without knowing the political allegiances of the dreamers. This ensured that they did not project their own values into the content analysis. This constituted the third step in the process.

- Collect
- Code
- Analyze

Finally, Bulkeley looked at the results. She used the coding to trace the differences in the dream narratives. In her summary, she wrote,

> [P]eople on the political right had more nightmares, more dreams in which they lacked personal power, and a greater frequency of "lifelike" dreams; people on the political left had fewer nightmares, more dreams in which they had personal power, and a greater frequency of good fortunes and bizarre elements in their dreams.[15]

Bulkeley argued that "these findings have plausible correlations to certain features of the political ideologies of people on the left and the right."[16] It made sense to her that those who felt less powerful would choose more authoritarian leaders, whom they felt could help them accomplish things. It also made sense to her that those who felt they were fortunate were more willing to share with those who they felt had gotten a hard deal out of life. She recognized that her study was exploratory, not definitive, due to its small numbers and the fact that her research subjects were all college students. She argued that her results were interesting enough, though, that they "merit future investigation in larger-scale studies."[17]

This is an important point. Yes, her study was small. And yes, her target group did not represent the population as a whole. When combined with other studies that have uncovered core attitudinal differences between liberals and conservatives, however, her work suggests a relationship between political allegiances and people's different ways of experiencing the world. Her creative addition was to apply content analysis to dreams as an aspect of that experience.

Other Texts

Investigators have treated other cultural products as texts to analyze. To take one example, Dominick Frosch and his colleagues did a content analysis of television drug ads, to see what techniques pharmaceutical companies use to convince viewers to buy their products.[18] They recorded ads on U.S. prime-time network television for four consecutive weeks, rotating among the four major networks to ensure equal access to all segments of network viewership. They captured and analyzed 103 advertisements, which included 31 unique "product claim" ads and 7 shorter "reminder" ads.[19] Though a small number, this is not a sample in the statistical sense because the researchers captured all the ads that appeared on the network during the prime viewing period. Their texts thus accurately reflect advertising practices at the time they did their analysis.

What did they find? In their words:

Most ads (82%) made some factual claims and made rational arguments (86%) for product use, but few described condition causes (26%), risk factors (26%), or prevalence (25%). Emotional appeals were almost universal (95%). No ads mentioned lifestyle change as an alternative to products, though some (19%) portrayed it as an adjunct to medication. Some ads (18%) portrayed lifestyle changes as insufficient for controlling a condition. The ads often framed medication use in terms of losing (58%) and regaining control (85%) over some aspect of life and as engendering social approval (78%). Products were frequently (58%) portrayed as a medical breakthrough.[20]

If you find this disturbing, listen to their conclusions:

Despite claims that [pharmaceutical] ads serve an educational purpose, they provide limited information about the causes of a disease or who may be at risk; they show characters that have lost control over their social, emotional, or physical lives without the medication; and they minimize the value of health promotion through lifestyle changes. The ads have limited educational value and may oversell the benefits of drugs in ways that might conflict with promoting population health.[21]

This content analysis raises huge questions about the U.S. policy of allowing drug companies to advertise directly to the public.

Content analysis is a relatively popular technique for analyzing politics. The Pew Research Center on Journalism and Media, for example, ran a content analysis of news reporting about the major presidential candidates during the run-up to the primary election season in fall of 2007.[22] By scoring news reports for both tone and topic, they found that Barack Obama was given much more favorable coverage than were the other major candidates. None of them received much coverage for their policy positions; more stories emphasized the candidates' backgrounds and the nature of the "horse race" in which they were engaged. Content analysis is truly a broad technique. It can search for hidden patterns in a multitude of sources.

Analyzing Discourses

So much for texts. Let's now see how content analysis can help us understand social life even more deeply. For this, we need to understand a new term: **discourse.** This is a powerful concept, but one that is frequently used with inadequate explanation. That's unfortunate. Understanding the discourses that are common in a given society is a useful way to understand how that society works.

What is a discourse? *It is an institutionalized way of thinking and speaking about things, embedded in language.* This language shapes people's thoughts and behavior. Just as eyeglasses filter what we see, our ways of speaking about things filter how we think. Our thinking then influences how we act. Examining a society's dominant ways of speaking about things helps us understand that society's behavior.

Cindy Myers's research on the different ways of talking about poverty in the *New York Times* and the *Wall Street Journal* is a good example of this. The *Times*'s language portrays poverty as an impersonal but active force, which "traps" and "mires" people, into which people can "fall" and from which they have a hard time "escaping." Such words lead directly to policy recommendations that promote government action. Why? Because only a strong organization can "overcome" such a powerful force. Just as we need governments to protect us from hurricanes, so we need governments to "lift people out of" poverty. In this discourse, individuals cannot do it on their own.

The *Journal* presents a completely different discourse. There, poverty (as a concept) scarcely exists; the discourse focuses on "poor people." Such people sometimes "choose" to be poor, or at least make "bad choices" that limit their ability to live a decent life. The discourse focuses on their deficits: their drug addiction, their lack of education, their inability to find jobs or housing, and in general their inability to be productive members of society. This discourse also praises those who "lift themselves up by their bootstraps." We can applaud those who do and feel sorry for (or give charity to) those who do not. This discourse leads us to programs that "fix" people (by giving them skills they lack) rather than to programs that change social structures.

These two approaches have long dominated American approaches to poverty. The first attempts to change organizational and governmental systems so that they let more people succeed. The second assumes that the current social system works well, so it focuses its efforts on giving individual people the skills they need to fit into the system. Both approaches have merit, but teaching people to write better résumés doesn't work when there are no jobs for them. Encouraging them to look for housing doesn't work when rents are too expensive for even those with jobs to afford.[23] The *Journal*'s discourse ignores such things, just as the *Times*'s discourse ignores the fact that poor people can improve their lives on their own. Discourses matter to how people behave.

Does this approach make poverty just a matter of talk? Not in the least. Calling something "a discourse" does not make it any less real. As Margaret Wetherell and Jonathan Potter wrote in another context,

> New Zealand is no less real for being constituted discursively—you still die if your plane crashes into a hill, whether you think that the hill is the product of a volcanic eruption or the solidified form of a mythical whale. However, material reality is no less discursive for being able to get in the way of planes. How those deaths are understood . . . and what caused them is constituted through our systems of discourse.[24]

As the early American sociologist W. I. Thomas put it, "If [people] define situations as real, they are real in their consequences."[25] Poverty is indeed a matter of discourse, but the particular discourse in use shapes (or destroys) people's lives.

Critical Discourse Analysis

Analyzing discourses is a bit more complicated than ordinary content analysis. As outlined by Norman Fairclough, one of its chief proponents,[26] it consists of three elements:

1. *The texts themselves.* This matches the examples we've seen so far. How does a given text convey its message? To whom is the text directed, and how does it conceptualize its audience? What metaphors does it use and what are their implications? What possibilities does the text offer and what possibilities does it hide? How do wording and even grammar affect the text's message? These, plus the counting process, constitute the first element in a discourse analysis.

2. *The analysis of the social processes that surround the texts*—what Fairclough calls "discursive practices." These include the processes by which the texts are produced, such as the ways that the editorial boards of the *New York Times* and the *Wall Street Journal* come to a decision about what to write. They also include the processes by which the texts are consumed; how the *Times* and *Journal* editorials reach their readers, are repeated in other (usually partisan) media, and so on.

3. *The analysis of the wider social practices of which these particular texts and discursive practices are a part.* The *Journal*'s way of framing poverty is but one of many examples of neo-liberal discourse, which treats humans as freely choosing actors and argues that unimpeded markets improve everyone's chances for a good life. The *Times*'s way of framing poverty harks back to the New Deal response to this ideology. Both speak for parts of the American "establishment." This conflict of discourses shapes much of our current public life.[27]

Figure 12.2 shows this nested relationship. The analysis of the text corresponds to regular content analysis; discourse analysis adds the other two elements.

FIGURE 12.2   The Three Elements of Discourse Analysis

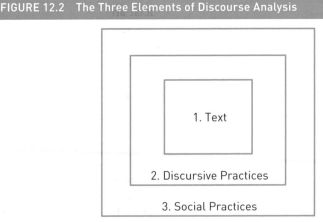

1. Text

2. Discursive Practices

3. Social Practices

Fairclough calls this approach **critical discourse analysis** because it is intended to lay bare the social processes by which discourse is created, shaped, and used. The word *critical* is not merely negative. Instead, it follows the European tradition of analytic criticism: A critical analysis seeks to understand how things work. These three steps let us see how discourses shape our everyday lives.

Two Examples

Here are two examples. The first is a critical discourse analysis of the official pastoral letters put forward by the U.S. Conference of Catholic Bishops. The second is a critical discourse analysis of the magazine *National Geographic*.

Like most religious organizations, the Roman Catholic Church puts forth periodic statements that apply church teachings to one or another area of public life. For example, the 1983 statement "The Challenge of Peace" addressed the morality of war in a nuclear age.[28] The 1986 statement "Economic Justice for All" examined the U.S. economy in light of Catholic social teachings.[29] These documents are produced according to specific procedures, and they go through many drafts, consultations, and so on before being approved. They conform to particular genres, use identifiable language, and the like. In short, as texts, they carry specific embedded social practices. Critical discourse analysis reveals these practices, how these practices shape the texts that result, who they influence, and who has influence over them.

In 2002, the U.S. Conference of Catholic Bishops issued two statements just a month apart: in November on the war in Iraq and in December on the clergy sex scandals and the protection of minors.[30] The textual differences between these documents reveal important aspects of the American Catholic Church as an organization.

Textually, the "Statement on Iraq" is written in a highly active voice, with active verbs and clear nouns that criticize U.S. officials' decisions to wage war. This active voice emphasizes the control that officials have over the war, and the fact that they could have made different choices to avoid the conflict. This was deliberate. The bishops wanted to combat any official attempt to avoid responsibility for the war's consequences. A passive-voice statement—"war was begun today"—would present war as a natural phenomenon that just happened without a responsible agent. So would a nominalization, such as "there was much destruction of the city center." Such language would let war leaders off the hook. The statement's active voice insists that war is always a choice and that other choices are always possible.

The statement on clergy sexual abuse of minors also uses active-voice language, but it does so differently. It does not attempt to avoid Church responsibility for the actions of wayward clergy. It does, however, use a much more bureaucratic tone, with some passive voice thrown into the mix. It wants to reassure Catholics that their children are safe, so it emphasizes that new procedures are now in place to protect them. The old procedures were not wrong, just incomplete. The document's tone tells

THINK ABOUT IT
Why might the Catholic Church use such different discourses on these two issues?

Catholics that the hierarchy had always had their best interests at heart and is now doing even more for them. The document says this both overtly and through the ways it uses language. Critical discourse analysis exposes such textual tricks, surfacing them for all to see.

The first step of the analysis looks at the texts themselves. The second step locates those texts in the wider circle of social practices of which they are a part. It describes the ways in which the texts were written and promulgated, the factional fighting that went into shaping them, whose voices were heard and whose were not, and so on. It then examines how the texts are used both inside and outside of the Catholic Church.

The third step broadens the analysis. It examines not just the American church hierarchy's actions but reactions from Catholic laity, the efforts of various Catholic intellectual factions to promote or denigrate the documents, the Vatican's private and public rejoinders, responses from other religious groups, government and politicians' efforts to spin the documents to support the government's own positions, and so on. Critical discourse analysis looks for the pattern of these reactions, especially as they sustain or undercut existing power relations—both within and outside of church organizations. Taken together, these three steps tell us a lot about the Catholic Church that is ordinarily hidden from view.

On a completely different topic, Catherine Lutz and Jane Collins applied critical discourse analysis to *National Geographic,* the popular middlebrow mass-market magazine through which many Americans get their knowledge of the rest of the world.[31] Lutz and Collins show how the magazine's photographers, editors, and designers select images and text to represent various world cultures. Then they provide a content analysis of hundreds of photographs to show how the magazine uses color, pose, framing, and vantage point to present a very American view of non-Western peoples.

National Geographic's 1986 article on Micronesian independence, for example, shows local people topless and dressed in grass skirts, practicing native crafts. This is not a realistic picture of island life. Photographs of the same scenes—given to me by the mother of one of my students—show locals dressed in shorts and T-shirts, watching their similarly dressed fellow villagers perform traditional dances. *National Geographic*'s editors chose the staged exotic shots rather than the more prosaic ones, because they wanted a story about "happy timeless people" who are facing the modern world.[32] This is a common American fantasy of the relationship between the old and the new, the traditional and the modern.

Lutz and Collins uncover lots of such stereotypes. Articles on Polynesia have high breast-counts; those on Japan present either a hypermodernity or an aesthetically beautiful traditionalism; those on Africa present faceless masses, poverty, and potential violence. These are American cultural images, not reality. As the publisher's blurb for Lutz and Collins's book puts it, "in purporting to teach us about distant cultures, [*National Geographic*] actually tells us much more about our own."[33] Critical discourse analysis is a powerful tool for bringing such things to light.

Analyzing Popular Culture: The Soaps

Popular culture is a prime arena for using content and discourse analysis. There are many hidden patterns to bring to the surface. For example, music historian Katherine Baber and I recently analyzed Disneyland's "Small World" ride, to show how the ride reflects American images of foreign peoples.[34] Other scholars have produced similar analyses on many topics.

One exemplary analysis is anthropologist Susan Bean's examination of American soap operas. She reviewed a summer's worth of these daytime television programs to show how they reinforce American ideas about the nature of family life.[35]

Soap operas began as an American radio genre in the 1930s.[36] Their daytime format, complicated, many-threaded plots, and melodramatic style were designed to appeal to American housewives, who were imagined to be bored with the cleaning and child care that made them such an attractive (and captive) audience. The name came from their first sponsors, makers of soap and cleaning products. Their style was unique among popular entertainment. Then, as now, they featured multiple simultaneous story lines, emotional plot twists, cliffhanger endings ("to be continued tomorrow"), and multiple love affairs, family crises, and disasters—all designed to keep women listening. By the end of the 1930s, "the soaps" represented some 90% of all commercially sponsored daytime broadcast hours.

The genre migrated to television in the early 1950s, where at its height it consumed 50 or more hours per week of network programming. Decline set in during the 1990s, as more women entered the workforce and younger women postponed marriage and children. Several long-running soaps were cancelled in the early 2010s, including *Guiding Light,* which had begun on radio in 1937. The rise of cable television, the development of cheaper "reality shows," and the growth of talk radio have all been cited as causes.

After their migration to television, soap operas soon spread around the world. British soaps, Australian soaps, Mexican *telenovelas*, and the like have similar features but their own particular cultural accents. British and Australian soaps often focus on working-class families, but American soaps tend to center on well-to-do professionals, whose family and relationship life is extremely complicated. As anthropologist Susan Bean summarized one mid-1970s plot moment in *Days of Our Lives,* a soap set in the fictional Midwestern town of Salem that revolves around two extended families, the Hortons and the Bradys:

> Bill and Laura are in love, but Laura is married to Mickey; Bob has divorced Phyllis to marry Julie, but Julie really loves another; Susan is married to Greg but his brother Eric is in love with her (will Susan fall in love with him?); Addie is married to Doug, but he and her daughter Julie used to be lovers (are they still really in love?). The triangle involving ties of love and marriage is the most frequently occurring plot. Each of the fourteen soap operas [on New York daytime television] features at least one triangle, some as many as five.[37]

Such separate plots rotate through each episode, each plot pausing at a dramatic moment to make room for another. They are never tightly connected and are sometimes not connected at all. If one resolves, others continue, and the characters later return with new troubles to endure. The audience has to stay tuned to follow the twists. This opens a market for plot-summarizing magazines such as *Soap Opera Digest,* sold at supermarket checkout stands, where the soaps' target audience—women—will see them.

Bean subjected the mid-1970s New York soap opera scene to an extremely interesting content analysis. She concluded that soap operas are about family life, but not in the simple way that you might think. By presenting the myriad ways in which families and couples fall apart, she argued, the soaps reveal the unconscious principles on which American family life is based. They do this by portraying what happens when those principles are violated. The continual churning of inappropriate relationships shows what American viewers think that ideal relationships should be.

Take the love triangles. The ideal pattern is that an available (unmarried) man and an available (unmarried) women fall in love, get married, and have children, which they raise together. This never happens in the soap opera universe. Instead, married people fall in love with someone new, which destroys their previous marriage because people cannot be in love with two people at once. Either they divorce (because new love is more powerful than anything else) or they stay married for practical reasons, in which case they are miserable. Soap opera viewers know this loveless marriage will fail, because marriage without love is a house built on sand.

Marriage also depends on sex and children. Bean tells one story about Doug and Eunice who are happily married but whose marriage falls apart when an accident leaves Doug paralyzed from the waist down, making sex impossible. He interprets Eunice's loving attention as pity and accuses her of sleeping with John. They divorce, but what will happen to their baby girl?

Parentage is the second most frequent problem in the soap operas that Bean analyzed. Sometimes the problem is that loving couples cannot have children. This usually leads to loss of love, separation, and divorce. Sometimes the problem is divorced couples competing for their children's affections. Both want custody, but the soaps seldom present joint custody as an option. Sometimes the problem is that children reject a loving stepparent, even in the case where the biological parent has died. The cultural message is that loving parents produce biological children together; any deviation from that norm results in marital and family trouble.

The last pattern Bean identified had to do with adult children and parents who will not let them be independent. She found several stories of long-absent mothers who try to interfere in their sons' marriage choices. This causes marital discord, but almost uniformly the meddlesome mother loses and retreats from the field. This makes sense, given soap operas' target audience. Few women want to identify with the meddling mother-in-law; they identify with the wife and cheer her when she wins in the end.

In Bean's analysis,

> the soap operas contain a coherent expression of the principles on which the American family is based. . . . [These principles] are revealed in dramatic dilemmas that violate the ideal order. . . . Resolution is sought in the restoration of the ideal, where this is possible, by uniting the several elements in a single relationship—the man marries the woman he loves; the child learns to accept his legal and loving mother as if she were his natural mother. The analysis . . . reveals the concepts . . . that are central to American ideas about the family: romantic and parental love, sex and marriage, blood [ties], and nurturing.[38]

These principles are not totally hidden, but Bean's content analysis of a summer's worth of soap operas shows in great detail how they operated at the time of her writing. The fact that the soaps at that time attracted a huge audience indicates the importance of their cultural message.

Note how this content analysis worked. Bean examined soap opera plots, diagramming them to show their underlying patterns. Despite surface differences, she found the same patterns over and over in all the soap operas she reviewed. To succeed, relationships had to have love, sex, marriage, and the possibility of children. Relationships that lacked any one of these dissolved. Parent-child relationships needed love, affection, and nurturing when children were young and independence when children grew up. Relationships that lacked any of these created much conflict.

Parent-child relationships also ought to be based on "blood": two parents, in love and married, should raise their own biological children. That is the American ideal. Unfortunately, this ideal is not always possible, so stepparents should love and nurture their stepchildren as if they were their own. Failure to establish this relationship also caused much grief.

These patterns structured almost all of the storylines, even though the surface details varied greatly. A crucial element of the structure was that it operated negatively. Rather than show relationships that work, the soaps show relationships that don't. Drama emerges when love is separated from marriage, when marriage is separated from sex, or when sex is separated from the ability to have children. The plots systematically violate the way things ought to be, to show that those violations turn out badly. They thus support American cultural norms. This explains part of their appeal to 20th-century American housewives, their target audience. The gendered division of labor of that era assigned family maintenance to women. Soap operas gave those women a lens through which they could see the principles that governed their lives.

Bean's content analysis worked qualitatively, through her detailed analysis of plots and her discovering of their similar structures. This chapter's early examples worked quantitatively, by

THINK ABOUT IT
What kind of patterns can you see in the TV shows you watch?

counting African American Oscar nominees, themes in unsigned newspaper editorials, or dream images. This is an important point about research in general. The logic of analyzing data to confirm or deny a hypothesis is the same, no matter what kind of data analysis you use. Choosing a method of analysis is the *last* step in designing research, not the first. Content and discourse analyses work using either quantitative or qualitative techniques. Which one you use depends on your research question, the nature of the hidden pattern that you are trying to expose, and the nature of the data that you are trying to analyze. Both have merit; neither one is a priori superior.

Note also how Bean followed the four steps of content analysis described earlier in this chapter. She did not do a full discourse analysis, because she did not look in detail at how soap operas are produced, how they are consumed, and how they fit into the wider social structure. As noted earlier, a content analysis is the first element in doing a discourse analysis. To that, a discourse analyst adds two more parts.

Research Ethics

Do content and discourse analyses raise any ethical issues? Certainly not, if the texts or cultural artifacts being analyzed are in plain public view. Analyzing public documents or performances violates no one's privacy; it forces no one to take personal risks; it does not limit people's freedom. It is always a good idea to refrain from identifying specific individuals unless it is crucial to your research question, but those individuals did put their texts out in public. So long as your analysis is accurate, there is no problem with using them.

That, of course, is the rub. You need to make sure that your analysis is accurate. This is particularly true when you base your analysis on a sample of texts rather than the total population of them. In her analysis of newspaper editorials about the nation-state, Adrienne Redd identified certain key years and chose all the editorials on her topic for those years. This avoided bias. Cindy Myers did the same with her analysis of 20 years of editorials about poverty. Both made sure they were getting the whole story. Often, though, you have to use samples. Then you need to be sure that the samples are large enough to represent your population accurately.

Beyond this, there are a few cases that call for caution. Some "public" texts are a bit less public than they appear at first. Facebook postings, for example, are often aimed at friends rather than at the public at large. That's why Facebook has privacy settings, though not everyone knows how to use them. Is it right to include postings in a content analysis when the only reason you have access to them is that the users have failed to set their privacy? Probably not. You wouldn't likely do this anyway, because analyzing posts from only those who don't know how to use Facebook very well is going to give you a biased sample.

How about doing a content analysis of Twitter? This raises different issues: Tweets are both public and searchable, but you need to make sure that your readers cannot trace those tweets back to their originators. Content analysis looks for general patterns, not information specific to individuals. It is good ethical practice to treat texts that could be traced back to individuals with caution.

Other than situations like these, content and discourse analyses are generally safe choices if you want to do ethical research. You will still need to submit your research proposal to your Institutional Review Board. It is likely, however, that the IRB will give you quick approval.

Review Questions

1. What kinds of hidden patterns can you find with content analysis?

2. What four steps do you follow in carrying out a content analysis?

3. What do we mean by *discourse?* What kinds of hidden patterns can you find with discourse analysis?

4. What three elements make up a full discourse analysis?

5. When should you use quantitative data analysis to find patterns in content and discourse?

6. When should you use qualitative data analysis to find patterns?

The open-access Student Study Site at **study.sagepub.com/spickard** has a variety of useful study tools, including SAGE journal articles, video & web resources, eFlashcards, and quizzes.

Notes

1. Edward T. Hall, *The Hidden Dimension.* Doubleday, 1966.

2. Joseph Tobin et al., *Preschool in Three Cultures: Japan, China, and the United States.* Yale University Press, 1989. Alongside the book, Tobin released a video of the same name. It is available from his website at www.joetobin.net.

3. Monika Goyal et al., "Racial Disparities in Pain Management of Children With Appendicitis in Emergency Departments," *Journal of the American Medical Association: Pediatrics* (November 2015): 996–1002.

4. William Smith et al., *The North Carolina Traffic Study,* 2003. Retrieved from https://www.ncjrs.gov/pdffiles1/nij/grants/204021.pdf

5. Ian Ayres et al., "Race Effects on eBay," *RAND Journal of Economics* (Winter 2015): 891–917.

(Continued)

(Continued)

6. Marianne Bertrand and Sendhil Mullainathan, "Are Emily and Greg More Employable Than Lakisha and Jamal? A Field Experiment on Labor Market Discrimination," *National Bureau of Economic Research Working Paper #9873*, July 2003. Retrieved from http://www.nber.org/papers/w9873.pdf

7. Daniel Butler and David Broockman, "Do Politicians Racially Discriminate Against Constituents? A Field Experiment on State Legislators," *American Journal of Political Science* 55 (2011): 463–477.

8. For a summary of several other studies, see Sendhil Mullainathan, "Racial Bias, Even When We Have Good Intentions," *New York Times*, January 3, 2015.

9. The charts are based on data posted in January 2016 by Kevin Drum on the *Mother Jones* magazine website (www.motherjones.com): "Raw Data: How #White Are the Oscars, Anyway?" and "#OscarsSoWhite Is Targeting Precisely the Wrong Thing."

10. Chris Rock, "It's a White Industry: One Black Man's Hollywood Adventure," *Hollywood Reporter,* December 12, 2014. Retrieved from https://www.hollywoodreporter.com/news/top-five-filmmaker-chris-rock-753223

11. Adrienne Redd, *Fallen Walls and Fallen Towers: The Fate of the Nation in a Global World.* Nimble Books, 2010.

12. Cindy Myers, "Talking Poverty: Power Arrangements in Poverty Discourse," PhD dissertation, Program in Human and Organizational Development, Fielding Graduate Institute, 2005.

13. Kelly Bulkeley, "Dream Content and Political Ideology," *Dreaming* 12 (2002): 61–78.

14. Calvin Hall and Robert Van de Castle, *The Content Analysis of Dreams.* Appleton-Century-Crofts, 1966.

15. Bulkeley, "Dream Content and Political Ideology," p. 61.

16. Ibid.

17. Ibid.

18. Dominick L. Frosch et al., "Creating Demand for Prescription Drugs: A Content Analysis of Television Direct-to-Consumer Advertising," *Journal of Family Medicine* 5 (2007): 6–13.

19. These are the two categories of advertisements that the U.S. Food and Drug Administration allows pharmaceutical companies to show. Only the "product claim" ads have to tell viewers about drug indications, efficacy, and dosage.

20. Frosch et al., "Creating Demand for Prescription Drugs," p. 6.

21. Ibid.

22. Pew Research Center, "The Invisible Primary—Invisible No Longer," October 29, 2007. Retrieved from http://www.journalism.org/2007/10/29/the-invisible-primaryinvisible-no-longer/

23. See Vincent Lyon-Callo, *Inequality, Poverty, and Neoliberal Governance: Activist Ethnography in the Homeless Sheltering Industry.* University of Toronto Press, 2004.

24. Margaret Wetherell and Jonathan Potter, *Mapping the Language of Racism: Discourse*

and the Legitimation of Exploitation. Harvester Wheatsheaf, 1992, p. 62.

25. W. I. Thomas and D. S. Thomas, *The Child in America: Behavior Problems and Programs.* Knopf, 1928, pp. 571–572.

26. Norman Fairclough, *Critical Discourse Analysis.* Longman, 1995. See also Louise Phillips and Marianne Jørgensen, *Discourse Analysis as Theory and Method.* Sage, 2002, pp. 60–95.

27. For a fascinating approach to this conflict, see Michael Burawoy, "Public Sociology vs. the Market," *Socio-Economic Review* 5 (2007): 356–367.

28. U.S. Conference of Catholic Bishops, "The Challenge of Peace: God's Promise and Our Response," 1983. Retrieved from http://www.usccb.org/issues-and-action/human-life-and-dignity/war-and-peace/nuclear-weapons/upload/statement-the-challenge-of-peace-1983-05-03.pdf

29. U.S. Conference of Catholic Bishops, "Economic Justice for All: A Pastoral Letter on Catholic Social Teaching and the Economy," 1986. Retrieved from http://www.usccb.org/upload/economic_justice_for_all.pdf

30. U.S. Conference of Catholic Bishops, "Statement on Iraq," November 13, 2002. Retrieved from http://www.usccb.org/issues-and-action/human-life-and-dignity/global-issues/middle-east/iraq/statement-on-iraq-2002-11-13.cfm; "Essential Norms for Diocesan/Eparchial Policies Dealing With Allegations of Sexual Abuse of Minors by Priests or Deacons," December 8, 2002. Retrieved from https://www.documentcloud.org/documents/335964-essential-norms-for-diocesan-eparchial-policies.html

31. Catherine Lutz and Jane Collins, *Reading National Geographic.* University of Chicago Press, 1993.

32. Carolyn Bennett Patterson, "In the Far Pacific: At the Birth of Nations," *National Geographic* 170 (October 1986): 460–500. My student's mother was doing economic development work in the islands at the time of the *National Geographic* photo shoot. You can see the front end of the *National Geographic* photographer's camera in some of her photos.

33. University of Chicago Press Books website, http://www.press.uchicago.edu/ucp/books/book/chicago/R/bo3697068.html

34. Katherine Baber and James Spickard, "Crafting Culture: 'Tradition,' Art, and Music in Disney's 'It's a Small World,'" *Journal of Popular Culture* 48 (2015): 225–239.

35. Susan Bean, "Soap Operas: Sagas of American Kinship," pp. 80–98 in *The American Dimension: Cultural Myths and Social Realities,* edited by W. Arens and Susan B. Montague. Alfred Publishing, 1976, pp. 80–81.

36. Robert C. Allen, "Soap Operas," in *Encyclopedia of Television,* edited by Horace Newcomb. Retrieved from http://www.museum.tv/eotv/soapopera.htm. See also Robert C. Allen, *To Be Continued: Soap Operas Around the World.* Routledge, 1995.

37. Bean, "Soap Operas," pp. 80–81.

38. Ibid., pp. 97–98.

CHAPTER 13

Ethnography: Exploring Cultural and Social Scenes

		Type of Data		
Data Collection Method	**Exploring Scenes**	**Acts, behavior, or events**	**Cultural knowledge**	**Hidden social patterns**
	Ethnography (participant observation)	X	X	X
	Grounded Theory			X

It was a quiet October day when I first walked into the San Francisco branch of the Church of World Messianity—the U.S. outpost of one of the 700 or so new religions founded in Japan in the 20th century.[1] One of my friends was studying to become a minister. I wanted to see what the group was like.

The church was located in the southwestern part of the city, in a small house that the group used for holding services. I knocked, and a kindly Japanese American woman answered the door. She said, "I see you have come to receive *johrei*." I didn't know what she was talking about, but being both young and adventuresome, I said, "yes," and she ushered me into what had once been the house living room.

The room contained several rows of chairs and a small altar holding a beautiful flower arrangement. Above it hung a large scroll with two Japanese characters. To the left was a photo of an older Japanese man holding his hand out in blessing. To the right of these was an image of a white circle with a yellow rim and crossed green bars inside it; at the center was a smaller circle, yellow in the middle and surrounded by red. The room was clean and spare and felt very peaceful.

Two chairs faced each other in front of the altar. The woman asked me to sit on one of them, and she sat on the other. After a moment's silence, she raised her hand in the same blessing sign as in the photograph. She placed her hand about one foot in front of my head and then slowly passed it down my body, taking perhaps 10 minutes to do so. At that point, she asked me to turn around, and then she repeated the gesture down my back. After another 10 minutes, she asked me to face forward again. She bowed and said, "Thank you for receiving *johrei*."

This was my introduction to the Church of World Messianity's chief spiritual practice: what members understand as using "divine light" to clean the clouds from people's spiritual bodies. I spent a good part of the next two years studying the group and its practices. I was engaged in **ethnography**: the intense examination of cultural and social scenes. I wanted to learn how the members of this church saw the world. I wanted to learn their rationales for doing what they did in it. I also wanted to understand the aspects of their group life that they, themselves, might not see.

These are the three main goals of ethnographic research, a data collection method often called **participant observation** by sociologists. Unlike detached observation (Chapter 11), ethnography involves participation in the cultural and social scenes being investigated. Ethnographers have three goals: (1) to learn to see the world as the participants see it; (2) to watch what those participants do that makes the scene possible; and (3) to understand the hidden patterns that those participants often fail to see, because they are too immersed in the scene to notice them.

Ethnographers have a hard job. They have to be part of the scene they are investigating, but they also have to be strangers to it. Being part of the scene tells you what the "natives" think and do; being a stranger to it shows you what the "natives" miss. The trick is to do both at once. That takes time, which makes ethnography one of the slowest ways to collect data. It is also one of the most rewarding.

The Three Goals

Let's take a look at how this works in real life. I'll take my own ethnographic study of the San Francisco branch of World Messianity as an example.[2] It reveals the three goals of ethnography in a particularly clear fashion.

Goal One: Seeing the World as the Participants See It

My first goal was to find out how the members of the church understood what they were doing. Many ethnographers use the term **worldview** to describe this. It is part of what we've previously called **cultural knowledge**, things that everyone in a particular social scene knows. Specifically, worldview is the part of cultural knowledge that involves seeing the big picture. Everyone knows practical things: how to crack an egg or diaper a baby, for example. Worldview is broader than this. It includes people's religious or spiritual beliefs, their shared sense of the meaning of life, and their shared ideas about the right things to do. We could equally call it a shared philosophy.

Most religious groups have such philosophies. World Messianity was no different. I learned about theirs by spending lots of time at the church and talking to members. For a bit under two years, I attended church functions on a weekly or biweekly basis, interacted with most of the regular attendees, and took part in church rituals. These involved worship services, *gohoshi* (cleaning and other odd jobs around the church), orientation classes in both Japanese and English, and more conversations than I could possibly count. I developed close relationships with one minister and with eight members, whom I repeatedly interviewed in depth. I also interviewed two dozen other members and four ministers at some length. Most of these interviews and observations took place in San Francisco and in Sunnyvale, California (where the church had a satellite center), but a few were in the larger churches in Los Angeles and Vancouver, British Columbia. For several years, I remained in contact with one of my original informants, who kept me aware of church developments.

What did I learn? First, I learned a lot about church history. The old man in the altar room photo was the church's founder, Mokichi Okada. He was a Japanese businessman who had long been interested in the direction that modern life seemed to be taking. Beginning in 1926, he had a series of visions in which he was visited by the Buddhist goddess of Mercy, Kannon. She gave him what he said were the keys to future history and to the salvation of the world. This led him to establish the church.

According to Okada, these visions showed him that the world stands at a crucial point in history.[3] He said there will soon be a supernatural transformation between the "Age of Night" and the "Age of Day," which he sometimes called the "Age of Water" and the "Age of Fire." Whereas the present world is filled with ugliness and evil, the new age will be one of truth and beauty. The enlightened teacher for the Age of Water— Jesus Christ—will make way for the great teacher for the Age of Fire, Okada himself. His followers called him *Meishu-sama,* meaning "Enlightened Leader" or "Master of Light." When that age comes, the world will be purified by what corresponds to the Christian "fire next time."

Okada divided the world between two planes: the "spiritual plane," on which God works, and the "material plane," where we mortals live. Our problem, Okada said, is that despite recent material progress, clouds—*kumo*—have accumulated on the spiritual plane. These separate us from God and cause war, poverty, disease, and pollution. In response, God has sent his Light to dissolve the clouds, through the use of a special tool to bring about human healing. That tool is *johrei.* Giving *johrei* dissolves the clouds that separate people from God. It raises individuals' spiritual levels, enabling them to live healthier lives and to work more effectively for paradise. It also raises the spiritual level of the giver or "channel."

Receiving *johrei* on my first visit, said the church members, brought me closer to God. It didn't matter that I had no idea what was going on at the time, nor did it matter whether I believed them. In their worldview, the important thing was that my clouds weakened and I could live a better life—whether or not I was aware of it.

Theologically, these teachings borrow much from Buddhism, Christianity, and Shinto. The eclecticism is overt. Except for a brief period in the mid-1970s, the church in America respected other religions. It sought to appropriate their "true" teachings while discarding what was "false" or "out of date." Okada himself described World Messianity as a combination of Christianity and Buddhism, West and East. That is the symbolism of the white, yellow, and red circle with crossed green bars hanging next to the altar. Church members call this the Izunome Cross. The vertical bar symbolizes the East, with its sense of order and hierarchy. The horizontal bar symbolizes the West, with its sense of equality and expansiveness. Okada taught that the coming Age of Day would require these two forces to work together harmoniously. That is why the church had to come to America: to help bring about the world transformation.

That's quite a worldview! I learned about it through conversations, classes, and interviews with pastors and church members, and by reading church literature. This is typical of ethnographic data collection. Ethnography is more eclectic than are most other data collection techniques. Anthropologist Renato Rosaldo referred to it as "deep hanging-out"—a phrase that captures both the need to learn from whatever is happening at the time and the sense that you have to pay more attention to everyday life than usual.[4] These data can be much richer than what you gather through more limited approaches.

My extensive "hanging out" with the church members, my frequent observations of their activities, plus my formal interviews gave me a great deal of insight into how church members saw the world. The theology that I've summarized here was accepted, in large part, by everyone. Individuals added their own nuances, however. In fact, there were three major theological subgroups in the San Francisco church, each of which emphasized a different part of the core philosophy.

One group of members emphasized the usefulness of *johrei* for physical health. These members talked about how they never had to see doctors; how their families used *johrei* to overcome colds, pains, and other ailments; and how they had witnessed medical miracles as a result of giving and receiving *johrei*. They described these miracles, testified about them at monthly services, and gave great thanks to God for the blessing that *johrei* brought them. In line with church teachings, they recognized that *johrei* cleared spiritual clouds, not physical ones, but they focused almost exclusively on the physical healing that resulted. Most, but not all, of this subgroup were second- and third-generation Japanese Americans. They saw themselves as embodying the unity of East and West that the church valued. They, in turn, valued *johrei*—the tool that it had taught them.

A second group of members specifically deemphasized physical healing. They focused on spiritual growth and saw *johrei* as a concrete tool for such advancement. Most of these were older English-speaking Whites, many of whom had been active in various spiritual and New Age groups for several decades. All saw value in many religions and appreciated the church's willingness to combine elements of Shinto, Buddhism, Christianity, and other faiths. They accepted that other church members found value in physical healing, but they did not think that it was very important. To them, it certainly did not compare to the spiritual benefits they got from *johrei*.

The third group of members was smaller and younger. It consisted mostly of former hippies and "graduates" of the 1960s San Francisco alternative arts scene. These people had been part of a young people's movement seeking social transformation, including San Francisco's famous "Summer of Love." As that movement declined, some people looked for another way to bring about the hoped-for new society. These church members saw *johrei* as a practical tool to raise San Francisco's collective spiritual consciousness. A few reported channeling *johrei* in the city council chambers; others directed *johrei* toward the police department and other public buildings. They hoped that clearing the spiritual clouds from key social institutions would bring a better life for all.

I must emphasize that none of these three groups rejected any of the church's core teachings. They all affirmed the theological package that I outlined earlier. They merely stressed different parts of that package. Had I encountered them outside the church context, I might have seen them as holding three different belief systems. They, however, saw themselves as holding just one.

Nearly two years of conversations and interviews at the San Francisco branch church gave me a pretty good picture of the group's cultural knowledge. This is the "what everyone knows" that ethnography captures so well.

Goal Two: Watching What Participants Do

The second goal involves collecting data on what the participants in a social scene *do*. Besides *johrei*, monthly church services, and periodic information courses, this included weekly or biweekly meetings at the Sunnyvale satellite center, classes in flower arranging, and lessons in "nature farming"—the use of *johrei* to grow healthier plants.

I have already described *johrei*, though in fact there is a bit more to report about the experience. Church members believe that not just anyone can do it. You have to take orientation classes to learn how to channel properly. They also believe that no one can channel without church authorization. All church members wore an *ohikari* ("sacred focal point") around their necks, which allowed them to channel *johrei* to others.

Members told me that *johrei* does not come from the channeler. Instead, it starts at the Mother Church in Japan, from which it is transmitted to the altar scroll in the Los Angeles church, then to the scroll in San Francisco, then to the *ohikari*, and finally through the channeler's hand to the person whose clouds are being dissolved. The Mother Church gets it directly from God. When members seek real healing, they go as far up that chain as they can afford. That's because—in the church worldview—the closer one is to the source, the more powerful the *johrei* becomes.

Yet giving and receiving *johrei* is not just a matter of worldview. It is also an experience. What does it feel like? I interviewed a large number of church members about what they felt physically, both while giving it and while receiving it. I used the **phenomenological interviewing** process described in Chapter 9.

As a rule, channelers reported feeling a tingling in the palm while giving *johrei*. Some reported a sense of heightened energy flow. Recipients mostly reported a heat passing over their bodies, starting at the head and moving downward as the channeler's hand focused on different parts of the body. A few recipients felt nothing; others reported sensations of extreme pressure, as if they were being sat upon or stunned; most were somewhere in between. Church members attributed the differences to the spiritual level of the recipient and also of the channeler. They explained that having fewer clouds on one's spiritual body lets more energy through. That, however, was an interpretation, not a description of the phenomenon itself. Ethnographers collect both, making sure to keep track of which is which.

What else did members do? Among other things, they went to monthly church services, which were something like a typical Protestant service, with *johrei* delivered by the minister to the entire group taking the place of a sermon. At a typical service, 20 to 30 members would fill the main church room. They would sing, recite prayers together in both English and Japanese, and hear announcements about church events. Members could testify to the blessings they had received since the last meeting or they could share important things going on in their lives. Then everyone would grow quiet and the minister would channel *johrei* to the whole group. Only ministers were allowed to do this; members could channel to only one person at a time. This marked a distinct status difference between ministers and members. Both interpreted this not in terms of worldly status, however, but as the result of the ministers' greater spiritual development.

Many members also practiced flower arranging and nature farming. Okada taught that beauty purifies both the world and the soul. As a result, he founded a school of flower arranging and an art museum, both of which brought the church fame in Japan. Some of the San Francisco members had been trained in arranging, so they taught classes to others. Okada also taught that the use of pesticides and chemical fertilizers on crops increased spiritual clouds. One of the San Francisco assistant ministers taught a course in nature farming that showed members how to channel *johrei* to their vegetables to keep the plants healthy. He was rather aghast that I was using goat manure on my own home vegetable crop. "How polluting!" he exclaimed. Dirt, water, and God's Light ought to be enough.

Members from all three subgroups took part in each of these activities. They worked together and all thought these activities valuable. They did, however, interpret them a bit differently.

I learned about the church members' cultural practices in the same way that I learned about their cultural knowledge: by watching, talking, listening, and asking questions. These are the ethnographer's key tools.

On Taking Field Notes

By now, it ought to be clear that ethnography is not a quick data collection method. You have to spend a lot of time in the field, to be sure that you've captured participants' ways of seeing the world and what those participants actually do—the first two goals of any ethnographic project. You thus have to take notes: extensive ones. Nobody has a good enough memory to avoid writing things down.[5] You inevitably forget things, so you depend on having good notes to remind you what you heard and saw.

There's a clear purpose to such notes: You have to separate what you actually saw and heard from what you *thought* about what you saw and heard. In my research on World Messianity, I wrote down what people were telling me in one notebook and put what I was thinking about what they were telling me in another. Had I gotten this mixed up, I might have mistaken my own thoughts for what I had been told. Ethnographers dare not do this. We want to make sure that we convey our observations accurately.

I've since developed an easy way to do this. Take a piece of paper and turn it sideways. Put a line down the middle and then divide each half with another line. That gives you four columns. Draw a line near the top, for column headings. Add these labels. You get four columns to record four different kinds of information:[6]

1. External Details	2. What I Observed	3. What I Thought About What I Observed	4. Other Thoughts
This column reminds me where the event was, who was there, etc.	This column contains a detailed list of what I observed.	This column allows me to record my thoughts about what I observed, ideally matched to the relevant spot in Column 2.	This column lets me record wilder ideas, including connections with other situations, readings, thinkers, etc.

- Use the first column to record all the external details of whatever you are observing: a meeting, a church service, an interview, and so on. Where was it? When was it? Who organized it? What was the topic? Who was there?
- Use the second column to record what you saw and heard, in as much detail as possible. *This is the key column,* as it gives you a clear record of your observations. The purpose of the other columns is to give you a place to put other things without them getting mixed in with your actual data.
- Use the third column for any comments, ideas, or the like that occur to you during the event. Or you can go back through your notes after the event and annotate them in this column. This might include questions that occur to you about future observations, ideas that you'd like to check out but can't just yet, and so on. Use it for things that relate rather closely to the event. You will certainly revisit this column as you are thinking through your data.
- Finally, put wilder or more extraneous thoughts in the fourth column. These might be intuitions, ideas for future projects, or anything that is tangential to the event and to your current research. The idea is to have somewhere to put things that catch your attention but that threaten to lead you away from your current focus.

You will, of course, focus most of your attention on Columns 2 and 3. Column 2 contains your raw data; Column 3 contains your first thoughts about that data. Keeping those separate will make your subsequent data analysis much easier.

When should you take these notes? As soon as possible after an event, if you can't take notes during it. Often you can't. You may be washing dishes with someone in the church kitchen and fall into a deep and meaningful conversation, during which you learn things that you hadn't previously known. You can't pull out your notebook right then. Not only will the dishwater ruin it, but your conversation partner may clam up or leave. So you stay engaged, remember as much as you can, and find somewhere private to take notes once the conversation is over. Sometimes you can head for the bathroom for some quick note-taking. Or you can wait until you leave the data collection site and take notes in your car. It's a good idea to drive a few blocks from the site for privacy. Don't drive too far, though. You don't want to forget what you heard and saw.

THINK ABOUT IT
Why is it so important to record what you see and hear <u>separately</u> from what you think about when you see and hear?

Goal Three: Understanding Hidden Patterns

Now for the third goal of ethnography: charting the hidden patterns that you find at your research site but that the participants in that site do not see. What hidden patterns did I find at the San Francisco Church of World Messianity?

The main hidden pattern was the fact that the church had the three distinct subgroups that I described earlier. Each of these groups engaged in the same church activities. Each affirmed the same basic theology. Each recognized the others as good members, part of the same movement to bring about the Age of Day. Yet the groups interpreted their activities and theology rather differently. Those differences led them to react differently to some events that happened toward the end of my fieldwork.

I've already mentioned the church founder's belief that the coming world transformation needed Japan and the United States to work together. That's why he sent missionaries to the United States and why the church worked so hard to get converts. The problem was, few Americans were converting. At the time of my fieldwork, the church listed about 16,000 American members, most of whom were inactive. Only 2,000 to 3,000 were active nationwide, most of them in Hawaii and Los Angeles.

The Japanese leadership decided that something was wrong with its American operation. They sent two senior ministers to the United States to locate the problem. These ministers decided to increase central control, so they ordered all members to attend special Rededication classes, at which they were to affirm their loyalty. Those who did not attend would lose their membership. Most inactive members chose to leave, but they had pretty much left already. A lot of the active members also left, however. The Japanese ministers underestimated the degree to which Americans do not like to be told what to think or do. The three subgroups responded differently to the two ministers' pressure.

The first group, remember, was mostly second- and third-generation Japanese Americans who used *johrei* for physical health. They were surprised when the two ministers condemned this attitude. *Johrei*, they were told, was a spiritual practice, not mainly a physical one. These members did not leave the church, however. Most of them decided to wait out the new program. They saw themselves as bridging East and West far more effectively than did the ministers themselves. As one of them put it to me, "The new ministers don't understand the American way. *Meishu-sama* [the church's founder] did, which is why he wanted Japan and the United States to work together. The Japanese leaders are too hierarchical. We'll wait until they realize their mistake."

The second group reacted differently. This was the group that emphasized the unity of all religions—another idea that the two Japanese ministers denied. Those ministers said that only World Messianity knew the truth and that all other religions were in error. Members of the second group disliked the new exclusiveness, and many left. Those who stayed often ignored the new messages. One of the latter told me that she had held a séance to consult her "guardian spirits" about what to do. She should stay, they said, "because *johrei* is too important a tool to let these small-minded ministers force you out."

The third group was the most affected by the new regime. They, too, were put off by the new exclusive message, but they also disliked the ministers' warnings that the predicted Age of Fire would not be a time of peace and harmony. In fact, the ministers accused those who believed in a peaceful new age as "being in the hands of dark forces." A higher proportion of this third group left the church than of the others.

When the dust had settled, the church had maybe 1,500 members left—a figure that did not grow significantly in subsequent years. This was not the outcome that the Japanese leadership had had in mind.[7]

How did I identify these three groups? They all participated in the same activities, and they didn't think of themselves as different. How was I able to discern their differences and then trace the results of those differences during the church's membership crisis? It took a bit more than simple "deep hanging-out" to do so.

As part of my ethnographic data collecting, I took an informal census of church members. I kept good field notes, in which I recorded which participants were friendly with each other and which moved in separate social circles. This gave me the outlines of the group differences. Over time, I was able to discover distinct networks of people who interacted more closely with each other than they did with outsiders. As I interviewed them, I also found that those who were in different networks gave me the different interpretations of church teachings that I described earlier. This combination of different social networks and different ideas led me to identify the incipient divisions.

This technique is called **network analysis**. It is a process of tracing the ties between people. Who sits together at lunch? Who talks to each other before and after services? Who carpools? Who visits each other's houses? Who does each member report feeling close to? Which people consider themselves friends?

Finding these networks involves both observation and interviews. I could watch what people did together, and I could ask them whom they were close to. I could gradually map their relationships. The three networks I found were not obvious, even to insiders. They were, however, present—and they explained why some people left the church in the membership crisis and why others stayed.

Ethnography is like that. You gather information in a lot of different ways. Censuses, observations, interviews, and the like all bring in bits of data. The ethnographer's job is to combine the data into a full picture of the social scene.

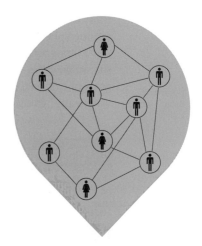

What Doesn't Matter

Clever readers will have noticed that I've left something out of my story about my time at the Church of World Messianity. I've talked about the church members' shared views of the world; I've talked about the things they did together; and I've talked about the hidden patterns that I saw in their community. Nowhere, however, have I said what *johrei* really is. I did say that it was the church's chief religious practice, and I described how the members experienced it, phenomenologically. I did not, however, tell you what is "really" going on when one person channels *johrei* to another.

That's because ethnography focuses on how people understand their own social situations. The church members all thought that *johrei* was a gift from God that could dissolve the spiritual clouds that are the source of humanity's troubles. Some used it to relieve illness; others focused on spiritual uplift; still other channeled it to bring about the Age of Day. For them, it really did these things. Ethnography gathers data about how people see the world.

Ethnography also focuses on the things that people do. Church members channel *johrei,* and I studied how they did so, when they did so, and how it felt to them while they were doing it. That is the second goal of ethnography: to describe people's social practices.

Finally, ethnography looks for hidden patterns in people's social behavior. It looks for things that the "natives" miss. The church members did not realize that they had formed three subgroups, each with a different interpretation of church theology. The only aspect of *johrei* that was "hidden" was the fact that no one questioned its presence. Affirming it was part of their common culture. The whole group agreed on this aspect of the church worldview.

Had I been engaging in something other than ethnography, I might have been interested in the question of *johrei*'s "real" nature. A physiologist might choose to examine church members' brain waves while channeling. A parapsychologist might want to look for ethereal radiation. These are, however, not the types of data that ethnographers pursue.

Ethnographers gather data about culturally shared knowledge and worldviews, shared practices, and hidden social patterns. Those data constitute the three main goals of this data collection method. As an ethnographer, I had no interest in what was "really" going on. I was interested in the people, not in the phenomenon.

ETHNOGRAPHY'S THREE GOALS

1. To learn to see the world as the participants in a social scene see it.

2. To watch what those participants do that makes the scene possible.

3. To understand the hidden patterns that those participants may fail to see, because they are too taken-for-granted to be noticed.

Steps to a Successful Ethnography

Besides the ability to talk with people, to observe what they do, and to identify patterns in their thoughts and behavior, a successful ethnography requires mastery of several specific skills. You have to gain access to the social scene you want to investigate. You have to develop rapport with the people in it. You have to listen carefully to their way of speaking. And you have to listen as much for what they *don't* say as for what they do.

Gaining Access

Ethnography is not like survey research. You don't just visit someone once, collect their views, and then go back to your office to tally them. You have to spend considerable time in the field. My research with the Church of World Messianity lasted a bit under two years. It wasn't full time, as I had a job and various family obligations. Yet I was a regular part of their community for long enough to gain a deep understanding of what was happening. Two years is not an unusual amount of time to spend on an ethnographic project.

This requires access. You first have to convince people to let you study them. This is easier with groups that welcome outsiders and easiest of all if you can find someone with high status in the community to serve as your sponsor. I was lucky with this particular church: I knew someone who was training to become a minister. She introduced me to the head minister, and when he found out that I was studying anthropology, he exclaimed, "That's wonderful! You can help us figure out how to make our Japanese religion appeal to Americans." This gave me a role, and his support gave me access. I can't say that I actually accomplished much on this task, but it did make my ethnography possible.

In short, I negotiated a role. I presented myself as an anthropologist[8] with an interest in understanding their church. The head minister saw the possibility of using my skills, so he presented me to others as someone who could help their church succeed. He also saw me as a potential convert. Though my ideas and his didn't quite match, both involved my learning as much as I could about the religion—a role that both he and I embraced. After a few weeks, I was so much a part of the social landscape that people didn't need to explain any longer why I was present.

Access is not always so smooth. On one of my later interview projects, the staff of a Catholic women's peace-and-justice center kept breaking their appointments with me. I'd drive two or more hours to reach their city, only to discover that they'd "forgotten" the appointment. They'd quiz me about my project, ask who else I'd interviewed, and then say they were too busy to meet with me and set a new appointment for a couple of weeks in the future. I'd show up again, they'd again have forgotten, would ask me the purpose of my project, and would again be too busy to cooperate. I finally got access when one staffer took pity on me and agreed to talk. We had a great conversation. When it was over, she said to the rest of the staff, "He's cool. He really listens." It turns out that they'd had a series of bad experiences with journalists who had misquoted them. They didn't want to talk with anyone who they suspected wasn't going to portray them accurately.

That was an interview project, not an ethnography. As a male, I would have had a hard time doing an ethnography in a women's center. The gender divide would have kept me an outsider and would also have interfered with their work. There would have been no suitable role for me. That didn't hinder my interviews, but it would have prevented ethnographic research.

This isn't to say that you can do ethnography only among people just like yourself. Whites can (and have) done ethnographic work in African American communities, and Americans can (and have) done ethnographic work in Japan.[9] Cross-cultural ethnography usually involves long-term interaction with people who differ from you in major ways. An ethnographer does, however, need a plausible role. Gaining access is a process of negotiating a role that the members of the target community can understand. They have to decide that your project is worth their while—even if they don't fully understand what ethnography is.

Developing Rapport

Once you have access, you have to develop rapport. You have to interact with people in such a way that they will open up to you, telling you what you want to know. Some ethnographers find this easy, whereas others find it more difficult. There's no one right way to do it. Your ability to get information from other people depends on your personality, but it also depends on the social rules of the group you are investigating. Not every group responds to the same kinds of invitation.

I'll give you a radical example. Anthropologist Napoleon Chagnon spent several years living with a village of Yanomamo Indians in the southern Venezuelan jungle.[10] He called them "the fierce people" and described in great detail their aggressiveness and their intertribal warfare. He estimated that over 20% of the male population died by violence.[11] This was no place for a self-effacing person to collect data. Chagnon reported having to show his informants that he was no pushover. He recounted one incident in which the villagers stole a bunch of boards he had collected to build himself a cabin. They used the boards as improvised canoe paddles, so that they could cross the river to meet a trading boat. Chagnon lost his temper at this, pursued them with his machete, and then, after threats of far worse, cut their canoes loose to float downriver. He then returned to the rest of the villagers, who congratulated him on finally learning how to be a Yanomamo. Information then became easier to obtain.

This is clearly an extreme case. Few ethnographic settings require this kind of self-presentation. Every ethnographer, however, has to figure out how to fit in to the group she or he is investigating. This involves an ongoing attention to the group's social dynamics and to its particular ways of sharing information. Just "being yourself" is seldom enough.

Typically, you will want to develop one or more **key informants**. These are people who know the culture well and who can guide you toward the information you seek. They may be **gatekeepers**: people in positions of power or authority in the group, whose goodwill toward you convinces others to cooperate. They may be so-called *native intellectuals*—observant people who both participate in group life and view it somewhat objectively. Finding such informants helps your project get going. You have to be careful, however, to double-check everything these informants tell you. Every informant has her or his own perspective. Some of them have axes to grind. It is your job to make sure that you get a clear, unbiased view, ideally from lots of different informants who have different things to tell you. Triangulation gets you a better picture.

There are dozens of books that describe how particular ethnographers have come to understand a social group's worldviews, practices, and hidden patterns.[12] It is always worth reading such "tales from the field." They can give you concrete clues about how to develop the rapport you need.

Listening to Language

What do you do after you've established rapport? Simple: You gather the information that you came to seek. Ethnographers have research questions just like other investigators. Those questions tell you that you need to collect a group's cultural knowledge, or to observe the things that its members commonly do, or to uncover its hidden patterns. So that's what you look for. Your questions focus your inquiry. Of course, you take notes on everything that you encounter, whether or not it relates to your question and whether or not you think it's relevant. You may later find that it leads you to the information you seek. In any case, your research questions give you goals toward which to steer.

While you're collecting that information, however, pay close attention to the words people use while they're talking to you. Words can tell you much more than you expect about how people really think. Attending to language gives you clues about people's underlying attitudes.

THINK ABOUT IT
Why do you need to talk with more people than just your key informants and gate-keepers?

You already know some examples. For instance, some adult men always refer to adult women as "girls." They may not mean this to belittle them; it's just the way they were taught to speak. Yet it usually does indicate an attitude that treats men as being the more responsible gender. So do phrases like "Man up!" "Take it like a man!" and "It's a man's job." Imagine someone saying "Boy up!" "Take it like a boy!" and "It's a boy's job." Those phrases set a whole different tone.

Just hearing these phrases from your informants doesn't justify you calling them sexist. It does, however, suggest that you ought to look for other patterns of language, belief, and behavior that might indicate underlying gender attitudes. You may or may not find them. Hearing the pattern gives you somewhere to start.

Other cases are more complex. In the late 1970s, Robert Bellah and his colleagues interviewed scores of Americans about their core values.[13] This was not an ethnographic study, but it did focus on the language that people use to describe how they make major life choices. They reported that their interviewees frequently used a language of individualism. These interviewees did not describe doing things because of civic duty or moral imperatives. Instead, they spoke of choosing what would be good for themselves and their families, or what best expressed their inner feelings. This wasn't just a matter of people looking out for themselves. The interviewees really did seem to think that society was nothing more than a collection of individuals, each pursuing her or his own ends. At least that's how Bellah and his coauthors framed the matter. They worried for American democracy if people could not conceive of putting civic duty or morality higher than themselves.

The point is not whether Bellah and colleagues were right or wrong about this.[14] The point is how they got there. They reached their conclusions by having deep conversations with people and listening to how those people phrased their ideas. Their classic example is an interview in which they asked Sheila Larson (a pseudonym) to describe her religion: "It's Sheilaism," she said. "Just my own little voice. . . . It's just try to love yourself and be gentle with yourself." This creates, they wrote, the logical possibility "of over 220 million American religions, one for each of us," each one centered on ourselves alone.[15] How, they wondered, could a society that thinks like this hold together? You don't have to agree with their worries to recognize that listening to people's language is a good way to understand those people's deepest views.

Being an Observed Observer

Ethnography is unusual in another respect. You are always being observed by the people you are observing. You watch them, and they watch you. You try to figure out what they think, and they try to figure out what you think. Detached observations, experiments, and surveys let you be a fly on the wall. No flies for ethnographers! Even interviews are more of a one-way street. Ethnography is a two-way street, because you spend so much time sharing your informants' lives that they also share yours. This creates both problems and opportunities that other data collection techniques do not.

The first issue involves figuring out how to live out in the open. Ethnographers are always on stage. People are always watching, so you have to keep up the front that got you access to the field site in the first place. If, for example, you are investigating a group that doesn't approve of alcohol, then you'd better not be caught buying beer. People might shun you, which would harm your research.

Ordinary life gives you backstage spaces to let down your guard. Adults go home after work. Teens go to their rooms to get away from their parents. Ethnographers can hide only by leaving the field, and that's not always practical. Even catching that beer in a different town might get back to your informants. To continue the theater analogy, you have to stay in character.

That's not all bad, depending on the role. An ethnographer friend of mine spent a year investigating a Presbyterian church in a small California town. He is actively religious, so he didn't have to pretend to be anything he wasn't. He was also young, single, educated, and very good looking. That caused a few problems, because many of the single women in the congregation saw him as a potential "catch." He didn't initiate this, but he's a clever guy and figured out very quickly what was going on. To maintain his fieldwork, he had to be careful not to get "caught" by any of the women. That would dry up his ability to talk to the others. Neither could he reject any of them, for the same reason. He certainly couldn't misbehave (by church standards). So long as he maintained both his single status and his virtue, he got invited to every event the church put on. Lots of people talked with him, of all generations. He used the role that they gave him to learn about the church community.

Another ethnographer friend found herself cast a bit differently. She, too, was investigating a church community, but one that was much more theologically conservative than the small-town Presbyterian church just mentioned. She was married, but her husband had his own job and did not join her fieldwork. That made it hard for her to fit in with a marriage-oriented congregation. Her interviews stayed formal, and she was kept at arm's length—until she became pregnant. That and the prominent ring on her finger opened doors for her to learn about how church women understood family, neighbors, and the meaning of life. Her pregnancy became a bridge. It shifted her role from highly educated outsider to expectant mother. It was all she needed.

The point is, ethnographers are always given roles. Sometimes the roles are of their own making, and sometimes they are not. The point is to shape them so that you get and keep access and rapport. That's how you get your data.

What About Objectivity?

This brings up another issue: How can you write objectively about a cultural or social scene when you are playing a part in it? Doesn't participation make you lose your objectivity? You'll inevitably know more about some informants and friendship groups than about others, just because you interact with them more easily. That could lead to favoritism and to a skewed description of the social scene itself. How do you make sure that you get a balanced view?

This is a real issue, but it is not as serious as it seems. Yes, ethnographic work is more personal than are some others methods of data collection. For example, surveys give you clear answers: A respondent does or doesn't identify as "male"; a person is "very happy," "pretty happy," or "not too happy." Nice, neat, clear. The problem is, that clarity has a severe cost: Your information is very shallow. Ethnography immerses you in a social setting precisely so that you can learn its complexities. You have to work hard to make sure you are getting as rounded a view of that scene as you can.

The issue is not whether your research is or is not "objective." That isn't the right way to think about this. So long as you collect good data, and you make sure that you are not consciously or unconsciously distorting that data, then your work is objective—that is, it is finding real objects in the real world. The problem is, all research is **perspectival**. It cannot see all aspects of that world simultaneously.

Here's an image for you: Research is like taking a photo. You grab your camera, point it, and shoot. Your photo will look pretty much like whatever you were pointing your camera at. You can't take pictures of dreamscapes or imaginary horses, nor can you get photos of 10-legged cows. You get what you point at: That's **objectivity**.

Now think about what you *don't* get, because your camera has a limited field of view. You don't get the scene behind you, nor do you get the scenes to your right and left. You don't get the sky or the ground, because your camera lens won't put all that into the picture. You get a clear view of what you're aiming at, but not of what is outside the frame. What you can see depends on where you point the camera.

It also depends on where you stand. I can stand on a mountaintop and get a fine photo of the surrounding countryside, but that viewpoint won't let me see down into the canyons and creek beds far below. I can stand in those canyons and get excellent views of their rocks, trees, and waterfalls, but from there I can't see the whole landscape. Neither of these places gives me photographs of bugs or flowers. Each, however, shows me something real.

What you see also depends on your camera's lens. I'm an amateur photographer, so I have several of them. Each one accomplishes something different. If I want a wide-angle photo, I use my widest lens. If I want a close-up photo, I use a macro lens. If I want to see something far away, I pull out my telephoto. My infrared lens shows certain things that the others don't. I can make pictures with any of them, but each one shows different aspects of the scene in front of me.

These three factors intertwine. You point your camera, you stand somewhere, and you use one or another lens. These shape what you can see. You can, however, see different things by pointing in a different direction, or by picking a different lens, or by finding a different place to plant your feet. Doing any of these lets you see different things than you could before.

Ethnography works the same way. You start your research from a standpoint, usually with some idea of what you are looking for. You can't always adjust that standpoint, though you can adjust your intellectual lenses and the direction you aim them. I can change my ways of thinking more easily than I can change the fact that I'm a late-middle-aged White American male. That identity gives me easy access to certain social and cultural scenes and bars me from others. It gives me rapport with some people and makes rapport with others difficult. I have a pretty large intellectual tool kit, so I can get past a lot of difficulties. But like camera work, there are things that my starting point and my tool kit don't let me see.

An early-career African American female ethnographer, for example, would begin her research with a different standpoint and a different intellectual tool kit; she would thus be able to see things that I cannot and she could not see things that I can. Our different standpoints would show us different sides of whatever we are investigating. We're both being objective, in that we are accurately reporting what we see. The issue is that our different standpoints and tools reveal different aspects of that scene.

To be concrete for a moment, several things made my ethnographic study of the Church of World Messianity possible. First, I had a friend in ministerial training. This eased my access. Second, I was young and had studied anthropology. This attracted the local church leader because he wanted someone to help translate their message for an American audience. I suspect that he also thought that a young person would be easier to steer. Being male in a male-dominated church didn't hurt, though a number of the older women treated me more like a wayward son than an authority figure. That helped me learn more from them than might otherwise have been possible. Finally, I was also comfortable with people doing what to an outsider might seem strange activities. In this case, I was comfortable watching people clean the clouds off of each other's spiritual bodies using *johrei*. Not everyone is comfortable with such things. I apparently am.

However, not being Japanese, middle-aged, or particularly accustomed to wearing suits kept me out of some places where I might have learned a great deal more about the church hierarchy. I could not penetrate that hierarchy, so I know relatively little about how the church leaders thought. Not speaking Japanese compounded the problem. My ethnographic descriptions thus focused on the ordinary people in the church more than they focused on the ministerial staff.

Every starting point has its strengths and weaknesses. Analyzing those strengths and weaknesses is a key step in doing what we now call **reflexive ethnography**. This is ethnography that pays attention to the human element in ethnographic investigation. It examines the effects of such things as friendship ties, age, training, gender, ethnicity, and the like on what one is able to learn in a particular field setting. Reflexive ethnographers chart the consequences for their knowledge of the personal characteristics that influence access and rapport. They ultimately paint a better picture of the limitations of what they know.

How do you maximize your strengths and minimize your weaknesses? Let's go back to the camera analogy. If one camera shows you a single side of a flower, two cameras will show you two sides. Three cameras will show three, and so on.

If you want to see more sides of a scene than you can see from your normal position, get out of that position and into another. The pregnant ethnographer mentioned earlier did that. As she moved from being a highly educated outsider to being an expectant mother, her access blossomed. I have another friend who experienced something similar in her study of women in a rural Irish community. She took her three children to the community, put the older two in local schools and took the youngest with her on her visits to farm wives. The Irish women opened up to her as they might not have to someone not so obviously motherly. She learned a tremendous amount about that community and credits much of that to her ability to take on a new role.[16]

Of course, not everyone can get pregnant, take babies to the field, and the like. Even if you can, there will be things you miss. Team ethnography is another way to get multiple perspectives. You build a team that gives you diverse access to the local community. Working together, you can see more than any single ethnographer can alone.

The issue is not that a single ethnographer lacks objectivity. It is that no one researcher can stand in all possible places, point in all possible directions, and master all possible intellectual lenses. Ethnography's ability to produce so much detail about a community brings this issue of standpoint to the fore.

Writing Your Results

The last step in any research project is writing your results. All researchers do this, but ethnographers have some special issues to handle. In brief, they have to write themselves into their reports. Standpoint shapes what data you can collect, which means you have to describe your standpoint so that your readers will understand better what you can and can't see. That will give them a more accurate picture of the cultural or social scene that you are describing. Readers will realize that they are not seeing the whole picture but only the part of the picture to which you had access.

Writing oneself into the text has been *de rigueur* for anthropologists at least since the 1980s. A series of books published in that decade showed how the old style of ethnographic writing had painted inaccurate pictures of the communities that anthropological ethnographers had studied. Writing as if one had an omniscient eye glossed over cracks in the ethnographers' data. This led to situations in which two different ethnographers could draw completely opposite conclusions about the same community. There was no way for readers to tell which had the more accurate view. Nor could readers use the views stereoscopically—treating each as revealing a part of the whole picture, which the readers could then assemble. James Clifford and George Marcus's *Writing Culture* and Clifford Geertz's *Words and Lives* were particularly influential in examining this issue.[17] They sensitized anthropologists to the ways in which who you are shapes what you can see, and how writing yourself into your research reports makes for better understanding.

Your first task as an ethnographer is to recognize your limitations during fieldwork and try to overcome them. Your second task is to give the readers details about those limitations, so that those readers can get a better picture of the people being studied.

Sociological ethnographers have been slower to take up this challenge. That may be because sociology still reveres quantitative analysis, which it often treats as more objective than qualitative data collection methods. As I've shown earlier, the issue is not objectivity. All research needs to describe its limitations. Ethnographers simply have to be more open about what they were and were not able to investigate while in the field.

Beyond this, writing ethnographic research reports is very much like writing up other kinds of research. You describe your *research question,* your *logical structure,* the *type of data* you were looking for, the *data collection method* you used, the *data collection site* where you looked for it, and the *data analysis methods* you used to come to your conclusions. Those are the six steps in designing research that we've encountered throughout this book. The difference is in the amount of detail an ethnographer has available to share. A two-year ethnographic project might well produce several books, each on an overlapping topic. For each of these, you need to let the reader know what you discovered, how it was discovered, and what things were not discovered because you did not gain access to them. Simple honesty about what you don't know is no failure.

A Word About Grounded Theory

Before moving on, I want to say a short word about **grounded theory**. I described that data collection method in Chapter 4. There, I pointed out that grounded theory shared a lot of ethnography's characteristics. Both seek hidden social patterns, both involve extensive participant observation in social scenes or communities, and both produce voluminous field notes. Both also start with relatively broad research questions that encourage investigators to pursue whatever unexpected patterns they find in the field. Both also typically describe the scenes they investigate rather than pursuing a causal or a correlational logical structure.

I also noted some differences. Grounded theory developed in the 1960s as a technique for investigating interpersonal interactions, particularly in social settings that were (at the time) not well understood.[18] Ethnography casts a wider net; as we've seen in this chapter, ethnographers also look for cultural knowledge and cultural practices—the things that everyone knows and does in a social scene or community. Hidden patterns are just part of the picture, and hidden interaction patterns are a subset of those. Grounded theory is thus a more limited data collection method, at least as it was originally designed. Contemporary grounded theorists also cast a wider net than was typical a generation ago.[19]

A major difference is the matter of standpoint. As I described earlier, ethnographers have learned to analyze their own social, cultural, and conceptual starting points, to see how those starting points shape the data they are able to collect. This is particularly true for anthropological ethnographers, but it is increasingly true for sociological ethnographers as well. Ethnographers have become reflexive; grounded theory practitioners have not yet followed suit. Perhaps someday they will.

Research Ethics

What ethical issues does ethnographic data collection raise? There are several, all driven by the kind of data you collect and the length of time you spend in the field. The principles are the same as with other data collection methods. You have to protect your informants, ensure their privacy, make sure they know who you are and what you are doing, and give them some control over the information they give you.

As you might expect, informants have less control over your observations in public places than over your observations in private. Patterns of public behavior are fair game, though you should make sure your reports focus on the patterns themselves rather than on particular individuals. Following the guidelines given in Chapter 11, on recording behavior, takes care of the concerns raised by that data collection technique quite well. As we saw in Chapter 9, interviews are more complex. There is no need to repeat that information here.

What ethical issues does ethnography raise that we haven't already encountered? Here are two.

First, there's the issue of all those notes. It takes time to discover people's shared cultural knowledge, so you'll take lots of notes. It also takes time to discover people's shared practices. That means more notes, including ones with details about specific people. You'd better write down specifics because you won't know at the beginning which practices are shared and which ones are unique to particular individuals.

One church I visited had a member who would do yoga in the corner during services. It was easy to see that this wasn't common practice, because none of the other participants stood on their heads during the sermon. What *was* a common practice, though, was the members' acceptance of such idiosyncratic behavior. One member rocked from side to side; another bowed deeply during the gospel readings; yet another sat in deep meditation. Only notes and my interviews with church members pointed me toward the shared behavior.

Hidden patterns are particularly tricky. These patterns aren't just hidden from you; they're also hidden from the other participants. Only extensive notes will help here. That's one reason I spent 13 years on a project with a radical Catholic commune. I had discovered some hidden patterns, and I continued my observations for a whole extra year, to make sure that I had captured them correctly.[20] All three of ethnography's goals call for extensive documentation.

The question is, how do you keep those notes private? How do you protect the privacy of the people you study, when you've written down so much about them? Even if you use code names or letters—and I suggest that you do—it would not take much to identify individuals from the mass of information that an ethnographer gathers. How do you make sure that nobody uses your notes to harm the people you have studied?

This is not a hypothetical issue. When introducing research ethics in Chapter 4, I mentioned Rik Scarce. He was a graduate student studying radical environmentalist groups when one of those groups vandalized a university laboratory. The local prosecutor subpoenaed Scarce's field notes, which he refused to release. He spent several months in jail for contempt of court for refusing to cooperate with his informants' prosecution. Mario Brajuha was similarly jailed for refusing to release his notes to prosecutors who were investigating an arson in the restaurant where Brajuha was doing his fieldwork.[21] These scholars chose to violate the law rather than endanger their informants.

Other researchers have taken other routes. I also mentioned Laud Humphreys's research on the "tearoom trade."[22] He collected data on men's impersonal homosexual sex in public restrooms, at a time when such activity was outlawed. On the positive side, he chose to keep his field notes in a safe-deposit box in a different state, out of reach of any prosecutor. On the negative side, he endangered the men by locating their addresses and interviewing them at their homes several months after his observations. Most scholars' professional organizations now have codes of ethics that would prevent the second of these but applaud the first.

Much more recently, sociologist Alice Goffman chose to destroy the field notes from her six-year study of a group of lower-class African American men in Philadelphia. Her book, *On the Run: Fugitive Life in an American City,* chronicled the effects of the War on Drugs in making these men's lives unlivable.[23] In it, she described a veritable police state that harassed these men constantly, no matter what they did. She described beatings and random arrests that systematically cut these men off from opportunity. Following the ethical guidelines of her academic discipline, she made it impossible to identify these men from her book's details. She used pseudonyms, relocated events in time and space, combined several incidents into one, and so on, all to prevent her book from causing them harm. She then destroyed her field notes to prevent them from being used to prosecute her informants for the very real crimes they had to commit during her fieldwork, just to stay alive. Those notes might have led to their convictions. Destroying them kept the focus on the patterns she discovered, rather than on individuals' behavior.

Unfortunately, that let her in for a good deal of professional criticism. She was accused of falsifying her observations, of making up her data, and even of aiding and abetting crimes—all because she was so good about protecting her informants. With her notes destroyed, she had no easy rebuttal. Fortunately, her undergraduate and graduate advisers had seen the field notes and could vouch for her accuracy. The case points out, however, the problems that paying attention to ethical standards can cause.[24]

The second ethical issue is a good deal more prosaic. It, too, stems from the fact that good ethnography takes a long time. After you've been in the field for a while, many of your informants will forget that you are an ethnographer. They'll think you're just one of them: a little stranger, perhaps, and certainly more inquisitive, but fundamentally part of their scene, not just a visitor.

You realize this at odd places. After several months of research on one of my projects, I found myself washing dishes in the kitchen with a homeless guy. We'd both been to a church service, then to a potluck supper, and now we were cleaning up. He knew me by sight and from previous conversations. We had a nice talk while our hands were immersed in water, making sure the pots got clean. At one point, he said (as guys do): "What do you do for a living?" I replied: "I'm a college professor." He gave me a surprised look. "Damn! I thought you were one of us!" he exclaimed. He paused for a moment, and then said, "But it's nice to know you." The gap between us closed again, and we went back to talking and washing dishes. It was good to know that our different paths in life didn't have to ruin our rapport.

The ethical question is how often ethnographers ought to remind their informants that they are researchers, not just human beings. We are both, but we have to remind them that we may someday leave and write up what we've learned about their lives. How often should we do so? How can we support their right to manage their participation in our project, while not bringing that project to a halt? These questions have no easy answers.

Review Questions

1. What are the three goals of ethnographic data collection?

2. What are the most important principles to use when you are taking field notes?

3. How do you locate hidden patterns in your field site? (These are the patterns that even the natives don't realize are there.)

4. What are some ways that you can gain access to your field site?

5. What are some ways of maintaining rapport with your informants?

6. Why should you listen carefully to the language that your informants use?

7. What does it mean to be an observed observer?

8. What ethical issues particularly affect ethnographers? What are some of the ways that ethnographers have protected their informants?

The open-access Student Study Site at **study.sagepub.com/spickard** has a variety of useful study tools, including SAGE journal articles, video & web resources, eFlashcards, and quizzes.

Notes

1. The name was a rather infelicitous translation of the Japanese *Sekai Kyusei-kyo*; it would be more accurately rendered as "the church that will save the world." For a very readable account of this and some other new Japanese religions, see Robert Ellwood, *The Eagle and the Rising Sun: Americans and the New Religions of Japan*. Westminster Press, 1974.

2. For details, see James Spickard, "Spiritual Healing Among the American Followers of a Japanese New Religion: Experience as a Factor in Religious Motivation," *Research in the Social Scientific Study of Religion* 3 (1991): 135–156; and "Globalization and Religious Organizations: Rethinking the Relationship Between Church, Culture, and Market," *International Journal of Politics, Culture, and Society* 18 (2004): 47–63.

3. Mokichi Okada, *Teachings of Meishu-sama*, Vol. 1 (1967) and Vol. 2 (1968). Atami, Japan: Church of World Messianity.

4. See Clifford Geertz, "Deep Hanging-Out," *New York Review of Books*, October 22, 1988, pp. 69–72.

5. There is one famous (but semi-apocryphal) exception. Edmund Leach wrote his famous *Political Systems of Highland Burma* (Harvard, 1954) after losing his original field notes in a river crossing as he fled Japanese troops during World War II. He was, however, able to reconstruct those notes' general outline, which he supplemented with notes taken later in the war and with archival materials. His notes were thus not entirely missing.

6. You'll find a more complete example of this grid in the "Research Guides and Handouts" section of this book.

7. I recounted the church's subsequent history in Spickard, "Globalization and Religious Organizations."

8. Though my formal degrees are in history, sociology, and religious studies, this was not a lie. I had at that time had more training in anthropology than in any of these disciplines.

9. Frances Kostarelos, *Feeling the Spirit: Faith and Hope in an Evangelical Black Storefront Church*. University of South Carolina Press, 1995; Timothy J. Nelson, *Every Time I Feel the Spirit: Religious Experience and Ritual in an African American Church*, New York University Press, 2004; and Matthews Hamabata, *Crested Kimono: Power and Love in the Japanese Business Family*. Cornell University Press, 1990.

10. Napoleon A. Chagnon, *Yanomamo: The Fierce People*. Holt, Rinehart, & Winston, 1968.

11. Others have questioned this figure, including Patrick Tierney (*Darkness in El Dorado*, Norton, 2000). For a summary of the controversy, see Steven Pinker, *The Blank Slate: The Modern Denial of Human Nature*. Viking, 2002, pp. 115ff.

12. Here are two: George Spindler, ed.: *Being an Anthropologist: Fieldwork in Eleven Cultures*. Holt, Rinehart, & Winston, 1970; and James Spickard et al., eds., *Personal Knowledge and Beyond*. New York University Press, 2002.

13. Robert N. Bellah et al., *Habits of the Heart: Individualism and Commitment in American Life*. University of California Press, 1985.

14. See, for example, Jeffrey Stout's critique in *Ethics After Babel: The Languages of Morals and Their Discontents*. Beacon Press, 1988, pp. 194–199.

15. Bellah et al., *Habits of the Heart*, p. 221.

16. I have deliberately not provided details about these three studies, though two are well-known books and the third is a well-known story in my subdiscipline. None of these authors, however, has published these tales, though they have spoken about them publicly at conferences.

17. James Clifford and George Marcus, *Writing Culture: The Poetics and Politics of Ethnography*. University of California Press, 1986; and Clifford Geertz, *Works and Lives: The Anthropologist as Author*. Stanford University Press, 1988.

18. Barney G. Glaser and Anselm L. Strauss, *The Discovery of Grounded Theory*. Aldine, 1967.

19. Adele Clark, *Situational Analysis: Grounded Theory After the Postmodern Turn*. Sage, 2005; and Kathy Charmaz, *Constructing Grounded Theory: A Practical Guide Through Qualitative Analysis*. Sage, 2006.

20. James Spickard, "Ritual, Symbol, and Experience: Understanding Catholic Worker House Masses," *Sociology of Religion* 66 (2005): 337–358.

21. Peter Monaghan, "Sociologist Is Jailed for Refusing to Testify About Research Subject," *Chronicle of Higher Education*, May 26, 1993, p. 10; and Mario Brajuha and Lyle Hallowell, "Legal Intrusion and the Politics of Fieldwork: The Impact of the Brajuha Case," *Journal of Contemporary Ethnography* 14 (1986): 454–478.

22. Laud Humphreys, *Tearoom Trade: Impersonal Sex in Public Places*. Duckworth, 1970.

23. Alice Goffman, *On the Run: Fugitive Life in an American City*. University of Chicago Press, 2014.

24. For a measured view, see Leon Neyfakh, "The Ethics of Ethnography," *Slate*, June 18, 2015, www.slate.com; for a critical attack, see Steven Lubet, "Did This Acclaimed Sociologist Drive the Getaway Car in a Murder Plot?" *New Republic*, May 27, 2015, www.newrepublic.com.

CHAPTER 14

Extended Example: Counting the Homeless

Most of us have encountered homeless people. Maybe we've seen someone in ratty clothes panhandling on a street corner or passed out on a park bench. Maybe we've volunteered in a soup kitchen. When we think about the homeless, we typically think of unkempt people, unemployed, mostly men, tired and ill from having no secure place to sleep. We think of mentally ill people who can't get care. Above all, we think of people who have no options, waiting because they have nothing to do and nowhere to go, living in public because they have no private place to be.

These people are, indeed, part of America's homeless population. They are not all of it, however. Many homeless people have jobs. Many have families. Many dress as neatly as "normal" people and hide their homelessness from others.

Some years ago, for example, one of my better students was homeless for much of a semester. She had broken up with her boyfriend and had neither money nor a place to live. You would never have known it, she covered her tracks so well. She slept in dorm lounges, in an abandoned broom closet, and three or four other places near campus. I learned of it because she needed somewhere to store her books and a few belongings. Is this not homelessness as well?

This chapter explores a single question about homelessness in America: "How many homeless people are there in the United States?" This is a complex issue, because homeless people are not easy to count. To put it bluntly, they hide. The street homeless hide for safety, both from criminals and from the police. People like my former student hide the fact that they have nowhere to live—in part from shame and in part so that others will not treat them badly. Nor is everyone who looks homeless actually so. I've had many conversations with people who appear to live in my town's parks or on its street corners but who are in fact relatively well housed. This makes counting the homeless complicated. Homeless people don't wear signs telling us who they are.

In this chapter, we'll review what social scientists have learned about counting homeless people. We'll go back a few decades to visit some early efforts; then we'll explore some later, more effective techniques. Finally, we'll evaluate current counting methods, weighing the choices that investigators have to make as they carry out the counts that the U.S. Congress has required of every city and county since the mid-2000s. These counts are supposed to track the seriousness of the United States' inability to provide housing for all its residents.

Unfortunately, these counts are often not funded, and if they are, they are seldom funded well. This is all too common with research on social problems. Well-designed research can produce excellent results, but only if there is enough money to collect the data properly.

What Caused the Homeless Crisis?

First, we have to understand a bit about the growth in the number of homeless people, beginning in the 1980s. The United States has always had homeless people.[1] Colonial authorities railed against vagrants. Early 19th-century elites moved poor people farther west. Authorities used debtors' prisons, work gangs, and the like to control those who could not or would not live a settled life. Economic good times brought stability by providing paying work for the majority of able-bodied men. Hard times set people on the road. The Great Depression of the 1930s was particularly difficult. That era established the image of the tramp in America's popular imagination.

The post–World War II era, however, brought both prosperity and stability to American life. Many people were still poor, but fewer were unhoused. City planners situated cheap "single-room occupancy" (SRO) hotels in their cities' warehouse districts, where poor, unskilled workers could live while they moved boxes, loaded trucks, and engaged in other forms of day labor. Often called "flophouses," "cage hotels" (from the anti-rat wire mesh overhead), or even "roach warrens," they were filthy places, but they were better than the streets. These "Skid Rows"[2] were full of poverty and drink. Yet they gave poor people, mostly men, a place to live indoors.

By the early 1980s, five separate socioeconomic trends combined to put more Americans on the streets than at any time in the previous 50 years. Experts differ about which of these were the most important, but they all agree that each of the five played a role:[3]

1. *A steep recession, the worst the country had seen since the 1930s.* The U.S. economy fell by an annualized 8% in the second quarter of 1980 and didn't begin steady growth again until the end of 1982. That affected all segments of the population, but especially those who worked in farming and manufacturing.
2. *The evaporation of low-wage, unskilled jobs.* Increased use of machinery, changing transportation patterns, and so on had eliminated many casual labor jobs just as America's Baby Boomer generation hit the job market and its troops returned home from Vietnam. The result was more workers in a contracting economy. After a decade of little economic growth plus high inflation, national unemployment peaked at 10.8% in December 1982.
3. *The disappearance of inner-city low-income housing.* City after city tore down SRO hotels in the name of urban renewal. Los Angeles, for example, once had more than 800 SROs; by the mid-1980s, only a tenth of those remained. Poor people had fewer affordable places to sleep, so more of them ended up on the streets.

4. *The closure of many state mental hospitals.* On the positive side, the development of new drugs made it possible (and more humane) to provide some mentally ill people with treatment in local clinics. On the negative side, those clinics were seldom fully funded, leaving their clients without easy access to medications or to the supervision they needed to continue taking them. Any relapse threatened to put them on the streets.

5. *The crack cocaine epidemic, which hit poor people particularly hard.* As sociologist Christopher Jencks noted, if one has a choice between a $5 high and a filthy $10 room, many will find the $5 high a better deal. That certainly put more people on the streets.[4]

Add these together, and the result was the highest level of street homelessness since the Civil War. This caught people's notice. A question arose immediately: How big a problem was this? How many homeless people did the United States have? Homeless activist Mitch Snyder claimed there were more than two million. The Reagan administration claimed the number was no higher than 300,000. Neither of these figures had much credibility. Snyder later admitted that he had guessed but wanted a big enough number to get people's attention. The Reagan officials just called some shelter operators and asked them to guess as well. The country needed actual data, so some pioneering sociologists pitched in.

Who Is Homeless?

The first step in counting homeless people is to define what we mean by "homelessness." That's obvious, but it's also far from simple. Different people define homelessness differently. Definitions clearly affect results. Nearly everyone would include these four groups:

- *People who live on the streets, under bridges, and in cars.* These are clearly not places meant for human habitation. People living in them are homeless in any reasonable sense of the word.
- *Those living in homeless shelters.* Technically, these people are "housed," but that housing is temporary and insecure. These people would quickly be on the streets if the shelters didn't exist, or if more people wanted spaces than the shelters could provide.
- *Those living in temporary shelters, such as the National Guard Armories that some cities open up when winter temperatures drop too low.* These people, too, would be on the streets, were it not for such emergency lodging.
- *Those who sleep in unusual covered places, even if they do so regularly.* These include the dorm lounges, garages, and empty buildings that my student used. They also include the tent encampments that spring up periodically in unused portions of city parks or around abandoned factories. Homeless people treat these as more-or-less permanent "housing," but they are not supposed to live there. Police sweeps can make such unofficial dwelling places disappear.

These four groups match the language in the Homeless Emergency Assistance and Rapid Transition to Housing Act of 2009—the law that governs U.S. Department of Housing and Urban Development (HUD) efforts to end homelessness. HUD adds, however, people who live in transitional housing. These people were once in shelters, but they have been moved to temporary housing to free up shelter space for others. They are on their way out of homelessness but are not quite there.

By the HUD definition, there were about 575,000 homeless people nationwide in January 2014. Of those, 400,000 were in shelters or transitional housing, and the rest were on the streets.[5]

How about homeless people who *don't* live on the street? These are people with no home of their own, but who double up with friends and relatives. If we really want to track homelessness, here are three groups we'd have to include:

- Young people who couch-surf because they have no place of their own.
- Families that double up for a week or a month while they're waiting for a new apartment.
- Women fleeing domestic violence, who have to go back to their batterers because they can't find any other dwelling.

None of these people have safe and stable places to live, and all of them experience considerable disruption. Are they homeless? How wide a net do we want to cast?

Schools count these last three groups as homeless, at least when they include children. The McKinney-Vento Homeless Assistance Act of 1987 says:

Students are counted as homeless if they lack a fixed, regular, and adequate nighttime residence at any point during the school year.[6]

By this definition, there were 270,000 homeless children in California alone during the 2012–2013 school year; nationwide there were almost 1.3 million. Seventy-six percent of the latter were doubling up with others, 15% were in shelters, and 6% were in hotels, while the rest were on the street or in other places.[7] The definition makes sense, because even short-term homelessness disrupts children's schooling.

To count homeless people, we need to decide whether to use the HUD definition, the McKinney-Vento definition, or something in between. It makes a great deal of difference to the numbers we will ultimately produce.

We also need to decide how long people have to be homeless for us to include them. Specifically, we have to decide whether we just want to count how many homeless people we can find on a single day—a **point-in-time (PIT) count**, to use the official term. Alternatively, we could include people who were homeless at any point during an entire year. The two graphs in Figure 14.1 show how different definitions of homelessness produce hugely different numbers.

THINK ABOUT IT
Why do we have so many definitions of homelessness?

FIGURE 14.1   Homeless Counts: (a) Unsheltered Population; (b) Doubled-Up Population

(a)

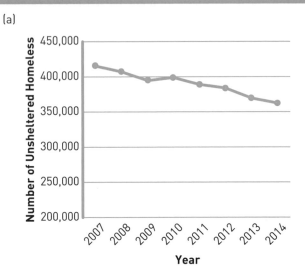

(b)

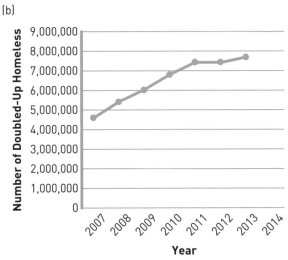

Figure 14.1a shows the unsheltered population for the HUD January PIT counts from 2007 through 2014. It includes just street homeless, not those in shelters or transitional housing. That's a very restrictive definition of homelessness—even more so than the 2009 act's definition. It's also a restrictive count. January counts are taken on a single day, often during a very few hours. If the homeless

people hid that day, or woke before the count started, they'd be missed. We'll soon see some other ways that PIT counts underestimate the homeless population. Still, the number of unsheltered homeless people appears to be falling. Several cities have made concerted efforts to provide more shelters.

Figure 14.1b shows a different set of figures, from the study of people who were doubled up at any time during one of the listed years. The numbers are large, even though they don't include the street homeless, people living in shelters, those in transitional housing, and so on. That's because even one episode of doubling up gets you counted.

The difference is striking: 362,000 street homeless on one night in late January 2014, versus 7.5 million people forced to double up at some point during the previous year. Which of these counts reflects the real homeless problem? Let's start with some plausible, but fictional, numbers. They will show us a pattern that will help us understand what is going on.

Imagine a city that has 9,500 people who are each homeless for 5 days in the course of a year—counting all kinds of homelessness. That's 47,500 person-days[8] of homelessness (9,500 × 5). Imagine that the city also has 500 people who are living on the streets year-round. That's 182,500 person-days of homelessness (500 × 365). Add together those two figures, and you've got 230,000 person-days of homelessness.

That's a lot of person-days. However, nearly 80% of them come from the 500 people who are homeless full time. Only 20% come from the much larger number of people who are homeless for a short time.

This means that on any day we choose, almost 80% of the people without housing will be long-term homeless and just 20% will be short-term homeless. A PIT count is going to miss most of the short-term homeless, but long-term homelessness is the real problem. They are the bulk of the homeless population at any given time.

These are invented figures, but are they realistic? Yes, they are. School data tell us that double-ups typically find housing rather quickly. A week or two weeks of instability and the children have someplace to live again. Their homelessness ends. Street homeless don't fare nearly so well. Though many long-term homeless people can afford occasional housing, and many cities open temporary shelters in the worst weather, most street homeless frequently sleep out of doors. At best, they cycle between shelters and streets and cheap hotels, sometimes for months, even years.

> **Person-Days of Homelessness**
>
> 9,500 people × 5 days = 47,500 (20.65%)
> 500 people × 365 days = 182,500 (79.35%)
> Total: 230,000 person-days

Street homelessness is thus the more serious problem. That's why most homeless counts use the HUD definition, focusing on homeless people living on the streets or in homeless shelters and transitional housing. That is the focus of this chapter. Remember, though, that street homelessness is just the tip of the iceberg. Many times more Americans are inadequately housed.

How Can We Find and Count Street Homeless?

That brings us to the central issue facing anyone who tries to count street homeless: How do we find them? The problem is straightforward: We can count only the people we find, and the harder it is to find people, the more we will underestimate the size of the homeless problem. How have researchers located homeless people in the past? Which ways of finding them are more successful—and which are less so? I'll give you three real-life examples.

Peter Rossi's Chicago Count

The best of these early efforts was led by Peter Rossi, a professor at the University of Massachusetts.[9] He and a team of researchers tried to count Chicago's street homeless in 1985 and 1986. They recognized how hard this would be, so they developed a two-pronged strategy. They surveyed homeless shelters, hospitals, and similar places to find homeless people who had shelter. They also scoured the streets, to see how many homeless without shelter they could find. For the latter, they went in pairs and were accompanied by off-duty policemen. This gave them both protection and the street knowledge that police have about where homeless people live. Chicago is a big place, and its homeless population was no longer concentrated on a single Skid Row. Rossi's team thus "searched a random sample of city blocks during the small hours of the morning, looking in every space they could reach without encountering a locked door or a security guard."[10] They questioned everyone they found, awake or asleep, and paid them for their information. This ensured that most would answer their questions. The team ran two censuses, one in the fall of 1985 and the other in the winter of 1986. Both were PIT counts, each done on a single night. That way, they could avoid double counting people, though they risked missing people who might have found a hotel room for that night or who remained too well hidden.

What did Rossi and his team find? Table 14.1 compares Rossi's two surveys with a similar study done by Donald Bogue in the late 1950s.[11] All three focused on Chicago, though Bogue's wider research covered other cities as well. The table shows us what happened to Chicago homelessness between the late 1950s and the mid-1980s.

As you can see from the table, Rossi and his team found about a third as many people on Chicago's Skid Row as had been present in the late 1950s. However, a much higher percentage of them, about 75%, lived on the street or in shelters. In 1958, 86% had lived in SRO hotels. By the mid-1980s, all but two of those hotels had been torn down. Chicago's poor had fewer options for cheap housing than a generation earlier. They had either gone elsewhere or had become homeless. The balance between street and shelter shifted between Rossi's two counts. This likely depended on weather and on an increase in shelter spaces as the homelessness crisis deepened.

THINK ABOUT IT
What are the advantages of counting at night?

TABLE 14.1	Chicago Homeless Counts		
Age and Location	**Bogue (Winter 1958)**	**Rossi I (Fall 1985)**	**Rossi II (Winter 1986)**
Homeless Adults			
Shelters	975 (10.5%)	1,106 (34.1%)	1,637 (56.1%)
Public places	110 (1.1%)	1,383 (42.7%)	528 (18.1%)
Hospitals	75 (0.8%)	80[a] (2.5%)	80[a] (2.7%)
Jails	85 (0.9%)	?	?
Other	60 (0.7%)		
Homeless Children	0	273[a] (8.4%)	273[a] (9.4%)
Total Street Homeless	**1,305 (14%)**	**2,842 (87.6%)**	**2,518 (86.3%)**
In SRO Hotels	**8,000 (86%)**	**400[a] (12.3%)**	**400[a] (13.7%)**
Grand Total	**9,305**	**3,242**	**2,918**

Notes: [a]Rossi's figures for hospitals, battered women's shelters, street children, and SRO residents are averages of his two surveys.

Why didn't the street homeless all go to shelters? The simple answer is that there weren't enough shelter beds, but there's another reason, too. Though shelters were much cleaner than the old SROs, the SROs treated their residents as paying customers. They didn't see them as charity cases and didn't ask them to "improve themselves." They let them be themselves. Like everyone else, homeless people have pride. Some of them preferred living on the street to being "rescued."[12]

Rossi's figures were, however, much lower than advocates for homeless people had estimated. They had expected him to find between 15,000 and 25,000 on the streets or in shelters. Part of this discrepancy could have been a result of the point-in-time survey method. A PIT count doesn't catch people who are homeless part of the time but can occasionally find places to stay. This is especially true in winter, when Chicago is notoriously cold. Among other things, families will often put up with misbehaving relatives rather than throw them out in the snow. Rossi also didn't report figures for those in jail, which is a common way for homeless to stay off the street in bad weather. Some may have migrated south to warmer climes. A non-PIT method, carried out at a warmer time of year, might well have found a larger number of people living out of doors.

Christopher Jencks pointed out another flaw. He noted that Rossi's team searched only places that were readily accessible, but that less accessible buildings are precisely the buildings in which [homeless seeking safe havens] are most likely to be found. People who sleep in automobiles and trucks also make an effort to park them where they will not be noticed. As a result, even the best early morning street count is likely to miss a significant fraction of the homeless.[13]

Jencks affirmed, however, that Rossi's count was clearly better than the mere guesses that were current at the time.

Martha Burt's Weeklong Method

A few years later, Martha Burt decided that she could do a more thorough job. She argued that homeless people are much easier to find by day, when they are more likely to be out in public, instead of hidden away, as many are at night. She also argued that counting over several days is more likely to catch people who spend some but not all of their time on the streets. By interviewing homeless people at soup kitchens, shelters, and daytime congregating sites (parks, train and bus stations, certain street corners), she hoped to learn where they had spent their nights during the previous week. Doing this for a sample of the visible homeless, she hoped to get a reasonable sense of the percentage who sleep in shelters and how often. As Jencks put this argument, "Since the number of shelter users is known with some accuracy, one can then estimate the overall size of the homeless population."[14]

Burt designed and carried out such a study in March 1987. She and her colleagues at the Urban Institute surveyed homeless people in a representative sample of cities with more than 100,000 population. They interviewed randomly selected homeless adults at daytime shelters, soup kitchens, and congregating sites. They returned to these sites for seven days, making sure they did not interview anyone twice. They asked about the reasons people became homeless and about family structure, among other things. They also asked where their interviewees had spent the previous seven nights. Paying them $5 for their trouble produced a 90% response rate—an excellent figure—which ensured that the sample adequately represented the homeless population in larger cities who frequent such locations.

Burt counted people as homeless if they met any one of three criteria: (1) They had no home or permanent place to live; (2) their home was a shelter, a hotel paid for by vouchers intended to assist homeless people, or a place not intended for habitation; or (3) they lived in someone else's home intermittently, but not regularly and not more than four nights a week. The last criterion is a bit broader than HUD's definition of street homelessness, but Burt's results showed that 96% of those meeting her definition had spent at least one of the previous seven nights on the street or in a shelter. This means that her definition matched HUD's in practice. What did Burt and her colleagues find?

First, they found that 18% of the street homeless were families with children, all but a few of which were headed by single parents.

THINK ABOUT IT
What are the advantages of counting during the day?

On average, each such family had two kids. Almost 96% of these families stayed in homeless shelters rather than on the street. This makes sense, because shelters will take in families with children before they will take in adults, and because parents do not want to risk having their children taken from them for "neglect"—as often happens if families stay on the street. It's better to find an official shelter than to risk losing their children. In fact, not a single family that Burt's team interviewed had spent the previous night on the street. Those who were not in shelters had doubled up with relatives or slept in a car. Homeless parents want to take care of their kids just as much as any other parents do.

Second, 74% of homeless people were single adults, and the remaining 8% were couples or pairs of buddies. On an average night, only a third of these adults slept in shelters. Four percent slept on friends' couches or paid for hotels using their own money.[15] The remaining 62% slept in the open, in cars, in abandoned buildings, and so on. This gives us a ratio of nearly two unsheltered nonfamily adults for every sheltered one.[16] That's about twice the ratio that Rossi found—evidence that his nighttime count probably missed a large number of unsheltered homeless. So did two of the three more recent homeless counts that we'll visit next. Trying to find unsheltered homeless adults at night seems not to be terribly productive.

Third, Burt and her team estimated that between 500,000 and 600,000 people were homeless during the week of their March survey. They got that figure as follows: First, they took the number of homeless families reported by shelter operators. They assumed this was close to the actual number of homeless families, because their figures indicated that almost all such families chose shelters over the street. Next, they multiplied the operators' reports of sheltered nonfamily adults by three to get the total number of homeless in this category; this used the two-to-one ratio of unsheltered to sheltered adults that their survey found. These two figures together gave them a total for their sample of large cities. They then extrapolated from that sample to the nation at large.[17]

I should point out that Burt and her team missed counting homeless people who do not use shelters or soup kitchens and who also do not regularly come to known congregating places—the parks, bus stations, and street corners where the team took its samples. There are surely some such people. Jennifer Toth's account of homeless living in New York's subway tunnels, for example, described a portion of that population that never came above ground.[18] There are likely not many such homeless, however. The strategy of interviewing homeless people by day and doing so over a week's time catches a much larger portion of the total homeless population than does any PIT night count—no matter how well run. Doing this, however, is expensive. As a result, Burt's survey has not, to my knowledge, been systematically repeated.

Nine years later, the U.S. Census Bureau carried out a National Survey of Homeless Assistance Providers and Clients (NSHAPC).[19] This survey focused on agencies that helped homeless people: soup kitchens, shelters, rescue missions, transitional housing authorities, and the like. It covered the country's 28 largest metropolitan statistical areas (MSAs, made up of large cities and their suburbs), 24 randomly selected small and medium-sized MSAs, and 24 randomly selected groups of rural counties or parts of counties.

The study collected three sets of data. The first, in February 1996, consisted of telephone interviews with representatives of all the service providers located in the areas sampled. This amounted to 6,307 service locations and the 11,983 programs that they reported offering. A follow-up mail survey tapped an additional 5,694 programs that had been identified in the telephone interviews. Finally, the study included interviews with 4,207 clients of a random sample of these programs, carried out in October of that year.

This survey did not itself attempt to count America's homeless population. It merely produced service providers' reports of their clients. Burt and her colleagues analyzed the study data and produced from it an estimate of the nation's homeless population.[20] More exactly, they produced two estimates. The first was based on the data from service providers. The second was from the client interviews. The first estimated that 842,000 people sought agency assistance in a typical week in February. The second estimated that 444,000 sought assistance in a typical week in October.

Both of these numbers have problems, albeit different ones. Burt and her colleagues noted that the February count is likely to be high. Service providers often overestimate the number of people they serve. Some homeless seek services from more than one agency. Some agencies serve both homeless and nonhomeless people—at least by the HUD definition of homelessness that we have been following—which opens the possibility of double counting. The October figure, by contrast, is apt to be low. Fewer programs are open in October than in February, as the weather is typically better in October, so fewer people need emergency services. Interviewing regular clients (as the study did) undercounts those who use services only infrequently. But the October data avoided the problem of double counting by interviewing clients, not providers, and the problem of including nonhomeless people. No wonder its figure was lower.

On the plus side, the NSHAPC data allowed Burt and her team to create one-day, seven-day, and annual projections of the number of people who seek some sort of homeless assistance. The weekly figures were higher, of course, but they allowed for a clear comparison with the Urban Institute's 1987 study (Table 14.2). The authors argued that the higher February 1996 estimate more accurately reflected homelessness at that date. They claimed that homelessness had thus increased over the nine years between the two studies.

This claim is, however, impossible to confirm. Whereas the 1987 study was an attempt to actually count homeless people, the 1996 study was not. Burt and her colleagues provided a plausible chain of reasoning, but they could not turn the NSHAPC data into a count of how many homeless there are in the United States. Too bad! The 1987 counting method remains the best example of what a good homeless count should look like.

TABLE 14.2 Weekly Homeless Estimates	
Date	Estimate
Burt: March 1987 (low)	500,000
Burt: March 1987 (high)	600,000
NSHAPC: Feb 1996 (service providers)	842,000
NSHAPC: Oct 1996 (client survey)	444,000

Counting San Bernardino

As good as Burt's weeklong count was, political events soon rendered it impractical. Congress's 2001 HUD Appropriations Act required every community to conduct a PIT count of street and sheltered homeless at least every other year. Local authorities could pick their own counting method, but they were limited to one- or two-night counts at a time of the year—usually late January—when cold weather was apt to keep homeless shelters full. The idea was to minimize the number of homeless who would stay out of doors. This made them easier to find and thus—ideally—made the counts more accurate.

Specifying that the count occur late in the month was strategic. Some homeless people get disability checks, Social Security checks, and other public assistance. This lets them rent hotel rooms until they run out of cash. A late-in-the-month count provides a better picture of the underlying homelessness problem. Had the counts been carried out earlier in the month, they would almost certainly have made the problem seem smaller than it is.

Unfortunately, neither Congress nor HUD paid for the counts. This discouraged communities from being thorough. Those that carried out counts, however, were eligible for HUD funding to serve their homeless populations. This encouraged participation. The counts began slowly, but by the late 2000s, HUD could provide a reasonable answer to our question about how many Americans are homeless—at least using HUD's restrictive definition of homelessness and the inherent problems that a PIT count brings.

HUD figures show that the number of street and shelter homeless declined about 12% from 2007 to 2014: from 650,000 to 578,000 (Figure 14.2, on the next page). Most of that decline stems from a lower number of street homeless, as the number of sheltered homeless stayed steady. This makes sense, as the overall economy recovered a bit in those years. Maybe the problem of street homelessness is finally getting solved.

Or maybe not. You see, there is a problem with the numbers. They show a decline in homelessness after 2012, but there's no spike in homelessness starting in 2008. There ought to be. That year saw a worldwide banking crisis, accompanied by a crash in the U.S. housing market. Big banks had bundled subpar mortgages into complex financial

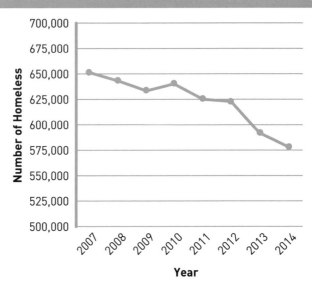

FIGURE 14.2   Count of Street and Shelter Homeless (HUD Definition)

instruments called derivatives, which they sold to unsuspecting investors. A lot of these loans soured, investors went broke, banks failed, credit dried up, and governments scrambled to keep the world financial system from collapse. It was bad. A million Americans lost their homes in 2008 and three million households were foreclosed in 2009. Federal Reserve chairman Ben Bernanke has been quoted as saying, "September and October of 2008 was the worst financial crisis in global history, including the Great Depression."[21] Shouldn't that crisis have shown up in the homelessness figures?

The short answer is yes. The mystery is why it did not. Part of the reason stems from the ways that homeless counts were carried out during and after the crisis. HUD does not specify exactly how counts are to be done; instead, it approves a variety of methods. HUD bases its nationwide figures on the data that various communities send it; its homeless estimates depend on their accuracy.[22] This isn't quite what computer geeks call "GIGO" (garbage-in, garbage-out), because some of the counts are very well done. But others are not. To my knowledge, no one has examined the process in enough depth to correct for the poor studies' undercounting. I'll later describe how this could be done.

Conflicting Results

First, though, I'll contrast two different counting techniques that came up with very different figures for homelessness in a single California county. Table 14.3 contains results from the San Bernardino County homeless counts in 2007, 2009, and 2011.[23]

The 2007 count used one counting technique; the 2009 and 2011 counts used a different one. The 2007 count was before the financial crisis. It was extensive and uncovered a relatively large number of homeless people, both in shelters and on the

TABLE 14.3 San Bernardino County, California, Homeless Counts			
	2007	**2009**	**2011**
Sheltered			
In Emergency Shelters	____	747	1,039
Individuals	281	a	a
Family Members	393	a	a
In Domestic Violence Shelters	____	*(included with emergency shelters)*	
Individuals	36	a	a
Family Members	97	a	a
In Transitional Housing	____	a	a
Individuals	292	a	a
Family Members	121	a	a
In Motels (Vouchers)	a	21	145
Total Sheltered	***1,220***	***768***	***1,184***
Unsheltered			
Individuals on street	2,927	616	439
Family members on street	167	a	a
Estimated uncounted people on street	____	352	1,253
People in cars	201[c]	b	42
People in RVs/Vans	712[c]	b	35
People in encampments	628[c]	b	101
Estimated uncounted in vehicles and encampments	1220[c]	b	438
People in parks	43	b	b
Total Unsheltered	***6,111***	***968***	***1,692/ 2,308[d]***
Total Homeless	***7,331***	***1,736***	***2,876/ 3,492[d]***

Notes: [a]Not reported separately. [b]Not collected. [c]Calculated from ratios in the 2007 report. [d]The first value leaves out those cars, vans, and camps; the second includes them.

streets. The 2009 and 2011 counts were much less extensive and found a lot fewer homeless—especially on the street. Each counting technique made certain assumptions, most of which were probably reasonable. Those assumptions go a long way to explaining the different numbers that each count produced.

The top half of the table records the three different counts of sheltered homeless—those living in shelters, transitional housing, and motels (using vouchers). The 2007 count found 1,220 people; the 2009 count found 768; and the 2011 count found 1,184. These differences are not terribly problematic. All three surveys used the same counting system: They called shelter operators and asked them how many people used their shelters on the count nights. The count for 2009 is lower than the others, but we don't know why. Was that the result of empty shelter beds? Or had one or two shelters closed that year, so fewer beds were available? The survey reports don't tell us. Still, the difference is not overwhelming; it's just not what we would expect, given the housing crisis that had hit San Bernardino County very hard in 2008.[24]

The differences on the bottom half of the table, however—the counts of *unsheltered* homeless—are huge. Here, the 2007 survey found vastly more than the others. The top three lines show the number of people each count found living on the street. The 2007 count found more than 3,000 individuals and family members—three times as many as in 2009 and twice as many as in 2011. This doesn't make much sense, given what happened to the housing market. Did both street and shelter homelessness actually *drop* with all those foreclosures? That's what the figures seem to show.

THINK ABOUT IT
What's wrong with this picture?

There's more. The 2007 count also found nearly 3,000 people living in cars, vans, and tent encampments. The 2009 survey did not include *anyone* with such living arrangements, even though the HUD definition includes such people as unsheltered homeless. The 2011 survey found about 600 people in cars, vans, and tents, but it did not include them in its summary figures. The authors of that study reported just 2,876 total homeless. They would have reported 3,492, had vehicle and encampment dwellers been included.

What's going on here? To understand, we have to see how each of the counts was done.

Two Different Methods Let's start with a key logistical problem: By land area, San Bernardino County is the largest county in California. In fact, it is the largest county in the United States. It starts at the eastern end of the Los Angeles Basin and extends north and east across the San Bernardino Mountains all the way to California's border with Arizona. The 2009 survey report notes that the county is so big

> that two states the size of Rhode Island, three the size of Delaware, and the states of Connecticut and Hawaii would all fit within the San Bernardino County boundaries with open space remaining.[25]

This is a huge area to survey, especially if we are seeking unsheltered homeless people. Fortunately, much of it is uninhabited mountains and desert, so the survey teams could concentrate on the area's 30 incorporated towns and cities, plus those few rural places where homeless folks were known to camp. All three of the counts focused on such known locations where homeless people congregate. The three surveys differed in how they located those "hot spots" and how they chose to cover them.

Let's look at the similarities. Each year's team assembled a few hundred volunteer canvassers, whom they split into groups of two or three. Each group was assigned an area to explore. Each group scoured that area, locating as many street homeless as they could find. They interviewed homeless people if possible, noting the first three letters of their names (to avoid having them counted twice) and their apparent age, gender, presence of family members, and so on. Sometimes they were not able to get these details, so they just noted their observations. Each team separately conducted longer interviews with a sample of homeless people, usually not on the same day as the street count. This produced information about how long people had been on the street, about veteran status, and about whether people were on the street alone, in couples, or in families. This information supplemented the actual counts, but the HUD guidelines did not require that the teams collect such information from everyone.

These aspects of homeless counts are relatively standard. There were, however, three major differences between the 2007 count, on the one hand, and the 2009 and 2011 counts, on the other hand. First, the 2007 count surveyed all of the homeless hot spots in the county's 244 census tracts. They did so over two days in late February 2007. They concentrated on early morning hours, when they presumed that street homeless would be sleeping or just beginning to stir. They counted both the individuals they saw and the tents, boxes, cars, and vans where some of the street homeless lived.

The 2009 and 2011 counts, by contrast, surveyed just a fraction of the county's homeless hot spots. Specifically, they visited hot spots in 199 of 1,094 **census block groups** in 2009 and in 174 of 1,027 in 2011. These are small numbers: 18% and 17%, respectively. However, this is not as bad as it sounds. The 2009 and 2011 teams included all of the block groups that San Bernardino County staff had identified as having large numbers of homeless. They also included a smaller number of the block groups where few homeless were said to live, and (in 2011) they included an intermediate-sized sample of the block groups with medium-sized hot spots in them.[26] This sampling relieved them of having to scour the whole county, while still letting them extrapolate from the number of homeless that were present in the block groups they visited to the number that were present in the county as a whole.

The 2009 and 2011 canvassers focused on the late evening, 9 p.m. to 1 a.m., when they expected unsheltered homeless people to have gathered but still be awake or easy to find. They used the number of homeless they found in the hot spots that they visited to estimate the number of homeless people in the hot spots that they skipped.

The second difference was how the hot spots were identified. The 2007 survey team hired homeless people to accompany the survey

THINK ABOUT IT
Why didn't the 2009 and 2011 teams survey the entire county?

groups and asked them to help those groups locate homeless hiding places. They paid them (by the hour) for their expertise. They argued that local homeless people have a far better idea of where other homeless folks sleep than do the social workers, police, and other outsiders on whom the 2009 and 2011 survey teams relied. The results appear to confirm this: The 2007 survey found nearly three times as many street homeless as did the 2009 survey and nearly twice the number found in 2011.[27] This could, however, have been caused by the latter two surveys' estimation technique. Or there could simply have been fewer street homeless in 2009 and 2011 than there were in 2007. (Yes, the housing crisis makes that dubious, but we have to admit that it's possible.)

The third difference was that the 2007 survey counted people sleeping in vehicles and encampments, and the 2009 survey did not. This is significant. The 2007 survey reported 2,761 people sleeping in vehicles and makeshift structures, whereas the 2009 survey reported none. It's not that the 2009 survey teams did not find homeless in vehicles and encampments; it's that they did not count them. Yet HUD guidelines specifically include cars, vans, tents, and boxes as places "not meant for human habitation." How did the designers of the 2009 study justify their exclusion? Two issues combined to create this situation.

First, all three survey teams respected homeless people's privacy by not knocking on car or van windows and not entering tents, boxes, and other shelters to count their inhabitants. (This was a safety matter as well.) The difference is that the 2007 team counted the number of such dwellings, whereas the 2009 team did not systematically record them.

Second, the 2007 team used their count of these dwellings to create an estimate of the number of unsheltered homeless living in them. Rather than assume that each such dwelling held only one person, they created a multiplier based on their subsequent interviews with selected San Bernardino homeless. In those interviews, they asked people if they had ever slept in cars, vans, and tents. If so, they asked, "How many people stayed in that car/van/tent with you?" This gave them a typical occupancy ratio. They then multiplied the number of cars, vans, and tents they had counted by the ratios they collected. The ratio for cars, for example, was 1.24: one of every four people who reported living in a car reported sharing it with another homeless person. Multiplying 201 occupied cars by 1.24 people per car gave them 249 people. (Table 14.3 includes those extra 48 people in the "Estimated uncounted in vehicles and encampments" figure.)

The 2009 team rejected this approach. They decided that they would report only people actually seen and would not treat cars, tents, and so on as occupied unless they had seen and counted the occupants. Far better, they thought, to undercount the street homeless than to count people that their canvassers could not guarantee were present. Moreover, they noted that "HUD explicitly prohibits using, 'unscientific "adjustment factors" to derive . . . counts of the unsheltered population.'"[28] They deemed the 2007 team's ratios to be unscientific, although—ironically—they used much the same technique to extrapolate from the block groups they surveyed to the block groups they skipped. At any rate, they left out any mention of homeless living in vehicles and encampments.

The 2011 survey team made an intermediate choice. They directed their canvassers to record vehicles and campsites, but they did not construct ratios and instead assumed that each car, van, tent, or box housed only one person. They also estimated the number of additional dwellings they would have found had they surveyed all of the county's block groups rather than just a sample—just as they did with people they observed.

Despite this, the 2011 team chose not to include the numbers in vehicles and encampments in their final total. They said that this was to make it easy to compare their numbers with the 2009 survey. They thus reported a 75% increase in the county's homeless population, compared with 2009. The report did not speculate on the causes of this increase. It did, however, say that the actual number of homeless people was likely higher than the numbers that were reported in either year. In their words, their method

> produced a conservative count. It does not, nor was it intended to, convey the total number of persons experiencing homelessness in San Bernardino County throughout the year in 2011. The method employed in this study is likely to have resulted in an undercount. Homeless persons not physically observed were not counted.[29]

The 2009 report contained almost identical language.

Which Method to Choose? Clearly, these two methods of counting homeless people produced very different results. Two elements stand out.

The first is the process that the 2007 team used to identify homeless hot spots: They hired homeless people to guide the canvassers. The 2009 and 2011 teams instead relied on county employees, social workers, and police to identify places that homeless people congregate. The first method turned up many more homeless people than did the second. Unless there were, in fact, far fewer street homeless in 2009—which is doubtful, given the housing crisis—hiring knowledgeable homeless guides seems to be a better idea. So is surveying all of the spots these guides identify rather than just visiting a sample. The 2009 and 2011 sampling technique was, however, probably not a major source of undercounting.[30] Not knowing exactly where to find homeless people probably was.

The second element is the 2007 team's decision to count homeless people living in cars, vans, tents, and other encampments and the 2009 and 2011 teams' decision to leave these homeless out of consideration. There are good reasons for each approach, especially as neither team actually entered those street-side dwellings to count the people in them. The choice was between two risks. The 2007 team risked overcounting, because the cars and tents might have been empty, not inhabited (though their homeless guides said otherwise). The 2009 and 2011 teams, however, definitely undercounted: Some of those cars and tents were certainly full. There is no doubt that the 2009 and 2011 teams left out homeless people who should have been tallied.

Which way should we go? Rossi solved this problem by having off-duty policemen accompany his canvassers and entering the homeless people's hiding places. The police kept people safe, and Rossi paid his informants for invading their privacy. Burt solved the problem by approaching homeless people during the day and asking about where they stayed the previous seven nights. Doing this over the course of a week ensured that she would catch as many people as possible while both respecting their nighttime privacy and keeping everyone safe.

Neither of these solutions was available to the San Bernardino teams. They had little money, which made Rossi's approach impossible. They were prohibited from using the weeklong method by HUD rules. So they had to decide whether to risk overcounting the homeless people in vehicles and tents or risk undercounting them. The different teams made different choices. You can see the result of those choices by their reports' final numbers.

Personally, I would have preferred to see the 2009 and 2011 teams follow the 2007 method. In my view, this would have given a much more accurate estimate of the homeless population than the later surveys provided. The 2008 foreclosure crisis should have produced an uptick in San Bernardino homelessness. Instead, we got just the opposite. This tells me that the 2009 count missed a significant part of the homeless population, something that its organizers admit. Our review of its method shows a couple of ways that this undercounting might have happened.

We can't, of course, know exactly how many people are homeless in San Bernardino County. We can safely conclude, though, that San Bernardino County's homeless population did not fall as steeply as a naive comparison between the 2007 and 2009 final figures shows.

That's the point, of course. Few people are going to read the details. Newspaper accounts crowed about the drop in local homelessness between 2007 and 2009 without bothering to notice that the two teams counted different things. This affected public policy, as such things typically do. In this sense, it was good for the 2011 count to continue the 2009 method: Either its report of an increased number of homeless reflected an actual change in the homeless population, or it had found a higher percentage of homeless people than had been found two years before. Put negatively, it, too, undercounted homeless people. Yet it did so in the same way as before, making a trend easier to see.

THINK ABOUT IT
Why does it matter if the numbers are too low or too high?

Still, the 2011 team could easily have replicated the 2007 team's method. That would have provided a different—and more accurate—comparison. Had I been asked, that is the choice I would have made.

What has happened since? Per HUD requirements, the San Bernardino County Homeless Partnership conducted surveys in 2013 and 2015.[31] Designed by a third set of consultants, these PIT counts took place between 6 a.m. and 10 a.m. on a single January morning.

TABLE 14.4   San Bernardino County Homeless Count Results, by Method

	Method 1	Method 2		Method 3	
	2007	2009	2011	2013	2015
Sheltered					
Emergency/voucher	807	768	1,184	518	468
Transitional housing	413	a	a	556	370
Unsheltered					
Street	3,094	968	1,691	1,247	1,302
Vehicles, camps	3,017	b	616c	b	b
Reported Total	**7,331**	**1,736**	**2,876**	**2,321**	**2,140**

Notes: aIncluded with emergency/voucher. bNot reported. cNot included in reported total.

Like the 2009 and 2011 counts, they targeted previously identified homeless hot spots. Though the reports are imprecise about just how the counts were organized, it appears that the teams visited all of the county's hot spots rather than just a sample of them. It also appears that they did not count people in vehicles, tents, or other encampments, unless they could speak to them directly. This makes the 2013 and 2015 counts comparable to those of 2009 and 2011, though perhaps a bit more accurate.[32] Table 14.4 summarizes the counts reported in each of these years.

Leaving aside 2007, you can see a clear trend. By undercounting homeless people in much the same ways, San Bernardino County has made little progress in giving shelter to its unsheltered population.

Correcting National Figures

My point is not to pick on San Bernardino County, nor to impugn the integrity of any of the counting teams. My point is that how we count homeless people determines how many we will find. Errors at the local level get multiplied at the national level, because HUD's *Annual Homeless Assessment Reports* basically add up the various reports that local counting teams send in. Changes in national figures may thus merely represent changes in counting methods, not changes in the number of homeless in any given year.

Remember where our problem started. Figure 14.2 showed a drop in national homelessness after 2012, but it didn't show a spike in homelessness after 2008. The drop makes some sense: The U.S. economy has improved and many cities have tried to find ways to get homeless people off the streets. The lack of a spike, however, does not make sense. It probably indicates a counting error. If there was an error then, why not in other years, too? We can't rely on the overall HUD figures to tell us what is happening.

Short of redoing the counts, is there any way to get a more accurate picture? I think there is, though to my knowledge no one has yet attempted it. The key is right here in the San Bernardino counts, if we would only see it.

The idea is simple. Each local agency sends HUD a count of its homeless population. It also sends in a report of the counting method used. The 2007 San Bernardino count used a method that maximized the homeless population. The 2009 and 2011 counts used a method that left out a major portion of it. We could examine all the reports that HUD receives, sorting them by the methods used. If the pattern of methods is stable from year to year, then we can put more faith in the stability of the overall numbers. If the pattern is unstable, then the overall numbers are probably shifting because the methods shift, not because the number of homeless is changing.

Here are some simplified numbers, so you can see what I mean.

Let's imagine that we've got 100 different homeless counts from around the country. Let's also imagine that we've got two counting methods, one of which finds on average half as many homeless as does the other. Where Method 1 finds 500 homeless, Method 2 would find 1,000; where Method 1 finds 1,000 homeless, Method 2 would find 2,000; and so on. We can't say for sure which method is wrong. Method 1 might be undercounting or Method 2 overcounting, or both. We simply know the ratio of one method to the other. Making this algebraic: If Method 1 finds x homeless people, then Method 2 will find $2x$. Clear?

Now, in Year 1, let's say that half of the counting teams use Method 1 and half use Method 2. Assuming approximately equal numbers of actual homeless people in each counting area, HUD will report *150x homeless people* nationwide:

50 teams using Method 1 find $50x$ homeless
50 teams using Method 2 find $100x$ homeless

Let's imagine that in Year 2, each team that used Method 1 now uses Method 2 and vice versa. We'll still get *150x homeless people*:

50 teams using Method 2 find $100x$ homeless
50 teams using Method 1 find $50x$ homeless

Stability! It doesn't matter which method each team uses; what matters is that the percentage using each method stays the same.

What happens, though, if in Year 3 only 25% of the teams use Method 2?

75 teams using Method 1 find $75x$ homeless
25 teams using Method 2 find $50x$ homeless

That adds up to *125x homeless people*! Change the percentage using each method and the total changes. What if, in Year 4, we reverse the numbers?

25 teams using Method 1 find 25*x* homeless

75 teams using Method 2 find 150*x* homeless

Now we've got *175x homeless people*—and again only the percentages using each method have changed.

Remember, we don't know if Method 1 is undercounting homeless people, if Method 2 is overcounting them, or both. So we can't say, exactly, how many homeless people there are. The point is, we want year-to-year stability. We want to be able to tell if homelessness is rising or falling overall.

The solution is simple: Introduce a weighting factor to compensate for the differences in counting methods. In our example, we'd likely leave the first two years' figures alone; they're already stable. In Year 3, we'd reduce the numbers produced by teams using Method 1 by one third and double those used by Method 2. This would return us to the 50:50 ratio we had before. We'd reverse this in Year 4, doubling the numbers produced by Method 1 and reducing by one third those produced by Method 2.

Table 14.5 shows us what this would look like with numbers and not just algebra. I've substituted numbers for *x* and let *x* vary from year to year. The raw total just adds up the reported amounts. The adjusted total shows what we would get by restoring the 50:50 ratio between our two methods.

You get the idea. This technique wouldn't tell us exactly how many homeless people we have nationwide in any given year. It would, however, correct for the errors introduced by different counting methods. It would give the national numbers year-to-year stability. That's what both policy makers and America's homeless deserve.

I hope that someone decides to do such a study. It would be tedious, but it's not conceptually difficult. An investigator would have to review all of the various homeless counts and sort them by the counting methods used. Then she or he would examine how the percentages using each method have shifted from year to year. Though my example imagines that counts using Method 2 find twice the number of homeless as those used by Method 1, those are just made-up numbers to show how different methods' ratios produce different results. We don't have to decide which methods risk undercounting and which methods risk overcounting. All we have to do is restore each year's ratio of methods to a baseline. Then we can compare year-to-year progress.

TABLE 14.5 Comparison of Count Methods With Hypothetical Data

| | Method 1 | | Method 2 | | | |
	%	Count	%	Count	Raw Total	Adjusted Total
Year 1	50	250,000	50	500,000	750,000	750,000
Year 2	50	230,000	50	460,000	690,000	690,000
Year 3	75	450,000	25	300,000	750,000	900,000
Year 4	25	112,500	75	675,000	787,500	675,000

If you want to take on this project, you can find the biennial count reports posted on most counties' websites. You can also get count data through HUD's Homeless Data Exchange.[33]

Research Ethics

As you might imagine, counting homeless people raises a whole host of ethical issues. Generally speaking, homeless people are more vulnerable than are people with secure housing. Living out of doors, often dependent on charity, they lack some routine protections. The challenges homeless people face can be as simple as not having a place to urinate and as complex as having to walk all day and night to avoid being beaten up by gangs or arrested for vagrancy. The United States has a long history of harrassing homeless people, both by private citizens and by police. Even those cities with no formal laws against homelessness typically provide little succor.

Legally speaking, however, adult, mentally stable homeless people are not a protected population for research purposes. U.S. law gives special status to children, prisoners, sick people, pregnant women, and some others who could easily be coerced to participate in a research project. It does not give such status to the homeless. The question is, how should an ethical researcher design a homeless count, so as to protect the people whom she or he is surveying?

Remember the three principles outlined in Chapter 4—the three core values identified by the 1978 Belmont Report on the treatment of human research subjects: *respect for persons, beneficence,* and *justice.* These principles ask us to design our homeless surveys so that they respect homeless people as persons and maximize the benefits to those people that knowledge about the extent and nature of homelessness might provide, while subjecting them to as little risk as possible.

The benefits are largely out of the counters' hands, simply because Congress has mandated a biennial survey. This prevents Institutional Review Boards from deciding that such a census does more harm than good. The task for the research team, then, is to maximize the respectful treatment of homeless people while minimizing the harm that collecting information about them might cause.

There are various ways to do this. I've mentioned some of these in my descriptions of the Rossi, Burt, and San Bernardino counts. Rossi and Burt asked permission to interview homeless people and offered them a reward for participating. They did not interview those who turned them down. The San Bernardino teams did not give money, but they respected the privacy of those who declined to answer questions and furthermore did not approach those sleeping in cars, vans, tents, or boxes. The teams also noted people's identities by codes. This was partly to avoid double counting, but it also made sure that no one could identify individual homeless people through the survey forms. A code such as "JNC25" or "MPF37" protects people's privacy—especially if those who tabulate the forms are not the same people who fill them out.

Belmont Concepts

- Respect
- Beneficence
- Justice

My own students took similar measures to protect homeless people during a survey they carried out at the request of our local police department in 2010. At the time, that department had a rather enlightened notion of how to treat homeless people. They are, the then-chief said, citizens just like everyone else. They deserve protection—just like anyone else. Given their circumstances, that calls for extra police effort, and the chief wanted to get more information about local homeless people than the 2009 count's sampling system provided. He came to my class, because he recognized that his officers could not ethically carry out research interviews. Doing so could put pressure on homeless people to respond. This would amount to precisely the kind of compulsion that the Belmont Report disallowed. My students agreed to do the survey for him, and, with the help of my university's IRB, worked out ways to protect the more than 50 homeless adults who agreed to be interviewed.

IRBs are good at this sort of thing. They are not, however, designed to ask questions about the impact that certain design choices have on research results. Nor is it their job to gauge the ethical implications of those results on the public perception of homelessness as a social issue.

Let's take the three San Bernardino homeless counts as an example. As I noted earlier, the 2009 and 2011 counting teams made a deliberate choice not to include homeless people living in cars, vans, tents, and other encampments. The 2009 team didn't count them at all. The 2011 team counted the numbers of vehicles, tents, and so on, but did not report those numbers in their totals. They wanted to avoid overcounting homeless people, and they did so.

The 2007 team, by contrast, specifically sought out such homeless dwellings. True, they didn't directly count the people in them; that was part of respecting those homeless people's privacy. They did, however, develop a rather sophisticated method of estimating how many homeless lived in such habitations. As a result, the 2007 team reported 6,111 unsheltered homeless in the county on the nights of the count.

The 2009 team reported 968 and the 2011 team reported 1,692. Those numbers were reported in the press as a major drop in San Bernardino's homelessness problem. Few people examined the reports carefully enough to see what was actually going on.

I think it is fair to ask about the ethical consequences of the 2009 and 2011 numbers for public perceptions of homelessness across those years:

- Did these numbers produce *respect* for homeless people—for example, by showing that the homeless problem is large enough that it cannot be just a matter of "personal choice"? Or might the deliberate undercounting have encouraged politicians and the public to blame homeless people for their own situation?
- Did homeless people *benefit* from being deliberately undercounted, in a political climate that predictably directs public money away from "minor" social problems and toward "major" ones?

● If the choice is between deliberately undercounting homeless people and possibly overcounting them (as the authors of the 2009 and 2011 reports wrote in defense of their research design), which choice produces the most *justice*? Is it the one that minimizes the problem, potentially drawing resources away from combatting homelessness and/or focusing resources on "fixing" homeless people rather than creating housing that they can afford? Or is it the one that demonstrates that the problem is much larger than people had realized?

We know that the 2009 and 2011 teams undercounted San Bernardino County's homeless. We don't know whether the 2007 team overcounted them. In this situation, which design choice *respects*, *benefits*, and provides *justice* for the homeless subjects of this research?

THINK ABOUT IT
What would you choose?

My students also asked that question, though they were attempting to interview our town's homeless people, not count them. They interviewed these people with respect, and the project did, in fact, also prove to be beneficial to them. Among other things, the survey showed that a large majority of local homeless people had long-standing ties to the community. They did not come from elsewhere to prey on the goodwill of the town's residents, as a few local politicians had suggested. Some of these homeless had grown up in town. Others had relatives there. Many had been living in town before they lost their homes.

The police chief had expected as much. The survey gave him data to show that the local homeless were part of the community just as much as were those who were housed. This let him push back against the politicians who wanted to drive homeless people to neighboring cities. Until his retirement a couple of years later, he did so rather effectively.

Reflections

What can we take away from this chapter? Quite a lot, actually. We began by identifying homelessness as an important social problem and wondering about the extent of that problem in American life. We learned how the current spate of homelessness arose, and about how homelessness has been variously defined. We learned about the effects that these definitions have had on concrete attempts to count homeless people. We also learned a great deal about some of the ways that scholars have counted homeless people in the past. Finally, we learned a bit about the consequences of these researchers' design choices.

Real research projects call for such detailed treatment. Major research projects are complex, and they always raise many difficult issues that have to be resolved. Life is full of hard choices; research is no different. The projects I have described here show you how the decisions that investigators make have consequences for the results they produce.

I hope that this chapter has given you a sense of what empirical research on a major social problem looks like in real life. That was its point. Despite the complexities, however, it is relatively easy to identify in these various projects the six basic steps that make successful research possible.

Summary of the Six Steps

- Our **research question**: How many homeless people are there in the United States?
- The project's **logical structure** is *descriptive*: We seek to describe the number of homeless people in various parts of the country and also to describe some of their demographic characteristics.
- Our **type of data** is bodies: the number of homeless people that we can count during our census.
- Our **data collection method** is the actual counting of homeless people,

using one or another method of locating and counting them. (Some techniques are better than others.)
- Our **data collection site** is the geographic unit that we want to survey (e.g., town, city, county).
- Our **data analysis method** is typically simple addition, though we may choose to extrapolate from a portion of our data collection site to the whole site, if we do not have enough surveyors to carry out the census in full.

The open-access Student Study Site at **study.sagepub.com/spickard** has a variety of useful study tools, including SAGE journal articles, video & web resources, eFlashcards, and quizzes.

Notes

1. For a good history, see Kenneth Kusmer, *Down and Out, on the Road: The Homeless in American History*. Oxford, 2002.

2. A slang term for Seattle's Yesler Way, where logs used to be skidded down the hills to loading docks on Elliott Bay. It is

still a place of cheap hotels, soup kitchens, "rescue" missions, and other signs of homeless life.

3. Christopher Jencks's *The Homeless* (Harvard, 1995) is still the best account of these origins. He provides a detailed

(Continued)

(Continued)

analysis of how many homeless there were in the 1980s and what probably caused their numbers to increase.

4. Ibid.

5. National Alliance to End Homelessness, "The State of Homelessness in America 2015," April 1, 2015.

6. California Homeless Youth Project, "FAQ: Homeless Students in California," 2014. Retrieved from http://www.kidsdata.org/advisories/FAQ_Homeless_Students_in_California.pdf

7. Child Trends Data Bank, "Homeless Children and Youth," March 2015. Retrieved from http://www.childtrends.org/wp-content/uploads/2015/01/112_appendix1.pdf

8. One person homeless for one day equals one person-day of homelessness. Ten person-days could be either 10 people homeless for one day or one person homeless for 10 days. Such calculations let us compare different kinds of homelessness with each other.

9. Peter Rossi, *Down and Out in America: The Origins of Homelessness*. University of Chicago Press, 1989.

10. Jencks, *The Homeless*, p. 18.

11. Table 14.1 is from Jencks, *The Homeless*, p. 19. Bogue reported his count in his book *Skid Row in American Cities* (University of Chicago Press, 1963).

12. James Spradley reported that Seattle's homeless referred to going to "rescue mission" shelters as "taking a nose dive."

They disliked the forced prayers before meals and bed. Spradley, *You Owe Yourself a Drunk: An Ethnography of Urban Nomads.* Little, Brown, 1970.

13. Jencks, *The Homeless*, p. 10.

14. Ibid.

15. This figure comes from Jencks's reanalysis of Burt's findings. See *The Homeless*, p. 12. His detailed reanalysis begins on p. 125.

16. Jencks estimated a ratio of between 1.86:1 and 2.13:1. See *The Homeless*, p. 132.

17. The range in their estimate comes from the margin of error in that extrapolation.

18. Jennifer Toth, *The Mole People*. Chicago Review Press, 1993.

19. The study report is posted online at http://www.huduser.org/portal/publications/homeless/homeless_tech.html.

20. Burt and her colleagues provided their own report in Burt et al., *Helping America's Homeless: Emergency Shelter or Affordable Housing*? Urban Institute Press, 2001.

21. Tim Worstall, "Ben Bernanke: The 2008 Financial Crisis Was Worse Than the Great Depression," *Forbes,* August 27, 2014. Retrieved from http://www.forbes.com/sites/timworstall/2014/08/27/ben-bernanke-the-2008-financial-crisis-was-worse-than-the-great-depression/#4e477677c074

22. Specifically, it uses a sampling system to extrapolate from the counties that send in data to the nation as a whole.

HUD's *Annual Homeless Assessment Reports* contain details for each year.

23. *No Place to Call Home: 2007 San Bernardino County Homeless Census and Survey*, Community Action Partnership of San Bernardino County and Applied Survey Research (Watsonville, CA); *San Bernardino County 2009 Point-in-Time Homeless Count & Survey*, San Bernardino County Office of Homeless Services and CLA & Associates (Santa Ana, CA); *San Bernardino County 2011 Point-in-Time Homeless Count & Survey*, San Bernardino County Homeless Partnership and CLA & Associates (Santa Ana, CA).

24. The San Bernardino/Riverside area (locally called the Inland Empire) had the third highest foreclosure rate in the country in 2008: 8%. Les Christie, "Foreclosures Up a Record 81% in 2008," CNN Money, January 15, 2009. Retrieved from http://money.cnn.com/2009/01/15/real_estate/millions_in_foreclosure/

25. *San Bernardino County 2009 Point-in-Time Homeless Count & Survey*, p. 47.

26. Their goal was to be 90% certain that their count of the medium-sized hot spots was within 10% of the actual number of homeless present, and to be 80% certain that their count of the smallest hot spots was within 10% of the actual number present. For details of the block groups chosen, see *San Bernardino County 2009 Point-in-Time Homeless Count & Survey*, pp. 47–50, and *San Bernardino County 2011 Point-in-Time Homeless Count & Survey*, pp. 5–7. See also the discussions of sampling in Chapters 6 and 8 of this volume.

27. These ratios do not include those found living in cars, vans, and encampments (e.g., tents, boxes).

28. *San Bernardino County 2009 Point-in-Time Homeless Count & Survey*, p. 52

29. *San Bernardino County 2011 Point-in-Time Homeless Count & Survey*, p. 1.

30. Remember that the 2009 and 2011 teams visited *all* of the sites where they expected to find large numbers of homeless people. They sampled only places where they did not expect to find many. This let them concentrate their effort while lowering their chance of missing people.

31. The reports are on the San Bernardino County website (www.sbcounty.gov): *San Bernardino County 2013 Homeless Count and Subpopulation Survey*, San Bernardino County Homeless Partnership and Institute for Urban Initiatives (Pasadena, CA); and *San Bernardino County 2015 Homeless Count and Subpopulation Survey*, San Bernardino County Homeless Partnership and Institute for Urban Initiatives (Pasadena, CA).

32. The 2013 and 2015 reports lack the detailed methodological descriptions that the previous three reports contained.

33. Not all counties make their reports easy to find. At this writing, San Bernardino County's 2009 count is among the missing. The data exchange is at http://www.hudhdx.info/. Anyone can sign up for an account.

Research Guides and Handouts

Six-Steps Graphic: From Research Question to Data Analysis

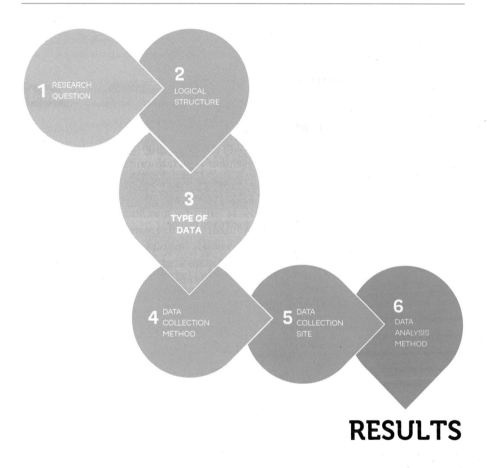

What Is a Concept Paper?

by J. Spickard

All research projects need a concept paper: a short summary that tells the reader what the project is, why it is important, and how it will be carried out. Even if no one else ever reads it, the concept paper helps you to spot any holes in your project that might later prove fatal. It is far better to be clear at the beginning than to put in a lot of effort for naught!

Typically, a concept paper contains these elements:

1. A clear description of the research topic, including a summary of what is already known about that topic.
2. A one-sentence statement of the research question that the project will seek to answer. (This is almost always something that is not known.) The concept paper should connect this question to the existing literature, something that almost always takes more than one sentence to accomplish.
3. A demonstration of why it is important to answer this research question: What good comes of this answer? Why is this project worth anybody's time?
4. A description of how you plan to answer the research question. This includes

    a. An outline of how the proposed project will be logically structured to answer the research question
    b. A description of the data that you plan to collect or use
    c. A description of how you will gather these data
    d. A description of where you will gather these data
    e. A description of how you will analyze these data

5. A statement of the limitations of this research, specifically the things that it cannot discover (and why).
6. A summary of any ethical issues that you expect to arise in the research process.
7. Longer projects (term papers, master's theses, dissertations, and professional research) also typically include a selected bibliography.

Concept papers typically range from two to five double-spaced pages (500 to 1,250 words), not counting bibliographies. Longer projects spend more time reviewing

(Continued)

(Continued)

what is already known about a topic, typically drawing on several different scholarly literatures to do so. Shorter projects do not need such depth.

Some projects, notably theses, dissertations, and professional research, later develop the concept paper into a formal research proposal, which covers the above points in greater depth. Different advisers and granting agencies call for different amounts of detail. It is a rare proposal, however, that takes up more than 20 double-spaced pages (5,000 words). A concept paper is a good first step in developing a proposal.

In any case, the point of a concept paper is to provide a clear summary of the research project. It should enable a casual reader to understand what you are investigating, why it is important, and how the investigation will proceed.

How to Choose a Data Collection Method

by J. Spickard

First, find the type of data you are looking for at the top. Then read down the column underneath the data type. Where you encounter an X, look to the left and note the suggested method. An X in parentheses means that the method can collect this kind of data, though it usually does so as a by-product of collecting one of the other types.

Data Collection Methods			Types of Data													
			1 Acts, behavior, or events	2 Reports of acts, behavior, or events	3 Economic data	4 Organizational data	5 Demographic data	6 Self-identity	7 Opinions and attitudes (shallow)	8 Opinions and attitudes (deeply held)	9 Personal feelings	10 Cultural knowledge (things everyone knows)	11 Expert knowledge	12 Personal and psychological traits	13 Experience as it presents itself to consciousness	14 Hidden social patterns
	A	Public and private records		X	X	X	X						(X)			
	B	Detached observation	X													X
	C	Ethnography (participant observation)	X	(X)		(X)			(X)	(X)		X	(X)			X
	D	In-depth interviews		X		(X)		X	(X)	X	X	X	X	(X)		(X)
	E	Surveys/questionnaires		X	(X)	(X)	X	X	X			X	(X)			
	F	Phenomenological interviews								(X)					X	
	G	Critical incident interviews		X					(X)	(X)		(X)	X			
	H	Focus groups							(X)			X	X			
	I	Psychological scales and their kin												X		
	J	Content analysis										X		(X)		X
	K	Discourse (or narrative) analysis										X				X
	L	Grounded theory														X

Reprinted from *Research Basics*, by James V. Spickard. Used by permission. This content is also licensed under Creative Commons-Noncommercial-ShareAlike (CC-BY-NC-SA) 4.0 United States License, http://creativecommons.org/licenses/by-nc-sa/4.0/. This guide may be distributed for non-commercial purposes.

A Template for Taking Field Notes

by J. Spickard

Many research projects call for field notes. We have to keep track of our observations, but we also need to keep track of what we're thinking about our observations. We need to keep these separate, lest we later mistake our thinking for what we've observed. I've found a four-column system to be very helpful. The two columns on the left are for two different kinds of observations; the two on the right are for two different kinds of thoughts about what we've seen. Putting them in separate columns keeps everything clear.

External Details	What I Observed	My Thoughts About What I Observed	Connections (Tame or Wild)
(This column reminds you where the event was, who was there, etc.)	(This column contains a detailed list of what you actually observed.)	(This column allows you to record your thoughts about what you observed, ideally matched to the relevant spot in the second column.)	(This column lets you record wilder ideas, including connections with other situations, readings, thinkers, etc.)
Mass at XYZ house, Denver. 9/27/04. Present: the core community, plus John Q., Fred R., Stacey P., plus five others I don't know and wasn't introduced to.	Mass began late. Roger R. was celebrant, introduced by Rick C. (as usual). Rick spoke at some length about the latest police raids in the local parish. Mike S. (in the audience) added news about the president's latest war speech. Roger acknowledged both of these, saying that it was in just such times as these that Jesus asked his disciples to come together, as we do now, in prayer for the state of the world. First reading from Isaiah, on the duty toward the poor. Second was parable of the sower. Roger spoke for 2.5 minutes on these, connecting them to the recent actions of the mayor's office cutting funding for anti-poverty work. In group homily, Mike spoke of the need to remain faithful, despite acts of our national "leaders." Kim spoke of the frustration at seeing so many people in need.	Note how negative tone is set, allowing (later) transition to positive tone in mass itself. Need to see this as part of the ritual, not separate from it. Celebrant draws explicit connection (which did *not* happen last time). These are not today's standard readings. I wonder who chose them—and why? Mike usually talks here, and often on the same subject. Do people have informal roles? Or do they just know each other well enough to rely on certain people for certain insights?	Those police raids are in M.D. parish; I wonder what Father Tony is telling his parishioners tonight? What passages is he using? How are they responding? The Sojourners Community has a very different approach, according to Jim W.'s description of their practices. So do most of the Quaker groups I've visited. Why? Do their rituals serve a different function in community life?

How to Write an Interview Protocol

by J. Spickard

My first research job was at a major East Coast university, where I was an assistant on a project evaluating two drug-treatment programs. I was not in charge of the research, but I learned a lot about what one *shouldn't* do. The project produced no usable results, largely because the project director didn't know how to construct an interview protocol. He didn't know what to ask, and he didn't know that he didn't know this. So he fished for answers, hoping that he'd catch something useful. He didn't. Good fisherfolk know that you need some idea of where to fish before you cast your line.

The sad thing is, it is pretty easy to put together an interview protocol—the set of questions that you plan to ask your informants. The process has two steps. Tom Wengraf covers the first of these in Chapters 3 and 4 of his *Qualitative Research Interviewing* (Sage, 2001). The second step turns Wengraf's questions into an interview experience that flows.

I'll describe these steps in brief and then note a third step that helps you turn your interview results into usable data.

Step 1: Identify a Central Research Question (CRQ), Theory-Based Questions (TQs), and Interview Questions (IQs)

Wengraf starts by noting that every piece of research has a central research question (CRQ). This is often a general question, such as "How do social activists use religious or spiritual resources to sustain their activist commitments?" In some cases, it can be rather practical: "How can the XYZ Charitable Agency weather its current organizational crisis?" In either case, the CRQ identifies what you want to know.

Any researcher, of course, has read a tremendous amount of literature on her or his research topic. Wengraf notes that this literature typically identifies possible answers to the CRQ—and often identifies several of them. The sociology of religion, for example, notes that people make use of (at least) two kinds of religious resources: "official" sources, endorsed by church authorities, and "nonofficial" ones, of which those authorities do not approve. Organizational development literature notes that all organizations—including nonprofits—go through several predictable transitions in the course of their lives. If we knew whether our social activists look to official or to nonofficial religious resources, we would be a step closer to knowing how they sustain their activist commitments. And if we knew whether the agency was in the midst of a predictable life-cycle transition, we would better know what actions to recommend.

(Continued)

Wengraf calls such questions theory-based questions (TQs). After identifying your CRQ, you need to identify several TQs that, taken together, allow you to answer the CRQ. Schematically, we have the following:

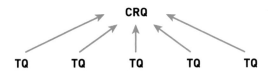

These TQs, however, are still too general. You need to "operationalize" them—break them down into smaller parts that real people can understand and answer. It would not be a good idea, for example, for us to ask our social activists, "Do you personally depend on official or on unofficial religious resources?" Few informants speak such academic jargon, and only some of those who don't will have the gumption to say, "Huh? What's that supposed to mean?" Most will say something that sounds like an answer, but they won't really tell us much. People need to understand clearly what they are being asked, if they are to provide details.

The researcher thus needs to create a series of interview questions (IQs) from each theory-based question (TQ). Informants' answers to these IQs should, collectively, answer the TQ. The answers to the TQs, taken collectively, should answer the CRQ. Schematically, it looks like this:

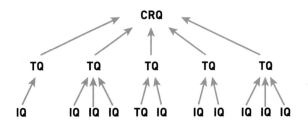

We might, for example, ask our social activists about the kinds of religious services they attend, about their own private religious practices, what they do under stress, and so on. We might ask them about their feelings about their church leaders. We should definitely ask them if they ever achieve a feeling of transcendence and (if so) when and how. All these questions, taken together, let us answer our TQ about the official or nonofficial sources of religious support. The answer to this TQ, together with the answers to our other TQs, should let us answer our Central Research Question.

Step 2: Turn the Interview Questions (IQs) Into a Usable Interview Protocol

Wengraf stops here. Though he might not agree with me, I think that this is still one step short of the goal. Interviews not only need to be logical and clear; they also need to engage our informants. Asking a long string of rather specific

(Continued)

questions seldom does so. Nor does it typically encourage informants to give us more than we asked for—the rich detail that enlivens their accounts and deepens our understanding of them.

Fortunately, this is relatively simple to correct. We take the list of IQs generated earlier and rearrange them so that they both engage informants and flow clearly. We might, for example, ask our social activists to tell us about a time when they were especially discouraged, and how they pulled themselves out of it. Depending on how the story unfolds, we might then probe about the usefulness of this or that religious resource. We would certainly want to know if such stories were typical of our informants' experiences—and we can ask this directly. The point is, you can call on your informants' imaginative creativity, as well as on their logic, to get a fuller picture of their experiences.

You just have to make sure that your protocol includes questions, stories, or reflections that elicit answers to all of your IQs. You don't need one-to-one correspondence, but you do need to make sure that you have everything covered.

One way to do this is to construct a table like the one shown below. Put your TQs and IQs across the top, and your interview protocol down the left side. Go through the rows, putting check marks beneath the IQs that each interview question answers. Make sure that every column has at least one check mark in it; if it does not, you need to revise your protocol so that the IQ in question gets answered.

	TQ1		TQ2			TQ3		
	IQ1	IQ2	IQ3	IQ4	IQ5	IQ6	IQ7	. . .
1. Do you consider yourself religious?							X	
2. What does "being religious" mean to you?						X		
3. With which religious group do you identify?	X		X					
4. What do you get out of belonging to that group?		X			X			
5. Tell me about a time when . . .			X	X			X	
6. Was this typical? How or how not?				X				
7. Can you tell me about a less typical instance?				X				
. . .								

(Continued)

Step 3: Interpret the Results

As you can imagine, using this method would have greatly improved the East Coast university project that I assisted many years ago. The method keeps things clear. It reminds you why you are asking each question. And it makes sure that you ask the right questions to get the responses you need.

It has the further advantage of helping you interpret your data. Remember that answering the interview questions (IQs) lets you answer the theory-based questions (TQs), which (collectively) answer your central research question (CRQ). *To answer any IQ, just read down the proper column, pulling together all of the answers in the rows that you have checked.* In the table provided here, for example, you would answer IQ3 by putting all of your informants' answers to questions 3 and 5 in a pile and then reading through them. *Voilá!* You'll know what your informants have to say about the matter. Do that for each column, combining the IQ answers to answer the applicable TQs, and you are well on the way to having answered the question with which your project started.

By the way: It makes no difference whether you sort your interview transcripts into piles on the living room floor, as we did in the old days, or with the help of qualitative data analysis software like NVivo or MaxQDA. The sorting logic is the same.

How Many Subjects?

by J. Spickard

A Flowchart for Interview Research

Students often wonder how many interviews they need for their projects. The answer, of course, depends on what they want to accomplish, but that doesn't seem to have penetrated to every corner of academic culture. Instead, people find magic numbers. In one place I worked, the magic number was 12. There, students initially proposed doing 12 "in-depth" interviews—no matter how many their project actually needed. I suspected that they (or their professors) had found this number in some "sacred" textbook—truly a bad research plan.

I developed an *Interview Rule-of-Thumb Flowchart* to help decide how many interviews you really need. Though the flowchart is pretty clear, it needs to be set in context. The key question is, "What are you trying to find out?" Here are three possibilities:

1. At one extreme, you may want to learn the relative distribution of traits, experiences, and the like among a population. For example, "What percentage of the population has experienced burnout? For what percentage of those was burnout caused by factors X, Y, and Z?" These questions call for a quantitative study of a true random sample of the target population. Depending on how large that population is and how detailed an analysis you seek, you aim for anywhere between 150 and 1,500 subjects, most likely using a questionnaire or structured interview. (Collecting data from 1,500 respondents will model the entire U.S. population within a few percentage points.) Response rate matters a lot. A low number of responses prevents you from generalizing to the population at large.

2. At the other extreme, you may want to describe a universal or near-universal process, often an experiential one. For example, say you are trying to learn how people enter a particular kind of trance state—perhaps one used in a particular type of nonmedical healing. You can interview a very small number of people, but the interviews must be both careful and deep: usually several hours spread over several sessions. Any indication that the process is not universal nullifies this research design.

(Continued)

3. The *Interview Rule-of-Thumb Flowchart* is designed for the cases in between. These are cases in which you know that your population's experiences vary, their interpretations of those experiences vary, or both. You don't, however, know the range of possibilities. In fact, this is what you wish to discover. And you don't care (at this stage) what percentage of the population thinks X and what percentage thinks Y.

    Thus, you need to conduct enough interviews so that you are sure you've found most of the possibilities, but you do not need to do them randomly. To use an example from religious research, if you are studying Christians, you need to make sure you have some Catholics, some Mainline Protestants, and some Evangelical Protestants, but you don't need a sample large enough to include Quakers.

    In short, you are seeking a good spread, but few enough interviews that you can explore issues in depth. The *Interview Rule-of-Thumb Flowchart* tells you when you've interviewed enough people.

Interview Rule-of-Thumb Flowchart for Nonrandom Samples

by J. Spickard

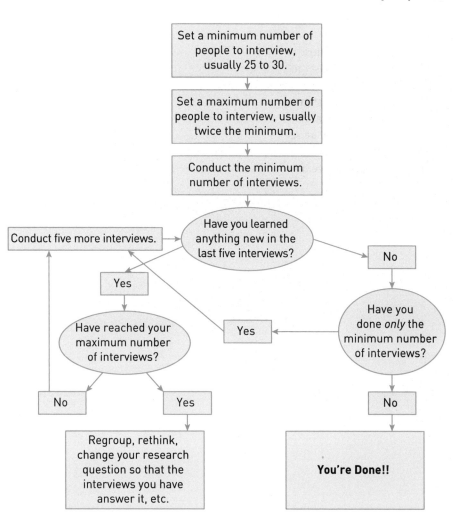

What Statistical Tests Should I Use?

by J. Spickard

A Decision Tree

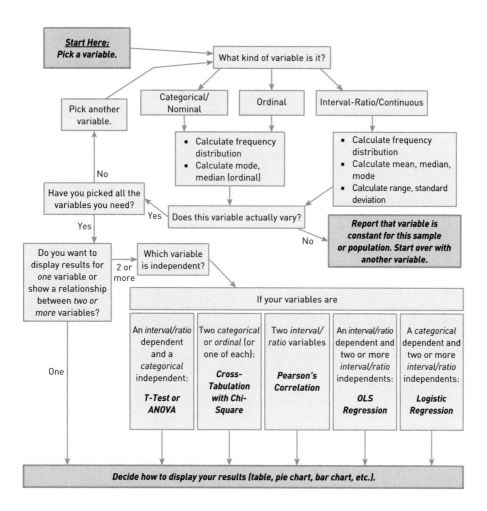

Reprinted from *Research Basics*, by James V. Spickard. Used by permission. This content is also licensed under Creative Commons-Noncommercial-ShareAlike (CC-BY-NC-SA) 4.0 United States License, http://creativecommons.org/licenses/by-nc-sa/4.0/. This guide may be distributed for non-commercial purposes.

Glossary

action research: (*logical structure*) Research designed to solve a problem, improve an organizational or technical process, or otherwise create practical knowledge. It focuses on finding and evaluating how to do things. In the process, it typically also describes or finds causal connections between things. It's focus, however, is on "how to," not "why" or "what." *See also* **participatory action research.**

acts, behavior, or events: (*type of data*) What people and animals do, plus things that happen. These are all observable phenomena. They are distinct from **reports of acts, behavior, or events.**

aggregate data: Data from groups, organizations, locations, and similar entities. The unit of analysis is whatever entity is involved. This can be states, cities, neighborhoods, or census tracts; companies, schools or school districts, or labor unions; and the like. These data are often collected individually but are reported collectively. The U.S. Census, for example, collects data from individual households but reports it by geographic area. This makes it easier to work with and also protects individuals' privacy.

analysis of variance (ANOVA): A statistical procedure used to test the extent to which two or more groups differ on an interval/ratio variable. Unlike a **t-test,** which tests whether two groups show different averages or **means,** an ANOVA can find the differences between three or more groups simultaneously.

average: *See* **mean.**

Belmont Report: The 1978 report of the National Commission for the Protection of Human Subjects of Biomedical and Behavioral Research, which forms the basis for research ethics as practiced in the United States. The report established three principles: **respect for persons, beneficence,** and **justice.** Research in the United States must adhere to these principles. Their application is typically overseen by **Institutional Review Boards**.

beneficence: The principle that research on humans and animals should do no harm, while maximizing the benefits of the research project and minimizing its risks to the research subjects. One of the key ethical principles of the **Belmont Report.**

bias: A strong inclination to interpret the world (or something in it) in a particular way, especially when that way does not stand up to intellectual scrutiny. Bias can be positive or negative. For example, you can be biased toward or against using a particular data collection method. This is more than just a preference; it is an unwarranted claim about the merits or demerits of that method. Bias is not the same as **subjectivity.** *See also* **objectivity, subjectivity**.

case study: (*logical structure*) Research that focuses on a particular case or instance, to see either what happened in that particular case or to show how well-known patterns and processes operate in particular settings. For example, you could investigate how a single school undertook curricular reform, or how a city reduced (or failed to reduce) traffic congestion by building a mass transit project. Case studies typically investigate complex cases in which several factors intersect to produce an outcome.

categorical data: Data organized by categories, such as male/female; graduated/did not graduate; Protestant/Catholic/Jewish/Other; Republican/Democrat/Independent; and so on. The number in each category can be counted, and the number of members of that category giving a specific answer to another question can be counted, to find its **distribution** in a **sample** or **population.** Statistical techniques such as **t-tests, ANOVA,** and **chi-squares** can tell whether or not there is a **significant** difference between the ways that the members of two or more categories answer that second question.

causal relationship: A relationship in which one factor causes another. Extreme rainfall, for example, can cause flooding, though the flooding cannot cause the rainfall. **Experimental and quasi-experimental research** seeks to locate the causes of particular phenomena.

census block: The smallest unit from which the U.S. Census Bureau collects information in the decennial census. The 2010 census had nearly 11 million blocks, of which some 5 million had no inhabitants. A block containing an apartment house, by contrast, could contain several hundred persons.

census block group: A combination of several census blocks, containing enough people so that no individual can be identified through reported census data. This is the smallest unit for which the U.S. Census Bureau reports figures.

census tract: The U.S. Census Bureau defines census tracts as "small, relatively permanent statistical subdivisions of a county," containing an average of 4,000 inhabitants. For the 2010 census, the smallest had 1,200 inhabitants; the largest about 8,000. A census tract is typically made up of several census blocks.

central tendency: *See* **measure of central tendency.**

chi-square: A statistic that measures the likelihood that an observed difference between the distributions of two sets of categorical or ordinal data arose by chance. It is typically used to see whether the results obtained by a random sample can be generalized to the population from which that sample was drawn. Technically called a Pearson's chi-square test.

coding: The process of analyzing interview transcripts, videos, and other forms of qualitative data to discover their patterns. You read through the transcripts, marking the presence of various elements—usually those suggested by the research question and by the scholarly literature on the research topic. You then bring together all of the passages with a given code and examine them to see what patterns occur. *See also* **external coding, internal coding.**

confidence level: In quantitative data analysis, a measure of the degree of confidence you can have that the results of your sample accurately reflect the population from which that sample is taken. It represents the percentage of samples of your chosen size that will be within your chosen **margin of error.** For example, researchers might say, "We are 95% confident that the true population value is within ±3% of the value we found in our sample."

construct validity: The degree to which a test measures what it claims to be measuring.

content analysis: (*data collection method*) A data collection method that examines texts, films, events, and so on, to identify patterns in them. It often does so by counting—for example, counting the number of violent incidents in television shows. You can also analyze content qualitatively—for example, by identifying the typical plot elements of soap operas.

continuous data: *See* **interval/ratio data.**

control group: One of the two (or more) groups in an experimental study. This group *does not* receive whatever treatment is being tested. *See also* **experiment, experimental group.**

control variable: In quantitative data analysis, a third (or fourth, or fifth, etc.) variable that might influence the relationship between the two (or more) main variables under investigation. You use statistical techniques to control for that variable; this removes the variable's influence, so that you can see the true relationship between the main variables.

correlation: A correlation measures the degree to which one set of values is related to another set of values from the same population. For example, states where people have to pay a high percentage of their income in rent are also states where people have long commutes to work. These two things are *correlated,* because they both happen in the same place. Highly educated people tend to read more than do less educated people; these are *correlated* because—generally speaking—the people who have lots of years of education read lots of books and those with few years of education read few books. Such correlations do not mean that every highly educated person reads more than every less educated person. Correlations describe tendencies, not absolutes. Neither do they determine cause. Two things may be correlated but have no **causal relationship** between them. *See also* **correlation coefficient, negative correlation, Pearson's r, positive correlation**.

correlations (strong, moderate, and weak): These measure the degree to which two **interval/ ratio variables** vary together. A strong correlation (either **positive** or **negative**) indicates a great degree of connection between the variables. A moderate correlation indicates a moderate degree of connection, and a weak correlation indicates a weak *but still important* degree of connection. *See* **correlation, correlation coefficient, Pearson's r.**

correlation coefficient: A measure of the degree to which two sets of interval/ratio numbers are correlated with each other. The **Pearson's r** is the most famous version.

correlational research: (*logical structure*) Research designed to see whether two (or more) things are correlated with each other. Do cities with large populations of homeless people also tend to be cities where affordable housing is scarce? Do wealthier families tend to spend a lower percentage of their income on food than do poorer families? (If yes, then the first of these is a **positive correlation** and the second a **negative correlation**.) The presence of a correlation between two variables does not indicate a **causal relationship.**

critical discourse analysis: A particular form of **discourse analysis** that emphasizes the social processes by which discourses are created, used, and sustained—often concentrating on the role of discourses in maintaining social inequality. Norman Fairclough's version has three elements: an analysis of how the texts being examined are created, an analysis of the discourse(s) they contain, and an analysis of how they are used to maintain certain people in positions of power.

critical incident interviews: (*data collection method*) Interviews that focus on a specific incident, asking interviewees to describe what exactly happened, what went right or wrong, and what they (and others) learned from the incident.

cross-tabulation: A technique for showing the relationship between two categorical or ordinal variables. You arrange these variables in a two-dimensional table and then use a chi-square (or other statistical measure) to see if there is a significantly different distribution of values between the various columns or rows of the table.

cultural interview: (*data collection method*) An interview that seeks to capture people's cultural knowledge. These interviews focus on the things that everyone in a social scene knows. They do not focus on individual idiosyncrasies.

cultural knowledge: (*type of data*) The knowledge shared in common among people in a given social scene. This includes **worldviews,** rules of behavior, and the like.

data analysis method: A technique for analyzing data, whether **quantitative** (**statistical**) or **qualitative** (**coding, thematic analysis**, etc.). Picking a data analysis method is Step 6 in the research design process.

data collection method: A technique for gathering a specific type of data. Different methods collect different types of data (*see* Table 4.1). Identifying an appropriate data collection method is Step 4 in the research design process.

data collection site: Where you collect your data. This can be a specific place, a specific population, or a specific sample of a population. Picking a data collection site is Step 5 in the research design process.

data type: *See* **type of data**.

deeply held opinions and attitudes: *See* **opinions and attitudes (deeply held).**

demographic data: (*type of data*) Data about the structure of populations. This includes breakdowns by gender, age, race and ethnicity, nationality, language use, and social class. Most countries collect such data in national censuses, which researchers can use to identify social trends.

dependent variable: A variable that is influenced or affected by one or more **independent variables.** For example, in the United States, income is frequently influenced by race and gender. Generally, Whites earn more than African Americans and men earn more than women—though the trend does not include everyone. Income is the dependent variable, because it can change. Race and gender are independent variables, because they are not influenced by income levels.

descriptive study: (*logical structure*) A study that describes a phenomenon, an event, a pattern, a historical trend, and so on. Descriptive studies generally answer questions that ask "what?" or "how?" To be distinguished from **causal research,** which tries to determine *why* a phenomenon or event happens or exists.

detached observation: (*data collection method*) A method of collecting data by the direct observation of behavior. The investigator typically does not interact with the subjects, but instead watches what they do. Detached observation can tell you *what* people do but cannot tell us *why* they do it.

discourse: A discourse is an institutionalized way of thinking and speaking about things, embedded in language. This language shapes people's thoughts and behavior. Just as eyeglasses filter what we see, our ways of speaking about things filter how we think. Our thinking then influences how we act. Examining a society's dominant ways of speaking about things helps us understand that society's behavior.

discourse analysis: (*data collection method*) A form of **content analysis** that tracks the discourses used in a particular text, film, or other cultural product. Different newspapers, for example, often use different ways of speaking about particular social problems; those ways of speaking can shape the kinds of solutions that their readers will find plausible.

dispersion: See **measure of dispersion.**

distribution: A pattern of data that describes how many of each potential value are present or, for geographic distributions, where the different items under investigation are located. For example, a demographic study may report the number of men and women, Whites, African Americans, Asian Americans, and the like in a population. A survey may tally how many people reported having been bullied at work and how many reported that they had not. An animal study may map the locations in which various species have been found. These are all examples of distributions.

ecological fallacy: The mistaken argument that the presence of a social pattern in a particular area allows you to make statements about particular individuals who live in that area. For example, the correlation between a high suicide rate and a high rate of residential mobility does not tell you that people who move often are more prone to suicide. It could well be that all of the suicides are by people who *don't* move.

economic data: (*type of data*) Data that report economic activity. Examples include the value of goods produced, delivered, or sold; changes in families' gross income over time; the profits and losses of companies in a particular city; and tax revenues.

ethnography: (*data collection method*) A method of collecting data that involves personal immersion in the social scene you are investigating. The investigator (or ethnographer) shares the daily activities of the people she or he is studying. This method is particularly useful for collecting **cultural knowledge** and for revealing **hidden social patterns.** Anthropologists traditionally use this term to describe what sociologists typically call **participant observation**.

experience: (*type of data*) More completely, *experience as it presents itself to consciousness.* This type of data describes what people report having experienced without regard to their interpretations of it. Psychological researchers, for example, may report the content of people's hallucinations, without seeking information about the cause of these experiences. Experience as it presents itself to consciousness is the main type of data sought by **phenomenological interviewing.**

experiment: (*logical structure*) Research that divides subjects into two or more groups, each of which receives a different treatment. The results from these treatments are compared with those from a **control group,** which does not receive any treatment.

experimental group: One of the two (or more) groups in an experimental study. This group *does* receive whatever treatment is being tested. Its results are compared with those from a **control group,** which does not receive the treatment, to see if that treatment makes any difference. *See also* **experiment.**

expert interviews: (*data collection method*) Interviews in which experts are asked about a particular phenomenon. It often makes sense to ask experts about something when exploring a topic about which most people know little or nothing.

expert knowledge: (*type of data*) The type of data sought in **expert interviews.** These are experts' informed views about something they have studied.

ex post facto research: (*logical structure*) Research that investigates a phenomenon or event after it has happened. Ex post facto research typically seeks the causes of phenomena or events where it is impossible to conduct actual experiments. You find a case and then examine that case in detail, to see if you can identify the factors that shaped it.

external coding: A **coding** scheme to interpret qualitative data whose codes are developed by the investigator or by an academic discipline rather than by the people being studied. A religion researcher, for example, may want to code interviews according to whether they exhibit "sectarian" or "denominational" attitudes. These concepts are probably meaningless to the people being interviewed but have proved useful to sociologists of religion. External coding is distinguished from **internal coding,** which sticks to the concepts used by people being studied.

factor analysis: A statistical technique for locating a set of hidden factors that shape people's responses on psychological and other tests that seek to identify people's traits. Factor analysis measures the degree to which people's answers on a number of test items indicate a common underlying trait.

fallacy: *See* **ecological fallacy, sampling fallacy, significance fallacy.**

first-order phenomena: Phenomena that investigators can experience or observe directly. In contrast to **second-order phenomena,** which are available through other people's reports.

focus groups: (*data collection method*) A group brought together to discuss something under investigation, typically because of their individual familiarity with one or more aspects of the topic. Their conversations shed light on that topic. Having multiple voices often stimulates deeper conversation than individual interviews might produce.

gatekeepers: People who control access to a data collection site. They can either help investigators by giving them access to the site or hinder research by closing the site to them.

General Social Survey (GSS): An opinion survey conducted in the United States almost every year from 1973 to 1992 and then every two years thereafter. Developed and run by the National Opinion Research Center (NORC), it models the U.S. noninstitutionalized adult population very closely. Many of its questions are asked on each survey. This allows researchers to track changes in attitudes over time.

grounded theory: (*data collection method*) A form of data collection that looks for hidden patterns of interaction in specific social settings. It involves a rather rigorous process of note-taking, hypothesis generating, and hypothesis testing that involves constant comparison of new observations with old ones. In many ways, this is a sociological version of **ethnography.**

hermeneutic circle: A process for understanding another person. You listen to that person, try to retell what that person says in your own words, and then ask if you are right. If you are not, the person corrects you, you reformulate your version, and ask again. You continue until the person confirms that you have understood him or her. This technique was originally developed to interpret Biblical and other texts. Because texts cannot speak, the reader comes up with an interpretation and then checks to see if that interpretation is supported or negated by other parts of the text.

hermeneutic interview: (*data collection method*) An **in-depth interview** that seeks to understand what the world looks like from another person's point of view. Understanding that point of view and confirming that understanding in the interview process involves using some form of the **hermeneutic circle.**

hidden social patterns: (*type of data*) Patterns of behavior, knowledge, or interaction that are not generally acknowledged (or even recognized) in a given social scene. For example, in most societies, men and women have differently patterned ways of speaking. To take another example, most Americans think that people are homeless because they are addicted to drugs or are mentally ill, when the real reason for homelessness is the lack of affordable housing.

historical research: (*logical structure*) Research that investigates events in the past. Such research often describes the past for its own sake, though it can also use past events as a way to throw light on current ones.

independent variable: A variable that influences or affects one or more **dependent variables.** For example, in the United States, race and gender frequently influence income. Generally, Whites earn more than African Americans and men earn more than women—though the trend does not include everyone. Income is the dependent variable, because it can change. Race and gender are independent variables, because they are not influenced by income levels.

in-depth interview: (*data collection method*) An interview that seeks people's detailed descriptions of something: an opinion or attitude, an event, a worldview, or the like. In-depth interviews seek detailed answers that may be rather idiosyncratic. Whereas **surveys** can get by with multiple-choice or short-answer questions, interviews must ask questions that allow their respondents to dive deeply into a subject. *See* **critical incident interviews, focus groups, hermeneutic interviews, phenomenological interviews.**

Institutional Review Board (IRB): A group authorized to examine research projects to ensure that they meet ethical standards. IRBs are charged with making sure that human and animal subjects are protected. In the United States, all universities, research institutes, and other organizations that receive federal grant money must have active IRBs. Other countries have similar bodies.

inter-decile range: One of several **measures of dispersion** of **interval/ratio data.** It calculates the full range and then removes the top and bottom 10% of the values. It is less apt to be influenced by outliers than is the full range itself.

internal coding: A **coding** scheme to interpret qualitative data whose codes are drawn from the people being studied rather than from the investigator or from the scholarly literature. A researcher studying motivation, for example, may code interviews according to how her or his informants describe their reasons for doing things. She or he will use the terms that the informants provide, rather than trying to fit those informants into standard categories. *See also* **external coding.**

inter-quartile range: One of several **measures of dispersion** of **interval/ratio data.** It calculates the full range and then removes the top and bottom quarter of the values. It is less apt to be influenced by outliers than is the full range itself.

interval/ratio data: Data that are ranked (as is **ordinal data**) but for which we know the exact distance between the various ranks. For example, the Fahrenheit and Celsius temperature scales are interval data, because the distance is the same between any two adjacent degrees. These scales are not **ratio** scales, though, because their zero point is arbitrary: 80° is twice as hot as 40° on the Fahrenheit scale, but more than five times as hot (26.7° vs. 4.4°) when converted to Celsius. **Ratio** scales have a true zero. Among temperature scales, only degrees Kelvin is a ratio scale; converting to Kelvin shows that 80°F is 12% hotter than 40°F (353.2°K vs. 313.2°K).

interview: *[data collection method]* The process of engaging in conversation with someone in order to learn specific knowledge from them. Interviews typically provide in-depth information, of the kind that cannot be gathered by less time-intensive methods. This can include that person's deeply held opinions, attitudes, and feelings, detailed descriptions of events or experiences, general knowledge about that person's culture, or specific knowledge based on that person's expertise. See **in-depth interview, interview protocol**. See also **critical incident interview, cultural interview, expert interview, hermeneutic interview, phenomenological interview**.

interview protocol: A written-out script for an in-depth interview. It usually contains the key questions that you intend to ask, in an order designed to make the interview flow smoothly and produce good results. It also usually includes several follow-up questions, to let the interviewee elaborate on various points. Few interviews use all of these follow-up questions, but it is wise to prepare them in advance.

justice: The equal and fair treatment of all people, including (sometimes especially) those who have less social, economic, and political power than others. One of the key ethical principles of the **Belmont Report.**

key informants: The people who give you the most useful information for your study. Ethnographers, particularly, depend on key informants to teach them about the community they are investigating. Experts are good key informants on a variety of research topics.

limitation: Elements that the investigator cannot control, which limit the applicability of research findings. This can be a matter of having a limited group of informants, whose views cannot be generalized to the population at large. It can involve an inability to measure certain factors that may have influenced the population you are studying. Such things limit the conclusions that your study can draw. All studies need to state their limitations clearly.

logical structure: What your research has to do in order to answer your research question. Some research questions ask you to *describe* a phenomenon. Other research questions ask you to identify a phenomenon's *cause.* Yet other research questions ask you to *compare* two cases or instances, examining their differences to learn more about each. Choosing your logical structure is Step 2 in the research design process. Table 2.1 lists 10 different logical structures that research can use.

longitudinal research: (*logical structure*) Research that traces change over a long period of time. For example, longitudinal environmental research traces changes in an ecosystem; longitudinal medical research traces changes in people's health; and longitudinal educational research traces people's educational experiences.

margin of error: The degree of error you are willing to accept when testing whether the results of a sample reflect the patterns in the total population. Used in combination with a **confidence level,** the margin of error lets you specify how far your sample distribution is from the population distribution.

For example, researchers might say, "We are 95% confident that the true population value is within ±3% of the value we found in our sample."

mean: The average value of a set of **interval/ratio data.** Add up all the values and divide by how many there are.

measure of central tendency: Any of several measures of where values cluster in a set of **interval/ ratio, ordinal,** or **categorical data.** Examples include the **mean,** the **mode,** and the **median.**

measure of dispersion: Any of several measures of the distribution of a set of **interval/ratio data.** Examples include the **range,** the **variance,** and the **standard deviation.**

median: A **measure of central tendency.** The middle value in the distribution of a set of **ordinal** or **interval/ratio data.**

meta-analysis: (*logical structure*) Research that combines several previous studies into one and then reanalyzes their data so as to draw more general conclusions than any of the individual studies could do alone.

method of data analysis: *See* **data analysis method.**

method of data collection: *See* **data collection method.**

Metropolitan statistical area (MSA): A geographic unit identified by the U.S. Office of Management and Budget as a unified urban area, encompassing several connected cities, towns, and even counties. Comparing MSAs with each other is usually better than comparing cities, because local political boundaries do not mean as much in an era of urban sprawl. At this writing, there are 381 separate MSAs in the United States.

mode: A **measure of central tendency** that indicates which values are most common in your data.

narrative analysis: A form of **discourse analysis** that uses narratives as its raw material. These can be stories, accounts, life histories, and so on. *See* **discourse analysis.**

natural experiment: (*logical structure*) A situation that naturally creates experimental and control groups, which for practical or ethical reasons an investigator could not have created artificially. In essence, real life has created the experiment and the investigator simply examines the results that occur for each group.

negative correlation: A **correlation** in which two interval/ratio variables vary together, but negatively. Items with a high score on one will have a low score on the other, and vice versa. With **aggregate data,** this type of correlation indicates that the two things tend to happen in different places, in different organizations, and so on. With **survey data,** this type of correlation indicates that the two things tend to happen to different individuals.

network analysis: The process of tracing who interacts with whom and in what ways in a given social setting. This is useful for understanding group formation and dissolution, patterns of influence, and the ways in which information is passed on, among other things.

nominal data: See **categorical data.**

nonnumeric data: Data that does not involve numbers. Interview data are typically nonnumeric, as they are filled with complex meanings that are lost if you try to analyze the data by counting.

nonsignificant: (*statistically speaking*) The statement that there is no significant relationship between two sets of data, and that the small difference found in a **random sample** cannot be generalized to the larger **population.** The actual determination of significance or nonsignificance depends on the chosen **confidence level** and the chosen **margin of error.** *See also* **statistically significant.**

numeric data: Data that involve numbers. This can be demographic data, economic data, counts of survey answers, or anything else that can be analyzed mathematically.

objectivity: The effort to avoid bias in research. Objective research seeks to understand a phenomenon as it is rather than as the investigator (or anyone else) imagines or might like it to be. The opposite of objectivity is *not* **subjectivity,** because every human investigator is subjective (i.e., occupies a social position that allows her or him to conceive of some things and not of others). A dedication to objectivity is the dedication to discover and overcome such limitations. **Bias** occurs when the investigator fails to account for this subjectivity and thus makes stronger claims for her or his research than is warranted.

opinions and attitudes (deeply held): (*type of data*) Data consisting of people's deeply held beliefs, opinions, and attitudes. These tend to be complex and idiosyncratic, so they call for data collection methods that allow such complexities to emerge. **In-depth interviews** are a common method for collecting this type of data, though they are not the only option.

opinions and attitudes (shallow): (*type of data*) Data consisting of people's shallower beliefs, opinions, and attitudes. These are typically relatively simple, so they can be collected relatively quickly using well-crafted **surveys** and questionnaires.

ordinal data: Data that indicate rank-order but do not specify the distance between ranks. For example, "very happy," "pretty happy," and "not too happy" are clearly ranked, but we have no idea whether the distance between "very" and "pretty" happy is the same as the distance between "pretty" and "not too" happy. This rules out the use of some statistical measures, such as the **Pearson's *r*** correlation, but other calculations are possible, including **cross-tabulations** with **chi-squares.**

organizational data: (*type of data*) Data collected from organizations. This includes everything from staffing demographics, sales figures, and net income to stock prices, customers served, and tax payments. The amount of such data available depends greatly on the nature of the organization.

outlier: A data point that is very unusual, compared with the other data points in its set. For example, the state of Nevada used to have much higher marriage and divorce rates than did other states. That was the result of how easy it was to get marriage licenses and divorces there, compared with the rest of the United States.

participant observation: (*data collection method*) A method of collecting data that involves personal immersion in the social scene you are investigating. The investigator (or participant observer) shares the daily activities of the people that she or he is studying. This method is particularly useful for collecting **cultural knowledge** and for revealing **hidden social patterns.** Sociologists traditionally use this term to describe what anthropologists typically call **ethnography**.

participatory action research: **Action research** in which the community or organization being studied participates actively. That community often hires the researcher, decides what needs to be investigated, collects and analyzes data, and draws conclusions. The researcher advises this process but does not control it.

Pearson's *r*: A statistic that measures the degree of **correlation** between two interval/ratio variables. It varies between +1 and −1. If *r* = +1.0, we say the variables exhibit *perfect positive correlation.* If *r* = −1.0, we say the variables are *perfectly negatively correlated.* If *r* = 0.0 (or is close to 0.0), then the variables are uncorrelated: This means there is no relationship between them.

perfect correlation: A **correlation** in which two interval/ratio variables vary together: The item with the highest value on one variable also has the highest value on the other, the item with the next highest value on one variable also has the next highest value on the other, and so on. A perfect negative correlation happens when the item with the highest value on one variable has the *lowest* value on the other, the item with the second-highest value on one variable has the second-*lowest* value on the other, and so on. *See also* **Pearson's r.**

personal and psychological traits: (*type of data*) This data type is found most often in psychology, though other fields use something similar. Psychologists argue that individuals have different inner traits that shape their attitudes, feelings, and behavior. This includes such things as personality, intelligence, and so on. There are many ways of measuring these traits and also many ways of defining them.

personal feelings: (*type of data*) The emotional analogue of deeply held **opinions and attitudes.** Personal feelings tend to be complex and idiosyncratic. They are best collected by methods that capture this complexity.

perspectival: The fact that human beings are not omniscient and, thus, inevitably see things from a perspective. These perspectives both enhance and limit what they can see and understand. This may be the result of their social status, because not everyone has access to all research populations. Or it may be the result of their culture or training, because people from different social milieus are taught to understand things differently. *See* **subjectivity.**

phenomenological interviews: (*data collection method*) Interviews that focus on people's descriptions of what they have experienced, leaving aside their personal or cultural interpretations of that experience. *See* **experience.**

point-in-time (PIT) count: A count of homeless people taken on a single day or during a short set of hours rather than across a span of days. Such counts systematically underestimate the number of homeless people, though some methods of PIT counting are more accurate than others.

population: The total number of people, animals, texts, or the like from which your research **sample** is drawn. Some research projects collect data from all members of the population; this is feasible if the population is small. Most projects, however, collect data from only a few population members. You need to specify your population carefully, especially if you are excluding certain parts of that population that readers might assume you are studying; this is part of recognizing your study's **limitations.**

positive correlation: A **correlation** in which two interval/ratio variables vary together. Items with a high score on one will have a high score on the other. With **aggregate data,** this indicates that the two things tend to happen in the same places, in the same organizations, and so on. With **survey data,** this indicates that the two things tend to happen to the same individuals.

psychological scales: (*data collection method*) A data collection method designed to measure people's psychological traits. These typically ask people a series of questions that research has identified as indicating particular inner states or tendencies. For example, an introversion/extraversion scale may ask people whether they would prefer to spend an evening with a crowd of friends or with a single friend, whether they draw or lose energy from being in public, and so on. Psychologists use **factor analysis,** among other techniques, to construct these scales.

public and private records: (*data collection method*) A data collection method that focuses on the records maintained by governments, businesses, nonprofit organizations, and other entities.

qualitative data: Data that capture the complexity of human meanings and behaviors, without reducing them to numbers. *See* **nonnumeric data.**

qualitative data analysis (QDA) software: Computer software that facilitates **coding** of qualitative data. Programs such as NVivo, MAXQDA, Atlas.ti, and QDA Miner let you assign codes to bits of text and then collect all the bits with the same codes in a single document. Conceptually speaking, this is the same as writing your data on 3-by-5 cards and sorting them into piles on the living room floor. Practically speaking, QDA software keeps kids, cats, and spilled coffee from messing up the piles of data. But crashed hard drives and coffee on the keyboard pose their own dangers.

qualitative research: Research that uses one or another method of qualitative data analysis to draw conclusions from its data. The distinction between qualitative and **quantitative research** is not basic. It arises, instead, in Step 6 of the six-step method.

quantitative data: Data that can be counted. These can be demographic data, economic data, counts of survey answers, or anything else that can be analyzed mathematically. Same as **numeric data.**

quantitative data analysis: Any system for analyzing **numeric data.** This includes various forms of **statistical analysis,** such as **t-tests, chi-square tests, correlations,** and **regression analysis,** among others.

quantitative research: Research that uses one or another method of qualitative data analysis to draw conclusions from its data. The distinction between quantitative and **qualitative research** is not basic. It arises, instead, in Step 6 of the six-step method.

quasi-experiment: (*logical structure*) An approximation of an experiment, used in cases where something prevents you from controlling all of the potential intervening factors, but you can control enough of them to learn something useful. Perhaps you cannot bring people into the laboratory, because doing so will change precisely the behavior that you hope to study. In such a situation, a quasi-experiment is a good second choice. **Natural experiments** are a form of quasi-experiment.

questionnaire: (*data collection method*) A set of questions to be used on a **survey.** Questionnaires typically ask people to report their acts or behavior, their relatively shallow opinions, simple demographics, and their surface self-identities. Some questionnaires can ask for more extensive comments, though this is practical only when they are administered to just a small number of people.

random sample: A sample of a larger population, selected so that every member of the population has an equal chance of being in the sample. This eliminates potential biases that other sampling methods introduce. It also lets you measure the potential **margin of error** of your results. Only random samples allow you to generalize from the sample to the wider population.

range: A **measure of dispersion** of a set of **interval/ratio** or **ordinal data.** It is the distance from the lowest value to the highest value in that set.

ratio data: *See* **interval/ratio data.**

reflexive ethnography: Ethnography that takes seriously the fact that ethnographers are as human as are the people they study. They have their own social locations and personal characteristics, and therefore they observe the social world from a perspective, rather than purely objectively. For reflexive ethnographers, pure objectivity is impossible. The best one can do is to bring one's own perspective into the picture, showing what that perspective can and cannot see.

regression analysis: A statistical technique used to see which of two or more independent variables influences a dependent variable. This usually requires **interval/ratio data** on all the variables and a sufficiently large number of cases.

regression line: On a **scatterplot,** the line that comes the closest to passing between all the points. The degree to which the points cluster around the line is an indication of the strength of their **correlation.**

reports of acts, behavior, or events: (*type of data*) What people tell you about what they have done or observed. Unlike **acts, behavior, or events,** these are not directly observable. You have to allow for lapses in memory, observation, and so on.

representative sample: A subset of the population under study that matches the whole population's characteristics. This often involves taking a **random sample,** though you can also take a **stratified random sample** to make sure that you include particular population categories that a true random sample might miss.

research ethics: The process of reflecting on the potential dangers that your research poses to the humans or animals that you are studying. In the United States, an ethical evaluation is required of all research that takes place at organizations receiving any sort of federal funding. *See also* **Institutional Review Board** and **Belmont Report.**

research logic: See **logical structure.**

research method: A technique for gathering a specific type of data. Better described as a **data collection method.**

research project: A medium-to-large research effort that frequently explores several related research questions. Each question can be answered using the six-step method. The project draws conclusions based on the answers to all the questions, not just the answer to any one of them.

research question: Identifies exactly what you want to find out about a piece of your **research topic.** Developing a good research question is Step 1 in the research design process. That question should specify exactly what kind of data you need to answer the research question. If it does not, it is still too broad.

research site: *See* **data collection site.**

research topic: Describes an area that you want to investigate. Broader and less specific than a **research question.**

researcher-centered analysis: Data analysis organized around concepts developed by the researcher or in the scholarly literature. It often looks for things that the respondents do not realize or that are not part of their worldview. *See also* **external coding, internal coding, respondent-centered analysis.**

respect for persons: The principle that researchers should protect the autonomy of their research subjects and treat them with courtesy and respect. This involves giving them full information in advance about the research, its benefits, and its dangers, while allowing them full authority to participate or not to participate—even to the point of withdrawing after the research has begun. One of the key ethical principles of the **Belmont Report**.

respondent-centered analysis: Data analysis organized around concepts drawn from the respondents themselves. This analysis looks for patterns in the worldviews and ways of thinking that the respondents claim as their own. *See also* **external coding, internal coding, researcher-centered analysis.**

sample: A group drawn from a larger **population** and used to estimate the characteristics of the whole population. A **random sample** allows you to measure the odds that your sample corresponds to the population. A nonrandom sample does not allow you to generalize to the population itself, though it may reveal patterns that later randomized research can explore. *See also* **sampling fallacy, snowball sample.**

sample size: How large your **sample** is. In general, the larger your sample size, the more likely it is that the patterns you find will match the patterns in the whole population. This is, however, only secure when you have a **random sample.** Interestingly, the sample size you need to generalize to a large population is often not much bigger than the sample size you need to generalize to a small one. The **General Social Survey,** for example, samples about 3,000 U.S. adults every second year; that sample is large enough to produce just a ±1.8% **margin of error** at a 95% **confidence level.**

sampling fallacy: The fallacy of drawing conclusions about a population from a sample of that population, when the sample is not chosen randomly. Only **random samples** allow you to generalize from the sample to the whole.

scale of measurement: The form that your quantitative data take: **categorical, ordinal,** or **interval/ ratio.**

scales: (*data collection method*) Measures designed to discover underlying traits of some sort. You ask a series of questions, each of which is intended to measure part of that trait. Then you use a technique such as **factor analysis** to create a scale that measures the trait more accurately than do any of the constituent questions. The most common are **psychological scales.**

scatterplot: A two-dimensional graph that charts the relationship between two **interval/ratio variables.** One is on the x-axis and the other is on the y-axis. Each case has a dot where its two values intersect. *See also* **regression line.**

second-order phenomena: Phenomena that investigators cannot experience or observe directly, but for which they must rely on people's reports. In contrast to **first-order phenomena,** which investigators can experience or observe.

self-identity: (*type of data*) How people understand or see themselves. This can be relatively shallow, in which case it can be collected through survey research; an example would be, "Are you a Republican, a Democrat, or do you identify with no particular political party?" Or it can be relatively deep, in which case in-depth interviews will be a much better data collection choice.

shallow opinions and attitudes: *See* **opinions and attitudes (shallow).**

significance fallacy: The fallacy of arguing that an observed difference between groups in a sample represents a real difference in the total population, when the sample difference is too small to be statistically significant. For example, men and women may have slightly different attitudes toward something on a survey, but that difference has to be statistically significant before you can claim that men and women in the population at large differ on the matter. Small differences on a sample are usually the result of the specific sample; a different sample might well produce different results.

significant: (*statistically speaking*) *See* **statistically significant.**

site: *See* **data collection site.**

six-step method: The research design process outlined in this book. The steps are (1) develop a good **research question;** (2) choose a **logical structure** for your research; (3) identify the **type of data** you need; (4) pick a **data collection method;** (5) choose your **data collection site;** and (6) pick a **data analysis method.**

snowball sample: A nonrandom sample collected by interviewing someone and then asking that person for suggestions about other people to interview. The name comes from the purported fact that snowballs rolling downhill can trigger other snowballs to produce an avalanche.

social survey: *See* **survey.**

standard deviation: A measure of the distribution of a set of **interval/ratio data.** It measures **dispersion:** how spread out that distribution is from the **mean.** Mathematically, it is the square root of the **variance.** This is often a more useful number than the true variance, because it has the same scale as the underlying data.

statistical analysis: Any of a set of mathematical operations designed to find relationships between quantitative data. Technically speaking, *statistics* refers to operations on data from samples, but in everyday speech, it can refer to operations on data from populations as well. Many statistical operations are available. Most researchers need to know only enough to be able to talk with a statistician about how best to design the data analysis portion of their research.

statistically significant: The statement that there is a significant relationship between two sets of data, such that you can generalize the results from a **random sample** to the larger **population.** This may be a **t-test,** in which the two categories or cases are shown to be sufficiently different that the difference is not possible as the result of chance. It may be a **cross-tabulation,** in which a **chi-square test** shows that the two categories have a major difference between them. The determination of **significance** or nonsignificance depends on the chosen **confidence level**, the chosen **margin of error**, and the **sample size.**

stratified random sample: A **random sample** of a **population** chosen to make sure that each major segment of that population is represented in the sample. For example, you could divide the population into men and women and then take a random sample of each. This would avoid getting a sample with an unequal gender division.

subjectivity: An often misused term that denotes the fact that all human knowledge is **perspectival.** Subjectivity is not **bias**. Investigators are human and, thus, cannot see all possible sides of any phenomenon. It may be that their social position denies them access to certain informants or their intellectual training focuses their attention on certain concepts and not on others. A dedication to **objectivity** is the dedication to discover and overcome such limitations. **Bias** occurs when the investigator fails to account for her or his subjectivity in the research process. Given the intellectual baggage associated with the term *subjectivity,* the term **perspectival** is increasingly preferred.

survey: (*data collection method*) A set of questions used to collect people's reports of their acts or behavior, their relatively shallow opinions, simple demographics, and their surface self-identities. Large-scale surveys should be done on a **random sample** of a population, so that you can generalize your sample's results to the population as a whole.

survey data: Data collected through a **questionnaire** or **survey.** This typically consists of people's reports of acts or behavior, their relatively shallow opinions, simple demographics, and their surface self-identities. Large-scale surveys produce **quantitative data,** which can be summarized through **quantitative data analysis.** Smaller surveys can produce **qualitative data,** but this is not usually generalizable from a sample to a wider population.

survey research: Research that uses **surveys** or **questionnaires** to collect data from large numbers of people.

thematic analysis: A form of **qualitative data analysis** that focuses on the themes raised in a set of texts, interview transcripts, and the like. It identifies the themes brought up in the text, traces the relationships between them, and often ties those themes to wider cultural patterns. **Discourse analysis** frequently makes use of themes to show the discourses that people use.

t-test: A statistical procedure used to test the odds that sample measurements from two groups have different **means** on an interval/ratio variable. Originally called Students's t-test, it was developed by William Sealy Gosset, an employee of the Guinness Brewing Company, to test the differences between batches of beer.

type of data: The nature of the data that will answer your research question. Different questions ask for different kinds of things. Acts, for example, are different from *reports* of acts: One is the actual doing of something and the other is talk about that doing. To take another example, *experience* is a different sort of thing from the *interpretation* of experience; the first presents itself directly to your consciousness, whereas the second involves your thoughts about whatever it is that has presented itself. Identifying the type of data you need is Step 3 in the research design process. It is central to the whole endeavor, because it lets you choose a data collection method, a data collection site, and a data analysis method that fit the type of data you are seeking.

unit of analysis: The unit you use when you analyze your data. This may be different from the **unit of observation,** from which the data were collected. For example, you might reorganize survey data from individuals to compare the percentages of the population in each of the 50 U.S. states that have graduated from college. In this case, the unit of observation is the individual but the unit of analysis is the state. *See also* **unit of observation.**

unit of observation: The unit from which you collect your data. A survey of people, for example, collects data from individuals. A survey of companies or organizations collects data from those organizations. *See also* **unit of analysis.**

variance: A measure of the distribution of a set of **interval/ratio data.** It measures **dispersion:** how spread out that distribution is from the **mean.** Mathematically, it is the average squared deviation of each number from its mean.

worldview: The way an individual or a group of people sees the world. Anthropologists use this term to describe culturally shared visions of reality: the fundamental ideas or beliefs that a group holds about the world and how it works.

Author Index

Subject Index